POLLY PEACHUM

*The Story Of Lavinia Fenton
and The Beggar's Opera*

From an engraving by E. Apostool.   after Hogarth.

"Polly Peachum."
(Lavinia Fenton afterwards Duchess of Bolton)

POLLY PEACHUM

*The Story Of Lavinia Fenton
and The Beggar's Opera*

CHARLES E. PEARCE

BENJAMIN BLOM  New York/London 1968

First Published London, 1913
Reissued 1968
by Benjamin Blom, Inc., Bronx, New York 10452
and 56 Doughty Street, London W.C. 1

Library of Congress Catalog Card Number 68-21222

Printed in the United States of America

To

MY FRIEND

JOHN FARLOW WILSON

CONTENTS

CHAPTER I

THE INCEPTION OF *THE BEGGAR'S OPERA*

CHAPTER II

WHAT WAS GAY'S INTENTION ?

CHAPTER III

EIGHTEENTH-CENTURY BALLAD SINGING

CHAPTER IV

REALISM OF *THE BEGGAR'S OPERA*

CONTENTS

CONTENTS

CHAPTER X

POLLY AND HER FELLOW PLAYERS

CHAPTER XI

OTHER THEATRICAL NOTABILITIES

CHAPTER XII

THE "TOAST OF THE TOWN"

CHAPTER XIII

THE PENALTIES OF POPULARITY

CHAPTER XIV

PURITANISM UP IN ARMS

CHAPTER XV

THE SPITE OF A DISAPPOINTED JOURNALIST

CHAPTER XVI

THE TRIUMPH OF *THE BEGGAR'S OPERA*

CHAPTER XVII

SIDELIGHTS ON EIGHTEENTH-CENTURY THEATRICAL MANAGEMENT

CHAPTER XVIII

A " GAY LADY " OF THE PERIOD

CHAPTER XIX

POLLY AND THE POWLETTS

CHAPTER XX

COLLEY CIBBER'S ABORTIVE RIVALRY OF GAY

CHAPTER XXI

A GREAT LADY'S CHAMPIONSHIP

CHAPTER XXII

RIVAL POLLIES

CHAPTER XXIII

THE BEGGAR'S PANTOMIME

CHAPTER XXIV

FROM COFFEE-HOUSE TO CORONET

CHAPTER XXV

THE CURTAIN FALLS

CHAPTER XXVI

FAMOUS POLLIES

CHAPTER XXVII

TRAVESTIES OF *THE BEGGAR'S OPERA*

CHAPTER XXVIII

FROM MADAME MARA TO MADAME VESTRIS

LIST OF ILLUSTRATIONS

INTRODUCTION

In adding another volume to the already ample store of dramatic bibliography, I venture to claim that for the first time an effort has been made to collect and fix, with as much exactitude as the circumstances would allow, the scattered fragments of theatrical history relative to " Polly Peachum " and *The Beggar's Opera*. The records of the English stage are, to say the least, somewhat bewildering. The material contained in innumerable biographies, reminiscences, and notices in newspapers and magazines, is overwhelming. One finds errors repeated over and over again ; dates are at variance, the same anecdotes are related of different people, and contradictory statements abound *ad infinitum*. The difficulty of correction is great ; while that of discovering original sources of information is at times almost insuperable. The few actors of the eighteenth century who have indulged in autobiographies (or have had such " autobiographies " written for them) trusted to memories weakened by age. If the notion of keeping a diary ever occurred to any one of them, their way of life made such a thing impossible. Moreover, documents, account-books, contracts, correspondence which to-day would be treasures, were thrown aside contemptuously, as in the case of the ledger and other " treasury " books relating to the early days of Covent Garden Theatre, which came into the hands of the " petty tradesmen " mentioned by Mr. R. J. Smith. Fortunately the books were not wholly destroyed, and the residue is incorporated in Mr. Smith's " Collection of material for a History of the Stage." I have extracted much that throws interesting light upon the details of theatrical management during the first half of the eighteenth century; and these extracts, together with Gay's agreement under which he assigned the copyrights of the *Fables* and *The Beggar's Opera* to Jacob Tonson and John Watts, see the light of print, I believe, for the first time. Whenever it has been possible I have gone to contemporary sources, and where necessary I have quoted chapter and verse more or less fully. To do justice to the subject no other method seemed adequate.

I have to express my indebtedness to Mr. A. M. Broadley for the many interesting prints he has placed at my disposal. Several of these have never before been reproduced, and the same may be said of other illustrations—notably Walker as Macheath, Charles Bannister as Polly, and Westcombe House, Blackheath, where lived and died " Polly Peachum," Lavinia, Duchess of Bolton.

CHARLES E. PEARCE.

POLLY PEACHUM

CHAPTER I

THE INCEPTION OF *THE BEGGAR'S OPERA*

Pope's Villa—"The Twickenham Hotch Potch "—Pope, Swift, Bolingbroke,
Arbuthnot, Gay—Gay's ambition and disappointments—He writes
"The Beggar's Opera "—Its good luck—Lady novelists of the
eighteenth century—Coarseness of the times—Voltaire—Pope.

NEARLY two centuries ago there stood on the banks
of the Thames at Twickenham a comfortable, if
hardly picturesque, house, surrounded by a model
garden, with shady groves, a cool grotto where a
spring continually rilled, and a lawn sloping down
to the placid river. This pleasant retreat was known
as Pope's Villa—a name which has been handed
down to the present day, but by some misconception
bestowed upon quite a different house, for the
original Pope's Villa has long since disappeared.
When it was for sale, the poet Rogers had a great
wish to buy it, but he feared it would fetch more
than he could afford, and in addition he dreaded
the epigrams and jibes which would certainly have
been levelled at him. He writes: "When the Villa was
finally dismantled, I was anxious that the obelisk
erected by Pope to his mother's memory should be
placed in the gardens at Hampton Court, and I
offered to contribute my mite for that purpose; but
no !—and the obelisk is now at Gopsall, Lord Howe's
seat in Leicestershire."

At Pope's Villa, in the early part of the year 1727,

1

a coterie of brilliant men were accustomed to fore-
gather—a coterie which, as representing wit, satire,
and poetry, it would be hard to parallel. There was
the host, misshapen, shrunken Pope, whose fine eyes
and melodious voice belied the spite and venom
(probably in a great degree the product of ill health)
which he could show when so minded. In 1727 he
was in his fortieth year, and at this date is said to
have been so weak that he had to wear " a bodice
of stiff canvas "; he could not dress without assistance, and his legs were mere drumsticks beneath
their coverings of three stockings. He was a
nervous dyspeptic, and his cravings for coffee, which
he insisted on having when he awoke in the night,
did not tend to add to the strength either of his
nerves or his stomach. The latter, indeed, he was
always taxing by his love of highly seasoned dishes,
and especially of potted lampreys ; of which luscious
fish no doubt the silver Thames skirting his grounds
gave him an ample supply.

The second was the pugnacious, fierce, and un-
compromising Dean of St. Patrick's, then in the full
possession of his amazing powers, his gigantic intel-
lect showing no signs of the decay which clouded his
last days. Swift had come to England in the spring
of 1726—his first visit to this country since the death
of Queen Anne—chiefly with the object of representing to Sir Robert Walpole, burly, astute, and cynical,
the distressed state of Ireland, and also, according
to some authorities, with a view of obtaining his own
preferment. He failed in the first—Walpole, mis-
trusting the motives of the intercessor, would do
nothing for Ireland—and as for the second, it is very
doubtful whether the Dean's proud, imperious spirit
permitted him to ask for favours. He returned to
Ireland in anxiety concerning Stella, who was showing signs of consumption ; remained with her until
March 1727, when, her health apparently improving,
he came back to England and took up his abode
with Pope. In the meantime, the most important

event in the Dean's literary career had happened. Gulliver had appeared, and at once achieved a fame which has not faded to this day.

While Gulliver was in preparation, Pope was busy selecting and arranging his own and Swift's fugitive pieces into three volumes of *Miscellanies*, Swift leaving everything to his friend, and bidding him act according to his own judgment and discretion. The *Miscellanies* were published in March 1727; and some of the keen onslaughts, especially a treatise on "Bathos or the Art of Sinking," acted as a stick thrust into a hornets' nest. The irony was bitter, and emphasised by a list of living writers as exponents, whose names were hardly concealed by letters of the alphabet. The minor poets and prose-writers were maddened, and retaliated in lampoons and libels, after the abusive fashion of the age. Pope, always sensitive, chafed under their stings, but Swift, more robust and conscious of his strength, cared little. No one knew better than the combative Dean that the giver of hard knocks must expect hard knocks in return. Swift was not one to wear his heart upon his sleeve to the boredom of his friends, and it may be taken for granted that he never allowed his griefs and disappointments to interfere with his wit. In 1727 he had no great personal trouble. The embarrassment of his love-affair with the ill-fated Vanessa, the tragedy of whose death took place in 1720, belonged to the dim past, and his only anxiety was the delicate health of Stella. She was destined to pass away in the January of the following year; but Stella was not believed to be in danger in the heyday of the " Twickenham Hotch Potch," as the gatherings at Pope's Villa were called by Nicholas Amhurst, better known under his pen-name of "Caleb D'Anvers," one of the crowd of literary gadflies who delighted in irritating the poet and his friends.

A notable component of the "Hotch Potch" was Henry St. John, Viscount Bolingbroke. St. John, after a stormy political career, followed by exile

and deprivation of a peer's privileges, had come back
from France four years before; and to use the words
of Sir Walter Scott, " Pope, Arbuthnot, Gay, Bathurst, and other old friends, received him with open
arms and with the melancholy pleasure of sailors who
meet after a shipwreck from which they have escaped
by different means." By an Act passed in 1725
Bolingbroke was enabled to inherit and purchase real
estate, and he settled at Dawley, near Uxbridge,
within an easy ride of Pope's Villa. When Pulteney
and Sir Robert fell out, he joined with the former, and
assisted Caleb D'Anvers in starting the *Craftsman,*
the first number of which appeared in December
1726. His idea was to enlist the aid of the Duchess
of Kendal (once known as Madame Schulemberg,
and nicknamed the " Maypole " from her excessive
leanness) in attacking Walpole, and through her he
sent a copy of the *Craftsman* to the King. George
treated the matter very lightly, and whatever might
have been Bolingbroke's next step was frustrated
by the King's death. For the time being Bolingbroke returned to his leisure at Dawley, and his intercourse with Pope during 1727 was very close.

Horace Walpole nursed his hatred of Bolingbroke
for many years, and in 1780 wrote thus bitterly of the
Twickenham coterie : " Bolingbroke was more than a
rascal—he was a villain. Bathurst, I believe, was
not a dishonest man, more than he was prejudiced
by party against one of the honestest and best of men
(? Sir Robert Walpole). Gay was a poor simple soul
intoxicated by the friendship of men of genius, and
who thought *they* must be good who condescended
to admire *him.* Swift was a wild beast who baited
and worried all mankind almost because his intolerable arrogance, pride and ambition were disappointed." Walpole spares Pope the rancour of
his tongue. Perhaps he recognised in the poet's
disposition something of his own finicking, petty,
spiteful nature.

Then there was Arbuthnot, the genial, witty

literary doctor, who had collaborated with Pope
and Swift, and who in real humour was allowed
to be superior to both. In 1727 medicine occupied
Arbuthnot's attention more than literature, but he
was constant in his visits to Twickenham. The
Memoirs of Martin Scriblerus, part of an extensive
scheme of satire on the abuses of learning in every
branch, devised by Swift, Pope and Arbuthnot, and
never completed, was almost entirely the work of
the doctor; and he joined with his two friends in
other productions, in which his style was so intimately blended with theirs, that it is hard to distinguish
the individual hands. No man was more beloved by
his associates or held in higher esteem for his talents.
" The doctor," once said Swift, " has more wit than
we all have, and his humanity is equal to his wit."
On another occasion with that quaint association of
the incongruous which was ever present in Swift's
mind, the Dean wrote : " Our doctor hath every
quality that can make a man amiable and useful, but
alas ! he hath a sort of slouch in his walk," a personal
touch which brings the doctor before us. Arbuthnot's
pen was rarely dipped in gall, and his humour was
as a rule less leavened by the coarseness in which so
many contemporary writers revelled.

Lastly, and from the point of view of the present
book, most important of all, comes John Gay,
careless, somewhat indolent and improvident, but
always good-natured and witty :

> "Of manners gentle, of affections mild ;
> In wit a man, simplicity a child."

Never had a man a larger circle of friends, and few
had greater triumphs as a poet and dramatist, but
at times he seems to have been under the impression
that he was hardly used—a not uncommon attitude
of those who love ease and good living. Gay was
really a very lucky man, and his mishaps were due
to his own mistakes. He had political aspirations,
but they were based on a desire to be comfortably

placed. Sinecures were plentiful enough in those days, but Gay was not destined to drop into one, and perhaps it was as well. It is doubtful whether he would have overcome his natural indolence, save under the spur of necessity. So far as his literary efforts are concerned, his successes more than counter-balanced his failures. His *Trivia, or the Art of Walking the Streets of London,* a poem which within its small compass presents a complete picture of the metropolis in the time of Queen Anne, on its appearance became at once the talk of the town. *The Shepherd's Week,* a burlesque on the so-called pastoral poems then in favour, was not less popular than the *Trivia,* and if his play *The Wife of Bath* had a chilly reception, his absurdity the *What d'ye Call it?*—a mock tragedy which so puzzled the audiences they did not know whether to laugh or to cry—made amends. About his comedy *Three Hours after Marriage* the less said the better. Pope had a hand in this, and Pope could rival Swift in coarseness when he was in the mood.

Gay was fortunate in having hosts of friends ever ready when help was wanted. In 1720 a collection of his poems was published by subscription, out of which he cleared £1,000. In an unlucky moment Mr. Secretary Craggs, of South Sea Bubble notoriety, made him a present of a parcel of the gambling stock. Gay lost his head; speculated, was eager for spoil, and waited too long. His imaginary profits vanished, and so also his real and tangible £1,000. His spirits fell to zero; his health gave way, and again his friends rallied round him. Dim hopes of court favour gave him the necessary impetus for exertion, and he wrote the famous *Fables.* It was a fitting rebuke for what must be deemed toadyism when nothing better than the post of a gentleman usher—not far removed from a footman—to one of the young princesses was offered him.

Gay refused the honour, and, again wounded in spirit, was plunged in disappointment. He could not

but come to the conclusion that, much as he yearned
for it, court life was not for him. The alternative
was literary work, free from the degradation of
waiting for crumbs from the rich man's table; and
to this new-found spirit of independence we owe *The
Beggar's Opera*, to which the year 1727 gave birth.

The Beggar's Opera for many reasons occupies a
unique position in the history of the British stage.
It is not necessary to dwell on its wit, its satire, its
rollicking humour—these qualities are patent, and
were recognised at its first appearance. That which
makes the Opera notable is the good fortune
which attended every step of its progress, cul-
minating in the happy selection of Lavinia Fenton
to play the part of Polly Peachum. Whether *The
Beggar's Opera* made Polly, or Polly the Opera, does
not matter very much ; what does matter is the fact
that, though for a century and a half nearly every
comedy actress who could sing was never satisfied
until she had appeared as Polly Peachum, not one
ever succeeded in eclipsing the fame of the original
Polly.   Polly Peachum is identified with Lavinia
Fenton, and will ever remain so.

While Gay was busy over *The Beggar's Opera*, his
mind was untrammelled. There was no need for
him to be on his best behaviour, as in the case of the
Fables—written professedly for the instruction of the
Duke of Cumberland, upon whom their polish and
elegance, if all the tales of brutality attached to
the name of the " Butcher " of Culloden be true,
could not have had a very softening effect. Gay was
able to write the Opera—as he wrote the *Trivia*
and the *Shepherd's Week*—to please himself. All the
elements of gaiety, all that served to stimulate
invention and high spirits were at hand in the surroundings amid which he worked. Nothing could be
more felicitous for the development of Gay's genius
than the society of the " Twickenham Hotch-Potch."
The freshness and the absence of effort, from the first
line of the Opera to the last, show this perfectly well.

The intellectual atmosphere of Pope's Villa was altogether exceptional, and was well calculated to counteract Gay's natural indolence. The wits of Twickenham were always on the top of the tide in politics, in literature, in everything that was going on or being talked about. Had there been a Boswell or a Pepys among them, what a chronicle of talk—wise, frivolous, satirical, playful, perhaps not too decorous —would have been handed down to delight future generations ! Everything recorded would certainly not be considered suitable for the reading of the " young person," but in an age which numbered Congreve, Wycherley, Vanbrugh and Farquhar among the playwrights, Swift and Pope among the satirists —to say nothing of a host of lesser lights with more coarseness than wit—and Astræa, otherwise Mrs. Aphra Behn, of whom Pope writes :

> "The stage how loosely does Astræa tread,
> Who fairly puts all characters to bed ! "

as the most successful novelist, prior to Richardson and Fielding, the " young person " was not considered.

Another lady novelist, who rivalled Mrs. Aphra Behn, but never attained to Astræa's celebrity, was Mrs. Eliza Haywood. Mrs. Haywood had neither the freedom nor the sprightliness which relieved the coarse audacity of Mrs. Behn. Her stories are a mixture of fustian and sickly sentimentality, interspersed with tedious details of intrigues. When her heroines are not puling maidens and her men insufferable prigs and bores, they are Messalinas and Tarquins. Mrs. Haywood was not fertile in invention, and to attract notice she adopted the method of taking living personages, inventing for each a highflown name after the taste of the time, and fastening upon them amatory adventures more or less questionable.

The Memoirs of a Certain Island adjacent to the Kingdom of Utopia and *The Court of Caramania* were

JOHN GAY.

From an engraving by J. Romney, after J. Thurston.

MRS. CIBBER.

From an engraving by Fairn, after Orchard.

8]

her most ambitious efforts among a dozen novels
or so, all dreary enough, and nowadays difficult to
wade through.   Yet we may suppose that they were
devoured with avidity at the time they first appeared.
To further stimulate curiosity, *The Memoirs of a
Certain Island* was published with " A Key " in
which the initials of the originals appeared opposite
to the pseudonyms.   The copy in the British Museum
Library has the blanks attached to the initials
filled up in pencil by some industrious and well-
informed person, and from this " Key " we learn
that hardly any man or woman moving in Society
between 1720 and 1730, from the Duke of Marlborough downward, escaped Mrs. Haywood's net
of scandal.   What was thought at the time of the
lady's " revelations " it is hard to conjecture.   Contemporary records at all events are silent as to the
effect on the fashionable ladies and gallants who
figured in the stories.   One can hardly imagine them
remaining silent under the imputations cast upon
them, yet there is no evidence to the contrary.   Perhaps they felt flattered !

Pope pillories Mrs. Haywood in *The Dunciad* in
a description, commencing :

> " See in the circle next Eliza plac'd,
> Two babes of love close clinging to her waist ;
> Fair as before her works she stands confessed
> In flow'rs and pearls by bounteous Kirkall dress'd."

The malodorous comparison which follows we
dare not quote.   Kirkall, it may be remarked in
passing, was the name of the engraver of the lady's
portrait published with some of her works.

Sir Walter Scott, in his life of Swift, says that " the
writings even of the most esteemed poets of that
period contain passages which in modern times
would be accounted to deserve the pillory.   Nor
was the tone of conversation more pure than that of
composition, for the taint of Charles II.'s reign
continued to invest Society," and in all probability
the Boswell of Pope's Villa would have imitated the

example of honest Samuel Pepys and have written
his journal in shorthand, of which the "judicious
editor" of after years would have given such extracts
as he considered fit for the public eye—a process
which might have resulted in the elimination of the
most interesting and illuminating passages, as it may
be presumed was the case with the "judicious"
editing of Bubb Dodington's *Diary*.

In Archibald Ballantyne's *Voltaire's Visit to
England* we read that "Owen Ruffhead, one of the
earliest of Pope's biographers, author of a so-called
Life of Pope, which appeared in 1769, started a story
for which Dr. Johnson, by substantially adopting it,
has secured a common currency." Ruffhead's strange
story is as follows : " Mr. Pope told one of his most
intimate friends that the poet Voltaire had got some
recommendation to him when he came to England,
and that the first time he saw him was at Twickenham, where he kept him to dinner. Mrs. Pope, a
most excellent woman, was then alive, and observing
that this stranger, who appeared to be entirely
emaciated, had no stomach, she expressed her concern
for his want of appetite, on which Voltaire gave her
so indelicate and brutal an account of the occasion
of his disorder, contracted in Italy (where Voltaire
never had been and never was, Mr. Ballantyne inter-
polates), that the poor lady was obliged immediately
to rise from table. When Mr. Pope related that, his
friend asked him how he could forbear ordering his
servant John to thrust Voltaire head and shoulders
out of his house. He replied that there was more of
ignorance in his conduct than a purposed affront;
that Voltaire came into England, as other foreigners
do, on a prepossession that not only all religion, but
all decency of morals, was lost among us."

Commenting on this, Mr. Ballantyne says :
" Supplied with this curious theme, following writers
mainly repeated it, indulging a pleasant fancifulness
by occasionally introducing some slight variations.
Johnson, who hated Voltaire, and who had no other

difficulty in regard to Rousseau and Voltaire than to settle the degree of infamy between them, says in his life of Pope that Voltaire ' had been entertained by Pope at his table, where he talked with so much grossness that Mrs. Pope had to leave the room.' A third version is circumstantially certain that the other guests at Pope's dinner table indignantly called Voltaire ' dog ' and ' scoundrel,' while a fourth insists that Voltaire's talk was ' blasphemous as well as disgusting.' "

Mr. Ballantyne discredits the whole story, and it is quite possible he is right. Loose talk is not unknown in the present day, but it would be absurd to argue that because there exists what is called " smoke-room conversation," such lapses from good taste are frequent. The point is not one that would be dwelt upon here but for the bearing it has on the style of *The Beggar's Opera*. The wonder is that, written as it was in the coarsest period of English literature, with its author in daily intercourse with and under the influence of the two great writers whose satire was never tempered by delicacy, Gay steered clear of all that can be called objectionable. Even in these squeamish times the play could be performed exactly as it was originally written, and no one need be shocked.

Macaulay wrote of the dramatic literature which followed the Restoration that it was clever and very entertaining, but that it was in the most emphatic sense of the words " earthly, sensual, devilish." It is true that in 1727 writers for the stage no longer dared attempt such outrages on taste as *Love for Love* and *The Double Dealer*, but the Congreve, Wycherley, and Farquhar plays—at least the most decent of them—were continually being performed, and there were others by inferior writers containing scenes which eventually became beyond toleration and were expunged. Remembering all this, and the lengths to which dramatic authors and actors are tempted to go to obtain a laugh, the restraint exhibited

by Gay in *The Beggar's Opera* is a fact deserving of
emphasis.

It would appear to have been the practice of the
literary brotherhood at Twickenham to submit their
productions to each other for criticism, emendation,
or omission.   Swift, however, was probably an exception, for, to quote again from Scott, "he produced and
read his poems to the little circle of friends where he
presided as absolute dictator.   Copies were requested
and frequently granted.   If refused, the auditors con-
trived to write down from memory an imperfect
version.   These in the usual course of things were
again copied repeatedly, until at length they fell
into the hands of some hackney author or bookseller,
who for profit or to affront the author, or with both
views, gave them to the public."   Such an autocratic
spirit did not, however, belong to Gay, nor did his
talents, great as they were, justify its assumption.
When, therefore, he handed the first draft of *The
Beggar's Opera* to the circle, it was with the expectation that it would be freely criticised and, maybe,
condemned.   Whatever literary merits the play possessed, it was a new departure in writing for the stage,
and one can well believe that however the Twickenham
critics may have differed on particular points, and
whatever they may have thought of the humour and
cleverness of *The Beggar's Opera*, they were all agreed
that success with the town was very doubtful, for
Gay's experiment not only went dead against the accepted canons and solemn traditions of the stage, but
was contrary to the vitiated taste and stilted fashion
of the day.   A return to nature after a long period of
artificiality often has the aspect of innovation, and
of this no better proof can be cited than the effect
produced by *The Beggar's Opera*.

CHAPTER II

WHAT WAS GAY'S INTENTION ?

Gay the sole author of *The Beggar's Opera*—Was it intended as a satire on the Italian Opera ?—The absurdities of Italian Opera in England—Clayton's *Arsinoë*—Handel's *Rinaldo*—The rivalry between the Drama and Opera—The popularity of Jack Sheppard—Did it further Swift's idea of a " Newgate Pastoral " ?

THE story of the origin of *The Beggar's Opera* told by Pope, and given in Spence's *Anecdotes*, has been quoted so often, that an apology almost is needed for repeating it once more; but the repetition is unavoidable, as it settles all disputes as to the authorship.

" Dr. Swift," we read, " had been observing once to Mr. Gay what an odd pretty sort of thing a Newgate pastoral might make. Gay was inclined to try at such a thing for some time ; but afterwards thought it would be better to write a comedy on the same plan. This was what gave rise to *The Beggar's Opera*. He began on it, and when first he mentioned it to Swift, the Doctor did not much like the project. As he carried it on, he showed what he wrote to both of us, and we now and then gave a correction or a word or two of advice, but it was wholly of his own writing. When it was done neither of us thought it would succeed. We showed it to Congreve, who, after reading it over, said, ' It would either take greatly, or be damned confoundedly.' " Elsewhere (Spence's *Anecdotes*) Pope records: " Dr. Arbuthnot was the sole writer of *John Bull*, and so was Gay of *The Beggar's Opera*. I own appearances are against the latter, for it was written in the same house with me and Dr. Swift. He used to communicate the parts

13

of it as he wrote them to us, but neither of us did any more than alter an expression here and there."

But nothing of this was known at the time to the outside world, and Pope and Gay having already been closely associated in the production of *Three Hours after Marriage*, it was not unnatural to suspect that the phenomenal success of *The Beggar's Opera* was due to the collaboration of the master wits of the day. The suspicion that Gay was not solely responsible for his dramatic efforts had indeed always existed. Pope certainly excited remark when he took the whimsical absurdity *What d'ye call it?* with a portion of the manuscript in his own handwriting, to Cibber and read it to the players, though Gay was standing by. Cibber, who did not love Pope, soon found occasion for sarcasm. " What," said he, on seeing a knife on the table with the name of Gay upon it, " does Mr. Pope make knives too ? " Little wonder, then, that Pope, rather than Gay, had at first the credit of all the smart things in *The Beggar's Opera*. There was another reason suggesting doubt whether Gay was the unassisted author : *The Beggar's Opera* is immeasurably superior to anything that the genial poet has left us in the way of dramatic writing. Indeed, it is hardly possible to believe that the natural gaiety and the touches of human nature in the Opera could have come from the hand which penned such rubbish as *Three Hours after Marriage*. The explanation is that Gay had a subject congenial to taste in his " Newgate Pastoral," and that he had the keener interest in the work because it portrayed certain phases of life in London, the London he knew and loved.

It has always been taken for granted that *The Beggar's Opera* was intended as a burlesque upon the Italian Opera, which at that time was in high favour. In his *Life of John Gay*, Dr. Johnson states that *The Beggar's Opera* was " written in ridicule of the musical Italian drama," and this opinion has been accepted by other biographers without, we venture to think, sufficient examination. We submit that Johnson's authority as to music and the opera is of no value. He indeed admitted that " there was nothing in which the power of art is shown so much as in playing on the fiddle," but he owned to Boswell that he was very insensible to the power of music. " I told him," writes Boswell, in his sentimental, high-flown fashion, " that it affected me to such a degree as often to agitate my nerves, painfully producing in my mind alternate sensations of pathetic dejection, so that I was ready to shed tears ; and of daring resolution, so that I was inclined to rush into the thickest part of the battle." Boswell received from the Sage the crushing retort : " Sir, I should never hear it if it made me such a fool." Omnivorous reader as Johnson was, it is doubtful whether he ever interested himself in Italian Opera and in its introduction into England in the early part of the eighteenth century.

In spite of the " general opinion," we cannot see the slightest internal evidence in *The Beggar's Opera* of any intention to burlesque or ridicule the Italian Opera, nor is there any recorded utterance on the part of Gay, or Pope, or Swift, that such was the idea. The Italian Opera of those days, as performed on the Continent at all events, was a tissue of absurdity, bound by cast-iron rules, and it certainly lent itself admirably to travesty ; but no travesty is to be found in *The Beggar's Opera* from beginning to end. Mr. Rockstro, in his *History of Music*, tells of the ridiculous laws to which the early operatic composers were compelled to submit, and probably they submitted unresistingly, for they knew no other. These laws were framed by Hasse and Porpora, and we learn from Mr. Rockstro's pages that : " The custom of the time demanded the employment of six characters only—three women and three men ; though in cases of necessity, the presence of a fourth man was tolerated, or a woman was permitted to take a man's part. The First Woman (*Prima Donna*) was always a high Soprano ; the second, or third, a Contralto. The First Man (*Primo Uomo*), who represented the hero of the pieces, was of necessity an artificial Soprano, even though he might be destined to play the part of Hercules, or Agamemnon. The Second Man was either an artificial Soprano or a Contralto ; the Third was sometimes a Tenor, the Fourth, if present, was nearly always either a Tenor or a Bass. But it was not at all unusual to confide all the note parts to artificial Sopranos or Contraltos, without the aid either of a Tenor, Baritone, or Bass.

"Each principal character claimed the right to sing an Air in each of the three Acts of the Drama. The Airs confided to them were divided into five distinct classes, each distinguished by certain unvarying characteristics, though the indispensable *Da capo* was common to all. . . . Each scene ended with an air of one or the other of these classes, but no two airs of the same class were ever permitted to succeed each other. The hero and heroine each claimed a grand Scena preceded by an accompanied recitative, and usually sang together in at least one duet ; but trios and quartets were rigidly excluded, though the last act always terminated with an *Ensemble* in which all the characters took part."

All this is ridiculous and artificial enough, and the variants of the Italian Opera dished up to suit English tastes were not less stilted and absurd.

What may be termed the first opera in the "Italian style" performed in England was *Arsinoë, Queen of Cyprus*, set by Thomas Clayton. Its libretto and music were equally feeble. Clayton's method was simplicity itself. He merely took a number of Italian airs, altered and spoilt them, and called them his own compositions. The narrative, following the "Grand Italian" fashion, was in recitative. *Arsinoë* as music, was beneath contempt, but it was a novelty and it took the town. *Camilla*, produced two years after (in 1707), was of greater merit. The music was mainly by Buononcini, Handel's rival, and the opera

RICHARD LEVERIDGE.

From an engraving by J. Saunders, after Fry.

held the stage for many years.   The critics denounced the new style of entertainment, but the public patronised it, and Addison did not scruple to consult the popular taste in *Rosamond,* an opera set to music by Clayton. *Rosamond* ran three nights—quite as long as it was worth.

Adaptation was freely employed in the various operas produced until 1711.   The music of Buon-oncini, Scarlatti, and other less known Italian composers, was imported, and English words written to suit the various airs.   The success of the Italian tenor Nicolini, whose combat with a lion in the opera of *Hydaspes* was the subject of Addison's gay humour in No. 13 of the *Spectator,* brought opera into still greater favour, and when Handel produced *Rinaldo* at the Queen's Theatre in the Haymarket in 1711 (it is said he wrote the opera in a fortnight) the musical world were sufficiently educated to recognise the genius of the master.   *Rinaldo* was received with great applause, and is notable not only because with its advent a new era of opera was commenced, but because of the lovely air " Lascia ch'io pianga," which survives to this day.

We need not go over the list of operas which were produced in England from 1711 to 1720.   It is enough to say that they brought fame to such talented singers as Nicolini, Margarita de l'Epine, and Mrs. Tofts, and plunged theatrical managers, actors and actresses, into despair at the loss of the patronage of the public.   The effect of the rivalry was felt as far back as 1707, when some sympathising persons opened a subscription " for the better support of the comedians acting in the Haymarket, and to enable them to keep up the diversion of plays under a separate interest from opera."   The rivalry, though not so acute, continued after 1720, and it is no exaggeration to say that the vocal gymnastics of Farinelli, Senesino, Cuzzoni and Faustina, with their eternal trills, turns, fioraturas and embellishments generally, were greater attractions to the world of

2

fashion than the acting of Barton Booth, Dogget, Wilks, Cibber, Quin, Mrs. Porter, Mrs. Oldfield, and other dramatic celebrities of the day.

If Gay had any notion of ridiculing the Italian opera, he would have found plenty of material in *Rinaldo*. The versatile Aaron Hill (among the pilloried in *The Dunciad*), speculator, promoter of joint-stock companies, theatrical manager and dramatist (a terribly dull one), who brought out *Rinaldo*, had a shrewd notion of what the public liked, and he was not content to rely upon Handel's music alone. As an additional attraction he introduced living birds into the scene representing the gardens of Armida. Addison was not slow to make sport of this novelty.

" As I was walking in the Streets about a Fort-night ago," he writes in No. 5 of the *Spectator*, " I saw an ordinary Fellow carrying a Cage full of little Birds upon his shoulder ; and as I was wondering with my self what Use he would put them to, he was met very luckily by an Acquaintance, who had the same Curiosity. Upon his asking him what he had upon his Shoulder, he told him, that he was buying Sparrows for the Opera. 'Sparrows for the Opera,' says his Friend, licking his lips,—'what, are they to be roasted ? ' 'No, no,' says the other, 'they are to enter towards the End of the first Act, and to fly about the Stage.'

" This strange Dialogue awakened my Curiosity so far, that I immediately bought the opera, by which means I perceived that the Sparrows were to act the part of Singing Birds in a delightful Grove ; though upon a nearer Enquiry I found the Sparrows put the same trick upon the Audience that Sir *Martin Mar-all* practised upon his Mistress ; for though they flew in Sight, the Musick proceeded from a Consort of Flagellets and Bird-calls which were planted behind the Scenes. At the same Time I made this Discovery, I found by the Discourse of the Actors, that there were great Designs on foot for the Improvement of the Opera ; that it had been proposed to break down a part of the Wall, and to surprise the Audience with a Party of an Hundred Horse, and that there was actually a project of bringing the *New-River* into the House, to be employed in Jetteaus and Water-works. This Project, as I have since heard, is post-poned 'till the Summer-Season ; when it is thought the Coolness that proceeds from Fountains and Cascades will be more acceptable and refreshing to People of Quality. In the mean time to find out a more agreeable Entertainment for the Winter-Season, the Opera of *Rinaldo* is filled with Thunder and Lightning, Illuminations and Fireworks ; which the Audience may look upon without catching cold, and indeed without much Danger of being burnt ; for there are several Engines filled with Water, and ready to play at a Minute's warning, in case any such accident Should happen.''

What Gay had in his mind in writing *The Beggar's Opera* was not ridicule, but rivalry, and he could not have selected a more striking contrast to the stucco pseudo-classic themes of Italian Opera than the realism of Newgate. No doubt Swift's suggestion was the germ of the idea, but that which gave rise to the dramatic form into which that suggestion materialised was, we are inclined to think, the furore created by the exploits of Jack Sheppard and his association with the no less famous, or infamous, Jonathan Wild. We are not concerned to enquire why Mr. Sheppard was made a popular hero. Putting on one side his daring escapes from prison, he was an ordinary housebreaker, and all that can be said in his favour is that personally he was infinitely superior to the much-vaunted Dick Turpin, who, thanks to the invention of Mr. Harrison Ainsworth and circus proprietors, has been handed down to the present generation as a model of what a chivalrous highwayman should be. The real Dick Turpin was little better than a common footpad and burglar, and his ride to York and his " Black Bess " are the creations of the fictionist.

Turpin in his own day never achieved the celebrity of Jack Sheppard, and the fact remains that during the year 1725 Jack Sheppard, his exploits and his execution, formed the one topic London people were never tired of discussing. Throughout the autumn of 1725 Sheppard provided sensation after sensation by his daring escapes from prison. The sympathy of the mob was with him, not so much on account of his hardihood as because of their hatred of Wild and his gang of informers, and of their delight in Sheppard's defiance of the brutal criminal laws in force in those days—the days of beheadings, of hangings, whippings, disembowellings, and the tortures of the press-yard and hulks.

On the eve of Sheppard's execution, *The Daily Journal* rose to the occasion, and published some verses in thieves' patter, entitled " John Sheppard's Last Epistle," the two last stanzas running as follows :

> " 'Tis in vain to hope for a *Reprieve*,
>   The Sheriff's come down with his *Warrant*.
> An Account I behind me must leave
>   Of my Birth, Education and Parents.
> My Darbys (handcuffs) knock'd off in the *Witt* (prison).
>   My Friends to die penitent pray me ;
> The *Nubbing Cull* (hangman) pops on the *Cheat* (rope),
>   And into the *Tumbler* (cart) conveys me.

> "I am ambled from *Witt* to the *Tree*,
>   As ordered by my sad *Sentence*;
> The Gownman (chaplain) he there comes to me
>   And talks a long Tune of Repentance.
> I am up to the Jagger dubb'd (done for) right,
>   Then I loudly must join in a *Chorus*;
> My *Peepers* (eyes) are hid from the Light,
>   The Tumbler wheels off and I Morris (swing)."

Sheppard's journey from Newgate to Tyburn was one long triumphal procession, and *The Daily Journal* of November 17, 1725, tells how, after the sentence was carried out, " the Populace having a Notion that it was designed to convey him to the Surgeons, carry'd off the Body upon their Shoulders to an Ale house in Long Acre, and the Undertaker and his men got off with great difficulty." The sequel, described in the same paper on the following day, was exciting enough even for those days of excitement. We read that " A Bailiff in Long Acre having procured the Body of John Sheppard the Malefactor to be brought to his Home after Execution with a sinister design, and thereby frustrating the Preparations of his real Friends for burying him in a decent manner ; the same occasioned a great Riot in Long Acre, whereupon several of his Majesty's Justices of the Peace went to the House and having sent to his Royal Highness the Prince and to the Savoy praying that they might be assisted by a Party of the Foot Guards in the Discharge of their Duty ; a strong Guard came immediately, when a Solicitor and two others who had been the principal Promoters of the Tumult were bound over to the Sessions and the body of Sheppard was delivered over to a Gentleman whom himself had desired to take care thereof, and the same night about 10 it was interr'd in an Elm Coffin at St. Martin's in the Fields with a Velvet Paul (sic) over it, and the Funeral Service perform'd, etc., the Guards marching on each side of the Coach (in which the coffin was carry'd) with Bayonets fix'd at the ends of their Muskets, so that no Disorder happened. The Justices also made an order in writing on the interment." Surely no malefactor, and he a common housebreaker, was ever so honoured as to have a company of the Guards attend his funeral ! And this was not all, for we read also in *The Daily Journal* that " Sir James Thornhill, the King's History Painter, took a Draught of Sheppard's face in Newgate."

During the following year the book trade was flooded with versions of the *Life and Adventures of John Sheppard*. Defoe did not disdain to write one, which became much sought after—so much so that it was translated into French. A very popular entertainment was *Harlequin Sheppard*, produced at Drury Lane, and written by J. Thurmond, a dancing-master and author of *Harlequin Dr. Faustus*, a piece which ran for many nights at the Lincoln's Inn Fields Theatre. In *Harlequin Sheppard* (of the production of which no mention can be found in Genest) the great attraction was a song in thieves' slang sung by Frisky Moll, which to-day requires a glossary to be understood, but which doubtless was then intelligible enough to the audience. Frisky Moll's song is in its way a curiosity, as very few of the words are to be found in the modern thief's vocabulary. We give it together with its interpretation :

"I, Frisky Moll, with my rum coll (good man),
    Wou'd Grub in a boozing ken (ale-house),
But ere for the scraw he had tipped the cole (paid for refresh-
    The Harman (constable) he came in.   ments)

"He broke all the rubbs (obstacles) in the Whitt (Newgate),
    And chiv'd (cut) his darbies (fetters) in twain.
But fileing (breaking into) in a rumbo ken (pawnbroker's
    My Boman is snabbled (imprisoned) again.   shop)

"A famble (ring), a tattle (watch), and his popps (pistols)
    Had my Boman when he was ta'en ;
But had he not boozed in the diddl'd shops (gin shops)
    He'd still be in Drury Lane."

What, however, concerns us most is the " farce " entitled *The Prison Breaker, or the Adventures of John Sheppard,* and " intended to be Acted at the Theatre Royal in Lincoln's Inn Fields." The author (whose name is unknown) appears to have made all the necessary preparations ; a prologue was written by John Leigh, a popular actor who had not long come over from Ireland, and this prologue was to have been spoken by Charles Hulet, who subsequently played Macheath in *The Beggar's Opera,* and was said to have eclipsed Walker, the creator of the part ; but for some reason the play did not see the light, save in print. Our contention is that Gay in some degree was indebted to *The Prison Breaker* for the form in which he cast *The Beggar's Opera.* This indebtedness, of course, only related to the plot of the Opera and the scene in which it is laid ; the introduction of the songs and the music was a different matter, and with this part of Gay's scheme we now proceed to deal.

CHAPTER III

The explanation of the title *The Beggar's Opera*—Popularity of ballads in England—Gay's love for ballad singing—His " Black-Eyed Susan "—His indebtedness to the farce of *The Prison Breaker*—Varied uses of the term " Opera "—Addison's satire—The Duchess of Queensberry's suggestion

IN the " Introduction " Gay tells us that the Opera was originally written to celebrate the marriage of two ballad singers, James Chanter and Moll Lay. A portion of the " Introduction," which consists of a short dialogue between a beggar and a player, may be quoted, as throwing a little light on Gay's object. The beggar who is supposed to be the author says : " I own myself of the Company of Beggars, and I make one at the weekly festivals at St. Giles's. I have a small yearly salary for my catches, and am welcome to a dinner there whenever I please, which is more than most poets can say."

He goes on to remark : " This piece, I own, was originally writ for the celebrating the marriage of James Chanter and Moll Lay, two most excellent ballad singers. I have introduced the similes that are in all your celebrated operas : the Swallow, the Moth, the Bee, the Ship, the Flower, etc. Besides, I have a prison scene, which the ladies always reckon charmingly pathetic. As to the parts, I have observed such a nice impartiality to our two ladies, that it is impossible for either of them to take offence. I hope I may be forgiven that I have not made my opera throughout unnatural, like those in vogue ; for I have no recitative ; excepting this, as I have consented to have neither prologue or epilogue, it must be allowed an opera in all its forms. The piece

23

indeed hath been heretofore frequently represented by ourselves in our room at St. Giles's, so that I cannot too often acknowledge your charity in bringing it now on the stage."

One is tempted to ask, Is all this to be taken seriously, or only as a piece of persiflage in keeping with the spirit of the Opera itself ? The point is one which must have given rise to much discussion among the " Twickenham Hotch Potch," but no record exists of the fact. Why did Gay call his play *The Beggar's Opera* ? If we accept the statement in the " Introduction " as literally true, a reason, of course, is provided, otherwise it is difficult to find an explanation.

What the editor of Bell's *British Theatre* (ed. 1797) has to say on the subject is worth quoting, if only as a specimen of the prim and priggish criticism in fashion in the days of " Farmer George " and " Good Queen Charlotte." He says, " The intention of the author in thus naming the piece (*The Beggar's Opera*) is not clear : it may refer to himself—it may refer to his audience—both ways it proved a misnomer. This design was originally caught from a hint by Swift, and as a man into whatever ground he may venture, usually carries his anger and his prejudice along with him, so *The Beggar's Opera* became a vehicle of his spleen, and those whose influence he could not obtain he lowered to the level of highwaymen and housebreakers. That the Court felt any soreness at the satire it is not easy to imagine—if the severity were insupportable they knew how to stop it. The anger of mortification usually vindicates where it injures—injustice heals the venom in which resentment steeps the shafts of the satirist. The Characters of this Opera are low and vicious; the good here can derive no encouragement of virtue, the bad no discouragement of vice."

This relic of sententious moralising can hardly be regarded as solid argument. It is little more than a reflection of the spirit in which the enemies of Swift and Pope attacked the objects of their hatred through

LINCOLN'S INN FIELDS THEATRE IN 1811.

From an engraving by Wise, after Shepherd.

24]

Gay, during the excitement which followed the success of the Opera. They could see in it nothing but a political skit with Swift and Pope as the real instigators, as we shall endeavour to show when we come to deal with the furore created by Polly and the Opera. Meanwhile we are content to advance the opinion that the weight of hypothesis as to the origin of the musical form of the Opera is on the side of Gay's familiarity with English ballad singing, while the popularity of ballads with people of every degree ought certainly to be taken into account.

The writer of an interesting article on English ballads in *The New Monthly Magazine* (1836) points out that : " In the reign of James I. the taste of the population for nature and simplicity kept up the profession of ballad singing." On the other hand " Minstrels and fiddlers " were excommunicated by Cromwell, but for no other reason than because they were considered low and undesirable visitors to the metropolis. The ballad singers were left alone ; yet very few ballads, if indeed any, can be found which extol the virtues of the Commonwealth. When the Restoration came, however, the singers burst forth to offer up thanks in verse and music to celebrate the return of the monarch. For years after, the political history of the country can be traced in the ballads which were sung about the streets and in the house. Lord Wharton boasted that he had rhymed King James out of the country by his famous song " Lilibullero." James's daughter, Queen Mary, warmly favoured the ballad singers ; and Sir John Hawkins tells us that at an afternoon entertainment of music, when tired of listening to Purcell's songs (accompanied on the harpsichord by the composer), she asked the lady vocalist if she could not sing the old ballad of " Cold and Raw." The lady answered yes, and sang it to her lute. " Purcell," says Hawkins, " was all the while sitting at the harpsichord unemployed, and not a little nettled at the Queen's preference of the vulgar ballad to his music."

The writer in *The New Monthly Magazine* goes on to say that " We are to look upon the ballad singers from this time forth in the light of a corporation. Custom had established yearly festivals for them in the classic regions of St. Giles's, which were much frequented by some of the wits of the day—Swift, Gay, Bolingbroke, Steele, etc. From these high followers of the Muses yearly contingents of ballads were expected. Swift contracted to furnish the humorous songs. Gay, who, as Goldsmith observed of him, had a happy strain of ballad *thinking*, was set down for the pathetic ones. . . . Gay and Swift had naturally a relish for low society, and were hailed by the fraternity and sisterhood as the most precious sources of profit." Gay's ballad " Black-Eyed Susan," for which the celebrated bass singer Leveridge wrote the music, was made popular through the sweet voice and charm of a ballad singer known as Clara. Bolingbroke fell in love with her, and his passion was no mere passing fancy. His affection was sincere, and when she disappeared for a time—it is to be surmised that the young lady had more than one lover—Bolingbroke meeting her by accident, afterwards wrote the lines beginning :

" Dear, thoughtless Clara, to my verse attend,
Believe for once the lover and the friend,"

and ending :

" To Virtue thus and to thyself restored,
By all admired, by one at least adored ;
Be to thy Harry ever kind and true,
And live for him who more than died for you."

" Black-Eyed Susan " or " All in the Downs," the name by which the song was called in Gay's time, was also set by Henry Carey, George Haydon, and a Signor Sandoni, but only Leveridge's version has survived. As originally written, the opening phrase is not quite as we know it.

Gay, to quote Spence, " was quite a natural man, wholly without art (*i.e.* cunning) or design, and spoke

just what he thought and as he thought it." He
was a Bohemian by inclination, as were Steele,
Swift, Prior, Savage, Otway (we read of Otway
" carousing one week with Lord Plymouth, and
drinking a month in low company at an ale-house in
Tower Hill "), Carey, and other poets; and his love
for music would make him well acquainted, not only
with the ballads of his own day, but with those popular
with preceding generations. Among other songs
for which Gay was responsible besides " All in the
Downs," one recalls " 'Twas when the sea was
roaring," a great favourite, thanks to Leveridge's
fine singing; and in a way Gay identified himself
with English ballads. It requires, therefore, no
great stretch of the imagination to suppose that the
idea of an English Opera occurred very naturally
to him ; and how this idea came to be incorporated
with Swift's odd notion of a " Newgate Pastoral " is
not so difficult to conjecture when Jack Sheppard
and the farce of *The Prison Breaker* are remembered.

The curious thing about *The Prison Breaker* is
that in a way it anticipates *The Beggar's Opera*. We
have Sheppard and his gang, just as Macheath has
his associates ; Jonathan Wild is introduced—the
Peachum of the Opera was, it is well known, intended
to point at the hated thief-taker—and there is Coaxthief, described as the " Master of a public-house."
Lockit, as Lucy reminds him in one of her songs,
was once in the " public " line, and in both plays the
principal action takes place in Newgate. Here,
however, all resemblance ceases. The only female
characters in *The Prison Breaker* are Mrs. Poorlean
and Mrs. Coaxthief—coarse, lay figures of women
who have little to do—and Sheppard himself is not
painted with any attractions. The author's object
was in a measure to portray the free and easy life
of Newgate, and how the prison was regarded as a
show-place by the public. The author introduces
two stock stage characters, which the audience knew
very well would be cause for merriment—a Quaker

and an Irishman. To ridicule Quakerism was a sure
card to play, and we have the Quaker in this instance
indulging in sentiments and expressions which to-day
would warrant the free use of the blue pencil. These
two are among the " glut of company to see this
Sheppard," as Rust, a sort of Lockit, puts it, adding
what was doubtless quite true, " He's worth very
much to us." With " Dr. Anatomy," who has some
sprightly things to say concerning his perquisites
in the interests of medical science, a Welsh attorney
—a class of professional gentlemen which for some
reason was obnoxious to the mob—and a pawnbroker
who all figure in the plot, such as it is, the characters
are complete. A significant reference to the state
of the prison is contained in Rust's lament on the
arrival of fresh prisoners that " we are straitened
for room in this Gaol," but he finds comfort in
the fact that " to-morrow being Execution Day, we
can dispose of them more comfortably."

With Gay on the look-out for material for his
" pastoral " it is hardly likely he would pass over
The Prison Breaker. The resemblance it bore to
The Beggar's Opera was apparent to theatrical
managers, eager to benefit by the unprecedented
popularity of Gay's Opera; and among the advertisements in *The Daily Journal* in 1729 concerning
Bartholomew Fair we find an announcement that
" at Lee and Harper's Great Theatrical Booth over
against the Hospital Gate " one of the attractions was
"that celebrated entertainment called *Hero and Leander*,
with singing and dancing performed by persons from
both Theatres, beginning at ten in the morning and
continuing playing till three in the afternoon, and no
longer, because of the vast concourse of people
which crowd to see *The Quaker Opera, or the Escape
of Jack Sheppard.*" This was in all probability a
" dish up " of *The Prison Breaker*; but in spite of the
inducement held out that the entertainment would
" begin at four in the afternoon and continue the
remaining part of the evening, and any person may

come before the last show not to be crowded by paying more," the show could not have proved a powerful rival to the genuine *Beggar's Opera*, "with all the songs and dances set to music as performed at the Theatre in Lincoln's Inn Fields," which was given at the same time in the George Inn Yard in Smithfield " by the Company of Comedians from the New Theatre in the Haymarket."

It would seem, from the advertisements of the period, that the word " Opera " was applied to dramatic entertainments *ad captandum*, and the average person accepted the term without troubling very much about its exact meaning. At Lincoln's Inn Fields Theatre was produced in 1725, to quote from the advertisements in the *Daily Journal*, " A Dramatic Opera : *The Prophetess, or the History of Dioclesian*, with alterations and vocal parts all new set to music." At the same theatre was given " A Dramatic Opera, *The Island Princess or the Generous Portuguese*, with singing by Mrs. Isabella Chambers," and " the ' Enthusiastic Song,' by Mr. Leveridge." As these " dramatic operas " were performed by " the company of Comedians," they could hardly have been operas in the Italian style. Tom D'Urfey's *Masaniello*, as altered by Walker (afterwards the original Macheath), seems to have been difficult to classify, and is advertised simply by its name. It had an " original ballad in praise of fishing by Mr. Leveridge," and " a solemn piece of music vocal and instrumental," the " vocal parts by Leveridge, Legar, and Salway." *Don John*, with the original Shepherd's Music by Purcell, was given at Drury Lane ; and *Acis and Galatea*, set to music by John Eccles and called " a Musical Masque," was another variety of the " Opera." In 1727 a company of Italian Comedians performed " a Comic Opera, *La Parodia del Pastor Fido* " (*Daily Post*, April 25) ; and in the same year an attraction at the King's Theatre in the Haymarket was what was termed " A Comedy within a Comedy," entitled *The Foppish Merchant turn'd*

Comedian for Love, " with singing, dancing, and seren-
ading after the Venetian manner."

Earlier in the century we find the following
advertisement : " At the upper end of St. Martin's
Lane will be presented an Opera call'd *Alaesta or the
Triumphs of Neptune*, with several surprising figures
performed by Powell from Bath," and in *The Daily
Postman* for November 14, 1710, we read that :
" At Punch's Opera at Litchfield Street end this
present Thursday the 16th will be seen Powell's
puppet show from the Bath called *The History of
Chast Susannah and the 2 wicked Elders*. The Figure
being drest in Hebrew and Babylonian Habits with
that diverting figure of the Jesuite, where you'll see a
woman Quaker Holding forth from his Head and
is deliver'd with an antic from his Body with the
Scaramonah and Tumbler, etc. All the Figures performed by Powell with Scenes and Machines with a
prologue coherent to the play. The Boxes are moved
to the Front of the House, made convenient and warm
for the Quality to begin exactly at 6 o'clock."

Powell was a famous puppet show entertainer,
to whom there is frequent reference in the *Spectator*.
In No. 31 will be found an amusing skit upon the
various amusements of the day, which has a bearing
upon our contention that the term " Opera " had a
very wide application. Addison going into a Coffee-
house not far from the Haymarket Theatre, describes
how he found a shabbily dressed gentleman " entertaining a whole Table of Listeners with the Project
of an Opera which he told us had not cost him
above two or three Mornings in the Contrivance, and
which he was ready to put into Execution provided
he might find his Account in it. He said, that he had
observed the great Trouble and Inconvenience which
Ladies were at, in travelling up and down to the
several Shows that are exhibited in different Quarters
of the Town. The Dancing Monkies are in one
Place, the Puppet Show in another ; the Opera in a
third ; not to mention the Lions, that are almost a

day's journey from the Politer Part of the Town.
By this means People of Figure are forced to lose
half the Winter after their coming to Town, before
they have seen all the strange Sights about it.   In
order to remedy this great Inconvenience, our Pro-
jector drew out of his Pocket the Scheme of an
Opera Entitled, *The Expedition of Alexander the
Great* ; in which he had disposed all the remarkable
Shows about Town, among the Scenes and Decorations of his Piece. . . .

" This *Expedition of Alexander* opens with his con-
sulting the Oracle at Delphos, in which the dumb
Conjuror, who has been visited by so many Persons
of Quality of late Years, is to be introduced as telling
him his Fortune.   At the same time *Clench* of *Barnet*
is represented in another corner of the Temple as
ringing the Bells of *Delphos*, for joy of his arrival.   The
Tent of *Darius* is to be peopled by the Ingenious Mrs.
Salmon, where *Alexander* is to fall in love with a piece
of Wax-work that represents the beautiful *Statira*.
When *Alexander* comes into that Country, in which
Quintus Curtius tells us the Dogs were so exceeding
fierce that they would not loose their Hold tho'
they were cut to pieces Limb by Limb, and that they
would hang upon their Prey by their Teeth when
they had nothing but a Mouth left, there is to be a
Scene of *Hockley in the Hole* in which is to be represented all the Diversions of that Place, the Bull-
baiting only excepted, which cannot possibly be
exhibited in the Theatre by reason of the Lowness of
the Roof.   The several Woods in *Asia* which *Alexander* must be supposed to pass through, will give
the Audience a sight of Monkies dancing upon Ropes,
with the many other Pleasantries of that ludicrous
Species.   At the same time, if there chance to be
any Strange Animals in Town, whether Birds or
Beasts, they may be either let loose among the Woods,
or driven across the Stage by some of the Country
people of Asia.   In the last great Battel, *Pinkethman*
is to personate King *Porus* upon an Elephant, and

is to be encountered by *Powell*, representing *Alexander* the Great, upon a Dromedary, which nevertheless *Mr. Powell* is desired to call by the name of *Bucephalus.* Upon the Close of this great decisive Battel when the two Kings are thoroughly reconciled, to show the mutual Friendship and good Correspondence that reigns between them, they both of them go together to a Puppet-show in which the ingenious *Mr. Powell Junior* may have an Opportunity of displaying his whole Art of Machinery, for the Diversion of the two Monarchs.''

Bearing all this in mind, it is not straining the point to conjecture that Gay had no particular object in calling his play an Opera, save as an indication that it was provided with songs and was in the fashion. An additional argument in favour of this hypothesis is that the songs were originally intended to be sung without any accompaniments. Pope and Swift were not musicians. Swift had as little interest in the drama as in music, and he once spoke very slightingly of Mrs. Oldfield, whom he calls a "drab"; and Pope so far as music was concerned was equally indifferent. He was, says Spence, quite insensible to the merits of Handel, and seriously inquired of Arbuthnot whether the applause bestowed on his music was really deserved. Thus the absence of instrumental music did not appeal to them, but Arbuthnot had a considerable knowledge of music, and Gay, we know, played the flute, and chose probably the majority of the tunes introduced into the opera. The credit of the addition of accompaniments is due to the Duchess of Queensberry, Gay's great friend, who when attending a rehearsal objected to the voices being unsupported by an orchestra, and, we may be sure, protested with her usual vehemence. She carried her point in spite of Rich's objection, and this no doubt was why Dr. Pepusch was called in to assist. It is difficult to suggest any convincing argument to show that Gay had the conventional opera in his mind, either to

JOHN RICH ("LUN") AS HARLEQUIN.

From a rare print by G. Vander Gucht. in Mr. A. M. Broadley's Collection.

satirise or to parody. Mr. H. B. Wheatley, in his *Hogarth's London*, says that he had so little acquaintance with the requirements of our Opera, that at first no songs were introduced until nearly the middle of the play. Nor does the announcement of the first performance throw any light on the matter. Nothing indeed could be less promising of novelty than the following advertisement, which appeared in *The Daily Journal* of January 29, 1728 : " Never acted before. By the Company of Comedians, At the Theatre in Lincoln's Inn Fields this present Monday being the 29th January, will be presented *The Beggar's Opera*. Boxes, 5s., Pit, 3s., Gallery, 2s."

No one could have possibly guessed from this the nature of the piece. Rich did not think it worth while to give the cast, or even to mention Gay's name. Doubtless it was a matter of common knowledge that Gay was the author ; but had the intention been to burlesque Italian opera, Rich, who was a keen man of business, would, it is to be supposed, have announced that such was the case. It may have been that he regarded *The Beggar's Opera* in the nature of an experiment, or that he wanted to spring a surprise upon his audience, but whatever may have been in his mind, he made no attempt to whet the curiosity of the public in any way.

Very seldom did the newspapers of the day contain a notice of a theatrical performance, but *The Beggar's Opera* furnishes an exception, and in *The Daily Journal* of February 1 we have the following : " On Monday was represented for the first Time at the Theatre Royal in Lincoln's Inn Fields, Mr. Gay's new English Opera, written in a manner wholly new and very Entertaining, there being introduced instead of Italian airs, about 60 of the most celebrated old English and Scotch Tunes. There was present there, as well as last Night, a prodigious concourse of Nobility and Gentry, and no Theatrical Performance for these many years has met with so much Applause." It is worthy of note that while

3

reference is made to old English and Scotch tunes
being " introduced instead of Italian airs," there is
not a word of any desire to ridicule the Italian style,
and on the whole it is pretty certain that the audiences
and the critics accepted the Opera not as a satire,
but simply as a novelty that was " very Entertaining."

Mr. John Ireland seems to put the matter very
clearly in his *Hogarth Illustrated,* when he says,
" Gay must be allowed the praise of having attempted
to stem the Italian liquid stream which at that time
meandered through every alley, street and square in
the metropolis—the honour of having almost silenced
the effeminate song of that absurd exotic Italian
opera, which a little previous to this time was the
grand pursuit of the fashionable world . . . To lay an
embargo upon sound so imposed—to make an echo
perform quarantine ?   Ridiculous !   He took a better
mood, drew up a song against sing-song, and to the
soft sonnetteering stanza of Italy opposed the nervous
old ballad of Britain."   " Saire," once said an irate
Italian, " this simple signor he tri to pelt mi countrymen out of England with Lumps of Pudding "—one
of the tunes in *The Beggar's Opera.*

Hogarth's caricature of Farinelli, Cuzzoni and
Senesino shows very forcibly how easily these celebrated singers could have been burlesqued, had Gay
cared to make the experiment.   In 1728 the three
operatic celebrities appeared in Handel's opera of
Ptolemais, and we learn from the satirical description,
given in a pamphlet entitled *Reflections on Theatrical Expression in Tragedy,* something of Farinelli's
style of singing and acting.   " What a pipe !   What
modulation !   What ecstasy to the ear ! " exclaims
the author in affected rapture.   But he adds,
" Oh heaven !   What clumsiness !   What stupidity !
What offence to the eye !   Reader, if of the city,
thou mayst probably have seen in the fields of
Islington or Mile End, or if thou art in the environs
of St. James thou must have observed in the Park,

with what ease and agility a cow, heavy with calf, has rose up at the end of the milk-woman's foot. Thus from the mossy bank sprang up the divine Farinelli, then with long strides advancing a few paces, his left hand set upon his hip in a beautiful bend like that of an old-fashioned caudle-cup, his right hand remained immovable across his manly breast, till numbness called its partner to supply its place, when it relieved itself in the position of the other handle of the caudle-cup." And how the great singer appeared in this attitude, the curious may see for themselves in Hogarth's ludicrous drawing.

The annotator of *The Dunciad* (ed. 1736), put forward no suggestion of satire or ridicule in referring to the well-known line :

" Gay dies unpensioned with a hundred friends,"

and he was writing but eight years after the Opera was produced. " Furthermore," he says, " it drove out of England for that season Italian Opera, which had carri'd all before it for ten years, as the idol of the nobility and the people, which the great critic Mr. Dennis by the labours and outcries of a whole life could not overthrow, was demolished by a single stroke of this gentleman's pen." But the victory was achieved by fair competition and by no other means. If further argument be needed, it is furnished by Arbuthnot, who writing in the *Daily Journal* says, " I take *The Beggar's Opera* to be the touchstone to try the British taste on, and it has accordingly proved effectual in discovering our true inclinations, which, how artfully soever they may be disguised by a childish fondness for Italian poetry and music in preference to our own, will in one way or another start up and disclose themselves ; " and at this the question may very well rest.

CHAPTER IV

REALISM OF " THE BEGGAR'S OPERA "

IT need not be assumed that because *The Beggar's Opera* saw the light in a complete form in 1727, Gay had not conceived the play long before. The truth is, Swift suggested the idea of a Newgate pastoral as far back as 1716. Writing to Pope from Ireland on August 30 of that year, he says : " There is a young ingenious Quaker in this town, who writes verses to his mistress, not very correct, but in a strain purely what a poetical Quaker should do, commending her look and habit, etc., etc. It gave me a hint that a Quaker pastoral might succeed if our friend Gay could fancy it, and I think it a fruitful subject ; pray hear what he says. I believe further the pastoral ridicule " (the pastorals of Ambrose Phillips had for some time been attacked both by Swift and Pope) " is not exhausted, and that a porter footman or chairman's pastoral might do well. Or what think you of a Newgate pastoral among the whores and thieves there ? "

From this it is evident that the idea had been a long time coming to fruition. Swift took a hurried journey to Ireland in August of 1726, torn with anxiety concerning Stella's health, and Gay probably had turned the notion over in his mind before the Dean left Twickenham. That he had been at work upon it when Swift returned to England in March

1727 is evident from the statement of Sir Walter Scott that, " about this time Swift is supposed to have supplied Gay with the two celebrated songs, afterwards ingrafted in *The Beggar's Opera*, beginning ' Through all the employments of Life,' and ' Since laws were made for every degree.' "

Those who are tempted to read *The Beggar's Opera*, and are reading it for the first time, may not unnaturally imagine that Gay's Newgate is an ideal and an impossible one. On the contrary it was as real as though he had placed the prison itself on the stage. We venture to suggest that the Opera was a caricature of Newgate life and manners, rather than a caricature of the Italian opera; but if the force of a caricature be the measure of its truth, then no closer copy of the original has ever been put into a dramatic form. In the year 1717 a most entertaining little book was published entitled *The History of the Press-Yard*, and the author gives such a grimly humorous description of his experience that, apart from its bearing on the question of the genesis of Gay's masterpiece, it is well worth quoting. He begins by telling us that—

" I was very decently Conducted in a Coach to the Place of my future Residence called Newgate, there to reflect with myself on my past Indiscretions and to cool my Heels. . . . I found myself in the Lodge encompass'd by a parcel of ill-looking Fellows, that eyed me as if they would look me through and examin'd every part of me from Head to Toe. . . . Quoth a Fellow with the most rueful Appearance that ever Creature with two Legs ever made, to his Doxy, that I understood was a Runner upon all Necessary occasions of the Gaol, *Dol, we shall have a Hot Supper to Night, the Cull looks as if he had the Blunt, and I must come in for a share of it, after my few Masters have done with him*, and began to Rattle a Bunch of Keys in his Hand to call for Half a Pint of Brandy to drink his new Master's Health; which was immediately brought by a short thick Protuberance of

Female Flesh not less than five Yards in the Wast,
and sent down Gutter-Lane instantly (as well it
might) being little more than the quantity of Half a
Quartern. Madam, said I to her, for I found the
Beast had that Appellation given to her, which are
the Persons that are to take care of me ? *Bring the
Gentleman a Flask of the best Claret, that which Mr.
Kent sent in last, quick, quick, Sirrah* ; was all the
Answer I could have from her. Whereupon I
repeated my Question and desired her to pledge me,
which she did in a Bumper and replyed, *A Bottle
of French White for the Gentleman. You shall have it,
sir, as good as any in England, take the word of an
honest Woman for it.* Now this *Honest Woman* as I
was afterwards told was an old Convicted Offender,
one that had gone through every Degree of Iniquity
and by receiving Sentence of Death for the same was
arriv'd at the Zenith of Perfection in that Art and
Mistery . . . all Hands were at Work in putting the
Glass round for the good of the House as they called
it, and six or seven Flasks were consumed in this
manner and the value of as much more in Brandy,
which was all paid down upon the nail for, before I
could get the Woman or Monster above mention'd
to tell me what Appartment I was to have my
Abode in, and then she took upon her to whisper me
and say, *Dear Sir, you seem to be a very Civil Gentleman
and will no doubt be treated as such by Mr. (Rou)se*
(the head turnkey) *and Mr. R(ussel)l, who know how
to distinguish Persons of Worth from Scoundrels.* . . .
  " In the meantime this pair of Irons and that
pair of Fetters were handed about from one to the
other behind me, and I had the mortification of being
Terrified with, *a Pair of Forty Pounds Weight will be
enough for him,* spoke by way of Wisper. *We ought
to send to the Governor to know whether he is to be
handcuff'd.* This made me ready to enter into a
Treaty by way of Prevention and again to enquire
for the Persons who had Authority to manage it,
which one or two sly Thieves about me laying hold

of insinuated to me that it was in their Power to make an Interest as to my Irons and that upon such and such Considerations they would serve me. Hereupon I without any Hesitation thrust the Purport of their Agreement into their hands. . . ."

Compare the above with the dialogue between Lockit and Macheath in the scene in Act II., where Macheath is brought into Newgate :

"LOCKIT: Noble captain, you are welcome ! You have not been a lodger of mine this year and a half. You know the custom, sir. Garnish, captain—garnish. Hand me down those fetters, there.

"MAC.: Those, Mr. Lockit, seem to be the heaviest of the whole set. With your leave, I should like the further pair better.

"LOCKIT : Look ye, captain, we know what is fittest for our prisoners. When a gentleman uses me with civility, I always do the best I can to please him. Hand them down, I say ! We have them all prices from one guinea to ten ; and 'tis fitting every gentleman should please himself.

"MAC. : I understand you, sir (*gives money*). The fees here are so many and so exorbitant, that few fortunes can bear the expense of getting off handsomely, or of dying like a gentleman.

"LOCKIT : Those, I see, will fit the captain better. Take down the further pair. Do but examine them, sir ; never was better work. How genteely they are made ! They will sit as easy as a glove, and the richest man in England might not be ashamed to wear them. (*He puts on the chains.*) If I had the best gentleman in the land in my custody, I could not equip him more handsomely ! And so, sir, I now leave you to your private meditations."

There is no exaggeration here. It is virtually what took place on the admission of every prisoner. He had to " garnish " if he could ; if not, woe betide him. The life inside Newgate was very much that which went on outside, excepting that the prisoners had to pay through the nose for everything. They could hardly look at a turnkey but it cost them the price of a drink, and provided they had money, the prisoners might as well have been in Drury Lane or at Hockley in the Hole as within stone walls. The author describes how some of his fellow prisoners " were Drinking with Friends, some Reading, others playing at Skittles where there was scarce room to set up the Pins, and a fourth sort were talking extravagantly of politics." The chronicler joined one of the politicians and discoursed to him " over a Pipe and a Pot of Stout and Ale for which I paid six-pense till Notice was brought to us by a Person in Grey Hairs . . . that all Things were ready for our Evening's Refreshment and that honest Tom, for that was the Name of our Sutler in the Garrison, had carried the Bottles, Pipes and Tobacco into our Refectory called the Tap-room."

Gay more than hints at this freedom in Act III. Polly refuses the " strong waters " which Lucy would have given her to make her tongue wag concerning her relations with Macheath, and sends Filch to bring her news of the trial of the gallant Captain at that moment going on. Later on she enquires of Lucy, " Why is all this music ? "

" LUCY : The prisoners whose trials are put off till next season are diverting themselves.

" POLLY : Sure there is nothing so charming as Musick ! I'm fond of it to distraction.—But alas!— now all mirth seems an insult upon my affliction. Let us retire, my dear Lucy, and indulge our sorrows. . . . The noisy crew you see are coming upon us. [*Exeunt.*

"*A dance of prisoners in chains, etc.*"

In the final scene a number of Macheath's fellow Knights of the road are admitted to talk with him, and the Opera concludes with the reckless Macheath and his hapless sweethearts singing :

LAVINIA FENTON.

From an engraving by Faber, after J. Ellys, in Mr. A. M. Broadley's Collection.

" Lucy : 'Would I might be hanged—
" Polly :   And I would so too.
" Lucy : To be hang'd with you—
" Polly :   My dear, with you.
" Mac. : Oh, leave me to thought. I fear—I doubt!
I tremble—I droop! See, my courage is out (*turns up the empty glass*).
" Polly : No token of love ?
" Mac. : See, my courage is out ! (*turns up the empty bottle*).
" Lucy : No token of love ?
" Polly :   Adieu !
" Lucy :   Farewell ! (*bell tolls*).
" Mac. : But, hark ! I heard the toll of the bell."

If the truth were known, it would be found that the last moments of condemned prisoners were of anything but the edifying character which the pious compilers of last speeches and confessions would have us believe. They showed rather the bravado and indifference of Macheath. The writer from whose informing pamphlet we have quoted gives a case in point. While he was reading the newspapers (every one, be it remarked, who paid so much a week to the turnkey, had that privilege) one of the prisoners charged with erasing endorsements on bank bills with the " juice of Limmons " who was certain he would be hanged, " very frankly came to me and cry'd, Sir, I am told that you are a Judge of things of this Nature, pray will you look over my last Dying Speech and correct what you shall find amiss therein." The Dying Speech is given at length, and is not quite the contrite and decorous effusion which the smug official in holy orders, who added very materially to his stipend by putting "last words" into the mouths of felons about to be " turned off," would have written. It certainly would have shocked the pious Ordinary who, as Goldsmith wrote some fifty years later, " has but one story for the life of every hero that happens to come within the circle of his pastoral care." The final paragraphs of the "Speech" will suffice :

"To conclude, for I may speak till my Tongue's weary before a Reprieve will come. You Ladies and Gentlemen that are Spectators of my last *Exit*, can bear me witness that I do not go out of the World whining and crying like many others that have gone before me, because I have been told that this is no abiding Place and find that saying to be verified now by Experience, and the Condition I am in.

"As for my Bodily Goods, if the Government and Captain S——k have left me any to dispose of, I bequeath them to the Undertaker who is to have the Care of my Interment, and this honest Friend here *Jack Catch* or *Mr. Marvell*, which you please, who is to put a stop to my Breath ; tho' I very much fear little more than what is in my Pocket will fall to the share of the latter, because they have been emptied lately at Whisk (whist).

"So much by way of Oration ; here *Jack* do your Office decently and with dispatch, these Cloaths Hat and Wig are yours. You will find Fifteen Shillings and some Grocery in my pocket. Now Mr. Ordinary you may sing the Psalm if you please and I'll endeavour as well as it is possible to bear a Bob with you ; but let it be none of the Penitential ones."

Life was held very cheaply in the eighteenth century. Does not Horace Walpole tell a story of a footman who, convicted of the murder of a butler, was visited in the condemned cell by George Selwyn, morbid on such matters, and urged to write his confession. Willing to oblige, the fellow, who was but nineteen, took a pen and commenced : "I murd——" then he stopped, and looking at Selwyn, said with the most complete sang-froid, "How do you spell 'murdered' ? "

It is very certain that, in the first half of the eighteenth century, Newgate and its associations were brought home to the people of London every day of their lives. The suppression of Jacobitism,

which filled Newgate to overflowing, was fresh in
their memories; the processions from Newgate
to Tyburn were of weekly occurrence, and highly
popular as spectacles; prisoners with means could
hold high revel, if they pleased, within prison
walls; there was no barrier to visitors other than
the rapacity of the officials, from the Governor
down to the turnkeys—in a word, Newgate was the
centre of life in London, and a recognised institution,
quite apart from its function for the housing of
criminals. It was the happiest idea possible to
select Newgate as the scene of an " Opera," and the
very incongruity of the notion was an element of
success.

While Gay was busy polishing his drama, and
anxiously conferring with his friends Pope and
Arbuthnot (Swift was not of the party, being away
in Ireland at the end of 1727 with Stella) how to
strengthen its points and situations—to say nothing
of the labour of ransacking the world of ballad music
for popular tunes—a sprightly damsel of nineteen
summers, with speaking eyes and lips made for
smiles, was engaged by John Rich, the manager of
the theatre in Lincoln's Inn Fields, to play Cherry in
Farquhar's lively comedy, *The Stratagem,* as it was
generally called in those days, although better known
in these as *The Beaux' Stratagem.* Everything was
conspiring to benefit Gay, who, unconscious of his
impending good fortune, was bemoaning his ill luck
because his novelty had been refused by Colley
Cibber, then manager of Drury Lane. In reality
Cibber's failure to see the merit of *The Beggar's Opera*
was the most fortunate thing possible. There were
not two Lavinia Fentons, and it may be safely asserted
that in the hands of any one but the ingenuous
damsel of Lincoln's Inn Fields Theatre, Polly Peachum
—we mean the Polly of the play and not her representative—would not have achieved celebrity, and it
is quite possible that *The Beggar's Opera* would have
simply taken its place in the long list of dramatic

productions the names of which have alone been handed down to the present day.

Polly—or Lavinia Fenton, to call her by her own name—was of humble origin. In this respect she resembles Nell Gwynne, Ann Oldfield, Peg Woffington, Ann Catley, Kitty Clive, Dorothea Jordan, Harriot Mellon, and many other more or less celebrated actresses who have won their way to fame by their natural wit and high spirits, apart from their talents. John Ireland speaks of Polly as having sold oranges in the theatre, evidently confusing her with Nell Gwynne. As a matter of fact Polly's early history is very uncertain, and mainly rests upon the statements contained in a so-called biography published in 1728, after the young lady became famous. It is entitled *The Life of Lavinia Beswick, alias Fenton, alias Polly Peachum,* and on the title page is a synopsis of the contents of the volume, as follows : " The whole interspers'd with convincing proofs of her *Ingenuity, Wit* and *Smart Repartees.* And concluding with some remarkable Instances of her Humanity to the Distressed." The little book of forty-eight pages was " printed for A. Moore near St. Paul's, and sold by the Booksellers and Pamphlet-Shops in London and Westminster," and the price was one shilling.

The "Life" is one of a class peculiar to the period. The chief object of the biographer is to make up a racy story ; fact and fiction are interwoven without any clue as to which is which, actual names are rarely given, and the style is what no doubt in those days was deemed smart writing. Most of the notorieties of the eighteenth century, from " Old Q " down to Jack Sheppard, were honoured or dishonoured in this fashion, and naturally the "memoirs" of the ladies of the day were most in demand, and lent themselves best to the imaginations of the hack writers. Polly was not the first damsel whose doings, real or imaginary, were dished up to suit the taste of the scandal-loving public ; she was preceded by the sprightly Sally Salisbury among others, whose memoirs if issued to-day would most certainly bear the announcement " privately printed."

Two things strike the reader of to-day who attempts to wade through these specimens of by-gone sprightliness—one is the amazing freedom of the biographer, and the other the apparent indifference shown by the subject of his pen to his " revelations." The ladies, whose " memoirs " were sold openly, could hardly have been ignorant of what was written about them, but they do not appear to have been sensitive. Hardly an actress of any celebrity escaped the doubtful honour of having her private life reproduced with embellishments. Peg Woffington, Mrs. Cibber, Ann Catley, Mrs. Oldfield, Mrs. Bellamy and Mrs. Billington, had the privilege of reading more or less fictitious and scurrilous accounts of their lives, and nothing followed. The practice was continued into the nineteenth century. Even Miss Farren, the blameless, did not escape the penalty of celebrity. Mr. R. W. Lowe, in his *Biographical Account of Theatrical Literature*, calls her *Memoirs* " a very sneering account . . . seasoned with a few gratuitous nastinesses." Mrs. Jordan the vivacious was not spared by the scribbler or by the cartoonist. Two infamous prints by Gillray are in existence, the only excuse for which—if an excuse for coarseness without humour *can* be admitted—is that the artist's genius had o'erleaped itself, as indeed was shown by the attempt Gillray made on his own life. Nearer our own times Miss Harriot Mellon was the subject of blackmailing writers, while Madame Vestris and her gaieties were especially favoured subjects for the free and unscrupulous pen.

CHAPTER V

THE BLUNDERS OF BIOGRAPHERS

Polly's parentage—Her mother a coffee-house keeper—Polly's school adventure—Her first love affair—The amorous Portuguese nobleman—She goes on the stage—The fictions respecting her first appearance—The true story—Her theatrical career in 1726–27 traced

ACCORDING to Polly's biographer, " the person who had the pleasure of having her mother's first affections was a Lieutenant of a Man of War, his name Beswick, and thus pretty Polly was the fruit of their Amours, and was born in the year 1708." The Lieutenant having loved, sailed away after writing a letter in which he advises his forlorn love to contrive " to lie in like a citizen's daughter, twenty or forty miles off in the country, and then come up and rejoice with your friends, that you have recovered from a fit of sickness." He promises, however, that if he lives to return home, he will make provision both for mother and child, and in a postscript says : " If Hans-en-kelder should ripen into a living Monument of our Love, call it Porteus if a boy, if a girl Lavinia. And now, adieu, my dear, for two tedious long years."

The lady carried out these prudent instructions, our facetious author quoting, as suitable to the occasion, Prior's lines :

" Ten Minutes after Philomel happened to wed,
And was brought in a laudable manner to bed,
She warbled her Groans with so charming a voice,
That one half of the Parish was stunned with the noise ;
But when Philomel deigned to lie privately in
Ten Months before she and her Spouse were akin,
She chose with such prudence her Pangs to conceal,
That her nurse, nay, her mid-wife scarce heard her to squeal."

46

Of course, the sailor, after the manner of his kind, did not return—he probably thought he had atoned for everything in having given a choice of names to provide for contingencies—and Polly's mother did the best thing possible under the circumstances—she married. Her husband was a Mr. Fenton. Of Mr. Fenton we are told nothing, save that he lived in the Old Bailey. Apparently he was of no account, for the author proceeds to say of Mrs. Fenton that she, " being a woman of a popular spirit, soon after her marriage set up a coffee-house in Charing Cross, where Polly, being a child of a vivacious lively spirit, and of promising Beauty, was a plaything for the Fops. She never failed to afford them an agreeable diversion, and though at this time she was but 7 or 8 Years of age, she had some singular talents of wit, which showed her of an aspiring genius, and one that would in time strive with Emulation to exceed the Bounds of her narrow Fortune.

" It was about this time that a Comedian belonging to the *Old House* (Drury Lane) took great delight in hearing her sing little Catches as she had heard from the humming Beaux, or the more lofty strains of her mamma, by whose intercession this Gentleman took a great deal of pains with Polly and taught her some Airs which have since been to her advantage, and in which she daily improved, till her Mother sent her to a Boarding School, where she stayed till she was about fourteen, and then came home again to live with her mother, who was removed once more into the Old Bailey."

We are not informed whether the boarding school was in Queen Square, or at Chelsea, or at Hackney, where in those days boarding schools most abounded; but by way, possibly, of compensating for this lack of information, the author goes on to stimulate curiosity by remarking that " there may be something entertaining to tell of the pretty little Pranks she played there " (at school). We are bound to say, however, that these pranks are of the slightest possible interest, and we omit them and pass on to what the biographer calls " a remarkable incident." The story is as follows :

" A gallant spark of the *Inner Temple*, seeing her one night at a Ball, fell deeply in love with her, and took occasion to let her know it, both by Letter and personal Application ; and though she was scarce thirteen, she felt such Immotions for young *Noverint Universi* that she suffered the Servant to take Bribes to let him into the Garden, and would frequently bless him with an Hour's Conversation. And here it is said (by those who are acquainted with her most private Actions from her Infancy to this time) that she fell as deeply in love with the Templer, as he could possibly be with her ; yet she had ever that Discretion to make a distinction between the secret Impulses of her Heart, and the Expressions of the Tongue, daily feeling by Experience, that when a woman lets the sentiments of her Soul out at her Lips, her Love is counted Fondness, and the man who was ready to die at her Feet will be ready to stigmatise her for a good-natured Fool. Hypocrisy being now made a necessary Ingredient in Affairs of Love, and downright Dealing the only Impediment that can make a promising View prove abortive ; she therefore kept him at a convenient Distance, and seemed to give way to his courtship only, as a grateful Complaisance to a man that merited something which she was incapable of granting. And with this pretended indolent Templer she made use of that infallible Net for catching Men in Love, a killing Coyness! Poor Polly! The spark happening in Company where her Name was mentioned, took occasion to enquire into her private Affairs, and finding her Birth and Fortune were such as would but bring a Disgrace to his Family, he left her.

" This disappointment made such an impression in her Mind that the company at the Boarding School became burdensome, and the pleasant Garden where she used to delight herself with the young Lawyer

SCENE FROM " THE BEGGAR'S OPERA."

From an engraving by Blake, after Hogarth.

48]

intolerable, and as an expedient to wear off the Dilemma she lay under, she left the School and came home to her Mother, who found her daughter's Temper altered from the Gay to the Melancholy. She took her to the Park, the Play, and to all entertainments that might conduce to recover her to her former vivacity."

Polly's first serious love affair (the biographer has his own way of describing this event) happened in 1725, when " about that time her mother had an Intrigue upon her Hands which began at the Play House and ended in the Bed Chamber. The Gentleman who was her mother's gallant would fain have been an humble servant of Polly's, but the Mother, notwithstanding she indulg'd the tempting Baits which were daily offered her, yet at last she kept her for some great man, and bade her above all *things* to observe this. *That the first market a woman made was always the best, and second-hand goods would fetch but a second-hand price.* And it's confidently reported that lest Polly should fling away her Charms on some one who could not purchase them at a Price more exorbitant than *Lais* demanded of *Demosthenes*, her Mother made overtures to a certain ludicrous knight known by the name of the *Feathered Gull*, and the bargain was made as followeth : That upon her first surrender Polly should have £200 in ready special and be decked in all the *Mundus Mulieris* at the knight's expense ; that she should have £200 per annum whilst she remained constant, but if she suffered the Enemy to beat up her quarters, she was to be divested of all her ornaments at once and driven out of Paradise.

" But whilst the Mother was thus bargaining for her Ware, Polly was no less active in providing for herself. A Portugueze nobleman, being her only favourite, she consented, unknown to her Mother, to give him the Prize, which he generously rewarded ; and, accordingly, on a Friday, in the year 1725, he sent his own Coach into the Old Bailey by Appoint-

4

ment ; and after the Coach had waited three Hours,
she went into it, and was carry'd to the Place of
Assignation, where the Nobleman kept her till the
Monday following, and then sent her home again
in the same coach. But this Person being unhappy
in his private Affairs, after some time spent in
Raptures at his own House, he brought her to her
Mother, and promised *he would make a provision for
her suitable to the merits of so fine a creature.* And
to do him justice, his Generosity was above his
Patrimony, insomuch that his stock was exhausted,
before his appetite was pall'd, and falling into the
Hands of some severe Creditors, he was arrested
and carried to the Fleet.

" Whilst the *Portugueze* Nobleman lay confin'd
in the Fleet, a Mercer's apprentice who now keeps a
Shop of that business near the *Royal Exchange,* then
living upon *Ludgate Hill,* fell deeply in love with
Polly. Seeing her one Night at the Play-house, the
poor smitten spark was so captivated at first Sight
of her that he could scarce forbear making love to
her before the Face of the whole Audience ; his
colour went and came, he sigh'd, trembled, and in
short felt all those emotions which Men in Love are
subject to. After the Play was over, he watched her
into a Coach, and lest he should miss her in a Throng
of Whirligigs, he very orderly got up behind, and
was set down at her door in the Old Bailey; but his
Love was so strong, as deprived him of any other
Strength, insomuch that when Polly stepped out of
the Coach into the House, his Soul was near stepping
out of his Body, he was so far overcome by his
amorous passion. All Night he waited about the
Door, sometimes sighing, and sometimes Raving,
fearing she was a marry'd Woman, or doubtless, if
she were not, such a fine Creature as she was, would
repulse him, being but a young Lad, and not out of
his Apprenticeship. But when the morning came, he
was eased from part of his Pain : for upon Enquiry
after her, he found that she was a single woman ;

and at the same time he heard who she was, that she was a person of a Noble Mind, tho' of but narrow Fortune, which did not put the least Damp to him, he having a pretty handsome Estate, when he came of Age, and was willing to lay both that and himself at her Feet, and the next day he pick'd up a little courage (yet with a Heart almost broken for fear of a Denial) and went to inform her of his Passion.

" Polly, who had ever a great deal of wit, as well as good Manners, received him like a Gentleman, and entertained him very courteously ; but at the same time, she assured him, that *tho' he came with seeming honourable pretensions, for which she could not but use him with civility, yet there were some private reasons which would keep her from a marry'd state, and make his pretensions to her of none effect.*

" This so dumb-founded the Spark that he could scarce make a reply, but at length recollecting his fleeting Spirits, he addressed himself in such generous and honest Terms that she could not but have some respect and Compassion for his Youth ; and as she saw he was sincere, she obligingly told him *that the gods dealt with mortals in a manner unaccountable, and the fate of things often came about by unforeseen accidents : therefore she would not obstinately give him a denial,* but told him *that her apartment was so far at his service, that he should be welcome to spend an hour there, when he could find leisure,* but bid him *not be too confident upon the little hope she might give him, by admitting this freedom, lest he should meet with a disappointment.* Overjoyed at this promising Success, the Youth knew not how to express himself, nor could she keep him from his Knees, to shew his Thankfulness with the greater Humility.

" He seldom miss'd seeing her every Day from the beginning of July 1725 to the latter end of August, and sometimes she would favour him with her company abroad ; when, tho' he was but a lad, he had always some pretty Thing to say to her, and she in return was at length as generous as to tell her Mind

freely, that he must never expect to have her, tho'
she condescended to please him with her Company,
for to deal plainly and honestly with him, she told
him her Heart was disposed of otherways. This
struck such a Damp to the Young Lover, he could
scarce contain himself ; yet, as she had never flattered
him with any real Expectations, he had nothing to
reproach her for. But Polly seeing his Passion rather
increasing every Day, resolved not to act dishonour-
ably by a Youth who acted so honourably by her,
and as she could not consent to marry him, since
she had given her Heart to the *Portugueze* Nobleman,
she feared if she should indulge this Passion longer,
the Conclusion might be attended with some dreadful effects. To prevent which, she told him he must
endeavour to set his Heart at Ease, for she could not
comply with his desires upon any terms or Con-
ditions whatsoever, and therefore he must desist from
coming to her House for the future, since it was
impossible he should conquer his Passion by means
which served only to inflame it ; which words, like a
dagger to his Soul, put him in the greatest Agony and
sent him home in deep Despair and Melancholy, not
stirring out of the House from Monday to the Friday
following."

Love letters of the usual high-flown type common to the wearisome novels of the time passed
between the two, and the Portuguese nobleman still
continuing in the Fleet, and her mother's health at
that time failing, Polly went and lived " within a door
of two of Coupland's, the great soap boilers in the
Old Bailey, and her generosity to this gentleman (the
Portuguese nobleman) was such . . . that she took
his Misfortunes to heart, and paying him a kind visit
*begged he would tell her how she might be serviceable to
him.* . . . He told her he would wait there with
patience till he could have money remitted over to
him from his own Country, and desired her in the
meantime that she would not make his troubles her
own, but take her Pleasure in the Town, and if she

would now and then condescend to bless him with an hour's conversation it would make his confinement tolerable, and if he lived once more to enjoy his liberty, his whole Life should be devoted to her Service."

Polly was so sensibly touched with this kind way of his expressing himself, that she immediately, without his knowledge, went and " sold all her rings, jewels and other valuable curiosities (the most part of which he had aforetime given her)."

According to the biographer it was " In this same year, 1725, that she began to think of treading the stage, and she having a lively imagination, joined with a good memory, and clear voice and a graceful mien, seemed as if Nature had designed her for the pleasure of Mankind in such performances as are exhibited at our theatres."

Some lines which she wrote on an empty fop, " that would have taken her into keeping, provided she would go down into the country and be cloyster'd up in a little village of his near Richmond in Yorkshire," having fallen into the hands of a " certain nobleman," he saw in her the possession of wit and spirit, and tried to get her into the playhouse. But this was not done without great difficulty. However " Mr. Huddy (now master of a strolling company) being turned out of the Play-house in Lincoln's Inn Fields in February 1726, had *The Orphan, or the Unhappy Marriage* for his benefit a month after, at the New Theatre in the Haymarket, which was in March, and at his Benefit Polly had the honour of first mounting the Stage,"

It has hitherto been accepted without question that Monimia was the part in which Miss Fenton made her debut. The assertion rests upon the authority of the " Life," and has been repeated by biographer after biographer without question, but it must not be forgotten that much of the matter in the " Life " ought to be taken *cum grano salis*. Mr. W. Cooke in *Macklin's Memoirs* enlarges upon what he found in the " Life," but gives no fresh facts. We find it here stated that " Her genius was entirely the gift of nature ; she discovered a talent for singing almost coeval with her speaking, and she improved it so much by continual practice as she grew up that at a very early age her adopted father took notice of it, and got her instructed by some of the best masters. She was said to have possessed a fine, simple melodious voice, and as Italian singing was little cultivated at that time, and perhaps out of reach of her father's finances, she was principally educated in the English ballad, in which from the reputation she has left behind her, on the authority of the best judges of that day, she must have greatly excelled. With these talents and in so conspicuous a situation as that of a coffee-house, it is no wonder that she readily found an *entrée* upon the stage. Being introduced to the manager of the Haymarket Theatre, he instantly engaged her—not, it appears, altogether as a singer, as her debut at this theatre was in Monimia in *The Orphan*, which happened in the year 1726, when she was but eighteen years of age."

It is very difficult to imagine the natural, unconventional Polly in the wholly artificial, tearful, terribly deceived Monimia, who ends her life by swallowing poison. Moreover it may be questioned whether a totally inexperienced *débutante* would be given a leading part in which, to please the punctilious audience of the day, she must preserve the traditional method of declamation, the pauses, the starts, and all the rest of the orthodox " business." It is a far cry from Otway's grief-stricken Monimia to Farquhar's Cherry, and the contrast makes the former the harder to accept. There is, however, a part in *The Orphan* almost made for the sprightly, adventurous Polly, and that is the Page Cordelio. The few lines Otway has put in his mouth are just those which a bright, coquettish, mischief-loving girl would deliver, with a provoking look in her bright eyes certain to bring down the house. One line, in view

of her subsequent history, was very appropriate—
" At least I'm not dull, and soon should learn,"
Cordelio tells the treacherous Polydore, while the
dialogue between the page and the unsuspecting
Castalio is such as would give full scope to archness
and feminine devilry.

But the truth must be told, and this truth we
only discovered after our doubts as to her playing
Monimia, and the possible chance of the part having
been Cordelio. A search in *The Daily Post* of 1726
brought to light the following advertisement in the
issue of February 23rd : " At the Desire of several
Persons of Quality, for the Benefit of Mr. Huddy.
At the New Theatre in the Hay-Market. To-morrow
being Thursday, the 24th Day of February, will
be presented a Tragedy call'd *The Orphan, or the
Unhappy Marriage*. Written by the late Mr. Otway.
With a new prologue to be spoken by Mr. Royer,
who plays the part of Chamont. The part of Acasto
by Mr. Huddy ; Monimia, Mrs. Haughton ; the page,
Miss Tollet, and the part of Serina by a Gentlewoman
who never appear'd on any Stage before. With
singing in Italian and English by Mrs. Fitzgerald.
And the Original Trumpet Song of Sound Fame, as
set to Musick by Mr. Henry Purcel, to be performed
by Mr. Amesbury." Thus is a time-honoured fiction
disposed of. Polly did *not* play Monimia, not even
Cordelio—she had hardly a speaking part !

There is no gainsaying this evidence. However
clever Miss Fenton may have been, she had no chance
of distinguishing herself in *The Orphan*, for Serina,
the daughter of Acasto, has but sixteen lines to
speak, and these are distributed over three entrances.
The part might be cut out and not be missed.
Lavinia's appearance was undoubtedly in the nature
of an experiment, or she would not have been described simply as a " gentlewoman."

The experiment was not repeated, if the absence
of any record in the newspapers is to be considered
evidence ; and the next we hear of the young lady

is contained in this advertisement in *The Daily Post*
of July 13, 1726 : " At the Theatre Royal in Lincoln's
Inn Fields on Friday next, being the 15th of July,
will be reviv'd a Comedy call'd *The Man's the Master*,
written by Sir William D'Avenant, and carefully
revised. The part of Lucilla by Miss Fenton, being
the first time of her appearance on this stage ; Don
John, Mr. Milward ; Don Louis, Mrs. Haughton,
Sancho, Mr. Bullock, Isdelel, Mr. Morgan, Stephano,
Mr. H. Bullock ; Isabella, Mrs. Herold ; Beatrice,
Mrs. Morgan ; Laura, Mrs. Martin. With singing by
Mr. Salway and proper Entertainments of Dancing
by Mr. Newhouse, Mr. Pelling, Mrs. Ogden, Mrs.
Anderson and others ; particularly a Chaconne by
Mrs. Anderson and the two Pierrots by Mr. Newhouse
and Mr. Pelling."

D'Avenant's play is a dreary production, and no
amount of careful revision could have made it acceptable. Lucilla is the second leading lady, but this is
not saying very much, for the action and the speaking are chiefly confined to the men characters. Nor
did the winsome Lavinia have much chance of
showing her charms, for during the greater part of
the time Lucilla is on the stage she is veiled. However, the revival had, we may suppose, a measure of
success, for it was repeated on the following Tuesday.

According to the author of the " Life," Lavinia's
acting in *The Orphan* gained her such applause
" that she had several presents made her and some
billets " ; one in particular from a young ensign.
This letter is so refreshingly free from the sickly
sentiment and extravagance which the elaborate
etiquette of the eighteenth century demanded from
lovers, that we are tempted to give it in full. The
amorous effusion runs thus :

" MADAM,
   " You may be a person of honour, for aught
I know to the contrary, and I hope you will be so
honourable as not to let a Man of Honour die Dis-

WALKER, THE ORIGINAL MACHEATH.

From an engraving by Faber, after J. Ellys.

honourably at your feet. For, by Heavens ! though I thought nothing so bright as my sword, yet I find your eyes are much brighter. My Dear, Dear Guardian Angel, could you conceive the anxiety I suffer on your account, you would surely pity me : for there's never an officer of our Regiment but takes notice of my being changed (since I saw you upon the Stage) from the most lively, brisk, fashionable, mannerly, genteel Beau in the whole Army, to the most dull, insipid, slovenly, out-o'-the-way-tempered Dunce in Christendom. D——n me, Madam, if I am not so over-charged with Love that my Heart which is the Bullet in the Barrel of my Body, will certainly burst and blow me into atoms if I have not your help to discharge the Burthen. And then Blood ! Madam, I am guilty of so many blunders and mistakes in the execution of my office that I am become quite a laughing-stock to the whole Army. Yesterday I put my sword on the wrong side, and this morning I came into the Park with one of my stockings the wrong side outward, and instead of applying myself to the Colonel, in the usual terms of Most Noble Sir, I looked pale, and with an affected d——d cringe, called him Madam. Thus, Madam, you see how far I am gone already. Then, to keep me from Bedlam take me to your arms, then I will lay down my arms, and be your slave and vassal."

There is plenty of spirit in this epistle, but we doubt its genuineness. It bears a strong family likeness to a number of effusions, purely fiction, published at the height of Polly's popularity, as will be seen from the specimens we give later on.

It is hardly likely, however many private admirers Polly may have had, that she would in three appearances in minor parts have attracted public attention, and it may be presumed that the " billets " and " presents," numerous enough when she became famous, at this period existed for the most part in the imagination of the biographer, who was perforce compelled to " write round " his subject. In regard to the statement as to Polly's next appearance, we are disposed to meet it with considerable doubt. We are told in the " Life " that five weeks after Mr. Huddy's benefit *The Beaux' Stratagem* was put on for the benefit of a Mr. Gilbert, an actor in Huddy's Company, and some noblemen present, the biographer adds, were so delighted that " they promoted her into the company of Young Comedians who acted twice a week, during that summer season, at the Playhouse in Lincoln's Inn Fields, and finally, Rich took her into the house as a steady actress at a salary of 15s. a week." A diligent search through the advertisement columns of *The Daily Post* and *The Daily Journal* failed to offer any corroboration of this assertion. That Polly subsequently essayed to represent the pert, intriguing Cherry is quite certain, and right well must it have suited her ; but we cannot find the slightest evidence that she played Cherry so early in her career as her biographer would have us believe. What we do find is an advertisement in *The Daily Post* of August 17, 1726, announcing that on the 19th " will be reviv'd a Comedy call'd *The Wits*, written by Sir William D'Avenant . . . Ginnet, Miss Fenton." Ginnet is maid to one of the other characters, and Polly had little to say and less to do than she had as Lucilla, while the play itself is as uninteresting as its predecessor. It was played only once. By an odd coincidence, in the number of *The Daily Post* containing the advertisement of *The Wits* appeared an announcement that " his grace the duke of Bolton has set out for the Isle of Wight, to take possession of his government of the said island." At that date it is pretty clear that Miss Fenton was nothing to him or he to her.

By this time it must have occurred to the management that Lavinia might be tried in some part which would give more scope to her ability ; and on October 3, according to *The Daily Journal*, she appeared as Mrs. Squeamish in *The Country Wife*, and again on November 16 in the same character. Mrs. Squeamish was certainly a great advance on the colourless Lucilla and Ginnet, and one can only hope that Lavinia relieved the coarseness of the wanton hoyden by her own lightness of touch. Wycherley's *Country Wife* must have been difficult to swallow, even in the times in which it was written. Some of the lines put into the mouth of Mrs. Squeamish are not the least objectionable of the many which Wycherley permitted himself to write in this, one of the worst of the many licentious plays of the Restoration period.

Thanks to the newspapers, we are in a measure able to follow Lavinia Fenton's career almost to the time when she leaped into fame. After Nov. 16, 1726, we do not find her name mentioned until Rich produced one of his greatest " Harlequin " successes, the entertainment entitled *The Rape of Proserpine*. This was on February 13, 1727. Harlequin was of course "Mr. Lun," John Rich's stage name, and " Miss Fenton " is announced among the " lasses." She had probably little more to do than to walk on. " Mr. Lun," we may be sure, had all the " fat," which was chiefly posturing and dancing. *Proserpine* was run throughout February and March with but two interruptions, one being *The Loves of Damon and Climene, or the Metamorphoses of Leander*, on March 15, and a revival of *The Country Wife* on March 23, for the benefit of Quin, with Lavinia in her old part of Mrs. Squeamish. The advertisement in *The Daily Journal* styles her, after the fashion of the day, " Mrs. Fenton." On the following night the run of *The Rape of Proserpine* was resumed " for the last time of performance until the Easter holidays." (See illustration p. 32.)

Rich hit the taste of the public with *Proserpine*, and it was continued until April 26, when *The Beaux' Stratagem* was played for the benefit of Hippisley and Mrs. Egleton (afterwards Peachum and Lucy), Cherry being taken by Lavinia. Until June 2 *Proserpine* held the stage, *The Country Wife* being put

on, for the benefit of some of the members of the
company, on May 16, with Lavinia as Mrs. Squeamish.
When the season commenced in October, Lavinia was
again in Wycherley's play for one performance, the
rest of the nights being taken up to the end of the
year by *Proserpine*.

It is quite clear from these announcements that
Lavinia was now a regular member of Rich's company, and it is equally clear that, save Cherry and
Mrs. Squeamish on benefit nights, she had nothing of
any importance given her. There was very little
speaking in Rich's pantomimes, and probably all that
the " lasses " had to do was to join in a dance with
the " countrymen." When this is remembered, the
salary of fifteen shillings a week, which some biographers have considered ridiculously small, was
really as much as a minor actress could expect in
those days.

There can be little doubt that while Lavinia
Fenton was learning her profession, Rich had an eye
on her abilities and was noting her progress. Though
she had never had a singing part, he must have known
that she had a voice which she was capable of using
with effect, for when he was considering *The Beggar's
Opera* there was no hesitation about his choice of
the lady in his company best fitted for the part.
Possibly too Gay had made Polly's acquaintance, and
with his love for ballad music knew how to appreciate
her talent.

So far as the " Life " is concerned we leave it at
this point, to take it up again when the biographer
gives his version of what happened to Polly in the
days of her success.

CHAPTER VI

THE MUSIC OF *THE BEGGAR'S OPERA*

A dry-as-dust composer—Dr. Pepusch's share in the music of the " Opera "—
Rich's contempt for singing actors—Quin declines to play **Macheath**—
The origin of " benefits "—Lincoln's Inn Fields Theatre—Its history

An interesting question in connection with the
preparation of *The Beggar's Opera* remains to be
discussed. Who was responsible for the selection
of the ballad music, and to whom must praise be
given for the skill shown in choosing tunes so expressive of the words ? Dr. Pepusch has always had a
good deal of the credit, but we take leave to doubt
whether he had anything to do with the matter,
beyond writing the overture and putting bases to
the melodies. Pepusch, indeed, was hardly the man
to have the extensive knowledge of old English
ballad music necessary for the task. He was a
scholarly musician, who loved the theoretical and
scientific side of his art. He had come from Berlin,
where he had held a court appointment of some
importance, which he threw up in disgust owing to
the abominable brutality of the reigning prince (it
was said that this personage, in the presence of
Pepusch, ordered an officer accused of some offence
to be decapitated without trial), and coming to
London, became a member of the Drury Lane band
out of sheer necessity. His taste was severe, and
his learning brought him the degree of Doctor of
Music at Oxford, after which the Duke of Chandos
appointed him *maestro di capello* at Cannons, where
he became intimately acquainted with Handel, who
numbered the duke among his warmest supporters
and patrons.

61

Pepusch was an enthusiast in the formation of the Academy of Ancient Music, and when in 1724 Dr. Berkeley conceived his strange project of a college at Bermuda—of all places in the world!— Pepusch was one of the professors selected, and he embarked with his associates for the intended settlement ; but the vessel was wrecked, and the whole design thereby defeated. Pepusch married a famous singer of the time, Margarita de l'Epine, who had made a handsome fortune, and the learned doctor was no longer compelled to do journeyman's work, which must at times have been very distasteful. His compositions are decidedly dry, and one can hardly believe that he was possessed of the qualifications to fit him for the selection of what he probably thought was light and trifling music. Mrs. Delany summed up Pepusch as a composer when she wrote : " I was to see the Opera of *Dioclesian,* but was very much disappointed, for instead of Purcell's music, which I expected, we had Papuch's, and very humdrum it was; indeed I never was so tired with anything in my life."

A strong argument against the assumption that the dry-as-dust Pepusch had anything to do with the selection of the melodies is found in his imperfect knowledge of English. A writer in *The Universal Magazine* (1778) says he " spoke English indifferently, and read it worse." How then was it probable he could fit the rhythm of Gay's verse to the music with such nicety as the Opera shows ? Pepusch, however, meant well, and conscientiously did his best to foster a taste for music in England. The writer whom we have just quoted tells us that when Pepusch came over " he found the practice of music in a very low state, very few but Professors being able to play in concert; and with a view to the improvement of it, he put twenty-four airs for two violins in all the variety of measures that music is capable of. These seemed to be but an introduction to Corelli's sonatas, which were then deemed much too hard to be put in the hands of learners." The writer might have added that for the greater part of the eighteenth century " fiddlers " were held in something like contempt by those who moved in polite society.

Lord Chesterfield's opinion of fiddle-playing by " gentlemen " has already been referred to, and in connection with Pepusch's praiseworthy efforts to popularise violin-playing it is worth while quoting the words of his supercilious lordship in extenso, as in most questions of taste and fashion his judgment was held to be supreme. " If you love music," he writes to his son, " hear it ; go to the persons concerned, and pay fiddlers to play to you. But I must insist upon your not playing yourself. It places a gentleman in a very frivolous, contemptible light, brings him into the middle of bad company, and takes up a great deal of time which might be better employed. Few things would mortify me more than to see you bearing a part in a concert with a fiddle under your chin."

Lord Chesterfield wrote this fifty years after the publication of Pepusch's duets, but he only put into writing what was the attitude of the bucks and dandies towards the violin during the eighteenth century. The flute was the fashionable instrument. It is shown to be so in one of the plates of Hogarth's *Marriage à la Mode*, and during the rage of *The Beggar's Opera* an arrangement of the songs for the flute was published by Watts, who with Jacob Tonson purchased the copyright of the Opera. In any case, prejudice and fashion or not, the amateur violinists of the day were hardly likely to be attracted by Pepusch's " twenty-four airs," as those of our readers who care to visit the British Museum Library can see for themselves.

The music of *The Beggar's Opera* with the score by Pepusch is given in the edition of 1729. The overture is arranged for two violins, two oboes, a tenor and a 'cello. The first and second violin played in unison with the first and second oboes, and to our ears the harmony would probably sound thin enough ; but, thin as it was, it sufficed. The songs merely had bases, and it was not until Arne rearranged the Opera, that they had anything like accompaniments. As for the melodies, their selection was in all probability that of Gay, perhaps at times assisted by Arbuthnot. Gay, as already pointed out, must have had a fairly intimate acquaintance with old English ballads, and he necessarily had the rhythm of the music in his mind before he wrote the words.

It may be assumed, then, after Cibber rejected the Opera and it was submitted to Rich, that the musical portion of the work was considered as of secondary importance. Gay could not have been sure of Rich. The manager was reputed to have a thorough contempt for actors who could sing. It is said that an actor once offered himself to Rich, and was requested to go through the scene of Othello before the Senate. On being questioned by the Manager whether or not he could sing, he answered in the negative. " I'm glad of it," replied Rich ; " it is a good sign ; I wouldn't give a farthing for a man that shall attempt Tragedy, who can sing ; there never was one able to turn a tune that could speak, except my friend Walker " (the original Macheath).

But Rich was a born showman. He understood the taste of the public, and he never allowed his own tastes or prejudices to interfere with his interests. Walker, to say nothing of Polly, must have convinced him there was money in singing actors. Art and necessity had made Rich a dancer and a posture-maker, but he had a secret belief that Nature had intended him for a tragedian. " I would rather play Cato to six persons in the pit than Harlequin to a crowded audience," he is reported to have said. He tried the experiment once, and that once convinced him he had better stick to dancing.

There are sixty-nine songs in the Opera, and those who are interested in the history of the old melodies to which they are adapted will find much interesting

WALKER'S BENEFIT TICKET.

Drawn by Hogarth.

SPILLER'S BENEFIT TICKET.

Drawn by Hogarth.

information in Mr. Hamilton McLeod's edition of *The Beggar's Opera*, published in 1905. Many of these melodies are delightful. They are all unaffected, and are wonderfully wedded to the verses. Rich, with his contempt for music, was probably not conscious of the Opera's chief attraction, and the rehearsals, the cast, the experiment of putting a comparatively unknown actress into the principal part, the novelty of the piece itself, and the doubt whether it would please the public, must have been a source of intense anxiety to all concerned, and especially to Gay, whose tendency it was to look upon the worst side of things. But he had the warm support of his "Duchess" and of Pope, to say nothing of Bolingbroke, Arbuthnot and Bathurst. For aught we know, the noblemen who, according to Polly's biographer, "promoted her into the Company of Young Comedians," were zealous in her interest, and maybe the Duke of Bolton was among them; and with such an influential following, Rich probably swallowed his dislike of singing actors and did his best to produce the Opera with credit to himself and the author.

He must have been terribly disappointed when Quin, who was to play Macheath, threw up the part. Nothing, however, could have been more fortunate. Quin was heavy and stagey, as indeed was every tragedian in those days when "dignity" was all in all. Rich actually discharged Macklin for speaking, as he called it, "too familiarly" on the stage. "I spoke so familiar, sir," said Macklin, "and so little in the hoity-toity tone of the tragedy of that day, that the manager told me I'd better go to grass for another year or two." A more unsuitable representative of the rollicking, devil-may-care Macheath than Quin could hardly be imagined. Moreover he could do little more in the way of singing than troll a ditty after dinner. He had luckily the sense to see that he would be a failure, and so the chief character in the Opera was handed to Walker, of

5

whom more anon. The rest of the cast gave no trouble. All the characters—Lucy, Mr. and Mrs. Peachum, the Lockits, down to the minor parts of Filch, Mat o' the Mist, and the rest—were admirably fitted, and here again Gay's luck was manifest.

The history of the theatre with which the fortunes of *The Beggar's Opera* were to be associated is of considerable interest. There have been three theatres in Lincoln's Inn Fields, and this has frequently led to considerable confusion. According to " Rainy Day " Smith, Killigrew in the year 1661 had a Theatre in the Tennis Court, Vere Street, Clare Market; and here in 1662 Sir William Davenant with his company removed from the theatre in Salisbury Court, Whitefriars; and the alterations made by Davenant justify the name of the second theatre. It opened with *The Siege of Rhodes*, a species of opera, when, says Mr. Timbs, " regular scenery was first introduced upon the stage." A delightful remembrance of Davenant's theatre is recorded by Pepys, who here first saw, and not only saw, but sat next to " pritty witty " Mistress Nell Gwynne. Pepys frequently called the Lincoln's Inn Fields Theatre " The Opera," though tragedies and comedies only were performed there—an additional piece of evidence in support of the theory of the indiscriminate use of the word.

In a roundabout way, the " benefit " system was the cause of the third theatre in Lincoln's Inn Fields being built. Colley Cibber, in his " Autobiography," referring to his experience at Drury Lane Theatre, says: " During the Reign of King Charles an actor's benefit had never been heard of. The first indulgence of this kind was given to Mrs. Barry . . . in consideration of the extraordinary applause that had followed her performance. But there this Favour rested, to her alone, till after the Division of the only Company in 1695, at which time the Patentees were soon reduced to pay their actors half in Good Words and half in Ready Money. In this precarious condition some particular actors . . . were too poor or too wise to go to Law with a Lawyer (Christopher Rich had been an attorney), and therefore rather chose to compound their arrears for their being admitted to the chance of having them made up by the profit of a Benefit Play. This Expedient had this consequence : that the Patentees, tho' their daily audiences might and did sometimes mend, still kept the short Subsistence of their actors at a stand and grew more steady in their resolution so to keep them as they found them less apt to mutiny, while their Hopes of being cleared off by a Benefit were departing. In a year or two these Benefits grew so advantageous, that they became at last the chief article in every actor's agreement."

At this time Christopher Rich was manager of Drury Lane Theatre, but his avarice, and unamiable qualities generally, caused constant quarrels between him and the proprietors. The actors were also aggrieved, and with good reason. To quote the "Answer" to Steele's statement of the case: "After Mr. Rich was again restored to the management of the Playhouse, he made an order to stop a certain proportion of the clear profits of any Benefit play without exception ; which being done and reaching the chief players as well as the underlings, zealous application was made to the Lord Chamberlain to oblige Mr. Rich to return the money stopped to each particular (? actor). The dispute lasted some time, and Mr. Rich was not giving full satisfaction ; upon that head was silenced (*i.e.* no performances were given), during the time of which silence the chief players set up for themselves and got into possession of the Playhouse in Drury Lane." Thanks to Collier, one of the proprietors of the patents, who had obtained a license and afterwards a lease of Drury Lane Theatre, " Rich in this business made out his right before the Attorney-General and other lawyers, and then petitioned the Council, who, refusing to determine the matter, referred him to law, and there

matters rested till he built a new house in Lincoln's
Inn Fields."

Old Rich died just before the theatre was opened,
and on the first night the interior was draped in black
in consequence.   Concerning the first night the *Weekly
Pacquet* of Dec. 18, 1714, contained the following
notice : " This day the new Play-House in Lincoln's
Inn Fields is to be open'd, and a comedy acted there
called *The Recruiting Officer* by the company that
act under the Patent, though it is said that some of
the gentlemen who have left the House in Drury
Lane for that service, are order'd to return to their
colours upon pain of not exercising their lungs elsewhere, which may in time prove of ill service to the
Patentee that has been at such vast expense to
make his theatre as convenient for the reception
of an audience as any one can possibly be."   Davies
(*Dramatic Miscellanies*) says of it : " It was finely
decorated.   The Scenes were new.   The Stage was
more extended than that of the rival theatre, and
superbly adorned with looking-glasses on both sides
of the Stage ;   a circumstance which Quin said was
an excellent trap to catch actresses who admired their
persons more than their profession of acting."

The theatre appears to have been redecorated some
eight years after John Rich's opening, according to a
paragraph in *The London Daily Post* of Sept. 24, 1722,
which records that : " On Saturday last (20th) several
of the most eminent painters met at the Theatre
Royal in Lincoln's Inn Fields to take a survey of the
ceiling, the House being thoroughly lighted for that
purpose ;   over the stage is represented Apollo and
the Muses ;   over the Pit a magnificent piece of
architecture, where is seen a group of figures leaning
over a long gallery—viz., Shakespeare, Jonson, etc.,
from the originals.   They seem in conference with
Betterton, the most celebrated Tragedian or Roscius
of his time.   The artists have given their opinion
that the performance excels anything of the kind
both as to design and beauty.   We hear that the

theatre will be finish'd and opened some time next week." John Rich removed with his company to Covent Garden in 1733, and the old theatre was shut up for about two years. Then Giffard from Goodman's Fields took it, but the glory of the House had departed, and it closed its doors as a theatre in 1737.

The house then saw many vicissitudes. In October 1745, when, by reason of the rebellion in the North, London was full of soldiers, it was lent to the Government for the purpose of a Guard Room; and afterwards we get a glimpse of it in the following advertisement, dated Sept. 1777 : " Old Play-House, Portugal St., Lincoln's Inn Fields. Mr. Hart requests the favour of his scholars and subscribers to observe the Tuesday night's subscription (which will be on a new plan) commences from Michaelmas. Those Ladies and Gentlemen who propose to honour him with their company are requested to call or send before that time, as the number of subscribers is limited. The minuet, cotillions, allemande, country dances, etc., taught privately at houses or abroad, as usual." At the end of the century it was a warehouse for the sale of china, and our illustration at p. 28 shows its appearance in 1811. Probably the exterior was much the same as in *The Beggar's Opera* days. The site is now occupied by the additions to the Royal College of Surgeons.

At first the theatre in Lincoln's Inn Fields had not the distinction of the rival house in Drury Lane in possessing a guard of soldiers; but in 1721 a disturbance arose in consequence of a nobleman, in a drunken mood, attempting to cross the stage while the play (*Macbeth*) was going on. Rich tried to exert his authority, and to protect Quin and the other actors from being interrupted: he and the intruder came to blows, and the nobleman's friends rushed to his assistance, to be met by a posse of actors, who supported the manager. The fashionable Mohocks were more at home at wanton damage than in fighting men who could defend themselves, and they attacked the hangings and fittings of the house, and as a result of their prowess the theatre had to be closed for two days.   After this the King granted permission for a guard to attend the performances.

Royalty was also pleased to bestow its patronage on the dramatic profession in the patents which Charles II. at his Restoration granted to Sir William Davenant and Henry Killigrew—a concession which led to much subsequent jealousy and heart-burning. The company acting at Drury Lane were called the King's Servants, and that at the Duke's Theatre in Dorset Gardens the Duke's Company. Colley Cibber in his "Autobiography" says that: "About ten of the King's Company were on the Royal Household establishment, having each two yards of Scarlet Cloth, with a proper quantity of lace allowed them for Liveries, and in their warrants from the Lord Chamberlain were stiled Gentlemen of the Great Chamber; whether the like Appointments were extended to the Duke's Company I am not certain."

Lincoln's Inn Theatre was the scene of the fatal affray between the dogmatic, pugnacious Macklin and Thomas Hallam, a fellow actor.   The quarrel was as stupid as it could well be.   It was over a wig of Macklin's which the other had taken.   In his rage Macklin thrust his stick into Hallam's face.   It entered the unfortunate man's eye and killed him. Macklin was tried for manslaughter, but escaped punishment.   The final closing of the theatre was for years identified with a curious story which gained credence among the ignorant and superstitious.   It had to do with Rich's successful pantomime *Harlequin and Dr. Faustus*.   We are told by Nightingale in his *Beauties of England and Wales* that during the performance of the pantomime, "when a tribe of demons necessary for the piece were assembled, a supernumerary devil was observed, who, not approving of going out in a complaisant manner at the door, to show *the devil's trick,* flew up to the ceiling, made his way through the tiling, and tore away one-fourth of the house, which circumstance so frightened the manager that the proprietor had not courage to open the house ever afterwards." Our ancestors had a great capacity for believing anything where the devil was concerned.

CHAPTER VII

EIGHTEENTH-CENTURY THEATRES

The surroundings of Drury Lane and Lincoln's Inn Fields Theatres—Their evil reputation—Gay's description in the *Trivia*—The building of the King's Theatre, and its effect on the "ladies"—The "appointments" of a theatre in 1728—Servants monopolise the gallery—Their insolence and rowdyism—Clare Market butchers and the theatre

THE student of stage history will not fail to notice that the two most popular theatres in London in the seventeenth and eighteenth centuries were situated among the slums of the metropolis. Drury Lane was notorious for its dirt and its ladies of "easy virtue." Gay does not mince the matter in his description in the *Trivia* of this world-famous thoroughfare :

"Oh, may thy Virtue guard thee through the Roads
Of Drury's mazy Courts and dark Abodes,
The Harlots' guileful Paths who nightly stand
Where Katherine Street descends into the Strand.
Say, Vagrant Muse, their Wiles and subtil Arts,
To lure the strangers' unsuspecting Hearts ;
So shall our Youth on healthful Sinews tread,
And City Cheeks grow warm with rural Red.

"'Tis she who nightly strowls with sauntering Pace,
No stubborn Stays her yielding Shape embrace,
Beneath the Lamp her tawdry Ribbons glare,
The new-scower'd Manteau and the slattern Air ;
High-draggled Petticoats her Travels show,
And hollow Cheeks with artful Blushes glow ;
With flattering Sounds she soothes the cred'lous Ear :
My noble Captain ! Charmer ! Love ! My Dear !
In Riding Hood, near Tavern-Doors she plies,
Or muffled Pinners hide her livid Eyes.
With empty Bandbox she delights to range,
And feigns a distant Errand from *the Change* :
Nay, she will oft the Quaker's Hood prophane,
And trudge demure the Roads of *Drury Lane*."

And let all Parties blame me, if they can,
Who're brib'd by Honours trifling as a Fan.

J. Smith Invt et Sculpt

THE STAGE OF THE LITTLE THEATRE IN THE HAYMARKET, 1735–6.

From Mr. A. M. Broadley's Collection.

Of Lincoln's Inn Fields the poet draws a picture as vivid as that of Drury Lane :

" Where *Lincoln's Inn*, wide space, is rail'd around,
Cross not with vent'rous step ; there, oft is found
The lurking thief, who while the Day-light shone,
Made the Walls echo with his beggar's Tone ;
That Crutch which late Compassion mov'd, shall wound
Thy bleeding Head, and fell thee to the Ground.
Though thou art tempted by the Link-man's call,
Yet trust him not along the lonely Wall ;
In the mid-way he'll quench the flaming Brand,
And share the Booty with the pilf'ring Band,
Still keep the public Streets, where oily Rays,
Shot from the Crystal Lamp, o'erspread the Ways."

The reputation of Lincoln's Inn Fields was no less evil than Drury Lane, but in a different direction. It was the happy hunting ground of the pickpocket, the cut-purse and the foot-pad ; and in that curious dingy little street, oddly named Whetstone Park, at the north-west corner of the " Fields," it had a sort of Drury Lane in miniature, so far as the lady residents were concerned.

The theatre in Goodman's Fields in St. George's-in-the-East was in quite a respectable locality in comparison. The rich ladies of fashion must have rejoiced when the King's Theatre (now His Majesty's) was built. The ladies of Drury Lane certainly did, if we may take the following whimsical assertion as having a basis of truth : " Talking of the fertility of the female sex has put me so in mind of the pretty baggages that I cannot forbear telling you that a Gentleman of my acquaintance who is a great admirer of the old game of Gingle de Flirt, has the curiosity of keeping an exact register of all the Nymphs and Goddesses in Drury Lane and all the little Courts and Alleys adjacent ; and he finds by his file, which is kept in as great order as a Bill of Mortality, that since the erecting of the new Play-house in St. James' they have decreased within a fortnight in their old precincts three hundred and odd, having removed their residence to the further part of Pick-a-dilly and the Haymarket, that they may be con-

veniently seated against the opening of the new
Theatre." This contribution towards a history of
gay London in Queen Anne's time is found in a MS.
note in R. J. Smith's collection of theatrical lore,
and its authority is given as " *Comical Observator in
a Dialogue between Captain Bluff and Mr. Merryman.
No. 1. Nov. 7, 1704.*" Further than this about the
"Comical Observator" we are unable to say.

During the days of the Stuarts many noblemen—
Lord Somers, the Earls of Bristol and Sandwich, and
the Duke of Newcastle among the number—had their
mansions in Lincoln's Inn Fields, but at the time of
the production of *The Beggar's Opera* it was the
haunt of truculent beggars and cripples, who had
no difficulty in extracting money from the timid.
There were no iron railings in those days, but simply
a series of wooden posts and bars, and the entrances
to the space enclosed are recalled by the present
Great and Little Turnstiles. The newspapers of the
early part of the eighteenth century abounded with
paragraphs telling of the dangers of the Fields. We
read how " last week a Gentleman coming from
Lincoln's Inn Fields Play House was robb'd of thirty-
seven shillings by two Men and one Woman. As he
was passing over the Fields to go to Little Turnstile,
they drew him off the Foot Path into one of the
Quarters. Each of the men held a pistol to his
breast and the Woman pull'd his waistcoat open and
held a penknife to his Breast which she scratched
with the same ; and although a great many people
were passing by he durst not cry out for help, for as
the people press'd them the Rogues made as if they
had been in friendly discourse with him. The three
made off undiscovered."

The thieves of Polly Peachum's day could give
points to our modern " dippers " and " snatchers "
and beat them. Listen to this : " Last Saturday
night a sharper snatch'd a cloak off a Gentleman's
shoulders at the Play-House Door in Lincoln's Inn
Fields ; but the Gentleman crying out ' Stop

Thief ' he let the Cloak fall, which one of his companions took up and carried to the Gentleman who gave him 5/- for his trouble, and directly offered his services to help him on with it, for which the Gentleman new thank'd him, and when he was turn'd about the Rogue snatch'd it away with his Coat and Wig and made clear off with them."

Wigs were valuable booty. They cost anything from five to fifty guineas. " Rainy Day " Smith tells in his life of Nollekens, the sculptor, of a favourite dodge of wig snatchers. A member of this fraternity dressed as a baker would walk along the street carrying a huge baker's basket on his head, as the custom of the baker then was, with a small boy concealed therein. An unsuspecting gentleman would suddenly have his wig spirited away, by the boy whipping out his hand for the plunder, and never imagine that the thief was the innocent-looking baker's man. When the trick oozed out, the bakers, to preserve their reputation for honesty, no longer carried the basket on their heads but at their backs, and the custom has not entirely died out even at this day.

Such were the surroundings of the theatre to which *The Beggar's Opera* was to bring fame and fortune ; and sadly Rich needed the latter, for although he had done pretty well out of his various " pantomimes " and his own performances under the name of Lun, as Harlequin, the adaptation of which character (now almost extinct) to English tastes he is entitled to claim, he found it very hard to fight against the attractions of Barton Booth and Mrs. Oldfield at Drury Lane.

To picture the first night of *The Beggar's Opera,* one has to imagine what the theatre was like in Gay's time. Nothing that we see in the sumptuously appointed play-houses of to-day suggests the slightest comparison. On each side of the stage were seats for the " quality," and their presence so close to the performers must not only have been a

source of embarrassment, but must have seriously
interfered with the action of the piece and the arrangement of " entrances " and " exits." However, the
custom had come down from the time of Shakespeare, and the incongruity did not occur to any one.
The " quality " still looked upon actors and actresses
as " rogues and vagabonds," and thought nothing of
taking liberties which must have led occasionally to
disturbances, as in the case of the drunken nobleman who crossed the stage while the play was going
on. They looked upon every part of the theatre as
open to them, and the managers had to make regula-
tions for their own protection.

The announcement at the end of an advertisement in *The Daily Journal* of May 25, 1727, is significant. " We hear that this Evening the famous
Captain Lemuel Gulliver is to be at the New Play-
House in Lincoln's Inn Fields, very handsomely
attended and dress'd in a rich Habit, the like of which
was never seen in England before. The two Stage
Boxes are kept for him and his Company ; the new
Dramatic Entertainment call'd the *Rape of Proserpine* is to be acted upon this Occasion, and in Honour
to the Captain some Decorations and Additions will
be made to it which have not been acted before.
The Master of the House has promised the Captain
that neither during the Play or Entertainment any
Person shall be admitted behind the Scenes, that the
Captain may not be too much press'd with the
Crowd."

The authority of Royalty was sometimes invoked,
as in the following : " The King's Theatre in the
Haymarket. No persons whatsoever will be admitted for Money, nor any Tickets sold at the Bar
but in the proper Offices. The Gallery 5s. By His
Majesty's Command, no persons whatsoever to be
admitted behind the scenes."

The seats on the stage for privileged persons were
not without their drawbacks, and managers found it
to their advantage to make special arrangements, as

indicated in this advertisement from *The Daily Post* of March 18, 1728 : " At Drury Lane for the benefit of Mrs. Booth. A play called *Double Falsehood or The Discreet Lovers.* Written originally by Shakespeare.

" N.B.—Servants will be admitted to keep Places on the stage, which (to prevent the ladies from taking cold) will be all enclosed."

The pit was chiefly occupied by the middle classes, who were lovers of the drama, and upon their judgment the fate of a play depended. In Dublin curious restrictions in regard to the pit were in force, as the following notice issued in 1744 shows : " Several Ladies and Gentlemen of distinction having applied to the proprietors of the theatre that Ladies might be admitted into the Pit at the same price as the gentlemen, which is the custom in London and in every Town in Ireland, but Dublin, the said Proprietors being willing to oblige all persons who encourage theatrical performance have given orders that for the future Ladies will be admitted into the Pit accordingly." On the other hand ladies were admitted free to the boxes of the Dublin theatres, with the result which may be imagined—few respectable ladies ever went.

The " gallery boys " of 1728 were far too rowdy to trouble to criticise. The merest trifle moved them to anger or mirth. Footmen were admitted free, a concession which these pampered gentry shamefully abused. Colley Cibber tells us how the custom came to be introduced. He says : " During this state of the stage it was, the lowest expedient was made use of, to ingratiate our Company in the Publick Favour. Our Master (Christopher Rich, John Rich's father), who had some time practis'd the Law, and therefore lov'd a storm better than fair Weather (for it was his own Conduct chiefly, that had brought the Patent into these Dangers) took nothing so much to heart as that Partiality, wherewith he imagin'd the People of Quality had preferred the Actors of

the other House to those of his own. To balance this
misfortune, he was resolv'd at least to be well with
their Domesticks, and therefore cunningly open'd
the upper Gallery to them gratis; for before this
time no Footman was ever admitted, or had presumed
to come into it, till after the fourth Act was ended.
This additional Privilege (the greatest Plague that
ever Playhouse had to complain of) he conceived
would not only incline them to give us a good word
in the respective Families they belong'd to, but would
naturally incite them, to come all Hands aloft, in
the crack of our Applause; and indeed it so far
succeeded, that it often thunder'd from the full
Gallery above, while our thin Pit, and Boxes below,
were in the utmost serenity. This Riotous Privilege,
so craftily given, and which from Custom was at
last ripen'd into Right, became the most disgraceful
Nuisance that ever depreciated the Theatre."

Cibber did not exaggerate. The intolerable
lengths to which the footmen carried their rowdyism
is shown in a mock advertisement in *The Female
Tatler* of December 7, 1709: " Dropped near the
Playhouse in the Haymarket a Bundle of Horse
Whips designed to belabour the footmen in the upper
gallery who almost every night this winter have
made such an Intollerable disturbance that the players
could not be heard and their masters were forced to
hiss 'em into Silence. Whoever has taken up the
said whips, is desired to leave 'em with my Lord
Rake's Porter, several noblemen resolving to exercise
them on their backs the next Friday morning."

The tyranny of the footmen continued until late
in the eighteenth century. John Taylor, in his
Records of My Life, says: " Another evil practice
of servants to the higher orders at that time was
carried to such a height that it wrought its own cure.
It was usual at the late Italian Opera House to allot
a gallery to the footmen, that when their masters or
mistresses had appointed a time to leave the theatre
their servants might be ready to attend. But these

livery men took it into their heads to become critics
upon the performances and deliver their comments in
so tumultuous a manner that the managers found it
absolutely necessary to close the gallery against them
and to assign it to those only who paid their admission.
Just before the abolition of this party-galleried tribu-
nal a wag, who was fond of music but who had more
wit than money, appeared at the gallery door, where
the porter demanded the name of his master. The
wag boldly answered, ' I am the Lord Jehovah's
servant,' and was admitted, one of the doorkeepers
saying to the other ' I never heard of that man's
master before, but I suppose it's some scurvy Scotch
lord or other ' ! "

It is odd that while the unruly behaviour of
servants was apparently endured by the audience
without active interference, an act of impoliteness
on one occasion was hotly resented. " Last night,"
says *The London Chronicle* of May 31, 1769, " a great
confusion happened at Mr. Foote's Theatre owing
to the obstinacy of some servants keeping places in
the boxes, in refusing to be uncovered ; which so
much irritated the gentlemen in the pit that they
severely thrashed the party-coloured gentlemen, two
of whom were obliged to be carried to a Surgeon."
It may of course have been that the cocked hats
obstructed the view of those behind.

The Daily Gazetteer of February 23, 1737, records
an instance of how far these liveried gentry could
carry their insolence : " On Monday night last," it
states, "a great Disturbance happened at Drury Lane
Play-House occasioned by a great number of Footmen
who assembled themselves there in a riotous Manner
with great outcries of burning the House and Audience
together unless they were immediately admitted into
what they call their Gallery ; and in order to Strike
a Terror they began to hew down the Door of the
Passage which leads to the said Gallery ; of which
Colonel De Veil (who was in the House) had immediate Notice and thereupon came out where they were

thus assembled, and notwithstanding they threatened
to knock his Brains out he read the Proclamation to
them, and admonished them to retire and desist
from so Unlawful an Undertaking; for that he came
as a Friend and not as a Foe to warn them of their
Danger. This Admonition and seasonably reading
the Proclamation had its desired Effect, for they all
went off in a few Minutes after the Proclamation was
read." Punishment, however, overtook some of the
ringleaders, for a few days afterwards *The Gazetteer*
informs its readers that two of the footmen were
brought before the justices at Hick's Hall, fined a
shilling, and sentenced to six months' hard labour.
In view of the last, it was hardly worth while to inflict
the first.

A truly modern grievance is brought to mind in
a paragraph in *The London Chronicle* of December 17,
1759, which moreover shows that a lady's maid could
make herself quite as objectionable in her own fashion
as the gentleman's gentleman in his. " On Tuesday
night," we read, " a Lady's representative in the
Middle Gallery at Covent Garden House, who had
on a black cloak, a round-eared cap, and an extravagant large hat, seemed very happy in depriving the
audience that sat behind her from seeing the performance ; she was entreated with great civility by
a Gentleman to remove that inconveniency to indulge
some of her own sex with a sight of the performance,
but she resolutely refused to acquiesce. She was a
second time entreated, and made no reply but showed
her disdain by standing up, which, being against the
rule that is observed she found herself obliged to [sit
down], to appease the clamor that prevailed ; but
showed a bold persevering spirit by cocking up the back
part of her hat, clinching her fingers and covering half
the stage from the sight of those behind her. The
Gentleman has too great a regard for the sex to expose the bitterness of her replies to the civil requests
in favour of the Ladies, but begs that when Masters
and Mistresses give leave to their servant-maids to

COLLEY CIBBER.

From Mr. A. M. Broadley's Collection.

see a play that they will oblige them to go without high-trimmed hats."

The servants were unquestionably a nuisance, whether inside or outside the theatre. We read in *The Daily Courant* of March 14, 1726, in connection with Handel's Opera *Scipio*, performed at the King's Theatre, that " complaint being made that the ladies who cannot get away so soon as the Opera is over are much annoyed by the Footmen coming within the first bars on each side of the house with lighted Flamboys ; To prevent the said inconvenience for the future it is desired that Ladies and Gentlemen will forbid their servants to come within the said bars with the Flamboys lighted, there being orders given not to suffer any of them to be admitted." No doubt these lighted " flamboys " were not only inconvenient but dangerous, but what of the inconvenience caused to the audience by the ladies leaving before the performance was over ? It will be seen that this inconsiderate practice, not altogether unknown at the present day, is of long standing.

The butchers of the adjoining Clare Market were great supporters of the Lincoln's Inn Fields Theatre. They were well-to-do people and spent their money freely. One of their favourites was the comedian James Spiller, who belonged to Rich's regular company and who played Mat o' the Mint in *The Beggar's Opera*. Another popular actor was Hippisley, the Peachum of the new piece. Gay, as already mentioned, was known to the public by his ballads, and maybe from his Bohemian tastes he had many personal acquaintances outside his circle of aristocratic friends, and in a very different station of life. St. Giles is not so far removed from Clare Market, but that the poet's delight in the ballad singers of the former might be known to the tradesmen and others who belonged to the latter. The pit and gallery were certain to be crowded, while on the stage and in the boxes author and manager had a right to expect a goodly attendance of the " nobility " and " gentry."

6

The eccentric and all-powerful Duchess of Queensberry—Prior's " Kitty "—Gay's generous patroness
and warmest admirer, would be certain to "assist,"
if not by her presence, at least by her purse ; the
Duke of Argyll, a great lover of the stage, was bound
to book seats ; the Duke of Bolton would come for
Polly's sake ; the Duke of Bedford and Sir Robert
Fagg, the sporting squire of Kent, for the same
reason. " Long Sir Thomas Robinson," as he was
called, though a staunch Walpolian, would not deny
himself the pleasure of seeing the new play, for his
fancy for all kinds of amusement amounted almost
to a mania ; while Sir Conyers D'Arcy, Bolingbroke,
Bathurst and many other friends of Gay no doubt
had pledged themselves to support him. Political
opponents of the " Twickenham Hotchpotch," eager
to hear what the wits had to say against the Government, were expected ; and last, but by no means least,
there were rumours that the great Minister himself,
Sir Robert Walpole, intended to be present. Everything therefore presaged a good " send off."

No adventitious aids in the way of modern lighting
arrangements were possible in 1728.   It is the custom
to-day to darken the auditorium in order to heighten
the brilliancy of the stage ; two centuries ago, the
body of the house was dim enough, but so also was
the stage, in spite of the incessant attentions of the
candle snuffers. There were no footlights, and the
lighting of the stage was not likely to be better than
at Covent Garden, which was illuminated, Mr. H. S.
Wyndham says in his *Annals of Covent Garden
Theatre*, by four hoops of candles hung on either side
of the stage. But audiences had never been used to
anything different, and it is all the greater tribute
to Lavinia Fenton's art both in acting and in facial
play that in spite of this disadvantage she achieved
a success unparalleled before and since.

CHAPTER VIII

THE " FIRST NIGHT " OF *THE BEGGAR'S OPERA*

The date of the production of the Opera fixed—Absurd theatrical traditions and the taste of the day—Mr. Gilfillan's imaginative description of the first night—His anachronisms—The audience dissatisfied—Jack Hall saves the situation—Sir Robert Walpole and the political allusions in the Opera—Success doubtful—Polly Peachum's ballad " Oh, ponder well " turns the scale—Macklin's version

THE play was produced on the night of January 29, 1728. It is well to lay stress on the date, for with tiresome persistency scores of writers perpetuate the inaccuracy of " 1727." Mr. W. H. K. Wright, in his Life of Gay, while mentioning the right date in one place, speaks of " November, 1727 " in another; the inscription on Hogarth's picture of *The Beggar's Opera* in the National Gallery says 1727, and the majority of Gay's many biographers fall into the same error. It may be presumed that the fashion of the day in dating plays not from the year in which they were produced, but from the theatrical season, led to the blunder. According to this fashion *The Beggar's Opera* was first performed in 1727–8, and subsequently through carelessness 1727 alone came to be mentioned.

An eighteenth-century audience soon made up its mind whether it liked or disliked a play, and it expressed its opinion for or against in unmistakable fashion. An important point in favour of *The Beggar's Opera* was its complete novelty. The play was totally different from anything which had preceded it. The critics had no standpoint. Had it been a tragedy, they would at once have thought of *The Mourning Bride, The Orphan, Venice Preserved,* or some of Aaron Hill's stupendously gloomy productions, all more or less specimens of stage fustian, judged from the modern standard of taste. On the other hand, if the " Opera " could have been regarded as a comedy pure and simple, it would have suggested comparisons with *The Beaux' Stratagem, Love for Love, The Constant Couple*, or *The Confederacy*.

These and other popular plays of the time were tests, and actors and actresses at the outset of their careers were expected to appear in the various parts with which the theatre-going public were familiar. Indeed, one is almost tempted to believe that some of the monstrously dull plays of that day attracted audiences not on account of their own merits but because the public liked to see its stage favourites solemnly pose and strut, and hear them mouth resounding lines with which it was already familiar. When Barton Booth quitted the stage on account of ill-health Quin succeeded him at Drury Lane. The play was *Cato*, and coming to that part where Porcius, Cato's son, brings the news of his brother's death, Quin, in speaking the line

" Thanks to the gods ! my boy has done his duty,"

so affected the whole house that the audience shouted " Booth outdone ! Booth outdone ! " This was not Quin's only triumph, for when he came to the famous soliloquy at the beginning of the fifth act he was encored and had to repeat the lines ! Quin, who outdid Booth, was himself put in the shade by an imitator of Booth, who apart from his power of mimicry had no stage qualifications whatever. This person was a button-maker in Paternoster Row. From constant attendance at the theatre, and especially when Barton Booth was playing, he was able to imitate this celebrated actor extremely well, especially in Othello. He became quite stage-struck, and when there was a vacancy in Rich's company, caused by Quin going to Drury Lane, the button-maker offered his services. He was engaged, and made quite a hit, especially in the passionate scene in the third act between Othello and Iago, the pit, in the obtrusive, obstreperous fashion of the day, shouting " Bravo ! Bravo! Better than Quin ! Better than Quin ! " Rich was delighted, and later on cast the button-maker for Polydore in Otway's *Orphan*, but he was a disastrous failure both in his acting and dress, and, says Davies, " the ladies more especially were disappointed with such a misrepresentation of the young gay libertine, dressed in the large full-bottom wig and red stockings, though they had been long laid aside by the politer part of the town."

Tradition governed the stage in its early days, and if such a thing as a " new reading " occurred to an actor he would hardly dare to introduce it, so conservative were the stern critics of the pit and boxes. Thomas Davies in his *Miscellanies* tells us that " it was a constant complaint of the old actors who lived in Quin's time that if Jonson's plays were intermitted for a few years they could not know how to personate his characters, they were so difficult and their manners so distant from those of other authors. To preserve them required a kind of stage learning which was traditionally hoarded up. Mosca in *Volpone*, when he endeavours to work upon the avarice of Corvino and to induce him to offer his wife to the pretendedly sick voluptuary, pronounces the word ' think ' seven or eight times, and with a different intonation on each occasion ! Many niceties of this kind were observed by the old comedians," adds Davies, " which are now absolutely lost to the stage."

Innovations, when they were once accepted, became traditions, no matter how absurd they might be, and were difficult to destroy. Wilks, when playing Hamlet, never spoke the Speech to the Players, and Davies conjectures that it was omitted from the time of the death of Betterton until Garrick revived it. Maybe Hamlet's advice was such as the mouthing players of the early eighteenth century

woefully needed, and therefore they objected to take
it. Booth, Wilks, and Cibber played Roman and
Greek heroes in full-bottom wigs. Some of these
luxuries cost as much as forty guineas apiece—an
expense which the actor himself had to bear. The
murderers in *Macbeth* were compelled by tradition to
chalk their faces, wear large whiskers and long black
wigs. This was an adornment of the comic actor,
Hippisley, the Peachum of *The Beggar's Opera*, when
he played First Murderer. Garrick abolished a good
many of these absurdities, but he introduced mannerisms of his own which were just as ridiculous. In
declaiming the lines

> "For some must laugh, while some must weep,
> Thus runs the world—away,"

it was his practice to pull out a white handkerchief,
and walking about the stage to turn it round with
vehemence. He always did the same " business " in
this scene. Perhaps he knew the audience expected
it, and did not care to disappoint them. Among
other traditional " business," the old actors always
wore huge plumes of feathers when they presented
characters of heroism and dignity. This fashion
came in at the Restoration and continued to Garrick's
time.

There was no chance of comparing *The Beggar's
Opera* with anything that had gone before. It was
sui generis. Gay, however, had already perpetrated
a dramatic riddle in the *What d'ye call it?* and maybe
the audience at first thought *The Beggar's Opera*
was a freak of the same nature. But long before
the first act was over it was seen that there was considerable method in the author's madness, and the
wit, the sprightliness of the dialogue, the natural-
ness of the characters, the charm of the familiar
ballads, the majority of which were household tunes,
and, above all, the acting, with the unctuous broad
humour of Hippisley, the quaint gravity of Spiller,
the gay recklessness of Walker, and the *naïveté*, the

mingled vivacity and pathos of Lavinia Fenton won every heart.

More than one writer has attempted an imaginary description of the first night, and notably George Gilfillan in his Life of Gay. " There was," he writes, " a brilliant assemblage. What painter shall give their heads and faces on that anxious evening ? Swift's lowering front ; Pope's bright eyes, contrasting with the blind orbs of Congreve (if he, indeed, were there) ; Addison's quiet, thoughtful physiognomy, as of one retired into some ' Vision of Mirza ' ; the Duke of Argyll, with his star and stately form and animated countenance, and poor Gay himself, perhaps, like some other playwrights in the same predicament, perspiring with trepidation, as if again about to recite *The Captives*. At first, uncertainty prevails among the patron-critics, strange looks are exchanged between Swift and Pope, till by-and-by the latter hears Argyll exclaim, ' It will do—it must do ! I see it in the eyes of 'em ! ' Then the critics breathe freely, and the curtain closes at last amidst thunders of applause ; and Gay goes home triumphant, amidst a circle of friends, who do not know whether more to wonder at his success or at their own previous apprehensions."

This is one of the most extraordinary efforts on record to picture the past. It certainly does not err on one side of the truth. Swift was not present at the first night. News of Stella's precarious health had sent him post-haste to Ireland, and the poor broken-hearted lady passed away on January 28, 1728, the very day before *The Beggar's Opera* was produced. It is extremely unlikely Congreve was present. He was very feeble, he was blind, as Mr. Gilfillan says, and he died in the spring of the following year. As for Addison, his " quiet, thoughtful physiognomy " could only have been seen in " another place," for he had been dead nine years when Mr. Gilfillan pictured him retiring into some " Vision of Mirza." What makes the blunder more inconceivable is that in his life of Addison, in the same volume, Gilfillan gives the date of the essayist's death correctly—namely, 1719.

Pope's account, the basis of Mr. Gilfillan's flight of imagination, as recorded in Spence's *Anecdotes*, still remains the one contemporary description. It is well known, but quotation is unavoidable : "We were all at the first night of it," says Pope, "in great uncertainty of the event, till we were very much encouraged by hearing the Duke of Argyll, who sat in the next box to us, say, ' It'll do—it must do—I see it in the eyes of them.' This was a good while before the first act was over ; and so gave us ease soon, for the Duke (besides his own good taste) has as particular a knack as any one now living in discovering the taste of the public. He was quite right in this, as usual : the good nature of the audience appeared stronger and stronger every act, and ended in a clamour of applause." Pope does not say whom he means by " we," and probably Mr. Gilfillan without investigation imagined the pronoun included all the "Twickenham Hotch Potch" ; but even so, how came Addison to be included ?

The sticklers for tradition, for the proprieties and for the unities, and the rest of the cast-iron laws which bound the drama of the times, were much exercised in their minds on finding that the Opera had no prologue. A play without a prologue was an unheard-of thing. True, there was a kind of prologue in the shape of a dialogue between a player and beggar in which, as already mentioned, the latter gives his reasons for writing the Opera ; but this did not satisfy the pit and gallery, who thought, as an overture did not usher in the programme, that they were being defrauded of their usual music. There were symptoms of a coming storm, and the comedian John Hall, who played Lockit, was sent on to apologise for the innovation and quell the threatened disturbance. He did it in a fashion as unpremeditated as it was unexpected. Anxious to hear what

Hall had to say, the audience received him with a chilly silence, which coming after a terrific uproar so disconcerted the apologist that he blurted out, " Ladies and Gentlemen, we—we—beg you'll not call for first and second music, because you all know there is never any music at all at an opera." The Irishism delighted the house, good-humour was restored, the dialogue was allowed to proceed, and was followed by the overture and the drawing up of the curtain.

But if the audience were slow to appreciate the novelties of the Opera, they were quick to seize upon any passage, whether in prose or verse, in which they saw some political allusion. The song with which the Opera opens, and a song of Peachum, the thief-taker, who is intended to represent Jonathan Wild, had a distinct reference to Sir Robert Walpole, and the presence of the Minister in the House gave a piquancy to the lines which was keenly enjoyed. The song runs thus :—

> " Through all the employments of life,
> Each neighbour abuses his brother :
> Whore and rogue they call husband and wife,
> All professions be-rogue one another.

> " The priest calls the lawyer a cheat,
> The lawyer be-knaves the divine,
> And the statesman, because he's so great,
> Thinks his trade as honest as mine."

This was not the only palpable hit. In Act III., where in the " condemned hold," after receiving sentence of death, Macheath trolls forth a whole string of ditties to keep up his spirits, he concludes with the famous song, set to the popular melody "Green Sleeves," beginning —

> " Since laws were made for every degree,
> To curb vice in others, as well as in me,
> I wonder we ha'n't better company
> Upon Tyburn Tree ! "

The quarrel between Peachum and Lockit was

thought to have reference to a disagreement between Sir Robert Walpole and Lord Townshend, although it is extremely doubtful whether Gay had any such intention. Lord Townshend, it was said, seized Sir Robert by the collar, Sir Robert laid hold of his in return, and both at the same instant loosing their holds, laid their hands on their swords. The belligerents made up their difference, but the affair got wind. Here, as elsewhere, it is impossible to be certain. Mr. Wilson Croker, in his edition of Lord Hervey's *Memoirs of George II.*, gives two authorities for the story, one putting it in 1729 and the other in 1730. Mr. Croker adds that " as *The Beggar's Opera* was played on the 29th January, 1728, it is certain either that the date of the historian's is an anachronism, or that Gay alluded to some earlier dispute, or that the story was made from the scene." The latter supposition is most likely correct.

Sir Robert Walpole never showed more tact and astuteness than while these daring shafts were hurled at him. He was an unpopular Minister, the house was full of his opponents, and a hostile demonstration was impending; but he adroitly turned aside the attack by smiling blandly and leading the applause !

Authorities differ as to the authorship of these two songs. It is agreed that they were not Gay's, and the honour is divided between Pope and Swift. " Warton," says Sir Walter Scott, in his Memoirs of Swift, " has assigned both to Pope, but the internal evidence is in favour of Mr. Deane Swift and Mrs. Whiteway who emphatically declared they were written by the Dean." Sir Walter adds in a footnote, " Swift never saw *The Beggar's Opera* in a complete state until it was printed, but it does not follow that he contributed no songs." Mr. Wright, relying on the authority of *The Mirror* (xi. 64), assigns both to Gay, and says that in Peachum's song Pope altered the last two lines, which in Gay's manuscript ran :

"And there's many arrive to be great
By a trade not more honest than mine."

The weight of evidence, however, is against the anonymous writer in *The Mirror*. A similar doubt is connected with Lockit's song in Act II., which certainly is as direct as the others :

> " When you censure the age
> Be cautious and sage.
> Lest the courtiers offended should be ;
> If you mention vice or bribe,
> 'Tis so pat to all the tribe,
> Each cries—' That was levelled at me.' "

According to W. Cooke's *Memoirs of Macklin*, the first song, "The Modes of the Court," was written by Lord Chesterfield, " Virgins are like the fair flower in its lustre " by Sir Charles Hanbury Williams, " When you censure the age " by Swift, and " Gamesters and lawyers are jugglers alike " is " *supposed* to be written by Mr. Fortescue, the Master of the Rolls." The compiler of the *Memoirs* adds in a footnote, " The above information came through the medium of the late Dowager Lady T——d," probably Lady Townshend. However, let the authors of the political verse be whom they may, the audience were quick to see the application, and all this contributed to the success of the night.

That which turned the scale in favour of the new venture is generally supposed to have been Polly's singing of the ballad wherein she appeals to her father (Act I. Scene viii). The surroundings amid which the ballad is set are highly humorous, and the unexpected pathos necessarily comes with greater effect. The entire episode, beginning with the ballad " Can love be controlled by advice ? " sung, one cannot doubt, with delicious unconsciousness by Polly, deserves quotation, and for convenience we take the condensed version from the modern acting edition :—

> " Can love be controll'd by advice ?
> Will Cupid our mothers obey ?
> Tho' my heart were as frozen as ice,
> At his flame 'twould have melted away.

When he kiss'd me, so closely he press'd,
'Twas so sweet that I must have complied,
So I thought it both safest and best
To marry, for fear you should chide.

"MRS. P.: Then all the hopes of our family are gone for ever and ever.

"PEACH.: And Macheath may hang his father and mother-in-law, in hopes to get into their daughter's fortune.

"POLLY: I did not marry him (as 'tis the fashion) coolly and deliberately, for honour or money—but I love him.

"MRS. P.: Love him! worse and worse! I thought the girl had been better bred. O husband! husband! . . .

"PEACH.: Dear wife, be a little pacified; don't let your passion run away with your senses. Polly, I grant you, has done a rash thing; but money, wife, is the true fuller's earth for reputation: there is not a spot or stain but what it can take out. A rich rogue now-a-days is fit company for any gentleman; and the world, my dear, hath not such a contempt for roguery as you imagine. I tell you, wife, I can make this match turn to our advantage.

"MRS. P.: I am very sensible, husband, that Captain Macheath is worth money, but I am in doubt whether he hath not two or three wives already; and then, if he should die in a session or two, Polly's dower would come into dispute.

"PEACH.: That, indeed, is a point which ought to be considered. The lawyers are bitter enemies to those in our way. They don't care that anybody should get a clandestine livelihood but themselves. . . . But now, Polly, to your affair—for matters must not be left as they are. You are married, then, it seems?

"POLLY: Yes, sir.

"PEACH.: And how do you expect to live, child?

"POLLY: Like other women, sir—upon the industry of my husband.

" Mrs. P. : What ! is the wench turned fool ? A highwayman's wife, like a soldier's, hath as little of his pay as his company.

" Peach. : And had you not the common views of a gentlewoman in your marriage, Polly ?

" Polly : I don't know what you mean, sir.

" Peach. : Of a jointure, and of being a widow.

" Polly : But I love him, sir. How then could I have thoughts of parting from him ?

" Peach. : Parting with him ! why, that is the whole scheme and intention of all marriage articles. The comfortable estate of widowhood is the only hope that keeps up a wife's spirits. Where is the woman who would scruple to be a wife, if she had it in her power to be a widow whenever she pleased ? If you have any views of this sort, Polly, I shall think the match not so unreasonable.

" Polly : How I dread to hear your advice ! Yet I must beg you to explain yourself.

" Peach. : Secure what he hath, have him 'peached the next sessions, and then at once you are made a rich widow.

" Polly : What ! murder the man I love ? The blood runs cold at my heart at the very thought of it !

" Peach. : Fie, Polly ! What hath murder to do in the affair ? Since the thing sooner or later must happen, I daresay that the captain himself would like that we should get the reward for his death sooner than a stranger. Why, Polly, the captain knows that as 'tis his employment to rob, so 'tis ours to take robbers ; every man in his business, so that there is no malice in the case.

" Mrs. P. : To have him 'peached is the only thing could ever make me forgive her.

" Air : Polly (*kneeling*)

" Now ponder well, ye parents dear,
O ponder well ! be not severe—
So save a wretched wife ;
For on the rope that hangs my dear
Depends poor Polly's life.

"MRS. P.: But your duty to your parents, hussy, obliges you to hang him. What would many a wife give for such an opportunity!

"POLLY: What is a jointure, what is a widowhood, to me? I know my heart—I cannot survive him.

"MRS. P.: What! is the fool in love in earnest, then? I hate thee for being particular. Why, wench, thou art a shame to thy very sex."

One can well imagine how this whimsical treatment of serious things tickled the fancy of the audience, hitherto accustomed to find its laughter in buffoonery and obscenity. Macklin, who was present on the first night, seems to have been of opinion that uncertainty prevailed even after this scene, and that success was doubtful until the opening of the second Act, when Spiller, the favourite of the " gods," as Mat o' the Mint in the carousing scene in a tavern near Newgate, led the spirited chorus " Let us take the rood," set to the march in Handel's *Rinaldo.* Then the applause was " as universal as unbounded." There is no contemporaneous evidence that Polly made her great success with the audience in " O ponder well," though one can well believe that it completed the conquest of the already enamoured Duke of Bolton. No doubt " the eyes of 'em " showed that at this point the audience were being won over; but Macheath after all was the character which appealed to pit and gallery. The dashing highwayman of real life was not an unpopular character with the people. If he got his money by questionable means, he spent it freely, and his daring imparted a romance to his deeds wholly wanting in those of the burglar. Highwaymen were not all ruffianly Dick Turpins. They came from all classes, and being eased of one's purse by somebody who had the manners of a gentleman may have softened the offence. At any rate, as a rule he robbed only the well-to-do, and this went for much in the opinion of an eighteenth-century mob.

CHAPTER IX

Hogarth's pictures of *The Beggar's Opera*—Their histories and description—The Duke of Bolton and the "nobleman look"—"Long Sir Thomas Robinson"—Hogarth's portrait of Polly Peachum

HOGARTH's picture (see p. 48) of the scene towards the end of the third Act has stamped the opera with an actuality without which we should have but a very poor idea of the theatre in the early part of the eighteenth century; for what the observant painter has given us of Lincoln's Inn Fields Theatre applied also to Drury Lane, and to the King's, the "Little Theatre" in the Haymarket. Hogarth was photographic in his accuracy, and the drapery above and the motto "Veluti in speculum utile dulci" may be taken as a literal reproduction of what he saw. So also the arrangement of the seats on the stage for aristocratic patrons. Hogarth painted three pictures of *The Beggar's Opera*, one for Sir Archibald Grant, another for Rich, and a third, which is inferior to the others and with fewer figures in the grouping. This picture was hung in the 1911–12 Exhibition of Old Masters at Burlington House.

The picture painted for Rich came into the possession of the Duke of Leeds, and its sale is thus recorded by *The London Chronicle* of April 2, 1762: "On Friday last, at the sale of the late Mr. Rich's pictures, jewels, etc., a clock by Graham was bought by the Right Honourable the Earl of Chesterfield for £42, and a Scene in *The Beggar's Opera* where Polly and Lucy are pleading for Macheath's life, painted by Hogarth, was sold for £32 14s. to his Grace the Duke of Leeds."

Mr. J. Ireland says "a duplicate of the picture of

95

The Beggar's Opera was painted by Hogarth for Sir Henry Gough," but from what original Ireland does not state. Indeed, the various statements concerning the copies extant of this world-famous picture make it very difficult to fix with certainty how many times Hogarth painted the scene. We have Mr. J. Nicholls, for instance, writing as follows : " Another copy of the same scene was bought by the late Sir William Saunderson, and is now in the possession of Lord Calthorpe. Mr. Walpole had a painting of a scene in the same piece where Macheath is going to execution." We confess our inability to settle this vexed question, and it is sufficient if we confine our attention to the one that is best known, the replica painted for Sir Archibald Grant.

Of the latter, Mr. Ireland says that " though Sir Archibald Grant paid half price for them " (Hogarth painted his picture of " The Committee " also for Sir Archibald Grant), " at the time he gave the order, I cannot positively assert that they were ever in his possession, for they afterward got into the hands of Mr. John Huggins, and at the sale of his effects the latter was purchased by the Rev. Doctor Monkhouse of Queen's College, Oxford." Sir Archibald Grant was expelled the House of Commons for questionable conduct in connection with the administration of a public trust fund, and probably cancelled his arrangement with Hogarth.

At the decease of Dr. Monkhouse the picture descended into the hands successively of the Rev. H. James de Salis and Mr. Thomas Bowerbank, and subsequently came into the possession of Mr. John Murray, and is now hanging in the National Gallery. On the frame is carved a medallion of Gay between two grotesque masks. The painting was in the Exhibition of Old Masters in 1875 numbered 127.

The incident illustrated by the painter is Macheath's predicament, when, after being called upon for trial, he is claimed both by Polly and Lucy. Lockit thus addresses him :

HIPPISLEY AS SIR FRANCIS GRIPE.

Drawn by Hogarth.

"Lockit : Set your heart at rest, captain—you have neither the chance of love or money for another escape ; for you are ordered to be called down upon your trial immediately.

"Peach. : Away, hussies! this is not a time for a man to be hampered with his wives—you see the gentleman is in chains already.

"Lucy: Oh, husband! my heart longed to see thee ; but to see thee thus distracts me!

"Polly: Will not my dear husband look upon his Polly ? Why hadst thou not flown to me for protection ? With me thou hadst been safe.

"Duet—Polly and Lucy :

Polly :	Hither, dear husband, turn your eyes !
Lucy :	Bestow one glance to cheer me !
Polly :	Think with that look thy Polly dies.
Lucy :	Oh, shun me not, but hear me !
Polly :	'Tis Polly sues.
Lucy :	'Tis Lucy speaks.
Polly :	Is thus true love requited ?
Lucy :	My heart is bursting !
Polly :	Mine too breaks¦!
Lucy :	Must I——
Polly :	Must I be slighted ?

" Mac. : What would you have me say, ladies ? You see the affair will soon be at an end, without my disobliging either of you.

" Peach : But the settling of this point, Captain, might prevent a lawsuit between your two widows.

" Air—Macheath :

" Which way shall I turn me ? how can I decide ?
Wives, the day of our death, are as fond as a bride.
One wife is too much for most husbands to bear,
But two at a time, there's no mortal can bear !
This way, and that way, and which way I will,
What would comfort the one, t'other wife would take ill.

"Polly: But if his own misfortunes have made him insensible to mine, a father, sure, will be more compassionate. Dear, dear sir ! sink the material evidence, and bring him off at his trial. Polly, upon her knees, begs it of you.

7

" Air—POLLY :

" When my hero in court appears,
　　And stands arraign'd for his life,
Then think of poor Polly's tears,
　　For ah ! poor Polly's his wife.
Like the sailor, he holds up his hand,
　　Distress'd on the dashing wave ;
To die a dry death at land
　　Is as bad as a watery grave.
And alas, poor Polly !
Alack, and well-a-day !
Before I was in love
Oh, ev'ry month was May !

"LUCY : If Peachum's heart is hardened, sure you, Sir, will have more compassion on a daughter— I know the evidence is in your power—how then can you be a tyrant to me! (*kneeling*)."

Two songs by Lucy follow, and we have Peachum exclaiming :

"PEACHUM : Set your heart at rest, Polly—your husband is to die to-day ; therefore, if you are not already provided, 'tis high time to look about for another. There's comfort for you, you slut !
"LOCKIT : We are ready, sir, to conduct you to the Old Bailey.

" Air—MACHEATH :

" The charge is prepared, the lawyers are met,
　　The judges all ranged (a terrible show !)
I go undismayed—for death is a debt,
　　A debt on demand—so take what I owe,
Then farewell, my love—dear Charmers ! adieu—
Contented I die—'tis the better for you.
Here ends all dispute, for the rest of our lives,
For this way, at once, I please all my wives.

"MAC.: Now, gentlemen, I am ready to attend you."

In the acting version of to-day, Polly's song is omitted, and the scene shortened considerably.

Indeed, as now published, *The Beggar's Opera*, compressed from three into two acts, hardly has justice done to it.

The picture is not only notable as a representation of the Opera, but as a collection of portraits not merely of the leading characters, but of the noble occupants of the privileged seats on the stage. To begin with the players : Macheath in his fetters (as represented in the person of Walker, Macheath has anything but a graceful figure ; Mr. J. Nicholls, indeed, calls him " a slouching bully ") occupies the centre of the picture, but it is Polly kneeling to Peachum (Hall) to whom one's eyes naturally turn.* Nicholls remarks that she " appears happily disencumbered of such a hoop as the daughter of Peachum within our younger memories has worn," and Macklin described her dress as " very like the simplicity of a modern Quaker." Whether by accident or design, no dress could have furnished a more effective contrast to the spirit of the play. It was a stroke of art to suggest innocence in the midst of vice and immorality. As years went on, it became the fashion, as Nicholls has hinted, to dress *The Beggar's Opera* in whatever might be the prevailing style of costume, thus losing the colour of the period the play represented. It was left for Madame Vestris, like the artist she was, to restore the original costumes. Of the other figures on the stage, Lucy, who is kneeling to Lockit (Hippisley) with her back to the spectator, is Mrs. Egleton, of whom contemporary critics have little or nothing to say. She was completely outshone by the glory of Polly. Peachum (Jack Hall) is made by no means bad-looking ; Polly of course is appealing to him. In the background, with his arm extended, is Filch (Nat Clark). Neither Mrs. Peachum nor Mrs. Lockit appeared in the scene, and so are not represented.

In the seats on the stage to the right we have the Duke of Bolton seated, his enraptured gaze unmistakably fixed on the lady who has won his

* See Appendix, Note 1.

heart. His Grace of Bolton is comely, dignified—an
unmistakable gentleman. " He had the nobleman
look," Spence records Pope saying of the duke:
" that look which a nobleman should have, rather
than what they have generally now " (1740). Pope
also saw the same " nobleman look " in the Duke of
Buckingham, while " Wycherley," he remarks, " was
a very genteel man, and had the nobleman look as
much as the Duke of Buckingham."   Other fortunate
possessors of the " look " were Lord Peterborough,
Lord Bolingbroke, and " one or two more."

Next comes Major Pauncefoot, of whom nothing
is known ; then Sir Robert Fagg, the horse-racing
baronet from Kent, one of Polly's most ardent admirers, whose name was coupled with hers in the
many lampoons which were written about the " toast "
of the town.   His gaze is not less intent than that of
his ducal rival. The name of the lady whose eyes
are turned upward is not given either by Ireland
or Nicholls. Beyond her is Manager Rich, who is
whispering to Cock, the picture dealer and auctioneer
of Poland Street, a very important person where
artists were concerned. Possibly Hogarth wanted to
stand well with him, and so introduced his portrait.
" By G——, I love you, Mr. Cock," said once that
vainest and most covetous of artists, Sir Godfrey
Kneller, " and I will do you good ; but you must
do something for me too, Mr. Cock : one hand can
wash the face, but two hands can wash one another."
A most excellent maxim for a man of business.   One
can hardly imagine Gay, who is standing half hidden
by Rich, putting it in practice. Mr. Nicholls describes
the poet as " saturated by public approbation " and
paying " no greater regard to the performance than
the manager." Gay has certainly a not dissatisfied
look on his good-humoured face, and as the picture
was painted in 1729, after the tremendously successful
run of the piece, the author had good reason to be
pleased, for his purse by that time was well lined.

On the other side we have two ladies, of whom

one is Lady Jane Cook. The name of the other Nicholls does not give. Then comes Anthony Henley —not to be confounded with "Orator" Henley— bending forward, his elbow resting on the ledge of the box and apparently holding something in his hand. If lorgnettes had been in use it might be said he had one. Perhaps it is a snuffbox. Lord Gage is standing behind Henley, and next to the latter at the end of the row is Sir Conyers D'Arcy. Forming the apex of the pyramidal group is Sir Thomas Robinson, called "Long Sir Thomas" to distinguish him from another Sir Thomas Robinson, afterwards the Baron Grantham. As the prefix to his name indicates, the Sir Thomas of the picture was tall and thin, whereas the other Sir Thomas was short and fat. The distinction gave great play to the wits. " I can't imagine why the one should be preferred to the other," said that lively lady of fashion, Lady Townshend, famed for her *bon mots*, some of which Horace Walpole has enshrined in his *Letters*: " I can see but little difference between them ; the one is as broad as the other is long."

Long Sir Thomas Robinson was just the man to be lavish in his patronage of the stage. Owing to his extravagance he was called " the Petronius of the present age," and his taste for the fashionable amusements of the day led to his being appointed a director of the entertainments at Ranelagh Gardens, in which place of gaiety he had a considerable pecuniary interest. One of his biographers tells us that his appearance was " often rendered still more remarkable by his hunting dress, a postilion's cap, a light green jacket, and buckskin breeches." It was Sir Thomas the long who was the cause of a ludicrous mistake on the part of a French Abbé, who, being introduced to him in Paris, said, " Excuse me, Sir. Are you the famous Robinson Crusoe so remarkable in history ? " Robinson was a close friend of Lord Chesterfield, who in his last illness said, in the jesting spirit which belonged to him, " Ah ! Sir Thomas; it will be sooner

over with me than it would be with you, for I am
dying by *inches*."

A charming portrait of Polly painted by Hogarth
is also in the National Gallery, and a reproduction
from an engraving of it by C. Apostool forms the
frontispiece of this volume. It was originally owned
by S. Ireland, and at his sale in 1801 was bought,
says Mr. W. H. Wheatley, by Mr. William Seguier
for £5 7s. 6d., and was afterwards in the collection
of Mr. George Watson Taylor. It fetched £52 10s.
when next sold; and was purchased by the trustees
of the National Gallery at the sale of the Leigh Court
collection in 1884 for 800 guineas. Mr. Dutton Cook
has gracefully described Polly as represented in this
picture. He writes of her: " with frank, open eyes,
delicately arched brows, well-shaped mouth, with
luscious cherry-red lips, and soft round chin, brown
hair, gathered lightly, not brushed, back from her
forehead, probably over a small pillow, surmounted
by a dainty lace ' mob ' cap with many flaps, a string
of pearls round her white neck, and dress of rich
but sad-coloured silk, with broad ribbon and cord
trimming *à la militaire* down the front, the dress high
on the shoulders, low in the bosom, edged with a
narrow frilling of lace, casting delicate reflections of
light on the superbly moulded bust."

While agreeing in the main with Mr. Dutton
Cook's piece of word-painting, one may be allowed
to question the accuracy of his observation in regard
to Polly's hair. The exact hue is difficult to define,
but it is certainly not brown. Pale straw with a
glint of gold is the nearest approach to its somewhat
peculiar tint. Mr. Dutton Cook draws no conclusion
as to Polly's character from her physiognomy, and we
are disposed to submit that it does not indicate extraordinary talent. Those "frank, open eyes " suggest
amiability and ingenuousness, but no latent genius
awaiting development. The picture was painted in
the plenitude of her charms—1734 has been named
as the date, but not with certainty—and she has a

matronly and a happy look. It can hardly be said that there are the makings of a great actress in that good-natured face. Polly was born to please; she succeeded, and we may be sure her friends crowded round her when the curtain fell, eager to pour out their congratulations. " Calls " before the curtain did not come into vogue until a much later date, but the lack of this modern institution was amply compensated for by the warmth of the compliments showered upon her behind the scenes by the occupants of the seats on the stage.

Neither were there any cries for " Author ! " Perhaps it was as well. Gay was corpulent and emotional, and might not have gone through the ordeal of bowing to the audience without mishap. The episode of his upsetting a screen in the royal presence, owing to his confusion, is well known. Genest says : " Gay seems to have been an awkward fellow—in *The Confederacy* Mrs. Oldfield was made to say :

" ' But hark ! Who's entering here ? I'll run away ;
For by the clumsie tread it should be Gay.' "

The suggestion may be hazarded that the performance was followed by a supper when compounds more potent than " mountain port " were consumed in inordinate quantities, and one may venture to surmise that among those who could boast of a headache the next morning was the genial dramatist and poet, John Gay.

CHAPTER X

POLLY AND HER FELLOW PLAYERS

Polly Peachum's fame—Her salary—The cast of *The Beggar's Opera*—Something about Hippisley, Hall, and Walker—Walker's popularity—His dissipated habits

LAVINIA FENTON awoke to find herself famous. The town talked of nothing but the new Opera and Polly Peachum. The name of the heroine—the daughter of a thief-taker !—tickled the fancy of the public and found its way to their hearts. Henceforth it was to be " Miss Fenton " no longer, but " Polly ! " After all, without prying too curiously into the why and wherefore, it may be said that the young lady had as much right to one name as the other.

From a pecuniary point of view Polly did not benefit much ; still her salary was doubled. She had been engaged at fifteen shillings a week ; it was now raised to thirty. The amount judged by the earnings of to-day sounds ridiculous, but one must not forget the " benefit." Actors and actresses, however, were paid better than singers, and in 1728 we learn from W. Cooke (*Macklin's Memoirs*) that " a first-rate singer could only obtain thirty shillings a week, which, according to the number of playing weeks in the season, amounts to forty-five pounds per year." Fielding considered that when compared with other professional men the actor was not so badly paid. He says in *The Covent Garden Journal*: " The stage at present promises a much better provision than any of the professions. . . . The income of an actor of any rank is from six to twelve hundred a year ; whereas that of two-thirds of the gentlemen

LAVINIA FENTON.

From an engraving by I. Tinney, after J. Ellys, in Mr. A. M. Broadley's Collection.

of the army is considerably under one hundred ; the income of nine-tenths of the clergy is less than fifty pounds a year ; and the profits of the law, of ninety-nine in the hundred, amount not to a single shilling." Fielding over-coloured the picture. The figures we give in Chapter XVII of the expenses of Covent Garden Theatre by no means support his roseate statement.

Something must be said on the gains from the "benefit" system. This addition to the actor's income did not necessarily mean the purchase of tickets at ordinary admission prices. After Macklin "created" Shylock (which before his time was almost regarded as a comic part), drawing forth the well-known eulogium " This is the Jew that Shakespeare drew," he took the play for his benefit, when " several Noblemen of the first distinction took what are commonly called *gold* tickets," the value of which depended upon the mood and generosity of the noble patron.

It was fortunate for Polly as well as for Gay and Rich that the other members of the company were already well known to and were in high favour with the public when the Opera was produced. The original cast, indeed, could hardly have been bettered. Each part fitted its representative like a glove. The following is the full list :

MEN.

PEACHUM	Mr. Hippisley.
LOCKIT	Mr. Hall.
MACHEATH . . .	Mr. Walker.
FILCH . . .	Mr. Clark.
JEMMY TWITCHER .	Mr. Bullock.
CROOK-FINGERED JACK .	Mr. Houghton.
WAT DREARY . . .	Mr. Smith.
ROBIN OF BAGSHOT . .	Mr. Lacy.
NIMMING NED . .	Mr. Pitt.
HARRY PADDINGTON . .	Mr. Eaton.
MAT O' THE MINT . .	Mr. Spiller.
BEN BUDGE . . .	Mr. Morgan.
Beggar	Mr. Chapman.
Player	Mr. Milward.

Constables, Drawers, Turnkeys, etc.

WOMEN.

Mrs. Peachum .	.	.	Mrs. Martin.
Polly Peachum	.	.	Miss Fenton.
Lucy Lockit .	.	.	Mrs. Egleton.
Diana Trapes .	.	.	Mrs. Martin.
Mrs. Coaxer .	.	.	Mrs. Holiday.
Dolly Trull .	.	.	Mrs. Lacy.
Mrs. Vixen	.	.	Mrs. Rice.
Betty Doxy .	.	.	Mrs. Rogers.
Jenny Diver .	.	.	Mrs. Clark.
Mrs. Slamakin	.	.	Mrs. Morgan.
Suky Tawdry	.	.	Mrs. Palin.
Molly Brazen	.	.	Mrs. Sallee.

Not a few of these actors and actresses merit something beyond the mere mention of their names. To take them in the order in which they stand we commence with John Hippisley (Peachum). He was very popular chiefly on account of his broad drollery, which, to his credit be it said, he kept under control. The licence which the dramatists of the day permitted themselves was an encouragement to coarseness on the part of the actor, and that Hippisley could, as Antonio, the " foolish debauched Senator " in *Venice Preserved*, not only induce an audience to tolerate him, but even earn its applause, is a tribute to his restraint. The dialogue between Antonio (supposed to be meant for Antony Ashley Cooper, first Earl of Shaftesbury) and Acquilena the courtezan is as silly as it is obscene, and Hippisley was the last actor who essayed the character. The whole scene was afterwards cut out, and is only to be found in old editions of Otway's play. By the special command of George II., when Prince of Wales, it was once revived, when Pinkethman played Antonio and the beautiful Mrs. Horton, Acquilena. Otway had the decency to spare the actress. All the silly and objectionable passages are put into the mouth of the foolish old man. Had it been otherwise, it is doubtful whether Mrs. Horton would have undertaken the part even to please a prince. " Mrs. Horton's beauty," Davies tells us, " was so remarkable in the early part of her life that few young men could see her without having a *tendresse* for her, which she never discouraged, and when on the verge of threescore she dressed like a girl of twenty. A nobleman some few years before her death offered her a very large fortune to live with him, which, says Davies quaintly, she " generously " refused.

According to the *Biographia Dramatica*, Hippisley's first connection with the stage was in a very humble capacity—he was a candle snuffer. He seems to have chosen very early the line which suited him, and with which he afterwards became identified. Davies says, " No Comedian ever excelled him in describing the excesses of avarice and amorous dotage." In such parts as Fondlewife in the *Old Bachelor*, Pandarus in *Troilus and Cressida*, Sir Francis Gripe in *The Busybody*, Polonius Corbaccio in *Volpone*, and Fluellen, he was admirable. Gay's good luck adhered to him when Hippisley was selected for Peachum. No actor of that day could have played the character better. Jonathan Wild, who furnished the model for Peachum, was one of the most notorious men of the times, and it is more than probable that Hippisley was familiar with the appearance and mannerisms of the famous thief-taker, and thus was able to introduce a little mimicry from life. Peachum's reading his Tyburn list is simply a reproduction of Wild's daily practice. The following dialogue between Peachum and Filch might really have been uttered by the notorious thief-taker and one of his creatures, and the close resemblance must have been keenly enjoyed by the pit and gallery :

" FILCH : Sir, Black Moll hath sent word her trial comes on in the afternoon, and she hopes you will order matters so as to bring her off.

" PEACH. : Why, she may plead . . . at worst; to my knowledge she hath taken care of that security : but as the wench is very active and industrious, you may satisfy her that I'll soften the evidence.

"FILCH : Tom Gagg, Sir, is found guilty.

"PEACH. : A lazy dog ! when I took him the time before, I told him what he would come to if he did not mend his hand.—This is death without reprieve ; I may venture to book him (*writes*) ' for Tom Gagg forty pounds.' Let Betty Sly know that I'll save her from transportation, for I can get more by her staying in England.

"FILCH : Betty hath brought more goods into our lock this year than any five of the gang, and in truth 'tis pity to lose so good a customer.

"PEACH. : If none of the gang takes her off, she may in the common course of business live a twelve-month longer. I love to let women 'scape. A good sportsman always lets the hen partridges fly, be-cause the breed of the game depends upon them. Besides, here the law allows us no reward. There is nothing to be got by the death of women—except our wives.

"FILCH : Without dispute she is a fine woman ! 'twas to her I was obliged for my education. (To say a bold word.) She hath trained up more young fellows to the business than the gaming table.

"PEACH. : Truly, Filch, thy observation is right. We and the surgeons are more beholden to women than all the professions besides."

Pecksniffian platitudes without number have been poured out from time to time, lamenting the immoral tendency of *The Beggar's Opera* in investing the highwayman with a halo of romance, and so recruit-ing the ranks of the Knights of the Road ; but none of the pious moralists seem to have noticed the ex-posure in the Opera of something worse than high-way robbery—the detestable practices of Wild and his gang, and the oppression, the inhumanity and the rapacity of the officials of Newgate, from Governor Pitt downwards.

Hippisley was a dramatist as well as an actor. He wrote an opera called *Flora,* an adaptation of

Doggett's *Country Wake* ; a farce, *The Journey to Bristol of the Honest Welchman*, and an interlude which went by the name of *Hippisley's Drunken Man*. This little sketch, Shuter, a comedian whose style resembled Hippisley's but was much broader, after Hippisley's death, brought out frequently for his benefit with success. It was the soliloquy of an inebriate, who affects the character of sobriety. Hippisley introduced it at his benefit at Covent Garden in 1742, when a play based on Hogarth's *Modern Midnight Conversation* was performed.

Shuter told John Taylor, the author of *Monsieur Tonson*, a farce which had some popularity in its day, that Hippisley suffered severely in his face at a fire, which gave such a ludicrous cast to his features that the audience always laughed when he appeared on the stage. He once consulted Quin on the profession to which he should bring up his son, whom he described as a very promising boy. Quin, who thought that all Hippisley's comic merit depended on the whimsical turn of his features, roughly said, " Burn his *face* and make him an actor." As this story is usually given, the cause of Quin's reply is omitted, and his suggestion appears as an unmeaning and gratuitous piece of rudeness. Taylor adds that Quin always pronounced the letter *a* broad, as in " brass," and Shuter mimicked his pronunciation of the word "face" in relating the reminiscence (Taylor's *Records*).

John Hall, who so distinguished himself on the first night by his naïve apology, was quite unknown until a portion of the fame of *The Beggar's Opera* descended upon him as Lockit. Nature had given him the requisite qualifications. He was portly, and he had a fair knowledge of music. He commenced life as a dancing-master, and afterwards acquired a proprietary interest in the Smock Alley Theatre, Dublin, one of his partners being John Leigh, known as "Handsome Leigh," a man of considerable merit. The theatrical speculation in Dublin proved a failure, and Hall and Leigh came to London, where they became members of the Lincoln's Inn Fields Company.

Hall had off the stage a quaint simplicity of expression which came very near unconscious humour. Moody, the actor, writing to *The European Magazine* in May 1807, from Barnes (where after his retirement from the stage he turned market gardener), gives some specimens of Hall's characteristic utterances. While he was a member of a Bartholomew Fair theatrical company, Hall wanted a pair of buckles, and asked the price of a stout pair of a shop-keeper near his booth. " As I am," said he, " a stout man, I find it hard to get a pair that will not break after two or three days' wear." " There, Master Hall, is a pair that will last for *ever*." " Will they ? " says Hall : " why, then let me have *two pair*." A second anecdote, neither better nor worse than the first, runs thus : " Hall upon coming to London was very desirous to see Rag Fair, with which he was highly delighted. On observing in this mart of *second*-hand articles a fine leg of mutton, he asked the price. The butcher told him half a crown. " Pooh ! " said Hall, " I can have a *new one* for that in Clare Market." Moody says with justice that " there are many traditional stories of Hall which were all in sober sadness, not arch, but simple. It is related of him that, his dresser having burned his shirt, he came to the Green Room in a high fit of laughter. Upon being asked why he so laughed : " Why," says he, " the dresser has let my shirt fall in the fire." " And do you laugh at that ? " " No," says he, " *but* (still laughing) *I have never another*." Moody claims Hall to be the actor who made the retort (ascribed to Walker) to Rich about his defective memory and the long run of *The Beggar's Opera*.

The story told in *The Era Almanack* of 1869 of Hall is quite in his naïve, simple vein. One night in 1739 the scene room at Covent Garden caught fire, and the audience being greatly alarmed, " the facetious Joe [? Jack] Hall " was ordered by Rich to explain the matter, " which honest Joe did in the following extraordinary address : ' Ladies and gentlemen, for Heaven's sake don't be frightened—don't stir—keep your seats—the fire is almost extinguished ; but if it was *not*—we have a reservoir of one hundred hogsheads of water over your heads that would drown you all in a few moments ! ' "

Quin, as already mentioned, was originally cast for Macheath. He was a poor singer and did not take kindly to the part. Moreover, he was one of the pessimists who prophesied the Opera would prove a " frost." But he hardly cared to offend Gay and his powerful friends, and he drudged through two rehearsals. At the end of the second one, a voice was heard singing some of the songs behind the scenes in a tone and liveliness of manner which Quin did not and never would possess. Quin was quite conscious of his shortcomings, and recognising the voice as that of Tom Walker, his own friend, exclaimed, " Aye, there's a man who is much more qualified to do you justice than I am." Walker was tried, and Gay with his knowledge of music saw at once that he had secured an ideal Macheath.*

Walker drifted into the profession, and, like scores of actors who afterwards achieved fame, gained his first experience as a member of a strolling company. He was acting the part of Paris in the " Droll " of *The Siege of Troy* in a booth at Southwark Fair, when by chance he was seen by Barton Booth, who recommended him to the manager of Drury Lane, where he made his first appearance in the character of Lorenzo in *The Merchant of Venice*, styled in the advertisements of this time *The Jew of Venice*, about the year 1716. Walker remained at Drury Lane until, as recorded, accident led him to call on his friend Quin, and his fortune was made. Macheath was totally different from any part he had hitherto played—so much so that it was said that " Booth found

* See Appendix, Note 2.

him a hero, and Gay dubbed him a highwayman."
Hogarth in his picture of Southwark Fair is supposed to have drawn Walker as Paris, who, with the
other characters in *The Siege of Troy*, is standing in
front of the booth.

Unhappily, success spoiled Tom Walker. His
popularity was only second to that of Polly, but in
a different direction ; the gay gallants of the town
patronised him, and in their company he was continually drinking. It is gravely stated in W. Cooke's
Memoirs of Macklin that he was frequently under
the necessity of eating sandwiches (or, as they were
then called, anchovy toasts) behind the scenes, " to
alleviate the fumes of the liquor." What a combina-
tion of odours ! One can only pity poor Polly and
Lucy when they had to endure the embraces and
salutes of the rollicking highwayman. After the run
of *The Beggar's Opera* was over, and Walker went
back to what might be termed the " legitimate
drama," he turned his attention to play-writing, or
rather play-adapting. He altered two dramas written
by Tom D'Urfey on the subject of Masaniello, and
boiled them down to one, choosing the seclusion of
Lincoln's Inn Fields Theatre at times when nothing
was going on, to do the work.

Leigh, the actor, who wrote the prologue to *The
Prison Breaker or the Adventures of John Sheppard*, to
which we have already referred, and a comedy called
Kensington Gardens, perpetrated a ballad, the first
line of which insinuates that Walker had some
reason other than quietude for selecting the theatre.
A couple of stanzas need only be quoted :

> " Tom Walker, his creditors meaning to chouse,
>   Like an honest, good-natured young fellow,
> Resolved all the Summer to stay in the house,
>   And rehearse by himself Masaniello :
> But as soon as he heard of the Baron's success,
>   He stript off his night-gown and put on his dress,
> And cried, ' D—mn my bl—d, I will strike for no less ! '
>   So he called O'er the hatch for Will Thomas.
>   Will Thomas, etc.

" THE BEGGAR'S OPERA " BURLESQUED.

From an engraving by T. Cook & Son, after Hogarth.

"'Go, tell my young Lord,' said the modest young man,
'I beg he'd invite me to dinner ;
I'll be as diverting as ever I can :
  I will, by the faith of a sinner.
I'll mimic all actors—the worst and the best ;
  I'll sing him a song—I'll crack him a jest.
I'll make him act better than Henley the priest.'
  'I'll tell him so, Sir,' says Will Thomas.
                Will Thomas, etc."

The " Baron " was Egleton, the husband of Mrs. Egleton (Lucy), and " Henley the priest " was of course Orator Henley, whose eccentricities at this time were the talk of the town, and whose chapel was in Clare Market, a little more than a stone's throw from the theatre. Will Thomas was a well-known waiter at the Coffee-house, Portugal Street, opposite the stage door of the theatre. According to W. Cooke, Orator Henley was taught to read by Walker. Cooke probably meant elocution. Henley was six years older than Walker.

It was said of Walker that at the seventy-second performance of the Opera, being rather imperfect in his part, Rich observed, " How's this, Muster Walker ? I thought you had a pretty strong memory." " So I have," replied the actor, " but you can't expect it to last for ever." This is the story which Moody said belonged to Jack Hall. It certainly sounds more like Hall than Walker.

Walker was the author of one of the numerous imitations of *The Beggar's Opera*. This was *The Quaker's Opera* (see Chapter III.)—acted at Lee and Hooper's Booth, Bartholomew Fair, 1729. Another of his efforts in this direction was *Robin Hood*, an opera, also performed at Bartholomew Fair. Dr. E. F. Rimbault, in a series of articles on Bartholomew Fair which appeared in *Notes and Queries* (Series 2, vol. 7), claimed to be the possessor of a copy of each opera, with the names of the actors in MS. in a contemporary hand.

Walker also tried his hand at a play, with the melodramatic title of *The Fate of Villainy*. It was

8

brought out at Goodman's Fields Theatre in 1730, but with very indifferent success. After this he seems to have lapsed further into dissipation, and when some years later he was dismissed from Covent Garden, he took his two pieces to Ireland, and at the Dublin theatre *The Fate of Villainy* became *Love and Loyalty*, but the fortune of the drama under its new title remained unchanged. Novelty drew an audience the first night, but the second being given out for his benefit, and not being able to pay in half the expenses of the house, the doors, by order of the manager, were ordered to be kept shut. " But that precaution was needless " (says Chetwood, who tells this anecdote), " as very few people came to enquire the reason of it." Dissipation and disappointment brought about a speedy end to the once popular Macheath. He died in great distress in Dublin, in 1744.

Tom Davies, who knew Walker personally, says : " He had from nature great advantages of voice and person. His countenance was merry and expressive ; and the humour, ease and gaiety which he assumed in Macheath and other characters of this complexion, rendered him a great favourite of the public. He knew little scientifically of music, other than singing a song in good ballad tune ; but that singing was supported by a speaking eye, and inimitable action."

Hogarth was very friendly with Walker, Hippisley, Spiller, and the rest of *The Beggar's Opera* Company, and passed many a merry hour with the comedians at the " Black Jack," at the south-eastern corner of Lincoln's Inn Fields, and at the " Bull and Butcher " in Clare Market. It is not so long ago that the " Black Jack " (famed for the daring leap Jack Sheppard took from one of the windows to escape capture) was standing—a picturesque old hostelry with a colonnade of rickety, weather-stained timber posts—and it had probably not altered materially since it was one of the houses of call for the " pros " of the theatre in Portugal Street. The " Black Jack " was kept somewhere about this time by Macklin's aunt, and Macklin himself was in her employ as a waiter.

Hogarth drew the design of the admission ticket for Walker's benefit, the grouping of the five principal characters being very much the same as that in the centre of his picture of *The Beggar's Opera*. The drawing was badly engraved by one Sympson, and is notable from the fact that it is the only instance of this style of etching in which the name of the engraver appears (see p. 64). Walker is represented in one of the figures in the doorway in No. 3 of the *Harlot's Progress*.

CHAPTER XI

OTHER THEATRICAL NOTABILITIES

Nat Clark—Bullock—Spiller—His artistic "make-up" and his popularity among the butchers of Clare Market—Mrs. Egleton and Miss Eliza Rogers—Mrs. Rogers of Drury Lane and Wilks—Her jealousy of Mrs. Oldfield—The other "ladies" of *The Beggar's Opera*.

NAT CLARK (Filch) lived for more than fifty years after the first representation of the Opera. He was a good all-round actor, whether in comedy or tragedy, but he never succeeded better than in the part of Filch, Peachum's right-hand man ; assisted as he was by his thin, meagre countenance, his shambling gait, and last but not least by his thorough knowledge of the thieves' patter of the day. Had he chosen to " gag," Clark could have delighted the " gods " with a few impromptus which, unintelligible to the " quality " on the stage, would have been thoroughly appreciated by the gallery. When the run of *The Beggar's Opera* was over Filch became second Harlequin to Rich. The two were very much alike, and one of the Company having quarrelled with Clark, waited until the performance was over on purpose to " have it out." Rich chancing to come off the stage first, was staggered by receiving a violent blow in the chest, and the assailant, seeing his mistake, did his best to apologise. " But pray, Muster," gasped Rich, " what could Clark possibly do to make you strike so hard ? " Unlike too many of his comrades, Clark was not a hard drinker. It is pleasant to know that he ended his days peacefully at Hammersmith, where he for some years lived in retirement, treating, so we are told, " his visitors with good ale and much theatrical anecdote."

Jemmy Twitcher, played by Bullock, has but a few lines to say, but they express the philosophy of the Opera. " Why are the laws levelled at us ? are we more dishonest than the rest of mankind ? What we win, gentlemen, is our own by the law of arms and the right of conquest." Of Bullock very little is known. All that need be said of him is that he is not to be confounded with his brother Christopher Bullock, who with seven or eight other actors quitted Drury Lane in 1714–15 to join Rich's Company at Lincoln's Inn Fields Theatre, and who afterwards was known as the author, or part author, of *A Woman's Revenge*, of which something will have to be said later on.

Spiller (Mat o' the Mint) was the son of a Gloucester carrier, who having acquired some property, apprenticed his only son to a landscape painter; but nature had made the lad an actor, and he drifted into the profession in the manner peculiar to the time by joining a company of strolling players. Comedy was his unmistakable line, and coming to London, his first engagement was at Drury Lane in 1710, when Aaron Hill found him a place in his company. He was an instant success—so much so that when he was but twenty-three years old, a piece was written especially to bring him under the direct notice of the public.

Spiller was regarded as a rival to Pinkethman, the great comedian of his day, and the two were very intimate. All would appear to be fair in stage rivalry, as in love and war; and probably Spiller held this opinion, if it be true that after a drinking bout with Pinkethman at the Gun Tavern, Billingsgate, Spiller picked his friend's pocket of a part in a new comedy written specially for Pinkethman. Spiller saw his way to get the better of his rival, and ran with his spoil to Christopher Bullock, who coolly appropriated the manuscript and wrote a piece called *The Cobler of Preston* on what Spiller had stolen, and so enabled Spiller to anticipate his friend by quite a fortnight.

Spiller and Pinkethman were both modern in their ways. Spiller anticipated the character actors of to-day in the care and attention to detail he paid to his dress and " make-up," and Pinkethman was a forerunner of Charles Mathews, J. L. Toole, W. J. Hill, and Arthur Roberts in his " gagging " propensities. Genest in his solemn style tells us that " he was apt to insert many things not in his part, and to take great liberties: if they succeeded all was well ; if he met with a rebuke he would say to himself, yet loud enough to be heard, " Odso I believe I'm wrong," which once was so well received by the audience that they turned their reproofs into applause. Steele in *The Tatler* banters the two actors delightfully in a comparison between their methods.

John Nicholls, in a note to the thirteenth number of the *Anti-Theatre*, says of Spiller that " he was a comedian who had a peculiar excellence above most of his brethren, who generally retained a sameness or at least a singularity to be known by in all characters, though however so various ; but he had the happiness of transforming himself into whatever character he represented—a remarkable instance of which occurred the first night of *The Artful Husband*, when his patron and admirer, the Duke of Argyll, literally mistook him for a new actor, and recommended him that night behind the scenes to Rich as a man who deserved encouragement." Spiller, it is quite clear, was an actor who regarded his art from a high standpoint, and was far removed from the ordinary comedian who is content to get his laugh from his mannerisms, and who is never so gratified as when the audience recognise him.

The profligate Duke of Wharton was one of Spiller's boon companions. According to Samuel Ireland (*Graphic Illustrations of Hogarth*): " The Duke, it is said, at a tavern proposed at each toast that every one in company should discard part of his dress, beginning with his peruke, coat, etc. ; when poor Spiller at the last toast, after making many apologies, owned he had mislaid his shirt; and to the high entertainment of his noble friend was obliged to appear in buff." If we are not mistaken, a well-known comedian of the present day, famous for his "gagging" propensities, once devised a similar practical joke, which for a time was very popular in certain circles.

Spiller's impersonation of old men seems to have been in every way remarkable. Riccaboni, a distinguished Italian actor who saw him in 1715 at Lincoln's Inn Fields Theatre, says that, "as he played the part of an old man I made no manner of doubt of his being an old comedian . . . but how great was my surprise when I learned that he was a young man of about twenty-six! I could not believe it; but I owned that it might be possible had he only used a trembling and broken voice and had only an extreme weakness possessed his body . . . but the wrinkles of his face, his sunk eyes and his loose and yellow cheeks, the most certain marks of a great old age, were incontestable proofs against what they said to me." Spiller always spent an hour or so in dressing himself, and "with the assistance of several pencils he disguised his face so nicely and painted so artificially a part of his eyebrows and eyelids, that at the distance of six paces it was impossible not to be deceived." The feeble lighting of the theatre of those days must, however, be taken into account. There was no revealing glare of the footlights.

Spiller was something of an author, besides being an actor and painter. He wrote, while a prisoner in the Mint for debt, a prologue which he spoke at one of his benefits when it preceded Addison's tame play of *The Drummer, or The Haunted House.* Nor was he wanting in wit. When he was being bantered by a minor Italian actress, who on a very small salary lived very extravagantly, concerning his poverty, he retorted, "What makes you rich, keeps me poor."

Hogarth was very partial to the light-hearted

comedian, and designed the ticket for his benefit which we reproduce at p. 64. The drawing for this ticket was much more carefully done than in the case of Walker. Spiller's portrait is said to have been extremely good, and the device exceedingly appropriate. Poor Spiller was always in financial difficulties, and of this unfortunate fact Hogarth made humorous and telling use. Spiller is standing in the centre of the picture knee-deep in theatre tickets for his benefit and with duns surrounding him. On one side of the scales is supposed to be the meagre contents of his pockets, and on the other are his debts. His tailor's bill is of prodigious length; other bills are for tripe, gin and tobacco. On the ground are " chalked " the amounts owing for drinks with his friends at his favourite " houses of call." A bailiff is clapping him on the shoulder, and in the background is a debtor's prison. At one time, it is said, he was so deeply in debt that, lest he should be arrested, he seldom ventured out of the theatre, where he shared an apartment with Walker—an additional proof of the real reason which induced the latter also to seek seclusion within the building.

The life of the merry comedian who was wont to set the table in a roar at the " Black Jack," the " Bull and Butcher " and other hostelries, ended in tragedy. He was cast for the Clown in the *Rape of Proserpine*, one of Rich's Harlequin productions, and during a performance before the Prince of Wales on January 31, 1729, he was seized with apoplexy on the stage and died within a week. His body lies in the churchyard of St. Clement Danes, and he was followed to the grave by a goodly assemblage of butchers from Clare Market who for years had delighted in his humour. To honour his memory the sign of the inn in the Market where he was always a welcome visitor was changed from the " Bull and Butcher " to the " Spiller's Head." The new sign was a portrait of the actor painted by John Laguerre, a clever ne'er-do-well, half actor, half painter, the son of a

SIR ROBERT FAGG AND THE GIPSY.

From a drawing by Hogarth.

120]

more celebrated artist of whose allegorical designs Pope wrote :

" Where sprawl the saints of Verrio and Laguerre."

The following epitaph is said to have been written by a Clare Market butcher, but it never found its way to his tombstone :

" Down with your marrow-bones and cleavers all,
And on your marrow-bones, ye butchers, fall !
For prayers from you who never prayed before
Perhaps poor Jimmie may to life restore.
' What have we done ? ' the wretched bailiffs cry,
'That th' only man by whom we live should die ? '
Enrag'd they gnaw their wax and tear their writs,
While butchers' wives fall in hysteric fits ;
For sure as they're alive poor Spiller's dead,
But thanks to Jack Laguerre we've got his head.
Down with your ready cole, ye jovial tribe,
And for a mezzotinto cut subscribe,
The markets traverse and surround the mint,
It shall go hard but he shall be in print.
For ' he was an inoffensive, merry fellow,
When sober hipp'd—blythe as a bird when mellow.' "

Laguerre presented the sign to the landlord a few weeks after the actor's death, but there is no record that the appeal to defray the cost of a " mezzotinto " met with any response. The sign itself, it is to be feared, has long since been destroyed.

The rest of the actors may be passed over, but of the actresses other than Polly some deserve mention. Mrs. Egleton (Lucy) was the wife of the actor who chose to call himself Baron Egleton, from his possession of a small patrimony in France which descended upon him, and which he soon got rid of by his extravagance. He was the " Baron " mentioned in John Leigh's skit *Will Thomas* (see p. 112). Mrs. Egleton was already well known as a comic actress of ability before the advent of *The Beggar's Opera*, and one of her many admirers was " that excellent judge John Duke of Argyll." To quote W. Cooke, " she died enamoured of Bacchus."

Mrs. Martin, it will be noticed, " doubled " the

parts of Mrs. Peachum and Dolly Trapes, and for
years she was in request as the former whenever
The Beggar's Opera was played. Her successor in
the same character was Mrs. Macklin, of whom
contemporary reports spoke very highly.

Mrs. Rogers (Betty Doxy) was no doubt Miss
Eliza Rogers, who was for some years a member of
Rich's company. She is not to be mistaken for Mrs.
Rogers of Drury Lane Theatre, an actress of some
celebrity, of whom Colley Cibber in his *Autobiography*
caustically wrote: " I have formerly known an
Actress carry Theatrical Prudery to such a height
that she was very near keeping herself chaste by
it. Her fondness for Virtue on the Stage, she began
to think, might persuade the world that it had made
an Impression on her private life, and Appearances of
it, and actually went so far that in an Epilogue to an
Obscure Play, the Profits of which were given to her
and wherein she acted a Part of impregnable Chastity,
she bespoke the Favour of some Ladies by a Pro-
testation that in Honour of her Goodness and Virtue
she would dedicate her unblemished Life to their
example. . . . But alas! how weak are the strongest
works of Art when Nature besieges it! for tho' this
good Creature so far held out her distaste to Mankind
that they could never reduce her to marry one of 'em,
yet we must own she grew, like Cæsar, greater by her
Fall! Her first heroick Motives to a Surrender was
to save the Life of a Lover, who in his Despair had
vowed to destroy himself, with which Act of Mercy
(in a jealous dispute once in my hearing) she was
provoked to reproach him in these very words,
' Villain! Did I not save your Life?' The generous
Lover in return to that first tender obligation gave
Life to her first-born, and that pious off-spring hath
since raised to her Memory several innocent Grand
children."

The " generous lover " was Wilks, but Cibber's
sneers concerning the lady's " theatrical prudery "
were quite misplaced. One of Wilks' biographers

gives her a high character for modesty and propriety. The truth seems to be that Wilks, a handsome man of great powers of fascination, was a general lover. Women easily came under his sway, but this was not so with Mrs. Rogers—hence the "long siege." Mrs. Rogers shared the weakness of vanity with every other actress, and she was not above losing her temper. When Ambrose Phillips' play *The Distressed Mother* was to be produced at Drury Lane it was intended that Mrs. Rogers should play the leading character, Andromache. Phillips and his friends, however, were of opinion that Mrs. Oldfield was much the better actress, as indeed she was, and insisted upon the part being given to her. Mrs. Rogers would not have been human if she had failed to be angry, but her method of retaliation is scarcely to be commended. To quote the words of a contemporary writer, she "raised a Posse of Profligates fond of Tumult and Riot, who made such a Commotion in the House that the Court, hearing of it, sent four of the Royal Messengers and a strong guard to suppress all Disorders. This being effected, the play was brought upon the stage and crowned with deserved success." (Egerton's *Life of Mrs. Oldfield.*)

The same writer is good enough to add: "I am from my own knowledge thoroughly convinced that Mr. Wilks had not any regard for Mrs. Oldfield, but what arose from the excellence of her own performance. Mrs. Rogers' conduct might be censured by some for the earnestness of her passion towards Mr. Wilks, but in the polite world the fair sex has always been priviledged from scandal, for which reason I shall here let fall the curtain and not mention any particulars of that unhappy woman or any of her descendants." Such high-minded consideration is indeed rare among the theatrical biographers of the eighteenth century. In the case of Mrs. Rogers it was almost superfluous, for she was more sinned against than sinning.

But she could never forgive Mrs. Oldfield, and as

she had a strong body of supporters, a heated controversy was carried on for some months between the
partisans of both ladies as to their respective merits.
At last it was decided to put the question to the test
of a competition—each lady was to play a part of her
choosing and the verdict was to be taken by vote.
Mrs. Oldfield selected the character of Mrs. Surewell
in *A Trip to the Jubilee,* but at the eleventh hour Mrs.
Rogers had the good sense to retire from the contest,
in which most assuredly she would have been defeated.

Wilks treated Mrs. Rogers very badly. After the
birth of their daughter he formed an attachment
to a lady of title, and he wanted to break off his
connection with the lady who had " saved his life."
Mrs. Rogers was not to be flung aside without showing
resentment, and of this she gave ample proof one
night when she was playing with Wilks in *Venice
Preserved.* In the scene where Pierre has to embrace
Belvidera very closely, she " laid hold of the opportunity and gave his cheek so handsome a bite that
the marks of her teeth remained and the blood flowed
very plentifully. This obliged the manager to take
care to divide their parts ever after." A wise and
reasonable precaution. The daughter of their union,
it may be mentioned, became the wife of Christopher
Bullock, of whom mention has already been made.

It may be noted, in passing, that one gets a very
good idea of the opinion of the supporters of the
" legitimate " drama and of their hostile attitude
towards opera in general in the final remarks of Mrs.
Oldfield's biographer, W. Egerton. He says : " The
Italian Opera, *The Beggar's Opera,* and other such-
like farcical and gewgaw Picture entertainments which
are of late introduced can leave no trace behind
them that can be of service beyond the present
moment. To sing and to dance are accomplishments
very few have any thoughts of practising, but to
speak justly and more gracefully is what everyone
thinks they do or wish they did." So far as *The*

Beggar's Opera was concerned it lived long enough to refute the critic.

Of the actresses who played Mrs. Coaxer, Dolly Trull, Mrs. Vixen, Jenny Diver, Mrs. Slammakin, Suky Tawdry, and Molly Brazen, nothing worthy of mention is known. Macheath hits off with such nicety the characteristic points of the ladies they personated, that one is tempted to quote his witty and lively description. He is carousing in the tavern near Newgate when the crowd of women enter :

"MAC.: Dear Mrs. Coaxer! you are welcome; you look charmingly to-day : I hope you don't want the repairs of quality, and lay on paint. Dolly Trull! kiss me, you slut! are you as amorous as ever, hussy? you are always so taken up with stealing hearts, that you don't allow yourself time to steal anything else. Ah, Dolly! thou wilt ever be a coquette. Mrs. Vixen, I'm your's ; I always loved a woman of wit and spirit ; they make charming mistresses, but plaguy wives. Betty Doxy! come hither, hussy ; do you drink as hard as ever? You had better stick to good wholesome beer ; for, in troth, Betty, strong waters will, in time, ruin your constitution ; you should leave those to your betters. What, and my pretty Jenny Diver too! as prim and demure as ever ; there is not any prude, though ever so high bred, hath a more sanctified look, with a more mischievous heart. Ah, thou art a dear, artful hypocrite! Mrs. Slammerkin! as careless and genteel as ever! All you fine ladies, who know your own beauty, affect an undress. But see, here's Suky Tawdry come to contradict what I was saying. Molly Brazen! [*She kisses him.*] That's well done! I love a free-hearted wench : thou hast a most agreeable assurance, girl, and art as willing as a turtle."

Different as their methods may be, the women are all bent upon the same thing—the betrayal of the reckless, amorous captain—and right well they do it.

CHAPTER XII

THE " TOAST OF THE TOWN "

Curious effect of the furore over Polly—The notorious Sir Robert Fagg—
Orator Hanley avails himself of *The Beggar's Opera*—Bartholomew
Fair performances—Mrs. Barbier, the Irish Polly—*The Cobler's Opera*—
Lacy Ryan and his acting—*Polly's Jests*—A duel over Polly Peachum

THE journals of the day assist one a little in forming
an idea of the way in which the town went mad over
The Beggar's Opera and Polly.   This assistance, however, is derived more from advertisements than from
paragraphs.   *The Daily Journal, The Daily Post,* and
the rest of the newspapers had very little space at
their disposal, and dramatic criticisms were almost
unknown.   In things theatrical the position was the
reverse of that of the present day.   Newspapers
paid the managers for the privilege of inserting their
advertisements!   A curious announcement in corroboration of this practice is furnished by an advertisement which appeared in *The Daily Post* in 1721,
running as follows : " The managers of Drury Lane
theatre think it proper to give notice that advertisements of their plays by their authority are published
only in this paper and the *Daily Courant,* and that
the advertisements of all other papers who presume
to insert advertisements of the said plays can do it
only by some surreptitious intelligence or hearsay,
which frequently leads them to commit gross mistakes, as mentioning one play for another, falsely
representing the parts, etc., to the misinformation
of the Town and to the great detriment of the said
theatre."   The practice had not died out in 1728,
and we have seen somewhere a statement that the

newspapers paid Rich as much as £60 during the year for inserting advertisements most of which related to *The Beggar's Opera*.

Here are a few of the advertisements which appeared during the run of the Opera : " This day is published A Sketch of the Beggar's Opera. Being a Lively Representation of that so-much *Admir'd* Performance with Suitable Instruments and Decorations. ' Ex cantare pares et respondere parato.' Virg. Sold by J. E. Sympson, Engraver and Print Seller in Bridges Street, Covent Garden." " A New and Entertaining Fan consisting of 14 of the most Favourite Songs taken out of the Beggar's Opera, with the Musick in proper keys within the compass of the Flute, curiously engraved on a Copper Plate. Sold for the author at Mr. Gay's Head in Tavistock Street, Covent Garden."

Over and over again one has read that besides fans, " screens " representing scenes from the Opera were sold in large numbers. It has always been taken for granted that these screens were of the ordinary kind, but it appears from an advertisement in *The Daily Journal* July 2 (1728) that they were nothing of the sort, but were probably some miniature imitation in cardboard. The advertisement of the screen, the adornments of which seem to have been of a decidedly personal character, runs thus : " This day is published the Beggar's Opera Screen, on which is curiously engrav'd on Copper Plates, the principal Captives of the All-Conquering Polly plainly described by Hieroglyphicks ; and on the Reverse their amorous Letters and Declarations to that celebrated Warbler of Ribaldry. The whole illustrated and adorn'd in their proper natural colours with Mottos suitable to their Quality. Printed for the Inventor and sold at the Fan Shop next door to White's Chocolate House in St. James Street ; at Mrs. Vuljohn's at the Golden Leg in Cranbourn Alley ; at Mrs. Jackson's at the Three Fans against Salisbury Street in the Strand ; at Mr. Markham's at the Seven

Stars under St. Dunstan's Church, Fleet Street ; and at Mrs. Robotham's at the Red M and Dagger in Pope's Head Alley against the Royal Exchange on Cornhill. Price 2*s*. 6*d*."

Before very long it may have dawned upon Polly that while she herself was drawing a salary of only thirty shillings a week other people were profiting by her fame. It is therefore not very surprising to find this solemn warning appearing in *The Daily Journal* : " Whereas my Name has been the Subject of several Songs and Pamphlets lately published, This is to inform the Town, That I never (before now) was privy or consenting to any one thing made public ; but being willing to entertain the Town with something diverting I have this Day with the Joint Interest of another Person, who performs in *The Beggar's Opera*, publish'd a Pamphlet by the Title of Polly Peachum's Opera : which containing a Medley of New Songs never before publish'd adapted to the several Tunes I sing in *The Beggar's Opera*, with the Song inserted in *The Country Journal* or *Craftsman* of Saturday, April 13, 1728, to which is annex'd A New Ballad inscribed to my Father, my beloved Captain Macheath and the Illustrious Gang of High-way Robbers. To the Tune of Green Sleeves alias Upon Tyburn Tree. Which is from your Humble Servant, POLLY PEACHUM. N.B.—This is dedicated to the facetious Sir R—— F—— and may be had at A. Dodd's without Temple Bar, E. Nutts' and A. Smith's at the Royal Exchange, and at the rest of the Pamphlet Shops in London and Westminster, price Sixpence."

Sir R—— F—— is of course our old acquaint-ance Sir Robert Fagg, who at this time seems to have been the most notorious man about town ; so much so that his son, anxious to obtain a seat in Parliament, considered it necessary to give himself a certificate of good character in the following adver-tisement which appeared in *The Evening Post* of January 27, on the eve of the production of *The*

RICH'S TRIUMPHAL ENTRY.

From an engraving by T. Cook, after Hogarth.

John Rich's removal from Lincoln's Inn Fields Theatre to Covent Garden.

[128]

Beggar's Opera : " Robert Fagg, Esq., only son of Sir Robert Fagg, Bart., who has a very large Estate in the Counties of Sussex and Kent (whose character is unquestionable and designs only the service of his country) intends to offer his Services at the next Election for the County of Sussex, in the room of the Rt. Hon, Sir Spencer Compton, now Lord Wilmington." Mr. Fagg is rather loose in his grammar, but there is no mistaking his meaning. His father's character was anything but " unquestionable." It is of course quite possible that Polly had no hand in the warning advertisement ; indeed, the tone of it suggests an adroit puff on the part of the publisher. Considering the reputation of Sir Robert Fagg, it is hardly likely Polly would voluntarily associate her name with his, especially as previous to 1728 Sir Robert was one of the many men about town who affected the society of that light o' love the notorious Sally Salisbury, of whom more anon. A single short ballad which found a good sale at the time is headed : " The case of a certain famous Sussex Baronet (as remarkable for his memorable atchievements among the Female part of the creation as for the many races he won at Newmarket) and Miss Sally." There is no occasion to go into the details of the " case." It may have been humorous reading at the time, but to-day it is as dreary as it is coarse. The first and last verse will, we imagine, more than suffice :

"I sing of a batter'd old knight,
In hunting and . . . . grown old,
  Brought into disastrous plight,
As quick to you I'll unfold.
  His honour and conscience he'll sell
For a pretty young girl or a nagg,
  His name it is needless to tell—
By the marks you will know it is Fagg.

  .   .   .   .   .

"The Knight is for wenches so mad
He spares neither widow nor Wives ;
  And maidens are always afraid,
And run as if 'twere for their lives.

9

Such a scarecrow to women is he,
Good Christians his like never saw,
He pays no regard to degree,
Not even his D—t— L—w."

The Daily Journal, on April 27, 1728, again finds material for its fun in Sir Robert, and published eight verses of doggerel under the title of "The Old Baronet behind the Scenes at *The Beggar's Opera*." They are to-day totally wanting in interest. The poet was also at work on April 19, when some verses in reference to Polly's forthcoming benefit appeared, headed "Advice to Polly." For a wonder the "old baronet" is not alluded to. The verses are exceedingly dull, but doubtless they served the purpose of advertising the divinity. The flute, as already mentioned, was the instrument favoured by amateurs. Gay, it will be remembered, played the flute, and one advertisement runs : "The Tunes to the songs in the Beggar's Opera transposed for the flute. Containing sixty-nine airs. Printed for John Watts at the Printing Office in Wild Court near Lincoln's Inn Fields. Price 1*s*."

Orator Henley, with the instinct of the born showman, seized upon the reigning attraction to advertise himself. Towards the end of 1728 we find, among other subjects—with puzzling titles intended to excite the curiosity of the public—upon which he proposed to discourse, the following cryptic, not to say startling announcement : "Captain Macheath not with child." And on another occasion, after the production of the Opera by the Liliputian Company, an account of which will be found later on, he advertises that "at the Oratory in Newport Market " (Henley seems to have removed from Clare Market at this time) "(1) the Liliputian orator, (2) Le Monde Traveste, being pull 32 of the Chimes of the Times to the Tune of Now comes in the Genius Year, or the Young Beggar's Opera, the Joy of the World."

The following paragraph in *The Daily Journal* of February 23—the twenty-second night of the Opera—

stimulates curiosity: "Last night a Welshman got into the Chariot of Stephen Fox, Esq., which was waiting at the Play-House in Lincoln's Inn Fields, in order as it is supposed to steal the Seats, but was taken by the Footmen in the very Chariot, who beat him with a great Oaken Stick as long as it lasted and then let him make his Escape." What temptation the seat of a chariot could present to a thief is difficult to understand. Perhaps the chariot was one of the cumbrous, capacious structures common at the time, intended for travelling purposes, and the seats may have contained lockers. Whatever may be the explanation, the unlucky Welshman suffered, and so apparently did the " great Oaken Stick."

The proprietors of the theatrical booths at Bartholomew Fair made full use of the leading attraction of the town. The " genuine Beggar's Opera with all the songs and dances set to music as performed at the theatre in Lincoln's Inn Fields " was given in the George Inn Yard in Smithfield " by the Company of Comedians from the New Theatre in the Haymarket. All the songs and dances set to music as performed at the Theatre in Lincoln's Inn Fields. N.B.—The clothes are chiefly new, as well as the scenes, which are painted by excellent artists and approv'd of and commended by the best masters."

Another advertisement informs us that " The Noted Yeates and the famous Posture makers is at the ' Great Booth ' in Smithfield Pound facing the end of Cow Lane, where during the Fair-time will be presented that most entertaining play called *The Beggar's Opera*, wherein is shown the vile practice of Peachum and his wife and the out-of-the-way management of their crew, the pleasant and melancholy strains of Polly Peachum and Lucy Lockit; the merry and half tragic flights of Captain Macheath, with the humourous dialogue between the Captain and his Seraglio of Dainty Doxies—and his parting with his dearly beloved Lucy; also the passages be-

tween the honest gaol-keeper Lockit and his daughter ;
almost all the songs by men and women ; likewise
his famous two postures masters, who perform such
surprising postures that they are really esteemed
the wonder of the world and age, Concluding with a
curious representation of his Sacred Majesty and the
present most illustrious House of Lords as sitting in
Parliament with curious machinery representing it.
Begin at 10 a.m. in the morning, ending at 10 at night."

There was certainly something very fascinating
about the Polly Peachum of the Opera, whoever might
take the part.   It had the " touch of nature " without
which a play can hardly endure the test of time.   The
Dublin gallants lost their heads and hearts over an
Irish Polly, Mrs. Barbier, a former member of Rich's
company and a popular vocalist, who took the city
by storm; and in *The Daily Journal* of February 24
appeared this advertisement : " For the benefit of
Mrs. Barbier, in which Mrs. Barbier will perform
between the Acts Three Opera songs and Three English
Ballets " (*sic*).

Theatrical rights appear to have been somewhat
loosely regarded at the beginning of the eighteenth
century.   It is hardly likely Gay had given permission to the Dublin manager to produce the play,
and Rich naturally was very angry, and on February 28 he inserted the following in the *Daily Journal*:
" Whereas Mrs. Barbier has advertised that *The
Beggar's Opera* is to be performed for her benefit on
the 10th March next.   This is to inform the Public
that such Advertisement was published without
consent of Mr. Rich, and that the same will not be
allowed of."   As Rich's grammar was often very
shaky, both in speaking and writing, it may be
presumed that the wording was strictly according to
" copy."   In spite, however, of its not being " allowed
of," Mrs. Barbier had her benefit, as appears from a
sheet ballad published in Dublin.   The heading runs
thus : " An excellent new ballad inscribed to the
Irish Polly Peachum on her Benefit of *The Beggar's*

Opera. Given at the General Desire of the Nobility
and Gentry of Dublin, April XI, Md,CC,XXVIII.
By a Person of Honour. Tune, ' Pretty Polly say.'
Dulce Decus. Hor."

The ballad is not remarkable for anything beyond its lavish eulogy and its nice discrimination,
which insists that the easy virtue of the London Polly
is not to be associated with the Polly of Dublin. The
innuendo thrown out concerning the former is both
ungenerous and uncalled for. The three concluding
stanzas will probably suffice as a sample :

VI

"Happy Johnny Gay,
Whose successful Play
Is made the theam of all we say,
And our Pills for Melancholy;
But this is all
Due to Poll—
When this house is full—
Who drew them there but Polly ?
For who can stay did Polly call ?
For who can stay did Polly call ?
Prevailing, lovely POLL.

VII

Miss be no longer vain,
Who with pleasing strain
In Lincoln's House did charm the Train
Of Belles and Beaux united.
Our Irish toast,
Can Virtue boast,
Which you have lost.
Then you Who've with Song Delighted,
Or Virtue, crowd in, crowd in all,
Or Virtue, crowd in, crowd in all,
So sweet, to Virtuous POLL.

VIII

Had Polly toy'd and kiss'd,
A benefit she'd miss'd,
But Virtue, which so long was Hist,
Is justly now requited.
Be angel still
In voice and Will
In face and Skill,
We're all with Each delighted.
Song and Virtue pleases all,
Song and Virtue pleases all.
And *both* are found in POLL."

The newspapers by this time were evidently alive
to the fact that the public took an interest in little
else but Polly Peachum, and *The British Journal* of
April 30 did not think it beneath its dignity to publish
this announcement : " We hear that there is now
in rehearsal, and will be performed next Friday at
Lincoln's Inn Fields Playhouse, a new Entertainment
called *The Cobler's Opera* for the benefit of Mr.
Hippisley, who has long entertained the Town in the
character of Peachum, in which it is said the pretty
Polly his daughter is degraded into an oyster girl."
The British Journal does not appear to have been
one of the favoured newspapers permitted to pay for
theatrical advertisements, as its paragraph contained
a serious inaccuracy. Polly did not then appear in
The Cobler's Opera, though some time later she played
in it for Hippisley's benefit. Exclusive information
seems to have been furnished to *The Daily Journal*,
but so jealously was this information guarded that
The British Journal was led into a trap. The first
intimation that Lacy Ryan had written a sort of
copy of *The Beggar's Opera* for Hippisley's benefit
was contained in the form of a letter to *The Daily
Journal* which appeared on the 24th, and in a way
was an indirect puff of *The Beggar's Opera*, since it
dwells more upon Gay's success than on the merits
of the forthcoming production.

The letter runs thus : " Sir, Upon your telling
me when I met you Yesterday Morning in Covent
Garden, there were Bills up for *The Cobler's Opera*
for the benefit of Mr. Hippisley on Friday next, I
called at Lincoln's Inn Fields Play House, to inform
myself upon what Plan this new Whim was built, and
was agreeably surprised with its being then in Rehearsal. I found our friend the Noble Captain, who
even in the character of a *dear inconstant varlet*, has
charmed the ladies, so changed in his behaviour, he
would have serv'd for the constant Hero of a Romance
in Folia. Mr. Lockit still fills up his character. Lucy
indeed seems here to be more vehement (not having

had her Man), and I may venture to say makes Amends for the Oddness and Violence of her Character by her Performance. She is still an enemy to poor Polly, and *not the only unjust one.* She (poor Polly, I mean) is still complaining, and upon my word both pleased and engaged my Pity. As for Mr. PEACHUM, he is the Proteus of the Farce. I would give you my opinion of the Whole, (i.e. *The Cobler's Opera*) but that the Reception of the Humour is doubtful, it following an Entertainment of such delicate Variety in *The Beggar's Opera*, tho' I'm very well assured 'tis no way brought on with the least Thought of vying, of which the Introduction will convince, for the AUTHOR, instead of laying any claim to merit, has fixed his utmost Hope on Favour. So that you may be satisfied of this, if you think it worth your while to hear half a score Ballads prettily introduc'd it will be rehears'd again To-morrow at 11 o'clock, and if you will ask for Mr. Ryan or me, you will find Admittance.—I am, Sir, Your Humble Servant, CHARLES EASEY."

Mr. Easey cannot be accused of protesting too much on behalf of the author. *The Cobler's Opera* is hardly good enough to be called even an imitation of *The Beggar's Opera*, save in the fact that the songs it contains, twenty-nine in number, were written to fit old and popular tunes. The scene is laid in Billingsgate, the leading lady is a fishwoman in love with the son of the master of an oyster vessel, and the cobler, like the beggar, is introduced only in the prologue. Hippisley doubled the parts of the cobler and the master of the oyster vessel. Mrs. Egleton, the Lucy Lockit of *The Beggar's Opera*, was the fishwoman, Peg Welfleet, and Miss Warren, who succeeded Miss Fenton as Polly Peachum, was the fishwoman's rival, Jenny Milton. The piece has but a thread paper of a plot, is in one act, and was played without a break or change of scene.

Lacy Ryan was an actor of considerable merit. His stage career may be said to have commenced in

1712, when he played Marcus at the first performance
of *Cato*. During the run of the piece he had a stroke
of ill fortune, which must have been brought to his
memory when he was writing *The Cobler's Opera*, if
indeed it had not something to do with his choice of
Billingsgate as the background of the play. To use
Chetwood's words, " he was accidentally brought into
a fray with some of our Tritons on the Thames, and
in the scuffle a blow on the nose was given him by
one of these water bullies who neither regard men
nor manners. I remember the same night, as he was
brought in the bier after his supposed death in the
fourth act of *Cato*, the blood from the real wound in
the face gushed out with violence ; that hurt had
no other effect than just turning his nose a little,
though not to deformity, yet some people imagined
it gave a very small attraction to the tone of his voice,
though nothing disagreeable." Charles Dibdin's account of Ryan's misadventures is that, " having first
received a blow on the nose in one affray which
turned it out of its place, and a brace of pistol bullets
in his mouth in another which broke his jaw, these
accidents so discomposed his voice that he became
a most ridiculous object of imitation, but that he
remained a very deserving stage favourite to the last."

Foote made full use of this " most ridiculous
object of imitation." The great mimic had been
very successful with his entertainment entitled *The
Diversions of the Morning* at Covent Garden in 1748,
but when he proposed to repeat it at the Haymarket,
the managers of Covent Garden and Drury Lane
became alarmed and invoked the powers of the
Licensing Act. The Lord Chamberlain sent to the
justices, and a posse of constables entered the house
and cleared out the audience. Foote was full of
resources, and he invited his friends and the public to
" drink Tea at the little theatre at the Hay-Market
every morning at the play-house prices." It was also
intimated that " while the Tea was preparing, as he
was then training some young actors for the stage,

DR. PEPUSCH.

From an old print.

ANASTASIA ROBINSON, COUNTESS OF PETERBOROUGH.

From an old print.

136]

he would with their permission proceed with his instructions." Under cover of this he introduced imitations of various actors, giving them a character suitable to each one's voice and style. Thus Quin, from his sonorous voice and weighty manner, appeared as a watchman; Peg Woffington, who according to Tate Wilkinson "had a most unpleasant speaking pipe," was an Orange woman to the Playhouse, and Ryan was—a razor grinder! Garrick and Woodward were also caricatured.

Ryan must have had not only determination, but also talent to overcome his physical defects; and proof of this is given by Garrick, who going with Woodward to scoff at Ryan's Richard, remained to admire, and " was astonished at what he saw working in the mind of the ungraceful, slovenly and ill-dressed figure that Ryan made, which told him more than he knew before and which caused Garrick to bring to light as his own that unknown excellence which in Ryan had remained unnoticed and buried." Indeed, if we may believe Foote, " all succeeding Richards " more or less imitated Ryan. Davies tells us that Ryan enjoyed a kind of prescriptive claim to all the lovers in tragedy and fine gentlemen in comedy at the theatres in Lincoln's Inn Fields and Covent Garden, for nearly thirty years. According to Dr. Doran, the modern actor whose style most resembled Ryan was Robson.

Among other methods adopted to give Polly due publicity, or to take advantage of the publicity she had herself acquired, was the production of *Polly Peachum's Jests*. This was quite in the mode. Most of· the favourites of the day compiled Jest Books or had such books compiled for them—if indeed they had any hand in the matter beyond allowing the use of their names. Excluding the *Merry Tales* of a century or so before, Joe Miller's *Jest Book* was probably the first of the kind bearing the name of the supposed author. Pinkethman, Quin, Garrick, Lord Chesterfield, all had Jest Books. These compilations bear a strong family likeness to each other, and the same anecdotes are dished up over and over again. The reading of any one of them is a wearisome task, while many of the stories would, we are afraid, bring a blush to the cheek of the " young person," if only she happened to understand what was meant.

Polly's Jests is neither better nor worse than any of the others. The title-page runs thus: " Polly Peachum's Jests, in which are comprised most of the witty apothegms, diverting Tales, and smart Repartees, that have been used for many years last past either at St. James' or St. Giles' : suited alike to the capacities of the Peer and the Porter. Printed for J. Roberts at the Oxford Arms in Warwick Lane." The solitary reference to the Opera the volume contains is this : " The other night his Grace the Duke of Argyll being at *The Beggar's Opera*, who says more good Things than anybody, met C-bb-r there behind the scenes; 'Well, Colley,' said he, 'how do you like *The Beggar's Opera* ?' 'Why, it makes one laugh upon the stage, but how will it do in print ?'—'O very well, by G—d,' reply'd the Duke, 'if you don't write the preface.' " It can hardly be said that this " repartee " makes one wish for more.

To make Polly's reputation as a " toast " complete, a duel was fought over her. The affair was not so tragic nor even so dignified as one, for the sake of romance, could wish. Quin is responsible for the story, and we give it in his words: " She was," he says, " in the upper boxes at the representation of a new performance, when a gentleman of the army who sat next to her said some civil things to her, which her *theatrical virtue* construed into an insult, and the Son of Mars had the mortification to find that all his soft things were thrown away upon her. The next time she appeared upon the stage, the captain happened to come somewhat surcharged with claret, and recollecting the lady's insolence a few evenings before, he began to give her a serenade of cat calls, which interrupted the play. *A man of fashion* who sat next to the captain, and had the lady's glory at heart, told him " he behaved very ill, and ought to be turned out." This was sufficient; they retired to an adjacent tavern in order to settle their difference in an amicable way, and cut one another's throats—whilst the tragedy went peaceably on, without any uproar or bloodshed. But the *man of fashion* having more prudence than to contend with any one in his profession, he declined fighting with swords ; but agreed meeting the next morning in Hyde Park to decide the matter with pistols. They met accordingly, and the *man of fashion* was, *à-la-mode de l'honneur*, mortally wounded—in the skirt of his coat ! "

CHAPTER XIII

THE PENALTIES OF POPULARITY

The poets let loose over Polly—Insinuations against the Duke of Bedford—
The Duke and Mrs. Oldfield—Caleb D'Anvers' lampoon—Hogarth's
caricature cartoon of *The Beggar's Opera*—Its exact meaning unknown

POLLY was a boon to the versifiers, the Grub St.
writers and the booksellers. Verses innumerable
were addressed to the divinity. Never was a favourite
of the stage so be-rhymed. In a duodecimo volume
was published a collection of skits entitled :
" LETTERS IN PROSE & VERSE TO THE CELEBRATED
POLLY PEACHUM, FROM THE MOST EMINENT OF HER
ADMIRERS AND RIVALS." These letters were certainly
less laboured than the majority of the many efforts
to which the charms of the young lady gave rise.
They are introduced by a sprightly " Advertisement "
which runs thus : " There are two things which
seldom fail to come to light—Murder and Verses.
These letters were dropped as the famous POLLY
PEACHUM took coach to meet His —— - I give
them to divert. If they succeed, I am pleased :
if they don't—I care not one farthing."

The first letter is supposed to be written by a silk
mercer from his shop at the Sign of the Seven Stars,
Ludgate Hill. Here it is : " Most Admirable Lady,
I am this moment returned from the Theatre, all
entranced with your most musical Harmony. Oh,
sweet singing Siren, I sacrifice my Heart at the
Altar of your Beauty, which is charmingly Divine.
In fine, I am quite Broke for my Trade; if the ladies
say ' Mr. Flush-Cheek, what is the price of this
silk ? ' I answer ' Polly—How—Peachum.' To the
tune of Sally, etc.,

140

I

"Oh that I were some mighty Prince,
  Or country Squire so jolly,
Or Lord, or Duke, or Gartered Peer,
  For my Beloved POLLY !

II

"Or that I was this happy Silk,
  (But wishing is a Folly,)
To kiss thy Breast as white as milk,
  Oh, my enchanting POLLY !

III

"Or that I was thy yielding Glove
  To press thy Hand—ah, shall I ?—
Or rather was thy dearest love,
  Oh, my engaging POLLY !

IV

"No longer now I dress my hair,
  For I am melancholy :
And for myself I little care,
  I care so much for POLLY.
                    "PHILANDER FLUSH-CHEEK.

"P.S.—I send a Piece of the newest Silk."
The next purports to be from a Barrister : "Most
Unaccountable Charmer, I curst the hour of Six,
which tore you from my Arms, and all Business. I
almost resolved to Sacrifice *Coke upon Littleton*. I
committed a Thousand tender Extravagances, kissed
the Chair on which you sat, insensibly blew out my
Fire, and mourned in Darkness over my Green cloth ;
where I drank the Coffee left in your Dish. Methought
I heard a tap of a Fan at my Door, which I had
folded against Gold itself. I flew to open it—but oh
Death to Love ! How I was surprised, instead of my
adorable Charmer, to find Doctor Drum Ear in my
Arms, who roared out. I called the Watch for Light,
who stared immoderately at us both, as we did at one
another. They run down Stairs, and cried out The
Devil, the Devil ! The Doctor's face was as black
as his Gown. In fine, I discovered that instead of
Coffee, I had drunk all my ink. Never was there such
an unfortunate Lover. I sent for an Apothecary,

took a vomit, washed my Face, and went to Bed, where I attend your dear Commands. Oh come and atone for these Disasters.—SULLIVAN SLAVER, Bencher. P.S.—I send you the key of my chambers. Would it were a Golden one for your sake."

The " Squinting Lawyer," who writes the third effusion, is allowed to burst into verse, and he attempts an imitation of the song Lucy Lockit sings at the commencement of the Third Act—a song omitted in the acting edition of *The Beggar's Opera* of later years. Lucy, addressing her father, recalls her education at the bar of an ale-house, and tells how it came about that Macheath won her heart, in the following naïve excuse :

> " When young at the bar you first taught me to score,
> And bid me be free of my lips, and no more :
> I was kissed by the parson, the squire, and the sot ;
> When the guest was departed the kiss was forgot :
> But the kiss was so sweet and so closely he prest,
> That I languished and pin'd till I granted the rest."

The letter runs as follows : "From a Squinting Lawyer : Desirable Lady, Tho' my Eyes look ten thousand Ways at once, they never saw anything so lovely as your fair self. All their various Beams are attracted by your Beauty, and they multiply every Charm. Imagine then the Height of my Passion, how much greater than any other Lover's can be. Let this, which the Vulgar duly call Squinting, turn to the advantage of my Love. But while I look so much on you I am blind to Interest, which was your Predecessor in my soul.

> " If Polly is generous she'll pity my Flame ;
> And if she but loves me I am not to blame.
> I suffer with Pleasure, if she crown my Desire ;
> If not, I will set the whole Commons on fire.
> The World now forsakes me, but I'll find it in thee.
> My papers I'll scatter to every Wind,
> And the Green Bag shall perish, if Polly be kind.
>   " ARGUS VELLUM."

The signature of the fourth letter, with its concealment of the last syllable, would suggest that a real person was hinted at. Rag Fair was in Rosemary Lane, not far from the Tower of London, hence the allusion to the " Lyon " in the Tower, where was, for nearly five hundred years before Gay's time, a menagerie, the lions being named after the reigning Kings, the populace firmly believing that when a King died, a lion of that name died after him. The Henley alluded to was, of course, Orator Henley.

" From the FOUR KINGS, RAG FAIR.—Madam, I have heard of the Great Sway you bear in Town to my Surprize ; for I have lived in Rag Fair these Forty Years, and without much success, tho' I sing to a Miracle, can roar with any Lyon in the Tower, and my Voice is as loud as H(enle)y's. I repeat verses like an Angel, and can make them, too. Pope, Swift and Gay are nothing to me ; yet I am forced to blow my own Blast. I have been at the Charge of framing all my works, and it has cost me Fifty Pounds in Leaf Gold to no purpose. The Town is fond and mad after you ; but I'll set it right, or I'll know why. I went into the Army to show my perfections, am a Captain in the Train'd Bands and discipline my Men in Verse. If you'll come and see us exercise, you may, and we'll have our Plumes new cleaned. 'Tis better than any Review. My height, my linen, my Manner are surprizing. If you'll be kind to me, I'll transmit you to Fame in one of the best Gilt Frames.

> " Women are fools, or they would ever chuse
> A Lover with a Fame bestowing Muse ;
> Who can to future Ages make them shine,
> They all shall hear you sing, if you'll be mine.
> " Your valorous Servant,
> " SHACKLET . . N."

The fifth letter in its spelling seems to anticipate Thackeray's Jeames Yellow-plush : " From my little RUM in Pel-Mel. ('Tis common to say the Hour.) Charming Mam, I No knot iff I heve Reson to acquse or blis me Stairs. I am entolerabel in Loof, and redust to a mere shado. Fram beeing halff a yard

on the Waste, I ame bot a Kuarter, and helplis as
ane Enfante. Me Peeple dres mee as they wil, that
i ame a mere Friwght. I am lacet to the Woarld,
and what is moar woarser tu my deet selff. I mett
Ladi Wesle Face in the Bax t'ather Nite, whu sterted
to cee me luke so pail.—Lard ! sase she, sur Friwght-
fooll, is itt yu, or yur Gost that hoavers neer Polly ?
I maid a lo Bough, and a Bluwsh—Gad, Gad, you
ar rewined. Huever I have satt for me Pictor to
Zincks at length, for your Ladyship's, wait till then
acksept itt in blawk and whight. I am fare in my
Face to a Wunder—mi Eise lawnguishen and swete.
Mon toup a Marveil bien poudere, but i am al yurs.
Me Leggs are small, mi Hands whight ; my tith
ivery ; my maner tout Charmant. Bot whither dose
my Buty lide me ? I'll be revenged and Knot loike
at Miself this Howre. Mi Talor tears Mee from you
with a nu Sute of Clowths. But I'll apere on the
Stage too Night.—SIR FRIWGHTFOOL FRIZZLE."

Of course the favourite subject of the day for
ridicule, Quakerism, is not forgotten, and the series
concludes with the following : " Dear Mary, If thou
inclinest to have Regard to this Friendly Invitation,
the Profits of my Tribe, and the choice of my Shop
shall be at thy command. I would seriously advise
Thee to beware of the Numbers that are daily fluttering about Thee, for they are of the wanton sort, and
unprofitable ; they will bring thee into a state of
Sorrow and Woe. My Loving Kindness towards
Thee is pure, internal, and truly unfeigned, and
therefore I shall remain to Thee most faithfully. The
other chaps will be frail ; for their Delight is in
Wickedness, and in leading aside silly women. Yet
I desire to be Secret in my concerns with Thee, and
rest in all Righteousness and Zeal, thy Loving Friend,
ELIJAH G——FOR.

   "From Gracechurch Street in the City of London
      the 11th day of the 6th Month 1728."

Other scribbling admirers are neither so sprightly
nor so decorous. Of three verses entitled " The

PEG WOFFINGTON.

From an engraving by H. R. Cook, after Peter van Bleek, in Mr. A. M. Broadley's Collection.

Amorous Lover" printed on a single sheet, the first and last only need be quoted :

> " While the Town agrees that Polly
> Best diverts the Melancholy,
> Let us toast the sprightly Lass,
> Heedless of Time and Treason
> Spent on her who gives such pleasure.
> Drink and fill about the glass.
> Polly's charms are so Extensive
> That the grave, the wise and Pensive
> Equally her Power obey.
>
> . . . . .
>
> " Everyone to Love Inviting
> Eager who should love her most
> Tho' her sex would vain outvie her
> And all Excellence deny her
> Polly's still the greatest toast."

" A new Ballad inscribed to Polly Peachum to the tune of Pretty Parrot say. By the Author of Leheup's Ballad," consists of nine stanzas in which the scurrilous versifier sets himself to enumerate Polly's lovers in a fashion more free than polite. In the first and second verse he makes pretty broad insinuations against Gay and Rich, and tells us in the third that,

> " But not only he (Gay),
> Men of high degree,
> Are as fond as fond of thee
> As the German Count, thy keeper."

Whether by the " German Count " the " Portuguese Nobleman " of the "Life " is meant, we are unable to say, but it is highly probable, as writers two hundred years ago were contemptuously vague where foreigners were concerned, and nationalities appear to have been flung about at random. In the fourth and fifth verses we have Sir Robert Fagg, the favourite butt, pilloried pretty severely. Very little is known of Sir Robert Fagg, beyond the fact that he lived his life to the full, which in the beginning of the eighteenth century meant, among other things, never going to bed sober if one could possibly help

10

it. We assume him to be the son of Sir John Fagg of Sussex, who during the Civil War sided with the Parliament, was made a Colonel, and was appointed one of the Commissioners to try the King, but took no active part in the proceedings. He had sixteen children, and died in 1701. Sir Robert Fagg in 1728 must have been getting on in years. Hogarth in the print which we reproduce on page 120 does not flatter him on the side of youth. It would be interesting to know the story of Sir Robert Fagg and the gipsy. Hitherto it has eluded us.

In the sixth stanza the libeller (we trust he was one) falls foul of the Duke of Bedford. This stanza is the only one we venture to quote in its entirety :—

> " B——d's pretty D——e,
> Wounded by a look,
> Would come on too for a Stroke
> When from the stage he had thee.
> O sweet Joy,
> Noble Boy,
> Pretty Toy,
> He will not upbraid thee,
> Tho' others on thee Fall,
> Tho' others on thee Fall,
> O pretty, pretty Poll! "

The innuendo implied in this verse we believe to be without foundation. There is no evidence of Polly having been the object of the Duke of Bedford's attentions, though it is quite likely, of course, that he proffered them. Like most of the titled gallants of the day, he was fond of dangling at the skirts of great stage ladies. Mrs. Oldfield was much in his favour, but she was more in love with a Mr. Mainwaring than with his Grace. Probably the Duke knew this, for he plumped his money-bags into the scale, and according to *The European Magazine*, " he called upon her one morning, and not finding her at home, left a paper on her dressing table, including a settlement on her for life of six hundred pounds a year. When Mr. Mainwaring next called and pressed a consummation of his happiness, she candidly confessed her regard for him, but told him ' He was an unlucky fellow, for that something had happened the day before which must postpone their intended happiness.' He pressed her to know the cause ; but she would not tell him till some days afterwards when she had returned the settlement to the Duke." Mrs. Oldfield had many lovers, but she was constant to the one who engaged her affections for the time being. Not until Mainwaring's death did she associate herself with General Churchill, by whom she had a son. Her amatory relations were no bar to her finding her last resting-place in Westminster Abbey. Leigh Hunt termed her " the fine lady of the stage in the most agreeable sense of the word." She dressed beautifully during her lifetime, and her ruling passion did not desert her when dying. Pope wrote of her in regard to this pardonable vanity :

> " Odious ! in woollen ! 'Twould a saint provoke,"
> (Were the last words that poor Narcissa spoke ;)
> " No, let a charming chintz and Brussels lace
> Wrap my cold limbs and shade my lifeless face ;
> One would not, sure, be frightful when one's dead,
> And, Betty—give this cheek a little red."

The seventh verse is devoted to " L——d T——y," the eighth to " Sir J—— H——d," and the ninth to " S——e." The identity of these three victims we have been unable to trace. " S——e " apparently held some Governmental position. The rest of the lampoon is but leather and prunella.

Polly had her defenders, and the slight on her fair fame received a just rebuke, the value of which, however, is considerably lessened if it be true that the hand which wrote the attack also penned the reply. A short time after the publication of the lampoon " An answer to Polly Peachum's Ballad " appeared with this introduction : " The following Lines being sent to the Author as an answer to the foregoing Ballad, he to shew what he Published was not done out of Malice to Polly Peachum, has annex'd them to this Edition, having so much value for the

Female Sex as to give them Fair Play to a Fair Woman." The author of the scurrilous ballad was believed to be Nicholas Amhurst ("Caleb D'Anvers"), and probably repenting his scurrility he wrote the "Answer" by way of apology. We give three of the four stanzas :

I

" Pray, Sir, who are you
That thus dares to shew
Polly's Pranks to open view,
And so loudly expose her ?
    Cruel Bard,
    This is hard,
    No Regard
To Polly nor those that knows her ;
For you do Lampoon 'em all,
For you do Lampoon 'em all
As well as Pretty Poll.

.   .   .   .   .

III

" Poll performs her Parts
With such Grace and Arts,
That each Night she conquers **Hearts**,
Both in Pit and Boxes ;
    Then refrain,
    Be n't so plain,
    Do not stain
Poll with common Doxies,
For she does charm us all,
For she does charm us all,
O Pretty, pretty Poll.

IV

" Since Poll has gain'd Applause
All vindicate her Cause,
And prodigious Crowds she draws,
All conspire to clap her :
    The House Rings
    When she Sings :
    Must such Things
Vanish in a Vapour ?
No, she out-shines them all,
No, she out-shines them all,
O pretty, pretty Poll."

Another catchpenny sheet was entitled *The Ladies' Opera*. It consisted of a number of doggrel verses on the events of the day. One verse runs :

"And now, dear Puss, what shall I say
About *The Beggar's Opera* ?
Nay it has rivalled dear Quadrill ;
Nor do they think that Night spent ill
If they can chorus Polly Peachum."

There were many other effusions, but it is hardly necessary to drag them from the obscurity which it must be confessed they justly merit.

Hogarth is closely associated with *The Beggar's Opera*, and did much to add to its fame. His cartoon, which will be found at page 112, seems at first sight to satirise the Opera, but he could hardly have intended to hold it up to ridicule. He had too many friends connected with it. The meaning of the print is by no means clear, and Mr. John Nicholls, who was intimately acquainted with Hogarth's work, confesses his inability to offer an adequate explanation. We subjoin his description from *The Genuine Works of William Hogarth*, vol. ii. :

" The Plate," he writes, " seems at once to represent the exhibition of *The Beggar's Opera* and the rehearsal of an Italian one. In the former all the characters are drawn with the heads of different animals ; as Polly with a Cat's, Lucy with a Sow's, Macheath with an Ass's, Lockit and Mr. and Mrs. Peachum with those of an Ox, a Dog, and an Owl. In the latter several noblemen appear conducting the chief female singer forward on the stage, and perhaps are offering her money, or protection from a figure that is rushing towards her with a drawn sword. Harmony flying in the air turns her back on the English playhouse ; and hastens towards the Rival Theatre. Musicians stand in front of the former, playing on the jew's-harp., the salt box, the bladder and string bagpipes, etc. On one side are people of distinction, some of whom as if making an offer to Polly or paying their adorations to her. To these are opposed a butcher, etc., expressing similar applause. Apollo and one of the Muses are fast asleep beneath the stage. A man is . . . under a wall hung

with ballads . . . A sign of the Star, a gibbet, and
some other circumstances less intelligible, appear in
the background." According to Mr. Nicholls, Hogarth
did two variants of the cartoon. One is inscribed
" Sold at the Print-Shop in the Strand near Catherine
Street," and the other has the title of " The Opera
House or the Italian Eunuch's Glory. Humbly
inscribed to those Generous Encouragers of Foreigners
and Ruiners of England." With the lines :

> " From France, from Rome we come,
> To help old England to b' undone."

Under the division of the Print that represents
the Italian Opera are the words " *Stage Mutiny* "—
" perhaps improperly added," says Nicholls. On
the two sides of this Print are scrolls containing a list
of the presents made to Farinelli. At the bottom are
the following lines :

> " Brittains (*sic*) attend—view this harmonious stage,
> And listen to those notes which charm the age.
> How Sweet the sound where cats and bears
> With brutish noise offend our ears !
> Just so the foreign singers move
> Rather contempt than gain our love.
> Were such discourag'd we should find
> Musick at home to charm the mind !
> Our homespun Authors must forsake the field
> And Shakespeare to the Italian Eunuchs yield."

Nicholls adds, " Perhaps the original Print was
the work of Gracelot, Vandergucht, or some person
unknown. The idea of it is borrowed from a French
book called *Les Chats*, printed at Amsterdam in 1728.
In this work, facing p. 117, is represented an Opera
performed by cats superbly habited. The design is
by Coypel; the engraving by T. Otten. At the
end of the treatise the Opera itself is published. It
is improbable that Hogarth should have met with
this *jeu d'esprit*, and if he did, he could not have read
the explanation of it." Hogarth may not have known
sufficient French to read the " explanation," but there
was nothing to prevent him getting it translated if

he were so minded. But the fact is, neither the explanation nor the plate furnishes the slightest basis for Hogarth's skit. The book *Les Chats*, which is in the British Museum Library, is a history of and a panegyric on cats—and the plate mentioned by Nicholls simply illustrates a whimsical idea of the author, who gravely states that he has been assured by musical connoisseurs that the song of cats could be rendered exactly by modern musicians, especially in regard to the recitative! He also contends that cats by their lightness are wonderfully qualified to perform a ballet.

No doubt the meaning of the print was perfectly well understood in Hogarth's day. As a rule the artist was direct enough, but his mind was so fertile that he sometimes overloaded his satire with details which, apt enough at the time, were of only passing interest, and once forgotten, all clue to their meaning was lost. The skit on the removal of Rich from Lincoln's Inn Fields to Covent Garden Theatre (see p. 128) is open to the same criticism in regard to its minutiæ, but its interpretation is not so difficult.

CHAPTER XIV

PURITANISM UP IN ARMS

Outcry against *The Beggar's Opera*—The Rev. Mr. Herring's attack—The brutality of the times—A contrast—A " revised version " of the Opera—Swift's defence of Gay in *The Intelligencer*

APART from Polly's celebrity, the Opera received splendid advertisement from the controversy it excited. The moralists, the rigid purists, the Pecksniffs were up in arms. Those apt to

> " Compound with sins they were inclined to
> By damning those they had no mind to,"

were outraged. The ball was set rolling, so far as the public prints were concerned, by a " correspondent " of *The London Journal* of March 30, 1728 ; but previously a sermon condemning *The Beggar's Opera* had been preached by the Rev. Thomas Herring, a militant divine, who was very much to the front during and after the rebellion of '45. Herring in 1728 was preacher at Lincoln's Inn, and naturally the theatre, and what went on there, came under his personal observation. The denunciation of the immoral tendencies of amusements generally, and of the stage in particular, has always been a pet theme of the clergy, and no doubt Mr. Herring saw his way to advancement by a vigorous onslaught on what the town most enjoyed. The letter in *The London Journal* we give in full, as it is a typical representation of the narrow views of the " unco guid " of the eighteenth century :

" SIR, It has, I think, been generally agreed among Moralists that all publick Sports and Entertainments should be so regulated as to have a tendency to the

152

KITTY CLIVE.

From an engraving by W. Greatbach, after G. P. Harding.

Encouragement of Virtue and the discountenancing of Vice and Immorality. This Practice, established by the wisest Legislators, who were sensible how great an Influence Plays and other Diversions have on the Minds and Manners of the Populace, has been conformable to this salutary Maxim. How shocking then wou'd it have appeared to the venerable Sages of Antiquity to have seen an Author bring upon the Stage as a proper Subject for Laughter and Merriment a Gang of Highwaymen and Pickpockets triumphing in their Successful Villainies, and braving the ignominious death they so justly deserve, with the undaunted Resolution of a Stoical Philosopher? The Courage express'd in the following Lines wou'd have become a Seneca or a Raleigh, but seems not so suitable to the character of a Criminal :

> " ' The charge is prepared ; the Lawyers are met ;
> The Judges all rang'd (a terrible Show !)
> I go undismay'd—For Death is a Debt,
> A Debt on Demand—so, take what I owe.'

The chief End of Punishment is to prevent the continuance of the like offences for the future ; and therefore all good Subjects should endeavour as far as it lies in their Power to heighten the Terrors of the Penalties annexed by the Laws to flagrant Crimes. But to place (on the contrary) these Penalties in a ludicrous light and to represent them as easie to be borne and contemptible is an effect blunting the Edge of the Civil Sword, and opening the Flood-Gates (if I may so speak) of the most outrageous Enormities. The Mischief will be still further promoted if the Lives of such abandon'd Wretches as Robbers and Night-Walkers are described as agreeable and full of Mirth and Jollity. How far a celebrated Entertainment may have contributed (contrary to the intention of the Author) towards these daring Attacks which are daily committed on the Property of the Subject in the Streets of our Capital (in Defiance of all Law, and I believe, beyond the Example of former ages) I will not pretend to say. But I am sure nothing can be more proper to foment these Violences than such Lines as these :

> " ' See the Ball I hold ;
> Let the Chemists toil like Asses,
> Our Fire their Fire surpasses
> And turns all our Lead to Gold.'

"The Agreeableness of the Entertainment and its being adapted to the Taste of the Vulgar and set to easy pleasant Tunes (which almost everybody can remember) makes the Contagion spread the wider and the Consequence the more to be dreaded. What Cicero says of the Poets in general may (with a little alteration) be more justly apply'd to the songs now in vogue. . . . I shall conclude with a very just observation of Mr. Addison in the 249th *Spectator*. . . . 'If' (says he) 'the Talent of Ridicule were employ'd to laugh Men out of Vice and Folly it might be of Some Use to the World ; but instead of this we find that it is generally made use of to laugh Men out of Virtue and Good Sense by attacking everything that is Solemn and Serious, decent and praiseworthy in human life.'—I am, Sir, Your very humble servant, PHILOPROPOS. P.S.—Since the Writing of the foregoing letter a Sermon has been preach'd in the Chappel of one of our Inns of Court, on the same subject by a celebrated Divine, which I doubt not will make a great Noise. It is to be hoped he will suffer it to be printed, out of regard to his own Reputation, as well as for the Service of the Publick. The judicious Critic was there display'd as well as the Christian orator. However this Discourse may be ridiculed by the fluttering Beaux and Belles of the Town, I will be so bold to say that (as low as our Morals are sunk) the clear reasoning, good Sense and manly Rhetorick in it will command the approbation of all persons of Virtue and Sobriety who have so much thought and consideration as to attend to the consequences of Things. It has been objected that the Subject was beneath the Preacher's Notice : To which it may be reply'd in the words of Horace, '*Hae mugae seria ducent in mala*,' and nothing which has a direct Tendency to promote a general Depravity of Manners can be thought unworthy the Rebuke of a Christian Divine."

Whether the sermon which so excited the admiration of " Philopropos " ever found its way into print, we are unable to say, but it formed the subject of much talk, and had the contrary effect from that which the preacher anticipated, for the theatre was crowded more than ever. One can well imagine what was in the sermon. Solemn warnings against vice have been thundered from pulpits time out of number, and it is doubtful if Mr. Herring had anything new to say on the subject. However, it brought him prominence, as he was made D.D. in 1728, and later in the year accompanied the King to Cambridge : and as this was the stepping-stone to future advancements, the reverend gentleman had reason to bless that which he cursed.

The chief objection the writer of the letter, and others beside him in later years, had to *The Beggar's Opera*, was that Macheath was reprieved instead of being properly hanged, and going to his death in an edifying manner. It is quite clear a highwayman ought not to possess the " undaunted Resolution of a stoical Philosopher." For a Knight of the Road to despise death was an outrage upon decency. " Philopropos," and doubtless the preacher as well, would have been satisfied if Gay had tacked on a " moral " and sent Macheath to the gallows whining and repentant, as, according to the many last speeches and dying confessions extant, thieves and murderers with properly constituted minds were in the habit of doing in the days when chaplains furnished material for Newgate Calendars.

Of the efficacy of brutal punishments, few " seriously minded men," with the parsons among them, had the slightest doubt. Two particularly revolting cases happened in the very year when Mr. Herring was so horrified at the unhanged Macheath and the free and easy Polly and Lucy. In *The Gloucester Journal* for March 5, 1728, we read that : " John Currie who forged Scotch notes was sentenced to be whip'd thro' that City to stand in the Pillory with his ears nailed to it, and afterwards to be transported, with Certification if he returned that he should be incarcerated during Life in that City and scourg'd thro' Edinburgh once a quarter." Shocking as this was, it is exceeded by a piece of brutality exhibiting a fiendish ingenuity worthy of a Torquemada. In *The British Journal* for May 18, 1728, we find it stated that : " Yesterday by Order of the Magistrates a Woman was whipt down the City, nail'd to the Tron, then had a Bit pinch'd out of her Nose with a new invented Machine, and was afterwards sent to the House of Correction for Thieving, House-Breaking, and other wicked Practice." Edinburgh has the credit of introducing this disgusting form of punishment. It is to be hoped that this " new invented machine " was promptly smashed, We fancy there is no other record of its being used.

Whipping, hanging, beheading, disembowelling, the horrors of the press-yard, the nailing of the ear to the pillory, branding and other forms of torture were common enough. Catherine Hayes was burned alive in 1726, and one would imagine that " the terrors of the penalties annexed by the laws to flagrant crimes " could hardly be heightened. It does not appear to have occurred to Mr. Herring, or to any other divine, that such legal enormities were worse than the immorality for which it may be said, without doing an injustice to very many respectable individuals from peers to peasants, the times were notorious. Nor do the moralists appear to have greatly concerned themselves about the amusements of the people other than those furnished by the " rogues and vagabonds " of the stage. We need not say anything about cock-fighting, as this sport may be considered quite refined by the side of other entertainments, which can only be matched by the wanton brutalities Hogarth depicted in No. 1 of his well-known prints " The Four Stages of Cruelty."

A few advertisements culled from the newspapers of the period will suffice to show what an ample field pious divines had for their labours, had the cause of humanity appealed to them, which apparently it did not. As a specimen of what the lower orders delighted in we take the following from *The Daily Journal* of May 2, 1727 : " Bear Garden, Hockley-in-the-Hole. A famous bull from Tothill Fields to be baited, which never fought before. Two dogs to fight. Ten let-goes, for a guinea each dog, at the Bull, the Dog that goes fairest and furthest in wins the money. Likewise the biggest Bear in England to fight two Dogs at a Time with other variety of Bull and Bear baiting. Likewise a Bull, Bear, and Ass, to be turned loose in the Game Place and Dogs after them." But this was quite mild fun in comparison to the pleasant novelty advertised in the same paper on July 25, wherein people were invited to see " A mad bull to be dressed up with fireworks, and a live cat to be tied to his tail and turned loose in the Game Place, with dogs after him ! "

After the foregoing it is almost refreshing to read that " At a public house in Leadenhall a Dog rubbed all over with a combustible Composition, was set fire to and being all in a Flame, the Dog took his way to the East India House, where if he had not been prevented by a Porter (who by kicking at him sprained his leg) he had ran directly into a Room where there were shavings and probably set the whole Neighbourhood on fire " ; and if this consequence had followed it would only have been a just retaliation on the part of the dog, which, as matters turned out, had to content itself with the porter's leg. As for other amusements, the holy minded probably took great delight in visiting Bridewell on whipping days ; while pious fathers considered they were inculcating

a highly moral lesson when they gave their sons a
treat in the shape of a visit to Bedlam to see the poor
raving, shrieking, mad people.

Slavery was looked upon as not only the proper
condition designed by a beneficent Providence for
negroes, but was tolerated even in regard to white
people. Kidnapping went on with impunity in
Bristol, the victims being sold as slaves in the West
India Plantations. As lawlessness was the rule
rather than the exception, this perhaps was not surprising ; but in the twentieth century one rubs one's
eyes to read the following in *The Daily Journal* in
December 1728 : " To be sold, a black boy about
16 years old. Enquire at Ned's Coffee House in
Birchin Lane." " A negro has a soul an' please
your honour ? " asked Corporal Trim doubtfully,
and Uncle Toby was inclined to think he had, but
had not considered the point.

The grounds of good Mr. Herring's horror of
The Beggar's Opera were political. The parson was
a rabid Hanoverian, and his zeal for the First George,
who could not speak a word of English and who was
only happy in his native country, was unbounded.
The offence of the Opera was that the author, the
friend of those enemies of Walpole, Pope and Swift,
had had the audacity to throw out innuendoes publicly
at the great Minister. The partisan preacher dared
not attack the play on this score, but he saw his
chance in condemning it on the ground that it was
an incentive to crime and immorality. The Rev.
Mr. Herring's championship of the King and his
Government was amply rewarded, for in 1737 he
obtained the bishopric of Bangor, and in 1743 was
made Archbishop of York. He was certainly industrious, and somewhat boastful, if we may make such
a charge against a meek and humble servant of the
Church. But what else is to be said of his statement
that during his progress through his diocese of York
—a period of six months—he was confident he had
confirmed above thirty thousand people ? The rising

of '45 stimulated all his pugnacity, and led to his stirring up the Yorkshire families to form an association for the defence of the Hanoverian monarchy, which resulted in the raising of a sum of £40,000 to aid in crushing the rebellion. Hogarth, in addition to painting the Archbishop's portrait, found material for a caricature in the prelate's warlike speech, when he addressed his clergy at York. A small portrait of the Archbishop, drawn as a headpiece to the printed speech, represents him half as a bishop and half as a soldier shouldering his musket. Above is the outline of a herring.

Archbishop Herring's warlike attitude on this occasion was the theme of a smart reply by that eccentric, but by no means foolish character, Orator Henley. The Clare Market preacher, when cited before the Privy Council for some alleged seditious expressions with reference to his Grace, was reproved by Lord Chesterfield for ridiculing the efforts made to suppress the rebellion of '45. " I thought there was no harm in cracking a joke on a red ' Herring,' " rejoined the unabashed Orator. Chesterfield thought he had scored off Henley when, the latter having defended his eccentric lectures by the plea that he must live, his lordship retorted, " I see no kind of reason for that, but many against it." Of course the laugh which a nobleman with a reputation for wit had a right to expect, followed. Henley, however, was equal to the occasion, observing that his lordship had said a good thing, but that it had been said before. The same comment may in a measure be made on Henley's own jocosity. Did not Archbishop Laud deliver himself of a paltry pun at the expense of the Welsh puritan divine, Julius Herring, whose tendency towards Nonconformity was so troublous to the authorities of the Established Church, to the effect that he " would pickle that Herring of Shrewsbury " ?

Baker in the *Biographia Dramatica* contends that the divines mistook the object of the new Opera,

" which was not to recommend the characters of highwaymen, pickpockets, and strumpets as examples to be followed, but to show that the principles and behaviour of many persons in what is called high life were not better than those of highwaymen, thieves, sharpers and strumpets. Nor can these characters be seductive to persons in low life, when they see that they must all expect to be hanged, ' 'Tis what we must all come to,' says one of them, and it is a kind of miracle if they continue six months in their evil courses." Half a century later an attempt was made to carry out the ideas of the parsons and render the Opera edifying. In October 1777 a Captain Thompson tried to put a moral to it. The play was produced at Covent Garden, and the audience, it is to be hoped, were gratified by seeing Macheath sentenced to the hulks. Here he is visited by Polly and Lucy. He persistently acknowledges his gratitude at being let off so lightly, and makes all kinds of good resolutions for the future. But the public preferred the old wickedness, and the revised version was a dead failure.

The militant Herring may be left to be dealt with by Swift. The Dean, staunch to his friend Gay, answered the reverend gentleman in *The Intelligencer*, a year after the famous sermon was preached. *The Intelligencer* was a paper started in Dublin by Swift and Dr. Sheridan, to carry on their political warfare against Walpole. It was published at a halfpenny, but in spite of its low price it came to an untimely end. Swift wrote nine articles for it, among them the one in defence of Gay and the Opera. We quote the main portion, as it throws light upon the point of view from which the great satirist regarded the Opera, and also what was in Gay's mind when writing it. After expressing the opinion that " the comedy or Farce (or whatever name the Critics will allow it) called *The Beggar's Opera* excels in humour, and upon that Merit to have met with much prodigious success both here (Ireland) and in England," the Dean goes

THE STAGE AT COVENT GARDEN, *cir.* 1770.

From Mr. A. M. Broadley's Collection.

[160]

on to deal with the "Common obtuseness that in *The Beggar's Opera* there appears to be some reflection upon Courtiers and Statesmen, whereof I am by no Means a Judge."

"It is true indeed that Mr. Gay, the author of this piece, hath been somewhat singular in the Course of his Fortune, for it hath happened that after Fourteen Years attending the Court with a large stock of real Merit, a modest and agreeable Conversation, a Hundred Promises, and Five Hundred Friends have failed of Preferment and upon a very weighty Reason. He lay under the Suspicion of having written a Libel or Lampoon against a great M(inister). It is true no doubt that great M(inister) was demonstratively convinced and publicly owned his conviction that Mr. Gay was not the Author; but having lain under the Suspicion, it seemed very just that he should suffer the Punishment, because in this most reformed Age, the Virtues of a great M(inister) are no more to be suspected than the chastity of Cæsar's wife.

"It must be allowed that *The Beggar's Opera* is not the first of Mr. Gay's works, wherein he has been faulty with regard to Courtiers and Statesmen. For— to omit his other Pieces—even in his *Fables*, published within two years past, and dedicated to the Duke of Cumberland, for which he was promised a reward, he hath been thought somewhat too bold upon Courtiers; and although it is highly probable he meant only the Courtiers of former Times, yet he acted unwarily by not considering that the Malignity of some People might misinterpret what he said to the Disadvantage of present Persons and Affairs.

"But I have now done with Mr. Gay as a Politician, and shall consider him henceforward only as Author of *The Beggar's Opera*, wherein he hath by a turn of humour entirely New placed Vices of all kinds in the strongest and most odious Light, and therefore done eminent Service both to Religion and Morality. This appears from the unparalleled Suc-

11

cess he has met with. All Ranks, Parties and
Denominations of men, either crowding to see his
Opera or reading it with Delight in their Closets,
even Ministers of State whom he has thought to
have most offended (next to those whom the actors
more immediately represent) appearing freely at the
Theatre, from a consciousness of their own innocence
and to convince the World how unjust a Parallel,
Malice, Envy and Disaffection to the Government
have made. I am assured that several worthy
clergymen in this city (Dublin) went privately to see
The Beggar's Opera represented, and that the fleering
Coxcombs in the Pit amused themselves with making
discoveries and spreading the name of those gentlemen round the Audience. I shall not pretend to
vindicate a Clergyman who would appear openly in
his habit at the Theatre among such a vicious Crew
as would probably stand round him, and at such
lewd Comedies and prophane tragedies as are often
repeated. . . . But when Lord Chancellors, who are
Keepers of the King's conscience, when the Judges
of the Land whose Title is Reverend ; when Ladies
who are bound by the rules of their Sex to the
strictest Decency appear in the theatre without censure, I cannot understand why a young Clergyman
who goes concealed out of Curiosity to see an innocent
and moral Play should be so highly condemned ;
nor do I much approve the Rigour of the great
P(relate) who said he *hoped none of his clergy were
there.* I am glad to hear there are no weightier
Objections against that Reverend Body planted in
this city, and I wish there never may. But I should
be very sorry that any one of them should be so weak
as to imitate the Court Chaplain not young who
preached against *The Beggar's Opera,* which will probably do more Good than a thousand sermons of so
stupid, so injudicious and so prostituted a Divine.

   " In this happy performance of Mr. Gay's all the
Characters are just. . . It shows the miserable Lives
and the constant Fate of those abandoned Wretches ;

for how little they sell their Lives and souls ; betrayed by their whores, their comrades, and the receivers and purchasers of these thefts and robberies.

" This comedy contained likewise a Satyr which although it doth by no means affect the present age, yet hath been useful in the former and may possibly be so in ages to come. I mean where the Author takes occasion of comparing those common Robbers of the Past and their several stratagems of betraying, undermining and hanging each other, to the several Arts of Politicians in Times of Corruption.

" This comedy likewise exposeth with great justice that unnatural Taste for Italian music among us which is wholly unsuitable to our Northern Climate and the Genius of the People, whereby we are over-run with Italian Effeminacy and Italian Nonsense . . . . upon the Whole I deliver my Judgment that nothing but servile attachment to a Party affecta-tion, a Singularly lamentable dullness, mistaken zeal or steady Hypocrisy, can have the least reasonable Objection against this excellent moral performance of the CELEBRATED MR. GAY."

Dr. Johnson, in his Life of Gay, sums up the matter with his strong common-sense. He charac-terises both the attack of Dr. Herring and the defence of Swift as " surely exaggerated. The play, like many others, was plainly written only to divert, without any moral purpose, and is therefore not likely to do good ; nor can it be conceived, without more speculation than life requires or admits, to be productive of much evil : Highwaymen and house-breakers seldom frequent the playhouse, or mingle in any elegant diversion ; nor is it possible for any one to imagine that he may rob with safety because he sees Macheath reprieved upon the stage."

CHAPTER XV

The Opera attacked for its political allusions—Caleb D'Anvers' onslaught in *The Craftsman*—The sequel of *The Beggar's Opera*—D'Anvers' spite against Polly—Polly's distanced rivals, Mrs. Oldfield, Mrs. Porter, Mrs. Younger and Mrs. Booth—Gay charged with plagiarism—The charge groundless

THOUGH the Opera, to quote Johnson, " was plainly written to divert," yet it is fairly evident that opportunities were not lost—whether initiated by Pope or Swift does not matter very much—of sending an arrow into the Governmental camp. Swift admits as much, for his argument that Gay, when " too bold upon Courtiers," probably meant " only the Courtiers of former times," must be dismissed as a piece of special pleading, which at the time answered its purpose, but which has now no particular value.

Political allusions under cover of lines supposed to have no reference to anything but the play itself were common enough in Gay's time. Walpole was a target against which too many shafts could not be hurled. On *Richard II.* being revived in 1744, the actor who personated Northumberland had a very methodical style of delivery, and when he pronounced the lines :

> " The king is not himself, but basely led
> By flatterers——"

the noise from the clapping of hands and clattering of sticks was deafening. Again, Ross has to say : " The Earl of Wiltshire hath the state in farm," and it was immediately applied to Walpole, " with," says Davies, " the loudest shouts of huzzas I ever

164

heard." On the other hand, the two lines " The king's grown bankrupt like a broken man " and " Reproach, and dissolution hangeth over him," were heard with " a dead and respectful silence." During some of the performances of *Venice Preserved* the audiences, divided in politics, fell often into riot and tumult. " The Senate of Venice," Davies points out, " was an excellent stalking-horse whence Otway took his aim at the House of Commons." Otway in his anxiety to support the cause of Royalty was, Davies adds, " ever in distress." Johnson in his *Life of Addison* speaks of the feeling which was excited by *Cato*. " The whole nation," he says, " was at that time on fire with faction. The Whigs applauded every line in which liberty was mentioned, as a satire on the Tories, and the Tories echoed every clap to show that the satire was unfelt." The climax came when Bolingbroke, calling Barton Booth, who played the leading character, to his box, gave him fifty guineas " for defending the cause of liberty so well against a perpetual dictator."

It was easy to attack *The Beggar's Opera* on the score of its political bias, and no one was surprised when on February 17, hardly three weeks after the Opera was produced, a fierce assault was made upon it in the form of a letter to *The Country Journal or The Craftsman*, edited by that political firebrand Caleb D'Anvers. The letter is signed "Phil Harmonicus," and we give it in its entirety.

" A key to *The Beggar's Opera* in a letter to Caleb Danvers, Esq. Sir :—I sent you some months ago an Account of the declining State of the Royal British Academy, occasioned by the Disputes between the two famous Rival Queens and their Contending Factions, whether the First part in the Opera belonged to Cuzzoni or Faustina, which have been since carried to such an Height that (like most other Animosities) they have almost brought that *mighty State* itself into Contempt. We have seen it Dwindle by Degrees for a year or two past till it is at *length* in a Manner *deserted*, even by its quondam *Admirers, Subscribers & Directors*—greatest O *Tempora*! O *Mores*! that ever the Theatre in the Haymarket should be obliged to yield to that in *Lincoln's-Inn-Fields*!—that the coarse Ribaldry and Vulgar Catches of a Newgate Hero should prevail over the melodious Enchantments of Senesino, whilst the once celebrated *Cuzzoni* and *Faustina* lay aside their former Emulation, and with united Resentment, behold the Palm of Precedence given to pretty Miss Polly Peachum—with a P!

" I hope the Beaumonde will give me leave to observe (which nothing but the present *melancholy* occasion could extort from me) that this is an undeniable Mark of a *vitiated Taste* and a *degenerate licentious Age*, which delight in seeing Things of the Greatest Importance turned to Ridicule. Who can help being surprized to find two of His Majesty's *Theatres* prostituted in this manner, and made the popular Engines for conveying not only *Scandal* and *Scurrility*, but even *Sedition* and *Treason* through the Kingdom. Have we not lately seen the awful Solemnity of a Coronation openly burlesqued at both Theatres? Have not the *Nobles*, the *Prelates*, the *Judges* and *Magistrates* of the Land been personated by Miller, Johnson and Harper at one House and by Harlequin and his Associates at the other? . . .

" Though I am a constant *spectator* of *The Beggar's Opera*, which affords me a *mighty Entertainment*, and have always had a great respect for Mr. R(ic)h ; yet I am often surprized at the late *unprecedented Insolence* and *Audaciousness of that Gentleman*, and *have often wondered that* such *Entertainments are suffered* to be exhibited Night after Night to the whole *Town* with Impunity. How could it enter into his head to turn the fine Songs of the Opera into such high Ridicule? He knows very well WHO goes to, and *takes delight in* these Diversions. . . . *Did he mean to insinuate by this that nothing but* sing-song empty Sound and Gesticulation *please and recommend* at an opera ? or *did he hope* that other harsh *Inferences would be made* by the Disaffected, *which I detest and He dares not name ?* . . . Nay, the very Title of this Piece and the *Principal Character* which is that of an Highwayman, sufficiently discern the mischievous Design of it, since by his Character everybody will understand *One* who makes it his Business arbitrarily to *levy* and *collect* Money on the People for his *own use,* and of which he always dreads to give any Account. Is not this *Squinting* with a Vengeance, and wounding *Persons in Authority* through the Sides of a *common Malefactor* ?

" But I shall go still deeper into this Affair and undertake to prove beyond all Dispute that *The Beggar's Opera* is the most venomous *allegorical Libel* against the G——t that hath appeared for many years past.

" There are some persons who esteem *Lockit* the *Keeper,* or *Prime Minister* of *Newgate* to be the Hero of the Piece ; to justify which opinion they take Advice that He is set forth on the Stage in the Person of Mr. Hall, as a very *corpulent* bulky man, and that he had a Brother named Peachum, who as represented by Mr. Hippisley appears to be a *little awkward slovenly* Fellow. They observe further that these *two Brothers* have a numerous gang of Thieves and Pick-pockets under their Direction with whom they divide the *Plunder* and whom they either *screen* or *tuck up* as their own Interests and the *present Occasion* require : But I am obliged to reject this Interpretation as erroneous, however plausible it may be, and to embrace another which is more generally received, namely that Captain Macheath, who hath also a goodly presence and hath a tolerable bronze upon his face, is designed for the *Principal Character* and drawn to asperse *somebody in Authority.* He is represented at the Head of a Gang of Robbers, who promise to stand by him against all the Enquiries and coercive force of the Law. He is often called a *Great Man*—particularly in the following Passage :

namely ' It grieves one's Heart to take off a Great Man in *Distress*,' which by the by seems to be an Inuendo that some Great Men will speedily fall into Distress. Soon after his first Appearance on the Stage, he is taken up and Confin'd for a certain slippery Prank on the Road but hath the Good Fortune to *escape* that Time by the Help of a trusted friend. He is afterwards re-taken in much better Plight and *Apparel* than before, and ordered for *Execution* which is prevented for no other reason that I can see than that the Poet is afraid of offending the Criticks by making an Opera end with a tragic *catastrophe* ; for he plainly tells us that this observance of dramatic Rules in one point have made him violate poetical Justice in another and spoil a very good moral, namely that the lower people have their vices in a Degree as well as the rich and are punished *for them—inuendo* that rich People *never are.* . . .

" His satirical strokes upon *Ministers, Courtiers,* and *Great Men* in general abound in every part of this most *excellent Performance.* In one place where Polly Peachum acknowledges her match with Captain Macheath her Father breaks out into a passion with these words, ' Marry an highwayman ! Why he'll make as bad an husband as a *Lord* '—inuendo that all Lords make bad husbands. Soon after that Miss Polly questions her spouse's constancy. He tells her that *you might sooner tear* a Pension out of the hands of a Courtier than *tear him from her—inuendo* that all Courtiers have *Pensions.* In the following song the employment of a statesman is by *inuendo* made as bad or worse than that of Jonathan Wild, represented under the character of Peachum, which he introduces by a general libel on Men of all professions even the most *sacred* in order to make that of a statesman more black and vile.

" 'Through all the Employments of Life,
Each Neighbour abuses his Brother,
Whore and Rogue they call Husband and Wife,
All professions be-rogue one another.

HACKWOOD PARK.

Seat of the Duke of Bolton.

From an engraving by J. Shury & Son, after G. S. Shepherd.

168]

> The Priest calls the Lawyer a cheat,
>   And the Lawyer be-knaves the Divine;
> And the Statesman, because he's so great,
>   Thinks his trade is as honest as mine.'

" The second Act begins with a Scene of High-waymen drinking together, who solemnly promise never to betray one another, for Interest or any other Motive, upon which one of them gets up and says : ' Show me a Gang of Courtiers *who can say as much*—*inuendo that Courtiers have less honesty than High-waymen*—in another place it is said that our Gang *cannot trust one another any more than other people*—*inuendo* . . .

" In a Scene between Peachum and his Brother Lockit, Peachum takes upon him to say *that he does not like those long Arrears of the G*——*t* (*inuendo* that the G——t *is in arrear*). Again says he, *can it be expected that we should hang our Acquaintance for nothing* when our Betters *will hardly save theirs without being paid for it*? *Inuendo*, that some persons have been well paid for *saving* or *screening their former acquaintances*. . . . He goes on with observing *that in one respect* their employment *may be reckoned dishonest, because like* Great Statesmen *they encourage* those *who betray* their friends—which contains by *inuendo* a confirmation of that ridiculous as well as scandalous vulgar error that *great Statesmen freely betray their Friends*.

" Upon this Lockit advises him to be more guarded, and sings the following air :

> " 'When you censure the Age
>   Be cautious and sage,
> Lest the Courtiers offended should be :
>   If you mention Vice **or** Pride
>   'Tis so pat to all the Tribe,
> Each cries—That was levell'd at me.'

" I submit it whether this is not a plain *inuendo* that every Courtier *is corrupt* either with Vice, or Pride, or with both ? . . .

" *What reasons induce the G*—— *to be thus passive*

under such repeated Insults, I do not take upon myself to determine, but though I am far from wishing, as I know it will be objected, to see the *Liberty of the Stage entirely abolished,* yet I think such licentious invectives on the most *polite and fashionable Vices* require some *immediate restraint,* for if they continue to be allowed they will become the censure of the Age, and no Man, even of the first quality or Distinction, will be at Liberty to follow his *Pleasures, Inclinations or Interest* (which is certainly the Birthright of every Free Briton) without danger of becoming the May-Game of the whole Town."

This letter, obviously from the pen of D'Anvers himself, was incorporated with other matter having special reference to Polly, and advertised thus in *The Daily Post* of May 22. " This day is publish'd for the Use of Dr. Swift, Alexander Pope, and Company, *The Twickenham Hotch Potch : Being the Sequel of The Beggar's Opera,* Containing. (1) The state of Poetry and Fate of Poets in England formerly. (2) The present War among authors, viz., Swift, Pope, Voltaire, Rolli, Trapp, Bundy, Ozell, and Parson Herring. (3) Pope corrected not wounded. Written by Mr. Theobald. (4) Seriosities and Comicalities with Two Dozen of Maxims equally useful for Court, Camp or City. (5) The Game of Flats, or, an Epistle from Signora F—t—na to a Lady. (6) The Rival Actresses, viz., O—f—d, P—t—r, B—h and Miss Y——g—r against Miss Fenton. (7) A Poetical List of Polly Peachum's Gallants. (8) A True Copy of Polly Peachum's Opera. Also Her Panegyric. Written by Caleb D'Anvers Esq. . . . N.B. This Design is to be carried on for the Good of the Publick."

In the " Introduction," D'Anvers sets forth the neglect which many distinguished men of letters, previous to Gay's success with a frivolous Opera, had to suffer, and proceeds in the following bitter fashion : " Thus have I set before the Reader's Eyes in as short a Method as I could, the cruel Treatment that so many extraordinary Men have received from

their Countrymen for these last hundred Years. If
I could now shift the Scene, and shew all the Penury,
and Avarice changed all at once to Riot and
Profuseness, and more, squandered away upon four
objects (an impertinent *Scotch*-Quack, a Profligate
Irish-Dean, the Lacquey of a Superanuated Dutchess,
and a little virulent Papist) than would have satisfied
the greater Part of those extraordinary Men, the
Readers to whom these Creatures should be altogether
unknown, would fancy them Prodigies of Art and
Nature, would believe that all the Great Qualities of
those extraordinary Persons above-mentioned were
centred in them alone ; that they had the Capacity
and Profoundness of *Bacon*, the fine Painting of
Spencer, the Force and Sublimity, and Elevation of
Milton ; the fine Thinking and Elegance, the Versifi-
cation of *Dryden* ; the Fire and Enthusiasm of *Lee* ;
the moving, melting, Tenderness of *Otway* ; the
Pleasantry of *Butler*; the Wit and Satire of *Wych-
erly* ; and the Humour and Spirit, and Art and
Grace of *Congreve*.   Instead of which this *Twickenham*-
Club cannot be justly intitled to any other Motto,
than that of the honest *Roman* :—

" ' Odi Imitatores Servum Pecus.'

Or what an *English* Poet has said of Longinus, may
be as justly applied to them :

" ' *Their own* Example, *strengthens all their* Law,
They are, Themselves, *the* Bathos *that they* draw.' "

Caleb D'Anvers was a disappointed man, and
after the manner of such his sword was for ever out
of its scabbard girding at foes real or imaginary.
Spite and jealousy were gratified when he dubbed
Arbuthnot a " Scotch-Quack," Swift a " Profligate
Irish-Dean," Gay "the Lacquey of a Superanuated
Dutchess (her Grace of Queensberry) " and Pope " a
little virulent Papist."   The retaliation of the mem-
bers of the " Hotch-Potch " must have wounded
D'Anvers' vanity beyond endurance—they treated

him with silent contempt. " Caleb " did not even have the doubtful honour of figuring in the *Dunciad* which Pope published during the following year, and one may search in vain in the correspondence of Pope and Swift for any reference to their assailant. They could not have retorted more effectively than by silent contempt. Nicholas Amhurst, who delighted to call himself " Caleb D'Anvers," was an industrious and pertinacious but hardly a formidable antagonist. His literary style was pretentious, and he had little claim to be called a wit, although no doubt he considered himself to be one. *The Craftsman*, which he founded, and to which Bolingbroke and Pulteney contributed, was one of the most successful political journals of the times, and D'Anvers carried it on with infinite spirit, but in his later years he fell upon evil days. He expected some permanent assistance from Pulteney, but the meanest and most selfish of Statesmen turned upon him the cold shoulder, and he died at Twickenham of, so it was said, a broken heart.

D'Anvers, whatever his abilities may have been, was not an amiable character, and not contented with attacking the Twickenham wits, he turned his venom on Polly, which was, to say the least of it, a cowardly thing to do. But Gay's triumph was gall and wormwood to him, and so he poured the vials of his superfluous wrath on the heroine of the Opera. There is nothing to excuse his joining the ranks of the scurrilous lampoonists who flung mud at her to suit the vulgar taste, and D'Anvers had not the defence that he tempered his spite by humour.

In the " Key " included in the book are a few scrappy skits on Polly, all more or less scurrilous. Most had appeared before, and the author was evidently so proud of his efforts that he republished them. The coarse effusion and its answer, already alluded to (see p. 148) are here, then follows what is termed an " Epigram to Miss Beswick, alias Fenton, alias Polly Peachum." It runs thus :

"Be not vain of your fancy'd Success, I desire you,
Nor think that *Lords* love you because they *admire* you;
A *Monster* does doubtless, deserve *Admiration*
As much as the *Prettiest Girl* in the Nation ;
And hourly Experience, Lavinia, will show you,
A *Granny* is star'd at, as much as a *Chloe.*"

Poor stuff indeed, while the note attached to it
is little more than coarse and senseless abuse : " This
Ballad-Singing-Beauty (which our present Race of
Beaus so much Admire)," says the carping critic,
" is a raw-bon'd, large-featured Female Virago and
having the necessary Qualification requir'd by Ser-
jeant Kite of being Six Foot high is no doubt born
to be a *Great Woman.*"

Sir Robert Fagg can of course no more be kept
out of the attacks on Polly than Mr. Dick could
keep the head of Charles the First out of his
thoughts. A string of doggerel is addressed to
him as " The old sportsman or the Antiquated
Baronet behind the scenes," under the heading
"*Polly Peachum's Opera or a Medley of New Songs.*
Published with her approbation." Then comes "A
Ballad by Caleb D'Anvers ; to the tune of Sally in
our Alley." It is hardly quotable. After indulging
in his malice, D'Anvers adopts his old trick, possibly
with a view of saving his skin, of applying the salve,
and winds up with :

"But these are all invented Lies
        And vile *outlandish* scandal
Which from *Italian* Clubs arise
        And Partizans of *Handel.*
Then let us toast the blooming Lass
        Whose Charms have thus ensnared me ;
I'd drink it in a brimming Glass,
        Though Parson H—ring heard me."

A footnote to the allusion to " Parson H(er) ring "
runs : " A mighty weak sucking Priest, who to show
his theological Capacity preached a sermon at Lincoln's Chapel against the Derision of the Age and *The
Beggar's Opera.*" The book winds up with parodies
on fourteen of the most popular songs in the Opera

sung by Polly, utterly wanting in wit and the majority casting reflections on her virtue. Not one is worth dragging to light. Just as an antidote to the poison, we give two verses which D'Anvers wrote in a more complaisant mood. They originally appeared in *Mist's Journal* of March 2, 1728.

> " While Polly charms the present Age,
> And Venus' train the Fair surrounds,
> Autumnal O-f—ld boils with Rage
> And rugged P-rt-r grimly frowns.

> " To the soft Flute B—th trips in vain,
> Nor longer charms th' applauding Throng ;
> E'en pretty Y—ng-er's Comic Strain
> Yields with the rest to Polly's song."

Polly's contemporaries, Mrs. Oldfield, Mrs. Porter, Mrs. Booth and Mrs. Younger, are here referred to. In 1728 Mrs. Oldfield was nearing the end of her career, and she died in 1730. Mrs. Porter was one of the finest tragic actresses of her day, and her success is made the more remarkable from the fact that she was a cripple, her hip joint having been dislocated through falling from her chaise in an encounter with a highwayman. She must have been a woman of extraordinary courage and energy, as she drew a pistol upon the fellow, who was hardly a Macheath, and frightened him into submission. A poetic ending to the affair is supplied by her giving the would-be robber ten guineas on finding that he was in want and afterwards raising sixty pounds for his family.

Mrs. Younger was a popular actress in Rich's company who was driven into the cold shade of neglect for the time being by Polly's success. Mrs. Younger indeed had no reason to love Polly, for after playing *Ariaspe* (one of her original parts) in Sturmy's *Sesostris* on January 17, 1728, the production and run of *The Beggar's Opera* shut her out of an engagement until December 7 of the same year, when she was *Artesia* in Burford's *Virgin Queen*. Mrs. Younger imitated Polly in one respect : she married into a noble family. Her husband, the Hon. John Finch, fourth son of the Earl of Nottingham, after " going the pace " in company with Sally Salisbury, settled down into matrimony.   The story of the Honourable John and the wanton Sally is told elsewhere.

Mrs. Booth was Barton Booth's wife, who, as Miss Santlow, made a hit in *The Fair Quaker of Deal* at Drury Lane.   Before then she was only known and admired as a dancer.   Cibber says of her performance in *The Fair Quaker*, " the gentle softness of her Voice, the composed Innocence of her aspect, the modesty of her Dress, the reserv'd Decency of her Gesture and the simplicity of her sentiments made her seem the amiable maid she represented."

The letter of " Phil Harmonicus " furnished a peg on which to attack the opera on grounds other than that of its alleged incentive to sedition.   This was the publication of Christopher Bullock's play *A Woman's Revenge, or a Match in Newgate*, produced in 1715 at the Lincoln's Inn Fields Theatre, and of sufficient attraction to take its place among other stock plays.   Christopher Bullock died in 1724; his brother was in the original cast of *The Beggar's Opera*, and the allusion in the eccentric dedication to " our dear Brother Mr. Christopher Bullock " must not be taken too literally, as it is hardly likely an actor would have any share in an attack on the very play in which he himself was playing.   Probably Caleb was at the bottom of the new assault, since the letter of " Phil Harmonicus " is printed along with *A Woman's Revenge*, and it may be that Christopher's brother had nothing to do with the publication.   The dedication, whimsical enough in its way, contains the new charge made against Gay, and we reproduce it in full :

"To

PRETTY MISS POLLY PEACHUM

" *Pretty* Polly *say*
What makes Johnny Gay
To call, to call, his Newgate *scenes*
The Beggar's Opera ?

" *Silly wretched Man,*
  Such a Flame to Fan,
To think of quenching Lover's Pains,
    That any Dungeon can.

" But hold me, dear *Duck*, whither am I running
in musical notes, when my only design is to Forewarn
and Admonish Thee in mournful guise of the great
Danger we are in from this Damn'd *Thieves Opera*
we are so merry about.

" Poll—pray retain in your memory what the
honest Cobbler says in Sir Fopling Flutter—*Ale and
History Master*, etc., for which Reason, take Notice,
my Girl, if we are put into the Crown Office, and
after that into Jail, for the Sins of other People, that
I here enter my Protest in Form against these Treason-
able Scenes, as they are fully proved to be by Phil
Harmonicus's *Key*.

" In the days of that Immortal Stuart, King
James the First, there lived one Mr. John Marston
who wrote Eight Plays.   One of which call'd *The
Dutch Courtezan*, was printed in the Year 1605, and
Eight and Twenty Years afterwards, 1633, it was
revived with great Success under the Title of *The
Revenge*—Or *A Match in Newgate*.   And in the
Year 1715, being the *second* Year of King George
the First (God bless his Memory), our dear Brother
Mr. Christopher Bullock, Re-viv'd this Comedy,
and call'd it *A Woman's Revenge* : Or *A Match in
Newgate*.

" And now you see in the First year of King
George the Second, that Mr. John Gay, who
turns the transactions of all the world into Fables,
has metamorphosed Mr. John Marston's *Dutch
Courtezan* into the Duchess of ——, and your
Mother Acts one Part, and does not prove her marriage.

" Every Page Gay has writ
Tho' 'tis stuff'd up with Metre :
Points out P(art)y and Parliament,
God bless the Speaker.

DR. ARNE.

From an old print.

" In short the truth ought to be told, our Brother Bullock's *Match in Newgate* is a harmless inoffensive Farce.

> " And dedicated was to me
> As you may very plainly see.

" *The Beggar's Opera,* Mr. Gay stole from Mr. Bullock, who only Borrowed it of Mr. Marston ; and the Law says ' the Receiver is as bad as the thief.' Besides it is most certainly a libel against the K— and G——t.

> " And we shall all be soused for our Folly
> Lockit, Macheath, Padwell, Peachum Polly,
> By other folks' crimes let us learn to beware,
> And keep our own Noddles, Girls, out of the snare.

" PETER PADWELL.

" PADDINGTON, St. David's Day, 1728."

The accusation that Gay went to Bullock's adaptation of Betterton's version of Marston's *Dutch Courtezan* for his *Beggar's Opera* is about as ridiculous a charge as can well be conceived. There is not the slightest resemblance between the two, beyond the circumstance that the last scene of *A Woman's Revenge* takes place in Newgate, and ends thus :—

" KEEPER : Sir, the Licence is come and the Ordinary waits above.

" THINKWELL : Come, young Fellows, take your girls by the Hands and lead up to the little old Gentleman in Black.

> " From this dire Place many to Death have gone,
> But to be Married very rarely one."

This is all. It is not worth while to explain what *A Woman's Revenge* is about. We may, however, remark that its author, Christopher Bullock, was an unscrupulous purloiner of other men's goods. We have already alluded to his smart use of a fragment of a play which James Spiller (Bullock dedicated *A Woman's Revenge* to " my merry friend and Brother

12

Comedian Mr. James Spiller) stole from Pinkethman while the latter was asleep ; and it is said he
passed off Savage's play *Woman's a Riddle* (adapted
from the Spanish) as his own, allowing the real
author a share of the profits. Another version,
according to the *Dictionary of National Biography*, is
that " the play was translated by Mrs. Price, the
wife of Robert Price, baron of the exchequer, and
that copies of it were given by her to Savage, to
Bullock, and to another writer unnamed, and that
Bullock in his position of manager was able to be
first in the field." However this may be is of no
consequence in the present connection, save that it
adds to the absurdity of the charge against Gay.
The Prison Breaker stands in a different category ;
but even here if Gay were indeed indebted to this
play, it would not amount to plagiarism. With the
mere mention of *A Town Pastoral* to " Miss Polly
Peachum written in imitation of the Fourth Eclogue
of Virgil. By J. W. of Cheapside, Linnen-Draper,"
which is tacked on to the reprint of Phil Harmonicus'
letter, the alleged indebtedness of Gay to *A Woman's
Revenge* may be dismissed.

CHAPTER XVI

THE TRIUMPH OF *THE BEGGAR'S OPERA*

The copyright of *The Beggar's Opera*—Gay's deed of assignment to Tonson and Watts—Legal proceedings concerning it fifty years later—Gay's letter to Swift on his success—Polly's mezzotints—Letters by Gay, Swift, and Mrs. Delany—Polly in *Love and a Bottle*, *The Beaux' Stratagem*, etc.

ONE of the favourite melodramatic actors of mid-Victorian days was Mr. R. J. Smith, better known as " O. Smith " from his remarkable performance of Obi in *Three-Fingered Jack*, an Adelphi drama of a full-blooded, transpontine type. Mr. R. J. Smith was an enthusiastic collector of matters relating to the stage, and left behind him some twenty-five volumes of manuscript notes and newspaper cuttings. There is not much attempt at arrangement. No doubt Mr. Smith intended at some future time to sift his mountain of material, but a little patience easily brings to light much that is valuable. One of these " finds " is a copy of the deed of assignment by which Gay sold the rights of publication in *The Beggar's Opera* and the *Fables* to Jacob Tonson and John Watts. Mr. Smith omits to give the source from which he copied the deed, but so far as we have been able to discover, it has not hitherto appeared in print, and we have every reason to believe the document has now the light of publicity for the first time. The deed runs as follows :

" Know all Men by these presents that I John Gay of Whitehall in the County of Middlesex Esquire for and in consideration of the sum of ninety-four pounds and ten shillings of good and lawfull money of Great Britain to me in hand paid by Jacob Tonson and John Watts of London stationer the receipt and

payment of which sume I the said John Gay do
hereby confess and acknowledge I the said John
Gay have and by these presents do grant bargain
sell assign and sell over unto them the said Jacob
Tonson and John Watts, all that the sole right and
title of in and to the copys and copyright of two
books, the one entituled fifty Fables written by the
said John Gay, the other entituled the Beggars
Opera as it is now acted at the Theatre Royal in
Lincoln's Inn fields and written also by the said
John Gay wch copy and copyright of the said two
books entituled fifty Fables and the Beggars Opera to
be and remain unto the said Jacob Tonson and John
Watts equally share and share alike and to their
heirs and assigns equally share and share alike for
ever, any Law now in being to the contrary notwithstanding. In Witness whereof the said John
Gay hath hereunto sett his hand and seal this sixth
day of February 1727. JOHN GAY. Sealed and
Delivered in the presence of

> Marggreat Cox.
> John Whitehead."

It will be seen that February 6, 1727, is given as
the date when the deed was executed. Either a
mistake was made by the original draughtsman or
by the copyist. Had not the words " the Beggars
Opera as it is now acted at the Theatre Royal in Lincoln's Inn Fields " appeared in the document, it would
have been reasonable to suppose that Gay assigned
the copyright the year before the Opera was brought
out, but as the deed stands it is clear some
one blundered. Whether this was the authority
on which so many writers on Gay and *The Beggar's
Opera* have gone wrong in regard to the date of the
production of the Opera, we are unable to say, but
it is clear that the newspapers of the period cannot
be gainsaid. An error of this kind is very difficult
to kill, and Mr. E. T. Brydges, who wrote an interesting letter to *Notes and Queries* (June 29, 1895) on a

Chancery suit arising out of this very assignment of copyright, apparently not knowing that the correct date was 1728, only repeated what he found in the legal papers before him. These papers, which Mr. Brydges found by accident in a solicitor's office, where they had been lying for years, consisted of a Bill in Chancery, dated October 26, pleadings, brief, etc., which set out, to quote Mr. Brydges' letter, "that some time in the year 1727 John Gay of Whitehall, composed and wrote a certain book and opera entitled *The Beggar's Opera*, which was represented and performed at the Theatre Royal, Lincoln's Inn Fields, and afterwards at the Theatre Royal, Drury Lane, and Covent Garden. That Jacob Tonson and John Watts became the purchasers from Gay of the Opera and also of fifty *Fables* written by Gay, and these books and the copyright thereof were on consideration of £94 10*s*. paid to Gay by Tonson and Watts, assigned to them by a deed dated February 6, 1727, and they duly entered the assignment in the register book of the Company of Stationers by virtue of an Act made and passed in the eighth year of Queen Anne. That Tonson and Watts printed and published a great number of the book of the Opera and sold them at sixpence each.

" Tonson and Watts some time afterwards dissolved partnership, and Watts assigned all his share and right in the copyright to Tonson, who also printed and sold a large number at sixpence each. Tonson died in the year 1766, leaving a will of which he appointed his brother, Richard Tonson, sole executor. Richard Tonson caused the book and Opera and the copyright thereof to be sold by public auction on August 8, 1767, and at such auction the plaintiffs (Andrew Strahan, William Griffin, George Kearsley, Thomas Lownells, Thomas Caslon, Samuel Bladon, and William Nicholl booksellers of London) became the purchasers thereof for the sum of £286 10*s*., and they also printed and published and sold copies of the book at sixpence each.

" The plaintiffs accuse the defendants (William Carell, Richard Dymott and Henry Sergeant, booksellers) of printing and publishing the Opera at the price of threepence each without their licence, and that at the bottom of the title page they give out that it is printed for the proprietors. It is also alleged that some variations, but few and insignificant, were made by the defendants in their copy, purposely inserted and omitted ' the better to cover the design of the defendants ' to deprive plaintiffs of their advantage. An account of sales and an injunction is prayed for.

" The defendants in their answer contend that under the Copyright Act of Anne the plaintiffs had a title for fourteen years only, and that at the end of that period the rights of printing and publishing the work reverted to the author, if then living, for another term of fourteen years. That inasmuch as the book was first published in 1727 the plaintiffs' right and Gay's right expired in 1741, and that from that time the book became common property, and that no right of assignment passed after Gay's death, as he died during the first term of fourteen years. Defendants admitted having printed 4,000 copies and sold 1,000, and received from such sale £15 12s. 6d.

" It appears that an interim injunction was granted, and a plea pleading the above statement was overruled. The bill was, however, some few months later dismissed for want of prosecution, and it must be assumed the plaintiffs gave up their contention."

Notwithstanding the clear terms of the Act of Queen Anne (1709) booksellers who had purchased copyrights really thought they had the rights in perpetuity—no doubt Tonson and Watts imagined they had overridden the Act when they inserted the words " any law now in being to the contrary notwithstanding "—and in 1759 a number of firms combined and raised a fund amounting to £3,150 for maintaining what they conceived to be their rights.

Injunctions were continually being applied for, and
any amount of litigation resulted, which was brought
to an end in 1774, when the House of Lords decided
by a majority of one that the right of perpetuity
had been taken away by the Act of 1709 and a term
of years substituted. Those booksellers who believed
they owned copyrights were very much surprised
and disgusted, and they presented a petition to
Parliament, praying to be relieved from the consequences of the decision; but though a bill for this
purpose passed the House of Commons, it was thrown
out by the House of Lords. The matter is of some
interest in the present connection, as it is an additional proof of the vitality of *The Beggar's Opera*,
seeing that the copyright had in a little less than
thirty years increased in value by nearly £200. The
assignment, it is true, included the *Fables*, but it is
pretty clear that the real bone of contention was
The Beggar's Opera. The *Fables* were never so
popular as to make the risk of an injunction and
legal expenses worth incurring.

Reverting to the puzzle of the date. It might
be said that the Opera was put into rehearsal in 1727,
and that this was what was meant by the words " as
it is now acted at the Theatre Royal in Lincoln's Inn
Fields "; but this theory does not explain away the
alleged signing of the document on February 6. It
may be safely asserted that the opera was not in
rehearsal then. As regards dates all is conjecture.
We know nothing for certain beyond January 29,
1728. What time Gay commenced writing the
Opera, when he finished it, when he offered it to
Cibber, how long Cibber retained the manuscript
before sending it back, when Rich decided to accept
it, the date of putting it into rehearsal—everything
is in the dark. We adhere, however, to our assumption that the date in R. J. Smith's copy of the
assignment is incorrect, and if so we may go further
and say that had Gay known his success would run
into sixty-two nights, he would have asked more than

£94 for the copyright with the *Fables* thrown in.
The date, February 6 (assuming that 1728 was the
year of the assignment), was but three days after his
first benefit, and he was probably deeply in debt,
and like all improvident men lived only for the
moment. He was little better than a child where
money was concerned, and no one knew this better than
his good friends the Duke and Duchess of Queensberry, who when he resided with them in his last
years insisted upon keeping his money or letting
him have small sums only at a time.

On February 15 Gay writes in high spirits to Swift :
" I have deferred writing to you from time to time
till I could give you an account of *The Beggar's
Opera.* It is acted at the Playhouse in Lincoln's Inn
Fields with such success that the playhouse hath
been crowded every night. To-night is the fifteenth
time of acting, and it is thought it will run a fortnight
longer. I have ordered Motte (*i.e.* the bookseller)
to send me the play the first opportunity. I made
no interest either for approbation or money ; nor
hath anybody been pressed to take tickets for my
benefit ; notwithstanding which, I think, I shall
make an addition to my fortune of between six and
seven hundred pounds. I know this account will
give you pleasure as I have pushed through this precarious affair without servility or flattery. . . . Lord
Cobham says that I should have printed it in Italian
over against the English, that the ladies might have
understood what they read. The outlandish (as
they now call it) hath been so thin of late that some
have called that *The Beggar's Opera* ; and if the run
continues, I fear I shall have remonstrance thrown
up against me by the Royal Academy of Music."
The word " Opera " is evidently omitted after " outlandish." The omission is however supplied in the
following from *The Daily Journal*: " We hear that the
British Opera commonly called *The Beggar's Opera* continues to attract at the Theatre in Lincoln's Inn Fields
with general applause, to the great Mortification of the

NANCY DAWSON.

From a mezzotint by James Watson.

performers and the admirers of Outlandish Opera in the Haymarket."

On March 20 Swift received the following from Gay, who by this time had received his benefit money, the receipts of four nights : "*The Beggar's Opera* hath now been acted forty-six times and was as full the last night as the first, and as yet there is not the least probability of a thin audience, though there is a discourse about the town that the members of the Royal Academy of Music design to solicit against its being played on the outlandish Opera days as it is now called. On the Benefit day of one of the actresses last week one of the players falling sick they were obliged to give out another play or dismiss the audience. A play was given out, but the audience called out for *The Beggar's Opera* and they were forced to play it or the audience would not have stayed. I have got by all this success seven or eight hundred pounds, and Rich deducting the whole charge of the house, hath cleared already near four thousand pounds. In about a month I am going to Bath with the Duchess of Marlborough and Mr. Congreve. . . . There is a mezzotinto published to-day of Polly, the heroine of *The Beggar's Opera*, who was before unknown and is now in so high vogue that I am in doubt whether her fame does not surpass that of the Opera itself."

When Gay was flush with the proceeds of his benefits he rushed off with the Duke and Duchess of Queensberry to Bath to spend his gains as speedily as possible, as we learn from Swift's bantering letter to Pope. "Mr. Gay's Opera," writes the Dean from Dublin, "hath been acted here twenty times, and my Lord Lieutenant (Lord Carteret) tells me it is very well performed ; he hath seen it often and approves it much. . . . I suppose Mr. Gay will return from the Bath with twenty pounds more flesh, and two hundred less in money. Providence never designed him to be above two and twenty by his thoughtlessness and gullibility."

Gay writing to Swift from Bath on May 16 alludes to Herring's attack upon him. He says: "*The Beggar's Opera* is acted here, but our Polly hath got no fame though the actors have got money. I have sent by Dr. Delany the Opera, Polly Peachum (i.e. the mezzotinto) and Captain Macheath. I would have sent you my own head (which is now engraving) to make up the gang, but it is not yet finished. I suppose you must have heard that I had the honour to have had sermons preached against my works by the court-chaplain, which I look upon as no small addition to my fame."

We give at p. 40 a reproduction of the mezzotinto. It is from a painting by J. Ellys, and the mezzotinto bears the name of the engraver " J. Faber " and the date 1728. Polly is here presented in quite a different aspect from that in which she appears in Hogarth's picture. She is not so handsome, not so placid, but has more character. She was then in the heyday of her fame, and she looks conscious of it. Ellys also painted her as a shepherdess (see p. 104), but to our thinking the pose is stiff and artificial, and the expression simpering. We may point out in passing that this portrait of Lavinia Fenton does duty as Kitty Clive in Mr. Wyndham's *History of Covent Garden Theatre*.

The correspondence between Gay's friends is evidence how they rejoiced in his success. In a letter from Pope to Swift on March 23, 1728, the poet writes : " Mr. Gay's opera has been acted near 40 days running and will certainly continue the whole season. So he has more than a fence about his thousand pounds ; he will soon be thinking of a fence about his two thousand." Bolingbroke's letter to Swift (undated) is in the same strain. " The only courtiers I know or have the honour of calling my friends," he writes, " are John Gay and Mr. Bowry. The former is at present so employed in the elevated airs of his Opera and the latter in the exaltation of his high dignity (that of Her Majesty's waterman) that I can scarce obtain a categorical answer from either to anything I say to them. But the Opera succeeds extremely to yours and my extreme satisfaction."

Towards the end of the year—the exact date is November 23, with once more the old blunder of " 1727," which the editor of the 1744 edition of Pope's works from which we quote should have corrected—we have Swift writing from Dublin to Gay thus : " I bought your Opera to-day for sixpence, a cursed print. I find there is neither dedication nor preface, both which wants I approve ; it is the *grand goût*. We are full of it *pro nodulo nostris* as London can be ; continually acting and houses crammed, and the Lord Lieutenant several times there laughing his heart out. I did not understand that the scene of Lockit and Peachum's quarrel was an imitation of one between Brutus and Cassius till I was told it. I wish Macheath when he was going to be hanged had imitated Alexander the Great when he was dying. I would have his fellow rogues desire his commands about a successor and he to answer let it be the most worthy, etc. We hear a million of stories about the Opera, of the applause at the song ' That was levelled at me,' when two great ministers were in a box together and all the world staring at them. I am heartily glad your Opera has mended your purse, though perhaps it may spoil your court. . . . Get me likewise Polly's mezzotinto. Lord how the schoolboys at Westminster and University lads adore you at this juncture ! Have you made as many men laugh as ministers can make weep ? . . . *The Beggar's Opera* hath knocked down Gulliver ; I hope to see Pope's Dulness (i.e. *Dunciad*) knock down *The Beggar's Opera*, but not till it hath fully done its job. To expose vice and make people laugh with innocence does more public service than all the ministers of State from Adam to Walpole."

Lively Mrs. Delany bears her testimony to the success of the Opera, but doubtless reflects the opinion of the " genteel " upper classes. " Yesterday," she writes, " I was at the rehearsal of the new Opera composed by Handel. I like it extremely, but the taste of the town is so depraved that nothing will be approved of but the burlesque. *The Beggar's Opera* entirely triumphs over the Italian one ; I have not yet seen it, but everybody that has seen it says it is very comical and full of humour ; the songs will soon be published and I will send them to you."

In a letter dated February 29, 1728, she tells Mrs. A. Granville that at a supper "we were very merry and sung *The Beggar's Opera*," and a fortnight afterwards returns to the one topic. " I desire," she writes, " you will introduce *The Beggar's Opera* at Gloucester ; you must have seen it everywhere but at Church, if you have a mind to be like the polite world." The Opera overcame all opposition, even that of the polite world, for it was given by amateurs. Again Mrs. Delany is the chronicler. " I desire," she tells her sister, on March 19, 1728, " you will pursue the scheme of performing *The Beggar's Opera*, but you must defer it till I come to you, for I put in for the part of Mrs. Slammerkin."

The victory of the English Opera was complete, and the defeat of the Italian variety was crushing by the end of 1729, to judge from Mrs. Delany's evidence. " The Opera (*i.e.* the Italian Opera) is too good for the vile taste of the town," she writes sadly. " It is condemned never more to appear on the stage after this night (December 20). I long to hear its dying song, poor dear swan. We are to have some old Opera revived, which I am sorry for. It will put people upon making comparisons between these singers and those that performed before, which will be a disadvantage among the ill-judging multitude. The present opera is disliked, because it is too much study and they love nothing but minuets and ballads ; in short *The Beggar's Opera* and *Hurlothrumbo* are only worthy of applause."

Polly was in great request at the many benefits which from time to time interrupted the run of the Opera. She was, we are certain—if it be true that physiognomy bespeaks the character—the soul of amiability, and her fellow actors and actresses did not have to ask her twice for her services. Her name in the bills must have put many pounds in their pockets. On March 14 she played Alinda in Beaumont and Fletcher's *Pilgrim* for Quin's benefit. Alinda is the leading female part, but it does not present much opportunity for effect. She had, however, to dress as a boy almost throughout, and possibly the costume was an attraction.

On the 18th of the same month she essayed a high flight—she played Ophelia. Genest is silent as to the representative of Hamlet, but we learn from an advertisement in *The Daily Journal* that it was Lacy Ryan. No record exists of her performance beyond the bare announcement, and whether she played well or ill it is impossible to say, but one may venture to think that she was sympathetic. On April 6 she assisted Walker as Leanthe in *Love and a Bottle*. The performance had a preliminary puff in *Mist's Weekly Journal* of March 16, in this facetious style: " We hear the late Mr. Farquhar's comedy *Love and a Bottle* is reviving at the New Play House for the Benefit of *Captain Macheath*. Two of his favourite wives will sing upon that Occasion, and gentle *Polly Peachum* is to—wear the breeches."

Lockit and Lucy, otherwise Hall and Mrs. Egleton, had a benefit on April 20, when was given " the second part of the comical *History of Don Quixote*. The part of *Marcella* by Miss Fenton with the song ' I burn—I burn,' " (*Daily Journal*). Tom D'Urfey wrote *Don Quixote*, a play in three parts ; Purcell put music to some of the songs in the first part, the well-known "Let the dreadful Engines" being one, and a duet, "Since times are so bad" in the second part. John Eccles is responsible for two in the second part, " I burn —I burn," and " Ye nymphs and sylvan gods." Eccles, a clever and prolific musician, aimed at being more than simply a song-writer, but it was his fate to be overshadowed by greater men. He composed music to Congreve's " Ode to St. Cecilia's Day," but it was never heard of after Handel's masterly setting. He was also responsible for the music in a revival of *Macbeth* in 1696—music bearing some resemblance to that of Matthew Locke, but not so good. " I burn—I burn " has nothing of the simplicity of *The Beggar's Opera* ballads, and one wonders how Polly dealt with it. As for the character of Marcella, when she is described as " a young, beautiful shepherdess of Cordona, extremely coy and averse to men at present, but afterwards passionately in love with Ambrosio," it can readily be imagined that Polly was suited with a part to which she was well qualified to do justice. Mrs. Bracegirdle was the original Marcella, so that she followed in good footsteps.

Three days after Mrs. Egleton's and Hall's benefit, Millward and Mrs. Berriman played in *A Bold Stroke for a Wife* "at the particular desire of several ladies of quality," with Polly as Betty—a chambermaid's part which gave her no trouble, for the maid appears but once, and has very little to say. On the 26th *The Busybody* was put on for the benefit of Hippisley, who played his favourite character of Sir Francis Gripe. *The Busybody* was followed by Ryan's *Cobler's Opera* with a part for Miss Fenton, but what part *The Daily Journal* advertisement does not state. Most likely it was Jenny Milton, originally played by Miss Warren. On the 29th Polly had her own benefit of *The Beaux' Stratagem* (alluded to elsewhere).

As in all probability all the benefit plays were new to Polly, it says much for her good nature that she took the trouble of studying fresh parts purely out of friendship. We make bold to say that Polly was as great a favourite inside the theatre as she was outside. There is no mention anywhere of squabbles or jealousies. The run of the opera proceeded without a hitch, and good luck followed wherever it went.

CHAPTER XVII

SIDELIGHTS ON EIGHTEENTH-CENTURY THEATRICAL MANAGEMENT

Extracts from John Rich's account-books—The profits of *The Beggar's Opera*—Gay's receipts from his benefits—Polly's benefits : the first one a failure—Sidelights from the account-books—Salaries, benefits, fines, cost of dresses, etc.

AFTER maintaining its position for sixty-two nights, on thirty-two of which it was played without a break, the run of the opera ended on June 19, the total receipts, including the various benefits, amounting to £9,183 19s. 6d. We take the figures as given by Mr. R. J. Smith, who has preserved in manuscript the names of the plays produced at the Lincoln's Inn Theatre, and their receipts, from the night when the new theatre was opened, in October 1714, to the year when Rich removed to Covent Garden. Mr. Smith does not give the source of his information in regard to the takings of *The Beggar's Opera*, but as in dealing with the accounts of 1735–6 he specifically mentions that they are from an old ledger kept by Richard Ford the treasurer, there is little doubt that he had access to Rich's books. That this was so is shown by the fact that the figures for the run of thirty-two nights given by " Dramaticus " in *Notes and Queries* (1st series, vol. i.), which we are told are from " the original account book of the manager, C. M. Rich," are identical with those in Mr. Smith's manuscript volume. Richard Ryan in his *Dramatic Anecdotes* puts the total receipts at £11,199 14s., but Ryan is not to be depended upon. His collection of stories is a very good (or bad) specimen of the many careless compilations relating to the stage which

191

exist, to the bewilderment and vexation of the student
of dramatic history. Nor is "Dramaticus" correct on
one or two points—that is, if Mr. R. J. Smith's figures
are to be accepted. Gay's benefits, he says, took
place on the third, sixth, ninth, and fifteenth nights,
and put £693 13s. 6d. into the author's pocket. But
according to Mr. Smith's records, there was also
an author's benefit on the eighteenth night, which
yielded £163 16s. 6d. making the total amount which
Gay drew £857 10s. Whether this be right or wrong,
Mr. Gilfillan and those who followed him without
enquiry are hopelessly out of it in fixing the amount
at £400.

It would be wearisome to give the receipts for
each performance ; roughly speaking, the sixty-two
nights work out at the average of £150 a night, the
highest sum being that taken at the forty-third performance, on April 11, when the figures were £198 17s.,
and the lowest on the fifty-first night, on May 10,
the amount dropping to £21 1s. No reason is
assigned for this sudden diminution, as on the night
before there was the respectable if not excessive
" house " of £69 12s. It may be, however, that as
four benefits took place immediately before, the
patrons of the theatre had spent their spare cash in
advance. At any rate, on May 17, when the next
performance of the opera was given, the receipts
rose to their former level and reached £134 18s. In
passing, it may be remarked that Richard Ryan gives
£53 6s. 6d. on the fifty-ninth night as the lowest
figures, and £194 13s. as the highest. He probably
had not the complete list before him, and in both
cases he was wrong. The King, Queen, and Princesses were present on the twenty-first night, but the
receipts were not anything out of the way.

In addition to Gay's benefits, there was one on
the thirty-third night for Mrs. Younger, a comedy
actress of great popularity and one of the mainstays
of Rich previous to the production of *The Beggar's
Opera*. Mrs. Younger, whose benefit realised £150 19s.,

NANCY DAWSON'S HORNPIPE DANCE.

From Mr. A. M. Broadley's Collection.

like Polly, as already mentioned, married into the aristocracy. Rich showed himself somewhat grasping in his reluctance to allow *The Beggar's Opera* to be put on for benefits. He probably could not well refuse Mrs. Younger, as she was not only a valuable member of his company, but must have suffered severely in pocket during the run of the Opera, but it was only natural he should look after his family or himself; and according to "Dramaticus" "an exception (in regard to benefits) was made in favour of John Rich, the brother of the manager," but this is a somewhat puzzling statement, as Rich's brother was Christopher Moyser Rich. The entry in Mr. Smith's records runs : "March 26. *The Beggar's Opera* for the benefit of Mr. John Rich, on the thirty-eighth night, £184 15s.," and if this be correct, the benefit was for Rich himself.

But until May 4 Rich would not permit any of the company to have the advantage of the Opera's success. Ryan had to put up with *The Fortune Hunters*, Quin with *The Pilgrim*, Mrs. Barbier with *Hamlet* (this was before her engagement for the production of *The Beggar's Opera* in Dublin), Mrs. Bullock with *The Bath Unmasked*, Mr. Leveridge with *The Fop's Fortune*, "Macheath Walker" with *Love and a Bottle*, and Hippisley with *The Busybody* and *The Cobler's Opera*.

The advertisement announcing *Love and a Bottle*, played on Walker's night, announces, among other attractions, "Leanthe, with singing in the character of the page by Miss Fenton"; and "Mrs. Trudge, with singing after the French manner by Mrs. Egleton" (Lucy Lockit). There was also dancing by two celebrated French exponents of the art, Nivelon and Poitier. Dancing was at this time inseparable from all theatrical productions, no matter what the play was, and M. Nivelon was an especial attraction. He was the author of *The Rudiments of Genteel Behaviour*, published in 1737, an elaborate treatise on dancing, walking, bowing, and deportment generally. The

13

book is illustrated with excellent engravings, and
throws an interesting light on eighteenth-century
fashion and deportment. Any one who desires to
know how the minuet ought to be danced, is advised
to consult *The Rudiments*, but with the warning that
the proper performance of this most courtly of
dances is not to be acquired without infinite study
and practice. Leanthe, a "breeches" part, must
have suited Polly extremely well, and a scene with
Pindress, a lady's-maid, who has fallen in love with
the page, indicates that she must have been much
slimmer than Hogarth has represented her in his
picture of *The Beggar's Opera*. "I could manage
him with one hand—See here, Madam," says the
amorous tirewoman, and the stage direction is,
"Takes him in her arms and is running away."
Leanthe has to sing one song " set by Mr. Richardson," but Mrs. Trudge's singing "after the French
manner " must have been interpolated. There is no
song for her in the 1728 edition of *Love and a Bottle*.

All the beneficiaries seem to have done very well
by the sale of tickets, with one exception, Nivelon,
whose amount does not reach £50 ; and this is somewhat curious, as Nivelon was paid better than the
stars of the company, Rich evidently regarding him
as a great draw. The receipts for tickets in every
case exceeded the amount taken at the doors, and
it may be that no *bénéficiaire* lost much by being
denied *The Beggar's Opera*. One would have thought,
however, that Polly, who had virtually made the
success of the piece, would have been privileged.
But this was not so, and she was expected to content
herself with Cherry in *The Beaux' Stratagem*, and
getting what advertisement she could out of heading
the bill with "*For the Benefit of Polly.*" The date of
her benefit was April 29, and on April 19 appeared
in *The Daily Journal* some poor verses, not worth
quoting, headed "Advice to Polly." They were
evidently intended to give a fillip to the benefit ten
days later. It would seem, however, that Miss

Fenton did not consider it fair that all the glory should be given to " Polly " and only a reflection descend upon herself, and maybe she gave Rich a piece of her mind, for the advertisement of April 27 is headed " *For the Benefit of Miss Fenton*," and announces " the part of Cherry by Miss Fenton, with singing by Miss Fenton." The lady, naturally enough, could not see why her benefit should be something like *Hamlet* with Hamlet omitted. " Polly " was all very well in its way, but it was only natural that she desired to remind the public that she was also " Miss Fenton."

For some reason dancing was not included in the programme provided for her benefit, but in addition to *The Beaux' Stratagem* were " Since Times are so bad, etc.," a duet sung by Mr. Leveridge and Mr. Salway, the music by Purcell to D'Urfey's words in the second Act of *Don Quixote*, " a Scottish ballad by Miss Fenton," and several " Ballad Duettos " by her and Mr. Walker. Lavinia evidently expected a bumper house, and special preparations were made. The pit boxes were " laid together " at 5s. each, 2s. was charged for the gallery, double the usual price, " and servants will be admitted to keep Places on the Stage which will be commodiously enlarged." According to the " Life," this " laying " of the pit boxes together " offended the best part of her Friends, in so much that she had a great many of her tickets returned, but the generosity of Mr. R(ic)h made amends for this disappointment, for he took the Money for that night to himself, and on the Saturday following gave her a benefit again, when *The Beggar's Opera* was acted with great applause before a crowded Audience, and Polly exerted herself so far that the Claps of her officious friends were so frequent and loud that it took half the beauty off the performance."

If the biographer is right as to the reason of the second benefit following the first so quickly, Rich of course is entitled to be credited with generosity. Whatever was the cause, the receipts from *The Beaux'*

Stratagem only amounted to £95 19s. 6d.—£47 15s. from tickets and £48 4s. 6d. in money—and the girl must have been greatly disappointed, especially as Walker, not nearly so attractive, though the principal character in the Opera, on *his* night made £167 16s., part of this perhaps being due to her own appearance in a " breeches " part. In spite of the statement in the " Life," we are inclined to think the failure of the first benefit was because she did not appear in the part over which the town had gone mad, and we can imagine that she did not hesitate to tell Rich so. Anyway, on her second benefit, the forty-eighth night, the takings amounted to £155 4s., of which only £17 12s. were from tickets—a pretty strong proof that she could rely upon the public without soliciting private patronage.

The opportunity Mr. R. J. Smith had of copying the accounts of the season 1735–6 contained in the old ledger enables one to form some idea of the salaries paid to actors and actresses of those days. A note preceding the figures states that the ledger " lacked many leaves that had by the devastation of some petty tradesman been turned to goth-like purposes and the remainder only preserved by the purchase of Mr. Richardson of the Hotel Piazza C. G., in whose custody same now is with proper appreciation for value and curiosity.—May 1818." Whatever may have been the amount of information devoted to " goth-like purposes," sufficient remains to make the old ledger extremely interesting.

We find that Hippisley contracted with Rich for £180 for the season; but this was not so good as it seemed, as the amount he was paid worked out at 155 nights at twenty shillings a night. Hippisley as a comic actor evidently was regarded as a greater attraction than Walker the singer, for the latter's contract was for 16s. 8d. " for every acting day throughout the season," which for 172 days comes to £143 6s. 8d. The entry under " Mr. Stephens " reads quaintly. " Acted under contract for Season of £200 and took on account monthly £24. His account charged with a forfeit in *Fair Penitent* of 4*s.* Also with a crutch stick lost, 10*s.* 6*d.*" Mr. Bullock (he played Jemmy Twitcher, a minor part in *The Beggar's Opera*), was paid at the rate of 6*s.* 8*d.* per day ; Aston, better known as Tony Aston, also had to be satisfied with 6*s.* 8*d.* a day, being charged two guineas for the services of Hippisley and Stephens, who played at his benefit. The scale descends with Mr. Houghton (Crook-Fingered Jack of the Opera), who though a decent actor could not draw more than 3*s.* 4*d.* a day. Clark (who played Filch) had also to be contented with 3*s.* 4*d.* and no benefit. Mr. Hallam, who met with so melancholy a fate at the hands of the irascible Macklin, was not considered worth more than half a crown a day and no benefit. Mrs. Hallam, on the other hand, drew as much as 16*s.* 8*d.* per day and—a touch of human nature this— " was mulct several times 4*s.* during the season." Fines presumably. Mr. Edward Thomas and Mr. Pritchard were probably supers. They were paid 1*s.* 8*d.* a night. The performer who was paid the highest salary, as already noted, was the French dancer Nivelon. He had £1 5*s.* a night.

Among the ladies the beautiful Mrs. Horton was a leading star. She received £250 for the season, with no benefit. Mrs. Bullock did better than her husband, receiving 16*s.* 8*d.* a day. Mrs. Martin had 5*s.*— if she was the Mrs. Martin who was the original Mrs. Peachum, one would have expected she would have had more—Mrs. Templar and Miss Eliza Rogers the like ; but Miss " Sue " Rogers, who perhaps was very young, drew but 1*s.* 8*d.* A dozen or more of ladies filling minor parts were paid salaries of various amounts, ranging from 1*s.* 8*d.*, which appears to have been the lowest depth, to 5*s.* A note tells us that the pages containing the salaries paid to the leading actresses other than Mrs. Horton are missing, which is a pity.

It is impossible to say whether the salaries of

1734 were more or less than those of 1728 ; probably
they did not differ much. The point to be remarked
is that the scale was based upon the " season," which
seems to have consisted of a fixed number of nights,
but that payments were only made on " acting
nights." This fact throws some doubt on the statement that Polly received fifteen shillings a week
when first engaged and thirty shillings after the first
night of *The Beggar's Opera*. No one was on a weekly
salary, and it is pretty certain that Polly's " contract "
would not be different from the rest. Of course the
" benefit " system must be taken into account when
the question of salaries is considered.

Some of the benefits at Lincoln's Inn Fields
Theatre recorded by Mr. R. J. Smith are of interest.
On March 19, 1730, *The Beggar's Opera* was played
for Quin's benefit, with the heavy stagey actor as
Macheath—the part he had once refused to play.
The receipts were £113 13s. 6d., of which £93 16s.
were from tickets. Leveridge put on *Hamlet* for his
benefit in April of the same year, being himself the
First Gravedigger—surely a most whimsical choice
on the part of the great singer. But strange liberties
were taken with Shakespeare in the eighteenth
century, and for anything we know the character
may have been played " with a song." At all events
he had a bumper house, no less than £235, evidence
enough of his popularity. Hulett, the vocal practical
joker, who sang Macheath's songs better than Walker,
could only draw £83 13s. 6d. when the Opera was
revived for his benefit. In March 1732 it was played
on behalf " of a gent of Eaton (*sic*) School," £154 2s.
being realised, and in the May following it was given
for the benefit " of the servants on account of their
arrears." It is to be hoped that the £66 7s. taken on
this occasion sufficed for their needs. Lastly, Miss
Norsa, who achieved great success as Polly during
the second run of the opera at Covent Garden, had
a benefit on May 26, 1733, and was the recipient of
£142 3s.

Actors have a curious fancy for attempting parts somewhat out of their line, and Walker was no exception to the rule. We find him taking a benefit at Covent Garden, when he played Pierre in *Venice Preserved*, with several " pieces of music between the acts." The advertisement announcing the performance informs the public that a " significant reason will be given hereafter for this undertaking, and in the meantime I cannot omit acknowledging my gratitude to the Master of this Company ; he has behaved upon this occasion in a most gentleman-like Manner. To my very good masters of the town. T. Walker." The " significant reason," no doubt, was that poor Walker was in very low water, and that the " Master of the Company," otherwise John Rich, had let him off some incidental expenses in connection with the benefit.

Many of the details of the accounts which Mr. R. J. Smith extracted from the old ledger are worth reproducing. Some of the women dressers were paid 1*s*. 8*d*. and others 1*s*. 6*d*., each acting day, the charwoman had 1*s*., the sweeper 1*s*. 6*d*., and the constable 2*s*. per day. The expenses of the leading ladies in the way of costumes were very heavy. For Mrs. Porter, the famous tragic actress, £63 were paid for " two rich suits of clothes." Mrs. Gould is debited with £7 17*s*. 6*d*. for " a black velvet gown and coat," and 12*s*. for " a widow's crape scarfe and three hoods." The men's dresses were equally costly. One entry runs : " To a suit of clothes for Mr. Ryan of Scarlet and Silver, £25 4*s*." Another : " For a coat and breeches of cloth laced with gold, and a green silk waistcoat trimm'd the same for Mr. Bridgwater, £15." A suit of olive-coloured velvet, laced with silver, figures at £13 13*s*., but for whom is not stated. Mr. Vincent is down for £1 11*s*. 6*d*. for seven pairs of stockings, and Mr. Smart's suit of crimson velvet trimmed with " a gold shape lace " cost £16 16*s*. An elaborate costume for some actor not named is described as " a blue cloth Coat faced with scarlet and a Waistcoat do. trimm'd with Gold and dark brown velvet coat embrd. with Silver and an orange coloured waistcoat embroidered with silk and silver." The mere description stimulates the imagination, and £43 possibly was not too much for such gorgeousness. It is to be presumed that the management paid the bills.

The forfeits or fines for the season amounted to £19 6s. Some of them were as low as 1s., and in one instance Mrs. Hallam—this lady seems to have been a systematic offender—is charged as much as £4 3s. 4d., which, however, appears afterwards to have been remitted. Other fines were incurred by Mrs. Hallam. One amounting to £3 4s. 10d., and another to £3 6s. 8d., seem to have been paid. Mrs. Hallam was corpulent almost to unwieldiness, and was most likely anything but punctual at rehearsals. Probably also she was good-natured and gave away more orders than the management would tolerate. Notwithstanding her portly presence, the public always liked to see her in characters which received no advantage from her figure. One can hardly imagine any part more unsuitable to her fifteen or sixteen stone than the melancholy, misled bride of a night, Monimia, yet she was fond of attempting it, and apparently the audience were satisfied. Of course her performance may have been amusing without being pathetic. Quin, who was never too delicate in his jests, observing at rehearsal one morning a tub on the stage, left from a performance in which it had been introduced, affected to be puzzled at what could be its use; then pretending its meaning had suddenly dawned upon him, exclaimed, " Oh aye, I see what it is. Mrs. Hallam's stays which she played Monimia in last night." Probably this sounded funny with Quin's solemn and weighty delivery, otherwise—— well, it was as good as the majority of the quips in the Jest Books of the day.

Coming back to the forfeits, Mr. Smith observes : " Mr. Stoppelaer was fined 16s. for sending in orders,

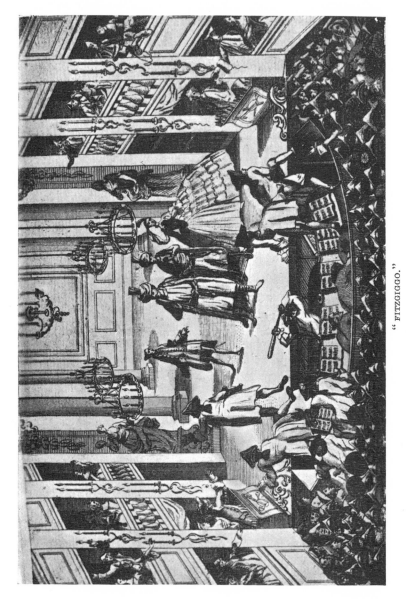

" FITZGIGGO."

From a caricature in Mr. A. M. Broadley's Collection, showing Miss Brent, John Beard and Signor Tenducci in the opera of *Artaxerxes*.

200]

and probably some of the other forfeits were only the amount in value for the admission when the actor took such a liberty as to write or overwrite. It is only Mr. Stoppelaer's case that in any way shows the ground of the forfeits."

There is an instructive note in regard to the visits of the Royal Family. " The usual charge," says Mr. Smith, "appears to have been £5 5s. There are entries upon their going eleven times, but only five have sums carried out, which in four instances were discharged afterwards. It might be the fact that on the other evenings Royalty carried ready money." Highly commendable if so. One is curious to know what is the practice nowadays. One of the women dressers supplied feathers, a very important adjunct to a lady's head-dress at that time, and she was paid £9 4s. for the season. When knee-breeches were worn, stockings were as indispensable as they were expensive, and it is not surprising to find that the hosiery bill came to £60.

The various taxes and other dues for Covent Garden ran thus : Land Tax for one year, £30 ; Window tax, £1 10s. ; Water (New River), £4 ; Doctor's rate and Church repairs, £18 6s. 8d. ; Scavengers, £5 ; Poor's rate, £15. The rates and taxes for Lincoln's Inn Fields Theatre were : Land Tax, £7 10s. ; Window tax, £1 10s. ; New River Water, £3 ; and Poor's Rate, £5 16s. 8d. The ground rent of Lincoln's Inn Fields Theatre was £87, less taxes. Half went to a Mr. Welchman, and half to Lord Chief Justice Reeve.

Among the miscellaneous items may be mentioned : " Oct. 13. Mr. Hippisley. Paid him a bill for treating the Company the 22nd day of January last, £11 10s. 11d." (Did Hippisley ever pay his score, one wonders ?) " Dr. Pepusch " (spelt Papush after the fashion of Mrs. Delany) " Paid on account at several times, £8 8s." (" For what reason ? " queries Mr. Smith). " Mr. Noon for Fireworks. Each night's fireworks in the Rape (of Proserpine) is 7s. 6d. Whole

Season after deducting forfeits 10s. amounts to
£8 2s. 6d." Then comes " Paid the tailor's men to
drink by Mr. J. Rich, 10s. 6d ; " " Paid the Guards for
the dismiss, 14s. ; " " Paid Mr. Robertson a bill for
Coffee drank behind the scenes, £2 3s. 2d." With
£14 10s. paid for lamps for 191 nights, we take leave of
the old ledger so far as general expenses are concerned.

The accounts conclude with a list of the moneys
debited to the various members of the Company
under the heading of " orders." Mr. Smith prefaces
the figures with the following : " It is impossible to
draw any certain conclusion as to the system, if there
was any, to regulate the number of orders that might
be given nightly, or otherwise, by any actor. The
profuse distribution of them by Mr. Ryan would
create a doubt, although regularly debited with the
full amount, if there was not some understanding or
drawback upon the total when settled at the end of the
season. He appears to have sent in ' by note or
orders ' only." About this one has nothing to say
beyond noting Ryan's lavishness, he having given
away during the Season, orders for box, pit and
gallery, amounting to £73 19s. Mr. Chapman comes
next with £16 19s. ; and the lowest donors are represented by Mr. Smith, Mr. Tench and Miss Brunette,
who gave away a two-shilling gallery order each.
It was probably as much as or even more than
they could afford. The only part about the orders
worth noting is that out of thirty-four members of
the Company, only five gave away box orders, all the
rest, even the beautiful Mrs. Horton, contenting
themselves with the pit and gallery.

Two items we should like to have seen recorded—
the sum paid for candles and the salary of the candle-
snuffer. They are perhaps in the sheets missing,
thanks to " the devastation of some petty tradesman."

CHAPTER XVIII

A " GAY LADY " OF THE PERIOD

Polly's biography resumed—The author's insinuations—He compares Polly
to Sally Salisbury—The history of Sally—The " gay ladies " of the
eighteenth century—Sally's frolic with Matthew Prior—Goldsmith's
favourite ballad—Henry Carey's remonstrance concerning his " Sally in
our Alley "—Sally's escapades in Holborn and at Hampstead—The Hon.
John Finch and his awkward adventure in a Chandos Street tavern

IN one respect Polly Peachum is without a parallel.
Amid the noise and hubbub created by her success
she pursued the even tenor of her way, so far
as we know, undisturbed and level-headed. She is
credited with no adventures, no escapades, no scandalous intrigues. One may venture to assert that she
fulfilled her engagement at the theatre with scrupulous
punctuality, that she had not the caprices of Peg
Woffington, or Kitty Clive, or Mrs. Abington, to vex
and harry the soul of the manager, and that she
never offended the audience by waywardness or ill
temper. We can fancy her always placid, always
natural, always in a good humour. Her portraits
seem to suggest that life went well with her, that
she was ever basking in the smiles of Fortune. Her
career during the run of the Opera and when she was
in the heyday of her glory, may not—apart from the
attentions of the Duke of Bolton—have been un-
eventful, but the records of the times are provokingly
silent on the subject. Horace Walpole had not then
fully developed his unapproachable skill in creating
and detailing lively and malicious gossip ; she was
too early for the journalists of the type of Lady Mary
Wortley Montagu, Mrs. Delany, and Lady Mary
Coke. The lampoonists did their best to suggest
scandal; the " Life " scattered insinuations broadcast,

203

but we fail to find corroboration or proof anywhere. Perhaps after all, as in the case of Canning's knife-grinder, there was no story to tell. In default of other sources of information, we can only fall back upon her solitary biographer, and dip once more into his prolix and, despite its pretensions, somewhat barren " Life."

It is somewhat odd that throughout the volume *The Beggar's Opera* is never once mentioned by name —perhaps the writer considered that what every one knew could be let alone—and he contents himself by remarking that consequent upon her success Polly became " the most celebrated Toast in Town ; she gained new Admirers every time she appeared on the stage, and Persons of the Highest Rank and Quality made love to her ; insomuch that by the presents she has received, she lives in ease and plenty, keeps her servants and appears abroad in as much Magnificence as a lady." This is only what was to be expected, and does not throw much light upon her daily life, her occupations, her amusements. One point in the foregoing extract, however, calls for comment in justice to Polly's fair fame. The writer speaks of the " presents," which enabled her to live in " ease and plenty," and in this connection it is only right to remember that in the eighteenth century presents to an actress did not carry with them an equivocal meaning. Macklin remarks that the giving of presents " was the mode of conferring favours on the Performers of those days without any impeachment of the latter's characters, either for manners, infidelity, &c. They were considered as pledges of public esteem, and as such shewn by the Performers to their friends and acquaintances."

One may assume that Polly had hosts of admirers, if not suitors. The statement has been repeated times out of number that she was so pestered by pertinacious and unwelcome gallants, that a number of young bloods formed themselves into a bodyguard, to see her from the theatre to her lodgings. It may have been so—we hope it was so—but we have not been able to find corroboration in any contemporaneous records. Certainly, if for no other reason than protection from the thieves and riff-raff haunting Lincoln's Inn Fields at night, such a bodyguard may have been necessary. The point is of no importance beyond emphasising the difficulty of ascertaining anything definite concerning this most elusive of popular actresses. Most ladies of the stage like to live in the glare of the footlights outside the theatre as well as inside, but not so Polly Peachum—there is, at least, no evidence of such an inclination.

Among the crowd of admirers that buzzed round her, we are told of " a noble knight of the Bath," a spark known by the name of " Horse-Courser-General," a description of whose wooing the author gives in too " racy " a fashion for present-day reading, and " a young amorous D—— (? the Duke of Bolton), who tired with Hymenical (*sic*) duty would needs be admitted among the Number of her humble Servants." While she was in the height of her popularity " the Portuguese nobleman mentioned before, hearing of Polly's fine success, gratefully remembered her generosity to him when he was under confinement, sent her £400, and fearing that she should be quite run away with by the Report he daily received of the Number of her slaves, he came over himself to enjoy the pleasures, which all the World covets, and to assure her that the Portuguese Ladies were mere Dowdies in Comparison of (*sic*) his dear Polly."

Considering the coarse taste and freedom of the times, the author is fairly considerate to Polly, but he oversteps the mark when he says " that her Amours are not inferior to those of the celebrated Sally Salisbury, nor have her Gallants been less generous to her than they were to that once famous Beauty." However, he is good enough to add, " to do Polly justice, she is not to be mentioned in comparison with Sally, for it is well known by those who have had the pleasure of Conversation with Polly, that she has a penetrating Genius, whereas the other had only some low life flights of Wit to recommend her, and by being twice in her company her Conversation became insipid, dull and nauseous." But to estimate the value of this apology—for the writer evidently places Polly in regard to morals on a level with Sally—it is only right to say something about this famous lady of pleasure.

Sally, indeed, cannot well be kept out of the chronicles of the times. She cuts a considerable figure in the fashionable, free-and-easy gaiety of the town. She introduces herself at every turn, and the evident delight the scribblers take in dragging in her name whenever they have the chance is quite typical of eighteenth-century life. Sally Salisbury, Nancy Dawson, and later on Kitty Fisher, Charlotte Summers, and Fanny Murray, not to mention their sister of a much lower grade, Kate Hackabout, were ladies who, if they existed nowadays, would not be known outside the circles which found attraction in their society. In Polly Peachum's time there was no such reticence, there was no attempt at concealment. The Sally Salisburys openly flaunted themselves, and their doings were retailed with much zest. The whirligig of profligacy went giddily round. The " bloods," whether young or old, never troubled to make the slightest apology for their amusements, no matter how debased they might be. Noblemen were not ashamed of sordid amours, and nobody was thought any the worse of for going to bed drunk every night, or for keeping a mistress, if not more than one.

All this is an oft-told tale. The picture as a whole is one of unbridled self-indulgence, and would hardly be worth dwelling upon, but for the bits of " character " which the student of the times comes across, and the glimpses of real life which the lifting of the veil discloses. The career of Sally Salisbury does both, and she has been referred to so often in these pages that it is hardly out of place to give her more extended notice.

Two biographies of the hussy are extant; one fairly soberly written, considering the nature of the material, and the other in which the author has not scrupled to let himself go. The title page of the first runs thus in the loose grammar of the day : "*The Genuine History of Mrs. Sarah Prydden, usually called Sally Salisbury, and Her Gallants, Regularly containing the real Story of her Life.* As well, the Adventures not yet known, as those Matters which are True in the Songs, Accounts & Memoirs already Published of her ; and rectifying what in those papers is related wrong. Together with her Behaviour in Confinement, and at her Trial, with the most material Passages that happen'd upon it. Done at the Instigation of certain Persons of Quality." The second is entitled "*Authentic Memoirs of the Life, Intrigues, and Adventures of the Celebrated Sally Salisbury, with True Characters of her most Considerable Gallants.* By Capt. Charles Walker." The *Genuine History* was printed for Andrew Moor in Paternoster Row, and the price was a shilling; the *Authentic Memoirs* bears no printer's name, and was sold for two shillings.

Sarah was a bricklayer's daughter. She was born at Shrewsbury, and her parents coming to London, her father enlisted in the foot guards, " to shield himself from his clamorous Creditors," and became an inhabitant of the Parish of St. Giles-in-the-Fields. Mr. Prydden appears to have been a very versatile personage, for besides being a soldier he also followed his trade of a bricklayer, and " having formerly been pretty conversant among the Country Attornies, as an Addition to his own Business, set up likewise for a Solicitor "—about as queer a jumble of occupations as one can well imagine. Sally seems pretty early to have gone her own road. She was apprenticed when she was nine years old to a sempstress in Duke's Place, near Aldgate, " to learn Plain worke," but soon after ran away and returned home, when she showed herself to be something more than a pickle. She stole a stuff-satinet petticoat from her mother, and decked herself out in it for a " Hopping Ball." " Dress and Dancing were the sole youthful delights of our Sally," says Captain Charles Walker, " and she never wanted a gallant suitable to her years to introduce her into every Hop of Eminence about the Town." This conduct so enraged the military and legal bricklayer that he " severely disciplined her with a horsewhip," whereupon Sally, to escape a second chastisement, which had been promised her, disappeared during the night. After her first escapade, she seems to have settled down to life in the streets, chiefly among the Covent Garden costermongers, and according to the season of the year " Shell'd Beans and Pease, cry'd Nosegays & Newspapers, peal'd Walnuts, made Matches, turn'd Bunter (*i.e.* a picker-up of rags in the streets) etc., well knowing that a wagging Hand always gets a Penny."

The author of the *Genuine History* contradicts this, as well as the story of her mother's stuff-satinet petticoat, but whether true or false is not now of the least importance. Captain Walker, impatient to get on to more important matters of an amatory nature, has nothing further to say about " our Sally's Childish pranks," and his rival fills up the blank by informing us that when she was fifteen she sold oranges at Drury Lane Theatre. All these fascinating waifs and strays of the stage appear to have tried their hands at this trade, if we may believe their biographers. Indeed, the term " orange girl " would almost seem to have been a euphemism for another profession. It is doing the pretty wenches no injustice if one ventures to suggest that more often than not they were not unwilling novitiates. One of the sons of Frederick, Prince of Wales, when a boy, innocently summed up the matter in a very concise form. Horace Walpole tells the story with great glee (also another equally naïve of the same lad for the details of which we refer the curious reader to the *Letters.*)

WESTCOMBE HOUSE, GREENWICH.

The re idence of " Polly Peachum."

From *Watts' Views*, after Paul Sandby.

208]

He writes : " T'other day, as he was with the Prince of Wales, Kitty Fisher passed by, and the child named her. The Prince to try him asked who that was ? ' Why, a Miss '—' A Miss,' said the Prince of Wales, ' why, are not all girls Misses ? ' ' Oh, but a particular sort of Miss—a Miss that sells oranges.' ' Is there any harm in selling oranges ? ' ' Oh ! but they are not such oranges as you buy—I believe they are a sort that my brother Edward buys.' "

Orange girl of " a sort " or not, Sally attracted the notice of Mrs. Barry, who, observing a peculiar sweetness in her voice, " had once an intention to instruct her in gesture and pronunciation in order to qualify her for the Stage," but, owing to an unguarded remark of a " Person of Quality " that it was a pity one so young and tender should be exposed to the temptations of the stage, the great actress took no further notice of the girl. Whether Mrs. Barry was really solicitous about Sally's future or was " jealous of the Nobleman's Affections, lest so charming an object should allure him from herself," the author is unable to decide. If Tom Brown's malicious banter of Mrs. Barry has any foundation—to the effect that she did not know who had given her five guineas the night before, unless the same sum were placed in her hand by the same person the next morning—jealousy may well have been the reason.

Perhaps Mrs. Barry was right, for Sally soon after attracted the notice of a Colonel Salisbury, who, wonderful to say, remembering the times, " thought her of too unripe a beauty to have an intrigue with, having others at his Devotion of fuller and superior charms, and went off to Bath, not dreaming that he was carrying little Sally's Heart away with him." Sally was not to be denied, and managed somehow to follow the Colonel with an idea of renewing the acquaintance, and " hearing that the cleverest Lasses were to dance for a Smock," she saw in the contest a good chance of bringing her admirer to her feet. " Several competitors," we read, " appeared upon

14

the Stage who delighted, tho' faintly, the eyes of
the Gentlemen gazers; while the Smock, the noble
object of their Efforts, was expanded in full view,
adorn'd with Ribbons and enrich'd with the finest
Lace. But immediately upon Sally's entering the
lists in a Party-coloured Petticoat and Lovely Shift,
the spectators were ravished with the sweet assurance
of her Air and the symmetrical Proportion of her
Limbs, her Legs and Feet having powers to excite,
like the face and voice of others." With such attractions no wonder Sally not only carried off the smock
but the Colonel as well.

After some months of gaiety at Bath she returned
to London, and falling on evil days sold " plays,
pamphlets, and other papers and stood to dispose of
them, or herself, at the corner of Pope's Head Alley
in Cornhill." The writer adds, " I remember still as
I went that way to school I was told there was the
beautifullest Wench who sold papers about Cornhill
that ever appeared on a Sunny Day," and after this
praise it is not strange to read that she was patronised
" by a wealthy Dutchman, but her fancy still dwelt
on the Colonel, whom she had met once more, and
appropriated his name." Apparently she could not
be constant, and the next we hear of her is that she
is lodging at " a Distiller's in New Street by St.
Martin's Lane," and here she got into sad disgrace
and was taken to the Bridewell in Tothill's Fields,
Westminster.

Her career after this is closely connected with
two notorious elderly ladies whose names were known
to every gallant about town. One of these dames—
Mrs. Needham—Hogarth has vividly drawn in No. 1
of *The Harlot's Progress*. The other was a Mrs.
Wisebourne, or Wybourn, described by the author
of the *Authentic Memoirs* as " a grave elderly
Woman in St. Martin's Parish, who was every day
very needful in the world; yet every day did a
World of mischief : who kept a House of free Hospi-
tality, but made folks pay vastly dear for what they

had." Under the skilful tuition of these experienced
ladies Sally had adventures without number. She
posed as "an Esquire's Daughter privately flown
from her solitary Friends in the country; at other
times she was a wealthy Tradesman's child in Cornhill, who being disappointed of her Lover by her
Father's Severity, for Revenge apply'd to Mother
Wisebourne for redress. At other times she was a
Nobleman's Niece, or the usual cant of a young
Miliner or Parson's daughter," from which we gather
that the wiles and devices of Aspasia are as old as
the hills. Moreover, we are told, thanks to the
wisdom of Mrs. Wybourn, that she was possessed of
a secret which would have enabled her to deceive
Henry VIII., or even that still more experienced
personage Colonel Charteris. Twenty-six times, the
veracious historian assures us, did Mrs. Salisbury
pass for a priestess of Diana!

Money came in plentifully; indeed, on one
occasion it was literally poured upon her. Captain
Charles Walker found the incident related unblush-
ingly in some broadside verses entitled *Remarks upon
Remarks on a Certain Lady and her Sparks* (in which
the inevitable Sir Robert Fagg figured, and not to
his advantage), and incorporated the details in his
Authentic Memoirs, to which we refer the curious
reader who would like further particulars. The
author of a single-sheet biography bearing the heading
Effigies, Parentage, etc., which, wonderful to say,
contains little to offend, describes her at the time
when she was at the height of her notoriety. The
broadside is adorned with a portrait (quaintly termed
"Effigies") which bears a striking resemblance to
another Sarah—her Imperious Grace of Marlborough
—so striking, indeed, that we cannot help suspecting
that the counterfeit presentment of one Sarah was
made to do duty for the other. Our biographer says:
"She's reckoned to be between thirty and forty
years of Age," says the author, "and still so handsome in her person that I could wish her mind was

within sixty, nay, an hundred degrees thereof. It is said that her beauty shone very bright about the age of five or six, when being at school her ready wit and quickness of apprehension gave very early proof of her extraordinary Parts and of her being a very wonderful Woman, for, in short, she soon outstripped the whole school as well at her Needle as her Books ; in a word, such was her bright Genius that she learned everything unless 'twas the Practise of Piety, and to walk in the Paths of Virtue, to which most believe her natural inclinations made her almost a stranger."

The author affects not to be too hard upon her frailty ; indeed, he treats her with great indulgence when he says : " Don't mistake me, I'm not going to accuse Mrs. Salisbury of the Crimes which are common to Town Coquets or the Ladies of Drury ; far from me be it so to act, for I could not say that ever I heard she was a common ——— ; no, she was totally unacquainted with those sort of ways, she understood neither their manners nor their customs, their Cant nor their Conversation, by a discreet (if modesty may upon any score be called discretion) Deportment won the Ears, Eyes and Hearts of her beholders and having captivated the Affections of several made them her Tool which she thought most encouraging and beneficial."

He then proceeds to tell us that after the Colonel's death she launched out into a free-and-easy mode of life and " was so much in vogue that even the populace composed a song about her, called ' Sally in our Alley.' What reason the vulgar had to do this I do not know, for nothing is more certain than that they had very little knowledge of her ; her whole time being spent in the society of nothing inferior to gentlemen, and I blush heartily to think what I dare not write—viz., that so many of our noblemen could delight in ———, and yet nothing is more sure than several of them did, for otherwise she never could have lived in that Pomp and made the appearance of—— A Cook Maid, a chambermaid, housemaid and footman, were generally the least of her equipage, a good house well furnished, and three or four dishes at Table were the least expense of one day."

In connection with the songs composed about Sally it is interesting to note that Henry Carey was sorely exercised lest his "Sally in our Alley" should be thought to have the slightest reference to the notorious wanton; and to protect himself he had the following printed on the copies of his song: "A Vulgar Error having long prevailed among many Persons, who imagine *Sally Salisbury* the subject of the Ballad, the Author begs leave to undeceive and assure them it has not the least allusion to her, he being a stranger to her very Name at the time this song was composed. For as Innocence and Virtue were ever the Boundaries of his Muse, so in this little Poem I had no other view than to set forth the Beauty of a Chaste and disinterested Passion, even in the lowest Class of human Life."

One of the most popular ballads concerning her was entitled "The Three Sallies." The author, evidently desirous of having as many strings to his bow as possible, brought in Sally Salisbury, Calico Sally, and "Sally" Faustina! Who Calico Sally may have been we have no idea—probably she was of Sally Salisbury's profession—and what Signora Faustina does in this galley is a puzzle. A passage in Forster's *Life of Goldsmith* bears upon the subject. "One day," he writes, "Goldsmith being in company where many ladies were, and a ballad singer happening to sing his favourite air of Sally Salisbury, under the window, his envy and vanity broke out and he exclaimed with some passion 'How miserably this woman sings!' 'Pray, Doctor,' rejoined the lady of the house, 'could you do it better?' 'Yes, madam,' was the answer, amid a general titter of distrust, 'and the company shall be judges.' He instantly began singing with some ear and no inconsiderable degree of pathos, and he obtained the universal suffrage of the company." What was this air ? There was certainly no song written about Sally in the time of her notoriety likely to have been sung by Goldsmith, especially in the company of ladies —yet one can hardly imagine *two* Sally Salisburys.

About this time Sally made the acquaintance of Matthew Prior, and once during a visit to Spring Gardens she played him, in one of the " critical " retreats, as Horace Walpole would probably call them, a cruel trick—probably when the poet was full of wine—" she privately clipp'd off all the End of his Periwigg, he knowing nothing of the matter (as a matter of fact his head was buried in his Cap at the time), and then running abruptly into the Garden among the Crowd of Belles and Beaux, he follow'd her hastily to the great Diversion of all the Company." Nothing came amiss to Sally in the way of daring adventure. A certain Lord Bul—k was fascinated by her charms, and she and another nymph fooled him in an escapade in Greenwich Park, the details of which may be left within the covers of the *Genuine History*. Then she was taken by Lord Ca(?rnarvo)n to Newmarket, and his lordship having lost at the races, Sally and one of her lady friends, fearing that in consequence they would go short, fled to London, taking with them the nobleman's best clothes, gold watch, rings, etc.

As Sally grew older, her impudence and the violence of her temper increased, and it was said " she learn'd her bullying way by going o'-Nights among the Mohocks drest like a beautiful youth," and once was rolled in a cask down Holborn Hill, and upon being taken into custody by the watch, her sex was discovered. She certainly upon emergencies could indulge in a wild luxuriance of forcible language, of which her biographer gives specimens, but this does not appear to have made her less acceptable to her noble friends, of whom she had any number. Nicolini, the operatic tenor, over whom ladies of title and fashion raved, was the hero of an adventure in which Sally came off second-best. It may be left untold.

For a long time she lived at rural Hampstead, at that time the resort of fashion, thanks to the medicinal spring in Well Walk. She held her own with the modish ladies at the Pump Room ; she was equally at home in the " Flask Kitchen," where she was fond of drinking with " a most humble and obsequious Adorer, who had an Estate of about £500 per annum and had almost spent the chief on her." She made a figure at the fashionable Belsize Gardens, and one night there had the fancy for proclaiming her Jacobitism. She was in company with two persons of Quality (" with two others who did not know her "), and " after they had drank several flasks she began a certain young gentleman's Health under the name of J—— the third ; it was readily pledg'd by three of those present ; but the fourth drank to the King's Health, whereupon she on a sudden snatch'd his own sword out and playing it before his Breast swore she'd let out his little Heart's blood if he would not drink it full, which Execution it was believed she would actually have perform'd. Upon which the Peer drank it ; but went the next Morning very prudently and acquainted his Majesty with the whole matter." But nothing followed : the whimsicalities of Sally Salisbury were too well known for any one to take her seriously.

Sally's frolics, her foolings, her drunken bouts, her sacrifices to Venus, were suddenly brought to an end by what was nearly a tragedy. We take the story from the evidence given at the Sessions House in the Old Bailey before the Lord Mayor and the Lord Chief Justice.

Late one night in the month of December the Honourable John Finch, fourth son of the sixth Earl of Winchilsea, entered the " Three Tuns Tavern," in Chandos Street, Covent Garden, and ordered a pint of Mountain wine. He was very cold, and was shown into a room where there was but a small fire. The " last Company being gone out of the House except two or three grave gentlemen who were drinking a glass of wine with the landlord in the little room behind the bar," and Mrs. Ditton, the bar-keeper, being told that Mr. Finch was cold, sent the drawer to ask him to come into the little room. The drawer found the Honourable John fast asleep, " with his Scarlet Cloak wrapp'd about him." He was awakened, he stumbled into the little room behind the bar, ordered some more wine, and sat by himself, the people of the house going to bed. About two o'clock in the morning the maid went to the drawer's room, and told him Mrs. Salisbury was come and wanted a pint of Frontiniac. The drawer got up, served the wine, and heard some discourse between Sally and the Honourable John about an opera ticket that, as he supposed, " Mr. Finch had given to some person unknown to Mrs. Salisbury." The drawer went on to say that, as they were talking, he having, with the Wine, "carried in a French roll and with it a Knife to cut it, as is usual ; he did perceive Mrs. Salisbury to have the knife in her hand and saw the motion of her hand towards Mr. Finch, but did not presently know what was done. That Mr. Finch was sitting open Breasted and Mrs. Salisbury next to him, that after the wound was given, Mr. Finch rose up and clapping his Hand upon his Breast said, ' Madam, you have wounded me.' Mr. Colthart, a surgeon, was fetched ; he cut the wound a little more in order to probe it the better, whereat Sally, at the sight of the blood shrieked, ' O Lord, Mr. Colthart, what are you doing ? ' and fell into fits. She recovered soon after, enquired of Mr. Finch how he was, and when he said he was worse, she rejoined, ' Jacky, you are not so bad as you imagine.' They drank some broth together, Mrs. Salisbury had some more Frontiniac and they went away in two chairs."

The story of Mrs. Ditton, the bar-keeper, was that there certainly was a drunken squabble over an opera

VERNON AS MACHEATH.

From the *Vocal Magazine.*

MISS BRENT AND MR. BEARD IN DR. ARNE'S
"THOMAS AND SALLY."

From Mr. A. M. Broadley's Collection.

ticket which Finch had given, unknown to Sally, to her sister. Sally seems to have flown into a passion, flung a glass of wine into the face of a Mr. Darley, and finished up by stabbing the Honourable John. Of course when she saw what she had done she became as penitent as before she had been furious, and cried out, " Jacky, do you forgive me ? " to which he replied, " I can, and can die with pleasure by your hand," that Mrs. Salisbury said she would go home with h'm and take care of him. That she said : " if you do forgive me, come and salute me," which he did. A vivid sordid picture indeed of drink, passion, and hysterics !

The Honourable John Finch was " bad of his wound for some two months," and when he recovered Sally was brought to trial, when the jury " found her guilty of assaulting and wounding, but as to her doing it with an intent to kill and murther, they acquitted her. She was condemned to pay a fine of £100, to suffer a year's imprisonment, and to give security for her good behaviour for Two Years more." The last-named penalty was, as events turned out, quite unnecessary, for before her year's imprisonment expired Sally was dead. A quaintly worded paragraph in *The Daily Post* while she was awaiting trial lets in a flood of light upon one of her weaknesses, and its interpretation is that poor Sally missed her drink. No wonder that, deprived of this solace, a few months' imprisonment sufficed to end her.

Walpole in a letter (April 10, 1747) to Horace Mann refers in his sprightly fashion to a piquant matter having a remote connection with Sally. " There has been," he writes, " an excellent civil war in the house of Finch. Our friend Lady Charlotte (Fermor) presented a daughter of John Finch (him who was stabbed by Sally Salisbury) his offspring by Mrs. Younger (*i.e.* the actress), whom he since married. The King, Prince and Princess received her ; her aunt, Lady Bel (Lady Isabella Finch) forbid Lady Charlotte to present her to Princess

Emily, whither, however, she carried her in defiance.
Lady Bel called it publishing a bastard at Court,
and would not present her—think on the poor girl.
Mr. W. Finch stepped up to his other sister, the
Marchioness of Rockingham, and whispered her with
his composed civility that he knew it was a plot of
her and Lady Bel to make Lady Charlotte miscarry.
The sable dame (who it was said is the blackest of
the family because she swept the chimney) replied
" This is not the place to be indecent, and therefore
I shall only tell you that you are a rascal and a
villain and that if ever you dare to put your head
into my house I will kick you downstairs myself."
Walpole adds, " Politesse anglaise! Lord Winchilsea (who with his brother Edward is embroiled with
both sides) came in and informed everybody of any
circumstances that tended to make both parties in
the wrong." How pleasant for every one concerned!

So much for Sally Salisbury, who may now be
allowed to rest. We have nothing to say against her.
She was neither better nor worse than hundreds of
her class, but to speak of her in the same breath
with Polly is an unpardonable libel on our heroine.
But the author of the " Life " had to think how to sell
his book, and he spiced it accordingly.

CHAPTER XIX

POLLY AND THE POWLETTS

IT is pretty clear the biographer's disparagement of Polly troubled his conscience, and to make amends he launches into extravagant eulogy. " Polly has so many smart as well as polite repartees, such a grace in the delivery," he declares, " and withal so little of that affectation which frequently makes a witty woman's company intolerable, that the oftener anyone hear her converse, the oftener he will desire it, and will improve himself by her profound Skill in every faculty as well as divert himself with her merry sayings and smart Returns of Gallantry ; for it must be acknowledg'd that her Beauty has not gained her so many Admirers as her sense, and the good Use she makes on't."

He then proceeds to give a specimen of the good qualities he admires so much. He says : " She was once in Company with a fop and a fine Gentleman, who each addressed her in their turns, but in a very different manner, and Polly very ingeniously gave each of them such suitable Answers, as converted the Fop, and made the man of sense a mere Fool. For from that time he was ready to lay down his life and estate at her service. ' Madam,' said the Fop, ' you have a very fine hand, which adds a great grace to your person.' ' Sir,' said Polly, ' you

219

have a very fine snuff-box, which adds a singular
grace to yours.' 'Madam,' said he, 'be pleased to
take a pinch out of it,' at the same time presenting
it with a ridiculous affected air; 'my snuff is very
good for the brain.' 'Sir,' said she, 'I verily
observe where the Brain is defective Snuff is of
great use, and though it cannot properly be called
either a Restorative or Provocative, yet certainly it
is a great Preparative to expel dullness.' 'You
are very witty and satirical, Madam,' said he. 'Sir,'
said she, 'if your snuff would inspire me with Wit,
I would satyrise upon your Box.'

    " The other gentleman finding Polly too many for
the Fop, and not willing to have him quite made a
sacrifice, very humanely interpos'd, and after desiring to be excused for interruption, 'Madam,' says
he, 'with that very air in which you this minute
appeared, the Town has obliged you with your
Picture in Mezzotinto.' 'Sir,' said she, 'the Town
may picture me as they please, but was the Town
to be pictured running to *The Beggar's Opera*, I
am sure it would be to my advantage.' 'I hope,
said he, 'you would not rally the Town for their
good opinion of your performance.' 'No, truly,
sir,' said she, 'I am glad the Town is governed by
opinion and not by caprice, but that is more than
I would have said to a gentleman of less penetration
and generosity than yourself. You, sir, discern things
in their proper light, and are satisfied that neither
Mr. Gay nor myself have outdone our Outdoings, as
Colley Cibber expresses it, but we in this have
spoke the Town on the Weak side, the Head, and
made it so giddy I fear in a little Time it will fall and
dash the Brains out of *The Beggar's Opera*.' This
she spoke with such pleasing Accents as took the
Gentleman she was speaking to, the weak Side the
Head in such a Manner, that he flung himself at her
Feet and told her, *Let the Town be mistaken in what
manner they would they could never be mistaken who
espous'd her Cause, for she was more than Woman.*

" And in short he fell so deeply in love with Polly that though his title is no less than an Earl he submits himself like a Slave at Polly's Footstool. And not only this, but several Noblemen who have distinguish'd themselves by great Actions both in the Field and the (——? Court) are now Polly's most humble servants ; for tho' she now is but in a mean capacity, yet she has something so Noble in her Presence, she is so sweet in her Conversation and withal so grateful and obliging to her Benefactors that her Lovers are not ashamed of their Amours forasmuch as they are devoted to the Shrine of one who is Mistress of so many Perfections."

The biographer is enthusiastic over her accomplishments. He declares that " she is a good Historian," that she argues " very profoundly both with regard to Politics and Plays," and that " she is such a Judge of Painting that the greatest of our Modern Artists in this Profession are glad to have her opinion of a Piece before it is shown to the World, knowing that if it escapes her Censure it will gain the Approbation of the Whole Town."

The climax of praise comes when he exclaims, " Notwithstanding her Wit and Skill she is the most humble, the most affable and the least conceited of any woman (that is both wise and beautiful) in the King's Dominions. Nor will she bear to hear encomiums on herself, it being a greater Affront to praise her before her Face, and she resents it more than if she was to be publicly called Gilt, Coquet, or even Common Whore or Strumpet."

So much for Polly's only biographer. He probably meant well, but one could have wished that his praise had been differently expressed. He concludes by giving some instances of Polly's " humanity and Good Nature," from which he thinks " she may pass for an accomplished worthy Lady, if the Public will allow an Actress the Title."

One of these instances is her generosity to her

stepfather, Mr. Fenton, to whom she allows "a decent maintenance." Another is best told in the biographer's own words. "A poor Milk-woman," he says, "who has marry'd a Black Husband was brought to bed of two tawny children at a Birth, and the Neighbours being mostly either too Rich to take notice of the poor woman or so poor and ill-natured that she could not be provided with Gossips at their being baptized, Polly hearing of it, sent her Maid to stand God-mother for her by Proxy, and gave her half a guinea to give the poor woman for an immediate supply, and after the Ceremony she went herself, reliev'd the woman very generously in that Exigency and ordered her to make free in sending to her House during the Time of her Lying-in, for such necessaries as she should have occasion for. This being rumoured about, a Taylor's wife being brought to Bed some time since and not being provided with Gossips, Polly went and offered herself to stand, which they gladly accepted of, and she called the Child by the Name of Polly Peachum, it being a girl." It may not be superfluous to explain that a couple of centuries ago, the word "gossip" was employed rather than godmother.

The final words of the paragraph with which the "Life" concludes must be taken with more than the customary grain of salt. There is not the slightest confirmation of the meaning conveyed to be found anywhere. Indeed, we are inclined to say of the Portuguese nobleman as Betsy Prig said of Mrs. Harris, "there is no sich a person." However, here is what the biographer states : "The latest and most notable of Occasions was but in April last, when the Portuguese nobleman mentioned before, and so well noted in Town, happened to fall again into some Trouble, when without hesitation she sent him £300 in Cash, which redeemed him from an arrest from which he knew not how to get clear, nor had he Courage to apply to her from whom he had received such unparallel'd favours before ; but her timely generosity put him out of anxiety and now they live together in one house enjoying the utmost Felicity and their Tempers exactly suiting each other makes up a complete harmony."

So much for the "Life," which was evidently rushed out at the height of the fashionable fever. The Duke of Bolton and Polly seem to have managed their affairs with great discretion, and the biographer could have known nothing of their attachment, or he would hardly have perpetrated the preposterous story of the Portuguese nobleman. It would certainly be safe to dismiss it as a ridiculous invention.

In the meantime the London theatrical season was drawing to a close, and the sixty-second night of the opera fell on June 19, when for the last time Polly faced the footlights. We are left to imagine whether it had leaked out that the idol of the public would never again delight the town. Perhaps at this time she had not made up her mind, or the Duke may have hesitated about taking a step which he naturally might think would lead to a scandal, seeing that he had already a superfluous duchess. The probability, however, is that if the news of his intimate association with Polly had got wind, the town would not have been very much concerned. It would most likely have treated the matter in the light style of Gay, who, in writing to Swift on July 6, 1728, casually mentions that "The d—— of —— I hear hath run away with Polly Peachum, having settled £400 upon her during pleasure, and upon disagreement £200." (This statement, by the way, has erroneously been often attributed to Swift.)

That Polly should leave the stage because she had become the mistress of the Duke of Bolton was probably regarded as wonderful. Few actresses of those days can be mentioned who had not had their lovers, and yet kept before the public; and why should Polly be any different from the rest?

But whether from wisdom or from inclination Polly quitted the theatre never to return. Of course

it may be that the Duke had a voice in the matter
(perhaps there was a prohibitory clause in the deed
of settlement), but the truth would seem to be that
Lavinia Fenton was not of the stuff of which great
actresses are made. She probably had neither the
requisite ambition nor the vanity, otherwise all the
prohibitory clauses in the world would have been
in vain. Whatever may have been the reason, she
showed a self-denial rare indeed among the female
favourites of the public. The sweet music of applause, the sense of personal attraction, the delights
of outspoken admiration are not easily resisted, and
less easily relinquished, yet Lavinia Fenton did both,
and she was right. Her departure from the stage
in the very zenith of success was as dramatic as the
blaze of triumph that attended her from the first to
the last of the sixty-two nights. Had she remained
she might have lived to see that triumph grow dim.
In all probability in any other part, if not a failure, she
would not have added to her fame. She was spared
that most melancholy future which falls to the lot
of all actresses who, outliving their day, have the
mortification of seeing the characters in which they
once thought themselves unapproachable, enacted
by younger and perhaps handsomer women, while
they themselves are faded, feeble, old or—fat! The
career of Lavinia Fenton was unique, and wisely she
left it to speak for itself.

So far as we have been able to ascertain, however
much Rich and the public were vexed at being deprived of the one and only Polly, no expression
of regret found its way into the public prints. Yet
it is quite certain Polly's retirement must have caused
an immense amount of talk; but it may be that only
when the autumn season began and the run of *The
Beggar's Opera* was resumed with its bright particular
star absent from the cast, did the public realise that
something had happened. Then, indeed, the story
would be in everybody's mouth.

Lavinia—one hardly dares now to call her Polly—

THE BOTTLE TRICK HOAX.

Showing the entrance to the Little Theatre in the Haymarket, 1748.

From a caricature in Mr. A. M. Broadley's Collection.

[221]

had made no insignificant connection. She had allied herself—in a left-handed way, it is true—with a nobleman whose ancestry could be traced back to the feudal times. The genealogy of the family is given in an article in Smollett's *British Magazine* of 1760, from which we learn that there were four branches of the Powletts, three having their own fashion of spelling the family name. These branches were Paulet, Marquis of Winchester ; Powlett, Lord Bolton ; Powlett, Duke of Cleveland ; and Poulett, Earl Poulett. The Winchester branch is the one with which we are most concerned, for it was one of its members who was captured by Polly. The writer of the article says :

" The first of the family that settled in England was Hercules, lord of Tournou in Picardy, who came over with Geoffrey Plantagenet, Earl of Anjou, third son of Henry II., and, among other possessions, obtained the lordship of Paulet, in Somersetshire, from whence the name was derived to his posterity. His son William de Paulet, residing at Leigh in Devonshire, added that denomination to Paulet, and with his son was written of Leigh-Paulet. William Paulet, the head of the family, was created Earl of Wiltshire in the reign of Edward VI., and appointed lord high treasurer of England. In 1551 he was made Marquis of Winchester, and sat as high steward upon the trial of Edward Seymour, Duke of Somerset. He enjoyed the treasurer's office for thirty years under three different sovereigns ; and being asked how he preserved himself in place, amidst such changes of government, he answered, ' By imitating the willow rather than the oak.' It was he that built the magnificent seat of Basing in Hampshire ; and lived till the age of ninety-seven, having seen one hundred and three descendants sprung from his body.

" His great-grandson John, Marquis of Winchester, adhered with unshaken loyalty to Charles I., and converted his house at Basing into a garrison, and

15

in person maintained a siege of two years; during
which he signalised his courage and conduct in a
series of most gallant actions. At last the place,
with himself and four hundred persons, was taken
by assault. He was so zealous in the cause of his
royal master that he inscribed every window with
the words *aimez loyauté* : a circumstance which
provoked the enemy to such a degree, that they
burned it to the ground; after having rifled it of
money, jewels, and furniture, to the value of two
hundred thousand pounds, including one bed estimated at fourteen thousand pounds. His son Charles,
Marquis of Winchester, born of his second wife,
Elizabeth, daughter of Thomas Darcy, Earl Rivers,
was influential in placing the crown of these realms
on the head of King William, who appointed him
lord lieutenant of the county of Southampton; and
on the 9th day of April, in the year 1689, created
him Duke of Bolton.

" The third Duke of Bolton was during his father's
life elected member of parliament for the county of
Caermarthen, and was afterwards called up by writ
to the house of peers by the title of Lord St. John of
Basing in the county of Southampton. He had
also commanded the royal regiment of horse-guards.
In the year 1722 he was elected Knight of the Garter,
afterwards appointed constable of the Tower, sworn
of the privy council, and nominated as one of the
regency when the King repaired to Hanover. In
1726 he was made governor of the Isle of Wight,
lord lieutenant and *custos rotulorum* of the counties
of Southampton and Dorset, the town and county
of Pool, and the town of Southampton; warden and
keeper of New Forest, *custos rotulorum* of Caermarthen,
governor of Milford-haven, and, in the sequel, lord
lieutenant of the county of Glamorgan. In the year
1733 he resigned all his places; but in 1740 he was
appointed captain of the band of gentlemen pen-
sioners, and one of the regency during the King's
absence. He afterwards resigned and accepted alter-

nately for several years; and when the last rebellion broke out he raised a regiment for his Majesty's service."

From this it would appear that the Powletts had an eye for their own interest, and that their main object in life was to be always on the winning side. It is also pretty clear that the writer in *The British Magazine* had instructions what to put in and what to leave out, and it is very astonishing to find no reference to what, apart from the siege of Basing House, is the most notable event in the history of the Winchester Powletts—namely the marriage of the third Duke of Bolton with Polly Peachum. The omission is all the more remarkable because Polly died Duchess of Bolton in the very year the article appeared, and though she had left the stage over thirty years, the fame of her personality had not only not faded, but the memory of her unique dramatic career was continually being revived by the perennial attraction of *The Beggar's Opera.*

Tate Wilkinson says that the Duke never had cause to repent making Polly his duchess, " as she filled every duty of that high station with becoming dignity—as a duchess, wife and mother. Admired by all, she enjoyed her envied laurels for many years, as the Bolton family can testify." One can only say that the Duchess had been dead quite six months prior to the publication of the " Genealogical Account," and had the " Bolton family " chosen to give this testimony, they had a very good opportunity. But what happened after the Duke's death in 1754 evidently gave much offence to his relatives, and probably the biographer was only obeying orders in ignoring the existence of " Polly."

Other and more important omissions in this colourless history were supplied some fifty years after by Cobbett, who, in reference to the revenues of Netley Abbey, amounting at the time of the suppression of the monasteries to £3,200 a year, estimated at the value of money in Henry VIII's time, wrote in his ruthless sledge-hammer style : " The possessions of the monks (of Netley) were by the wife-killing founder of the Church of England given away (though they belonged to the public) to one of his Court sycophants, Sir William Powlett, a man the most famous in the whole world for sycophancy, time-serving, and all those qualities which usually distinguished the favourites of such kings as the Wife-Killer. This Powlett changed from the Popish to Henry VIII.'s religion, and was a great actor in finishing the Papists. When Edward VI. came to the throne this Powlett turned Protestant, and was a great actor in punishing those who adhered to Henry VIII.'s religion. When Queen Mary came to the throne this Powlett turned back to Papist, and was one of the great actors in sending Protestants to be burned at Smithfield. When Old Bess came to the throne this Powlett turned Protestant again, and was, until the day of his death, one of the great actors in persecuting, in fining, in mulcting, and in putting to death, those who still had the virtue and the courage to adhere to the religion in which he and they had been born and bred." Admirably indeed did the first Marquis of Winchester (the premier Marquis in England) carry out his maxim of imitating the willow rather than the oak. The vicar of Bray was not more chameleon-like.

In the opinion of some authorities, too much has been made of the defence of Basing House and the alleged sacrifice and loyalty of the fifth Marquis. The truth seems to be that he was really fighting to maintain his own power and profit. Carlyle says : " Basing House had long infested the Parliament in those quarters, and been especially a great eye-sorrow to the Trade of London with the Western Parts. With Denrington Castle at Newbury and this Basing House at Basingstoke, there was no travelling the Western roads except with escort or sufferance." Of the first Duke of Bolton, the *British Magazine* biographer can find nothing more particular

to say than that he was " influential in placing the
crown of these realms on the head of King William "
—a blunder on the biographer's part, for it was the
second Duke who was William's partisan.   His grace
was, we are told by Bishop Burnet, " a man of most
profane expenditure and of a most ravenous appetite,
to support that in which he only followed the example
set him by the founder of the family."   His second
wife was a lady who owned large estates in Yorkshire,
and Wensleydale in the North Riding was subsequently the favourite residence of the third Duchess,
the Polly of these pages.

The second Duke was made Lord Lieutenant of
Ireland as a reward for his services to the Prince of
Orange, and his youngest brother, Lord William Powlett, after the fashion of the scions of the noble
families of that day, obtained a fat sinecure.   It was
this Powlett who was the hero of an anecdote which,
though it has been told fairly often, will bear repeating.
The authorship of a pamphlet entitled *The Snake in
the Grass* being attributed to his lordship, a gentleman alluded to in it sent Lord William a challenge.
The latter protested innocence, but the aggrieved
person would be satisfied with nothing less than
a written denial, whereupon Lord William took a pen
and began, " This is to scratify that the buk called
the Snak——" " Oh, my lord," hastily interposed
the challenger, " I am satisfied ; your lordship has
clearly convinced me that you did not write the
book."

Weak orthography and penmanship appear to be
failings common to the Powletts.   Mrs. Piozzi writes
thus of another member of the family :   " I don't
know whether this Lord Harry Powlett or an uncle of
his bearing the same name was the person of whom
my mother used to relate a ludicrous anecdote.
Some lady with whom she had been well acquainted,
and to whom his lordship was observed to pay uncommon attentions, requested him to procure her
' a pair of small monkeys from East India '—I forget

the kind. Lord Harry, happy to oblige her, wrote
immediately, depending on the best services of a
distant friend whom he had essentially served.
Writing a bad hand, however, and spelling what he
wrote for with more haste than correctness, he
charged the gentleman to send him over two monkeys,
but the word being written ' too ' and all the
characters of one height, 100, what was poor Lord
Harry Powlett's dismay when a letter came to hand
with the news that he would receive fifty monkeys
by such a ship, and fifty more by the next convey-
ance, making up the hundred according to his lordship's commands ! "

Lord Hervey was very bitter against Polly's duke.
Five years after she linked her fortunes with his, the
Duke joined the Duke of Argyll in opposing Sir
Robert Walpole's scheme of relieving the gentry from
the burden of the land tax, at that time four shillings
in the pound. Of course it was to be done at the
expense of those who did not own land. Already
Walpole had taken off a shilling by taxing one of the
necessaries of life, salt; and he proposed further to
assist the wealthy by imposing fresh excise duties on
tobacco and wines.

The opponents of Walpole strongly resisted—not
so much, probably, because they wanted to help
the people, as that they hated Sir Robert; and Lord
Hervey, a devoted Walpolean, wrote a vitriolic passage
in his best style concerning the Duke of Bolton. He
says in his *Memoirs of George II.* :

! " The Duke of Bolton, being out of humour and
Sir Robert Walpole's declared enemy, consider what
he held from the favour of the Court under this
administration, would have been more extraordinary
than all the rest, if it had not been for that great and
common solution for the many over-wise unaccountable riddles in people's conduct, which was his being
a great fool, but this explains a multitude of differences
in judging of multitudes of people as well as the Duke
of Bolton, for when one can once without hesitation

pronounce a man absolutely a fool, to wonder at any
of his actions afterwards, or seek a reason for them
is only putting oneself in his class, and I am no more
surprised to see an understood fool act against his
interest than I am to see a blind man go out of his
way. The Duke of Bolton was at this time Governor
of the Isle of Wight, Ranger of the New Forest, and
had a regiment, yet with all this the Duke of Bolton
was not satisfied, for being as proud as if he had been
of any consequence besides what his employment
made him, as vain as if he had some merit, and as
necessitous as if he had no estate, so he was trouble-
some at Court, hated in the country and scandalous
in his regiment. The dirty tricks he played in the
last (? reign) to cheat the Government of men, or
his men of half a crown, were things unknown to any
Colonel but his Grace, no griping Scotsman excepted.
As to his interest in Parliament, by the members he
nominally made there, these were all virtually made
by the Court, as they were only made by him in consequence of the powerful employments he held from
the Court."

One of the alleged " dirty tricks " formed the
subject of the uncomplimentary lines, in allusion to
secret profits out of army contracts, attributed to
Sir Charles Hanbury Williams, running :

> " Now Bolton comes with beat of drums,
>   Though fighting be his loathing,
> He much dislikes both guns and pikes,
>   But relishes the *clothing*."

As to Hervey's opinion that the Duke was a fool,
there would seem in the words which we have itali-
cised to be an allusion to his publicly associating himself with the heroine of *The Beggar's Opera*. Whether
this was intended or not, the statement of Lord
Hervey in reference to the Duke's appointments con-
victs the writer in *The British Magazine* of a mis-
representation possibly made with intention. His

Grace did not resign his various posts. They were
taken from him. The third Duke of Bolton, if he
were at all like the Powletts and Paulets in general,
would not be one to resign anything if he could
possibly keep it.

DRURY LANE THEATRE IN GARRICK'S TIME.

From Mr. A. M. Broadley's Collection.

CHAPTER XX

COLLEY CIBBER'S ABORTIVE RIVALRY OF GAY

Miss Warren as Polly's successor in *The Beggar's Opera*—Fluctuations in the receipts—Performance by the " Liliputians "—Who originated the idea ? —Madame Violante the tight-rope dancer in Dublin—Peg Woffington as a child—Did she play Polly or Macheath ?— Peggy and Garrick surprised— Rich removes to Covent Garden—Colley Cibber tries to rival *The Beggar's Opera* with *Love in a Riddle*—Its failure—Cibber's explanation

WHEN Lavinia Fenton left the stage to become the *chère amie* of his Grace of Bolton, the particular glory of *The Beggar's Opera* departed, but the Opera continued to attract on its own merits. Miss Warren, who followed the original Polly, was a painstaking actress, but she had no individuality and she could not supply Lavinia's place in the affection of the public. While Miss Warren was playing, the receipts varied considerably. On September 20 they were £75 7s.; at the end of November they fell to £23; and on December 11 they jumped to £112 9s. 6d. No especial reason is discoverable to account for this violent fluctuation. Throughout the season it may be said, roughly speaking, that the receipts averaged £70 each night. Up to the end of the year the Opera was played nineteen times in addition to the sixty-two nights ending June 19—besides the performances at the New Theatre in the Haymarket on November 30 and December 30, when a Mrs. Pullin was Polly. The rest of the cast does not appear in the advertisements.

Miss Warren making no sensation, another Polly appeared on May 5, 1729, in the person of Miss Cantrell, but she was no more successful than her predecessor. In the meantime, to whet the appetite of the public, an experiment (anticipating a similar one with Gilbert and Sullivan's *Pirates of Penzance* a century and a half later) was tried of a performance of *The Beggar's Opera* by a company of children, who were called the " Liliputians."

A curious question arises concerning the " Liliputians " : Was Rich the originator of the idea, or was it Madame Violante, the famous tight-rope dancer, whom Hogarth introduced into his " Southwark Fair " ? Theatrical historians are as slipshod over this as in almost everything else. Dr. Robert Walsh in his *History of the City of Dublin* says that " the exhibition of infant performers on the public stage is of very early date, and during the rage of *The Beggar's Opera* in London was a favourite project in Dublin." Dr. Walsh tells us in a footnote that in the year 1578 the children of St. Paul's " performed dramatic entertainments in London. In the beginning of the reign of Elizabeth the children of the Royal Chapel were formed into a company, and a few years after another company was formed, called the ' Children of the Revels.' These two juvenile companies became very famous ; all Lily's plays and many of Jonson's were first performed by them. So great was the estimation in which they were held that the adult companies in Shakespeare's time grew jealous of them. It is said in *Hamlet,* ' There is, Sir, an airie of young children, little Eyases that cry out on the top of the question and are most tyrannically clapped for it. These are now the fashion ' (Act II. sc. ii.)."

Dr. Walsh possibly had chapter and verse for his antiquarian researches, but when he came nearer home, and when one would expect him to be unimpeachable, he fails woefully. He has a good deal to say about the Dublin theatres ; and his story of the " Liliputians " is that " in the year 1731, Madame Violante had attempted to establish a booth for the performance of rough dancers, but the public were soon tired of the exhibition, and she converted the booth into a theatre. To make her performance more attractive by its novelty and singularity, she exhibited all theatrical pieces with a company of children under ten years of age. It is remarkable that *The Beggar's Opera* was first introduced to the notice of a Dublin audience by these infants." But it is still more remarkable that Dr. Walsh should have made this assertion when the evidence of Dean Swift that the Opera was the rage in Dublin in 1728 was readily accessible, to say nothing of Mrs. Barbier and the enthusiasm created over her Polly, of which Dr. Walsh seems not to have heard. Mr. Fitzgerald Molloy, no doubt following Dr. Walsh, has fallen into the same pit.

Dr. Walsh is very circumstantial in his account. After stating that the house in which the Dublin Liliputians performed was situated " where Fownes Street is now (1818) built and was approached by an avenue called Fownes Court," he goes on to say: " At the entrance of this court the mother of Mrs. Woffington kept for many years a stall or shop and sold fruit to those who frequented the theatre. Here it appeared her daughter was first seen and noticed by Madame Violante, and introduced to the public among her infant company. She afterwards removed with her to George's Lane. Her first appearance at Aungier Street was as a dancer, and the first speaking character she performed was Ophelia. When arrived at some eminence on the Dublin stage, she was called on by several persons of quality to attempt the character of Sir H. Wildair. In this she succeeded so admirably that she was immediately invited to London, where the novelty of the attempt and its astonishing success attracted immense crowds for twenty nights in succession." Horace Walpole grudgingly praised her : " She was a bad actress," he wrote, " but she has life."

In contradiction to Dr. Walsh we have W. Cooke in *Macklin's Memoirs* fixing the date of Peg

Woffington's appearance in the Liliputians in 1728.
Peggy was then ten years old, and had been one of
a troupe of children engaged by Madame Violante to
assist in her acrobatic show. The child, with others,
we are told, used to hang to Madame's feet in one
of her exhibitions of skill. Cooke, as we shall show,
was right in his date, but appears to be wrong in a
most important detail. Dr. Walsh tells us that the
part of Polly was played by Peggy, and there would
seem to be no doubt about this ; Cooke, however,
says that she was Macheath, and that when *The
Beggar's Opera* was produced and Peggy was the
Captain " the spirit and address of the little hero
was the theme of every theatrical conversation."

Cooke most likely was led astray by Macklin's
defective memory, but it evidently did not occur
to him to doubt the aged actor's statement, for he
adds : " Here was not only an early and accidental
decision of her genius for the stage, but for her
future excellence in breeches parts, as had not the
character of Macheath been assigned her it is more
than probable she would have gone on in the usual
line of acting without ever being celebrated as the
best male rake of her day." Following up his
Macheath assertion, Cooke is able to relate, apropos,
how the free-and-easy Peggy was once able to get
out of a very embarrassing situation, thanks to her
celebrity in " breeches parts." The story may
possibly be objected to by the purist, but the fact
remains that there would be very little to tell about
the actresses of the eighteenth century if Mrs.
Grundy had to be consulted at every turn. Every
actress, of course, had not the excessive tolerance of
Mrs. Barry, but to put the matter mildly, it may
be doubted whether the ladies of the stage in those
days, generally speaking, were inclined to take
Lucretia as their model.*

However this may be, Peg Woffington soon after
her return from Dublin in company with Garrick,

* See Appendix, Note 5.

somewhere about 1743, stayed for some time in Macklin's house, and on one occasion " a noble lord who was much enamoured with Mistress Woffington's many qualifications called." Unfortunately, on this particular night Garrick was occupying the lady's room, and alarmed by the knocking the actor jumped out of bed and hurried away with his clothes to Macklin's apartments, only discovering when he reached his friend's room that he had left his scratch wig behind !

In the meantime, his lordship, entering Peggy's room in the dark, had the misfortune to stumble over something, and when a light was brought the " something " was found to be a scratch wig ! The nobleman burst into a torrent of jealous rage, which Peggy took very calmly, begging of him not to make himself so great a fool, but to give her wig back to her. " What, madam ! " shouted the irate peer, " do you glory in your infidelity ? Do you know the wig, then ? " " Yes, to be sure I do," said she. " I'm sure it was my money paid for it, and I hope it will repay me with money and reputation too." This, however, did not satisfy the noble lord, whereupon she went on to say, " Why, my lord, if you will thus desert your character as a man, and be prying into all the little peculiarities of my domestic and professional business, know that I am soon to play a breeches part, and that wig which you so triumphantly hold in your hand is the very individual wig I was practising in a little before I went to bed ; and so, because my maid was careless enough to leave it in your lordship's way, here I am to be plagued and scolded." "We are further informed," adds Cooke gravely, " that this speech had all the desired effect. His lordship fell on his knees, begged a thousand pardons, and the night was passed in harmony and good humour." All that we dare say of this is that it is quite in the spirit of Boccaccio, behind whose name we take refuge.

Cooke's statement that Peggy played Macheath is, however, not altogether without foundation, but he confused Dublin with London. Mr. W. G. Lawrence, writing to *The Athenæum* on July 11, 1903, quotes, on the subject of Peg Woffington's first appearance in London, the following advertisement from *The Daily Post* of September 4, 1732 : " At the particular Desire of several persons of Quality. For the Benefit of the famous Signora Violante, who has just arrived with the new extraordinary fine Company at the New Theatre in the Haymarket, this present Monday, being the 4th of September, will be presented the most surprising performances that were ever shown in the English theatre. To which is added *The Beggar's Opera* after the Irish manner, which was performed 96 times in Dublin with great applause. The part of *Macheath* by the celebrated Miss Woffington, *Mr. Peachum*, Mr. Morrice ; *Mr. Lockit*, Mr. Daly ; *Filch*, Mr. Roan ; *Mat o' the Mint*, Mr. Dease ; *Polly Peachum*, Miss Jennie ; *Mrs. Peachum*, Miss Woffington ; *Miss Lucy Lockit*, Miss Corbally ; *Mrs. Diana Trapes*, Miss Woffington, and all the other parts to the best advantage."

Mr. Lawrence adds : " The comparison of the cast of characters in *The Beggar's Opera* with the original cast of the piece as represented by the Liliputian company in Dublin shows that there were serious defections existing—not only the compression of the Opera but also the doubling of certain characters. It is generally agreed that Peg Woffington appeared in Dublin as Polly, but at the Haymarket (when her age must have been about sixteen) we find her openly doubling three rôles. Not only this, but she was the first of the long line of female Macheaths extending down to within living memory. Her success in the character affords a clue to her early predilection for " breeches parts." Perhaps after all, Cooke in some measure was correct. It is possible that on an emergency Peggy may have played Macheath in Dublin, but if so it is curious that

Robert Hitchcock the historian of the Irish stage, should not have unearthed the fact.

Hitchcock, in other respects, does much towards settling the discrepancies of W. Cooke and Dr. Walsh. Hitchcock says that Madame Violante took the house in Fownes Court in 1727 and converted it into a booth, and brought over a company of tumblers and rope-dancers. But the novelty died away, and she converted her booth into a playhouse. Again she failed, owing to the badness of the actors, and it was then that she formed a company of children, the eldest not above ten years of age. " These she instructed in several *petit* pieces, and as *The Beggar's Opera* was then in high estimation she perfected her Liliputian troupe in it." This would indicate that the Liliputians were brought out in 1728, as Cooke has it, and not, as Dr. Walsh says, in 1731. As to whether Peg Woffington played Polly or Macheath, Hitchcock also settles this by giving the cast, which proves Cooke to be hopelessly in the wrong. Miss Betty Barnes was the gallant highwayman; the " afterwards well-known " Master Isaac Sparks played *Peachum*; Martin Barrington, " afterwards so celebrated for Irishism and low comedy," *Filch*; Miss Ruth Jenks, *Lucy*; " and from the Polly of that day sprang the beautiful, elegant, accomplished, captivating Woffington."

Dr. Walsh's error seems to have arisen from the fact that Madame Violante in 1730 removed from Fownes Court to another booth in George's Lane, where she again exploited her company of young comedians ; and here Peggy took part in a Liliputian performance of Christopher Bullock's *Cobler of Preston*, which, to suit the taste of the times, was converted into an opera. This was the play a portion of which in its manuscript form Spiller was said to have stolen from his fellow comedian Pinkethman and handed over to Bullock (see p. 117). Bullock always denied the story, and frankly admitted that he wrote his play on the basis of the introduction to *The Taming of the Shrew.* The operatic version leaves no doubt that this was so. The printed copy of the opera is dated 1732 and bears the announcement that it was " performed at the New Booth in Dublin." The cast is given, from which we learn that Kit Sly, the cobler, was taken by Mark Peters ; Joan, Kit Sly's wife, by Miss Violante ; Cicely Gundy, a country Ale-wife, by Miss Woffington ; and "a countryman" by Mark Woffington, presumably Peggy's brother. Peggy also spoke the prologue.

If we may take Hitchcock as a reliable authority on the question of dates it would appear that Rich was indebted to Madame Violante for the idea of the Liliputians. Hitchcock and Cooke agree that she brought out the children's opera in Dublin in 1728, while so far as London was concerned the first intimation that Rich contemplated anything of the kind is contained in this paragraph in *The British Journal* of November 30, 1728 : " We have advice from the Theatre in Lincoln's Inn Fields that *The Beggar's Opera* will speedily be acted there by a sett of children whom the Master of the said House has collected with great application from several parts of the town ; and that the youngsters perform so well in their rehearsals that there is no doubt but the town will be agreeably entertained by them." According to *The Daily Journal* the first night was January 1, 1729.

The experiment of the " Liliputians " was quite justified. The last two performances in 1728 at Lincoln's Inn Fields of the regular opera, with Miss Warren as Polly, drew but £72 between them, while on the first night of the Liliputians £116 11*s*. was taken, £69 1*s*. on the second, and on the fifth night, given " by the command of the Prince of Wales," the receipts rose to £118 14*s*.

Genest, in referring to the " Liliputians," says : " If I am not greatly mistaken I, many years ago, saw an edition of *The Beggar's Opera* as acted by children with Woodward's name to one of the charac-

MRS. ABINGTON AS THALIA.

From an engraving by Bartolozzi, after Cosway, in Mr. A. M. Broadley's Collection.

ters—in the Thespian Dictionary ; he is said to have acted Peachum at this time with great success." Woodward, who in such parts as Mercutio, Bobadil and Marplot, was unequalled in his day, made his first appearance on the stage in the Liliputian version of *The Beggar's Opera.* He was then fifteen, and Rich, seeing his capabilities, retained him in the company and instructed him in harlequin and other characters.

The Liliputians played for fifteen nights during January 1829, and then the opera reverted to its old form, Miss Cantrell on May 5 succeeding Miss Warren. Including the " Liliputian " performances, *The Beggar's Opera* was acted more than forty times in its second year. On May 21 it was played, together with *The Tavern Bilkers,* by command of the Prince of Wales, and after this it was not performed until December 17, when it was bespoken by the Duchess of Richmond and realised £106 7s. 6d. In the season of 1730 it was produced four times, and each occasion for a benefit, with Quin as Macheath (possibly to show that he could play the part if he cared to do so, though he never repeated it) on March 19, when he had the bumper house of £206 9s. 6d. Another benefit was that of Hulet, when he played Macheath, Miss Cantrell being Polly. The Opera was revived at intervals during 1731, drawing an average of £45, but in 1732, the year of Rich's removal to Covent Garden, it does not seem to have been played at Lincoln's Inn Fields. The preparations for shifting to the new theatre no doubt materially interfered with it. The Opera, however, was selected for the opening night at Covent Garden. Covent Garden Theatre was opened on December 6, 1732, when, according to *The Daily Journal,* " to prevent the scenes being crowded " the price of the stage seats was raised to half a guinea, and the pit and boxes were " laid together " at 5s.

Hogarth caricatured Rich's removal to Covent Garden Theatre in a print entitled " Rich's Triumphal

16

Entry" (see p. 128), of which Nicholls gives the following explanation : " This plate represents the removal of Rich and his scenery, Authors and Actors, etc., from Lincoln's Inn Fields to the New House. . . . The scene is the area of Covent Garden, across which, leading toward the door of the Theatre, is a long procession consisting of a cart loaded with 'thunder and lighting,' performers, etc., and at the head of them Mr. Rich (invested with the skin of the famous dog in *Perseus and Andromeda*) riding with his mistress in a chariot driven by Harlequin and drawn by Satyrs. . . . Pope is represented in his tye wig at one corner of the Piazza."

Meanwhile Cibber's mortification at the success of *The Beggar's Opera* and at his own blunder in throwing away his chance of producing it led him to making a further mistake. Quin writes that the " uncommon reception of *The Beggar's Opera* induced Colley Cibber to attempt something of the same kind next year, under the title of *Love in a Riddle* ; but how different was its reception from Gay's production !—it was damned to the lowest regions of infamy the very first night ; which so mortified Cibber that it threw him into a fever, and from this moment he resolved, as soon as he conveniently could, to leave the stage, and no longer submit himself or his talents to the capricious taste of the town." The play was produced at Drury Lane Theatre on January 7, 1729, and all that is to be learned of the fiasco from the newspapers of the day is contained in a paragraph in *The British Journal*, wherein we read that "His Royal Highness the Prince" continues frequently to honour both theatres with his presence. On Tuesday night he was at Lincoln's Inn Fields a second time, to see *The Beggar's Opera* performed by the Liliputians, and the next night to see *Love in a Riddle*, written by Mr. Cibber, being the second time of acting, at which there was such an extraordinary disturbance occasioned by the general disapprobation of the audience, that they would not suffer the performance to be continued till Mr. Cibber assured them it should not be acted any more than that night." *The Daily Journal* contents itself with saying that the Prince left early owing to the disturbance.

Undoubtedly the audience was right. The four first lines sufficiently stamp the play's trite artificiality. They run thus :

> " Hail to the rising Day ! Hail ! Waking Nature !
> Ye verdant Plains, ye Hills, and fertile Valleys,
> Ye lowing Herds and fleecy bleating Flocks,
> Ye warbling Groves and murmuring Fountains, Hail ! "

There is any amount of this flowery stuff, with but a modicum of wit, and the melodies to which the songs were set are inferior to those in *The Beggar's Opera*. One exception has, however, to be made— the charming ballad " Phillida flouts me." Cibber's lines, commencing " Oh what a plague is love ! " are above his ordinary level. From *Love in a Riddle* also comes the line " Such was the joy of our dancing days," the refrain of a fairly sprightly song " When I followed a lass that was froward and shy."

Cibber in describing the " damning " of his play asserts that the opposition it met with was due to an impression which had got about that he had been instrumental in getting Gay's sequel to *The Beggar's Opera* suppressed. " Stepping forward to the pit," he writes, " I told them that since I found they were not inclined that this play should go forward, I gave them my Word that after this Night it should never be acted again. But that in the meantime I hop'd they would consider in whose presence they were (referring to the Prince of Wales), and for that Reason at least would suspend what further Marks of their Displeasure they might imagine I had deserved. At this there was a dead silence, and after some little Pause, a few civilized Hands signify'd their approbation, when the play went on. I observed about a Dozen Persons of no extraordinary appearance sullenly walk out of the pit. After which every Scene of it, while interrupted, met with more applause than my best hopes had expected. But it came too late."

Cibber in his *Autobiography* not only apologises for having perpetrated *Love in a Riddle*, but pays a handsome tribute to Gay. Speaking of *The Beggar's Opera* he says : " The year following, I was so stupid as to attempt something of the same kind, upon a quite different Foundation—that of recommending Virtue and Innocence, which I ignorantly thought might not have a less Pretence to Favour, than setting Greatness and Authority in a contemptible, and the most vulgar Vice and Wickedness in an amiable light. But behold how fondly I was mistaken ! *Love in a Riddle* (for so my new-fangled Performance was call'd) was as vilely damned and hooted at, as so vain a Presumption in the idle cause of Virtue could deserve. Yet this is not what I complain of ; I will allow my Poetry to have been as much below the other, as Taste, or Criticism, can sink it. I will grant likewise, that the applauded Author of *The Beggar's Opera* (whom I knew to be an honest good-natur'd Man, and who, when he had descended to write more like one in the Cause of Virtue, had been as unfortunate as others of the Class) I will grant, I say, that in his *Beggar's Opera* he had more skilfully gratified the publick taste, than all the brightest Authors that ever went before him ; and I have sometimes thought, from the Modesty of his Motto, *Nos hæc novimus esse nihil*, that he gave them all that performance, as a satyr upon the Depravity of the Judgment (as Ben Jonson, of old, was said to have given his *Bartholomew Fair* in Ridicule of the Vulgar Taste, which had disliked his *Sejanus*), and that by artfully seducing them, to be the Champions of the Immoralities he himself detested, he should be amply revenged on the former severity and ignorance."

CHAPTER XXI

A GREAT LADY'S CHAMPIONSHIP

Polly, Gay's sequel to *The Beggar's Opera*—The Lord Chamberlain refuses to license it—*Polly* published—The Duchess of Queensberry solicits subscriptions within the Royal Circle and is forbidden to appear at Court— Sir Walter Scott's, Lord Hervey's and Mrs. Delany's account of the affair—*The Female Faction*—Death of Gay—Tributes to his memory

WHILE *The Beggar's Opera* was pursuing its triumphant way Gay was preparing the sequel alluded to by Cibber, which he called *Polly*. Like most sequels, it was terribly inferior to the original. Perhaps Gay was persuaded by his friends that, not having done poetic justice to Macheath by hanging him, he ought to make amends by devising an edifying end of some kind. He accordingly sentences the dashing highwayman to the Plantations, where the Captain, having robbed his master, runs away, blacks his face, turns pirate and calls himself Morano. Polly goes to the West Indies in search of him, meets Mrs. Trapes (one of the questionable dames in *The Beggar's Opera*), who tells her he has married Jenny Diver, " a transported slave." Polly is in great distress, not merely because of Macheath's faithlessness, but because she is now a wretched vagabond exposed to hunger and want. Mrs. Trapes sells her to Ducat, a rich trader, she has adventures in which two native chiefs, Pohetohee and Cawwawkee (whose names surely qualify them to figure in a modern comic opera), and eventually when she meets Morano she does not recognise him as Macheath, and only learns that he is the once gallant Captain after hearing of his death. She ends by marrying one of the Indian chiefs. *Polly* is a very poor production,⁵ and had it been put upon the stage would have met with a fate not very different from that of *Love in a Riddle*. But once more fortune was kind to Gay. The Lord Chamberlain refused to grant a licence. Let Gay himself tell the story :—

" 'Twas on Saturday morning, December 7, 1728," he writes in the preface to *Polly*, " that I waited upon the Lord Chamberlain ; I desir'd to have the honour of reading the opera to his Grace, but he ordered me to leave it with him, which I did upon expectation of having it returned on the Monday following ; but I had it not till Thursday, Dec. 12, when I received it from his Grace with this answer, that it was not allow'd to be acted, but commanded to be suppress'd. This was told me in general without any reasons assigned or any charges against me of having given any particular offence."

Gay proceeds to defend himself from the charge that he had in *Polly* encouraged sedition and criminality, and winds up by saying that " I am conscious to myself that my only intention was to lash in general the reigning and fashionable vices and to recommend and set virtue in as amiable a light as I could ; to justify and vindicate my own character I felt myself obliged to print the opera without delay." He did not, however, imagine how good a turn the Lord Chamberlain had done him. He writes : " I have submitted and given up all present views of profit which might accrue from the stage," and he could well endure the sacrifice, for as a matter of fact he made more money out of *Polly*, which was not acted, than out of *The Beggar's Opera*, which was.

Gay's circle was terribly enraged at the indignity cast upon him by the Lord Chamberlain's action. Her impetuous Grace of Queensberry threw herself into the fray with all the ardour of her nature, and when Gay decided to have the prohibited play printed she got into sad disgrace at Court through her excess of zeal. Mrs. Delany tells us how " The Duchess of Queensberry, to the great amazement of the admiring world, is forbid the Court only for being solicitous in getting a subscription for Mr. Gay's sequel to *The Beggar's Opera,* which the Court forbid being acted on account that it reflected on the Government. The Duchess is a great friend of Gay's, and has with him much endured, upon which to make him some amends, for he is poor, she promised to get a subscription for his play if he would approve it. She indiscreetly has urged the King and Queen in his behalf and asked subscriptions in the Drawing-room, upon which she is forbid the Court—a thing never heard of before to one of her rank. One might have imagined her beauty would have secured her from such treatment. The Vice-Chamberlain went with the message, and she returned the answer which I have enclosed."

The answer is quite in keeping with the spirit of " Prior's Kitty," who did not know what fear was. Her Grace wrote on February 27, 1729 : " The Duchess of Queensberry is surprised and well pleased that the King has given her so agreeable a command as to stay from Court, where she never came for diversion, but to bestow a civility on the King and Queen. She hopes by such an unprecedented order as this that the King will see as few as he wishes at his Court, particularly such as dare to think or speak truth. I dare not do otherwise, and ought not nor could have imagined that it would not have been the very highest compliment that I could possibly pay the King to endeavour to support truth and innocence in his house, particularly when the King and Queen both told me that they had read Mr. Gay's play. I have certainly done right, then, to stand by my own words rather than his Grace of Grafton's, who hath never made use of true judgement, nor honour through this whole affair, either for himself or his friends.—C. Queensberry."

In the British Museum is a volume of Swift's letters annotated by Sir Walter Scott for use in preparing his life of the Dean, and we find that Sir Walter has written in the margin : " The Duchess was so vehement in her attempts to have the embargo removed from Gay's play that she offered to read it to His Majesty in his closet that he might be satisfied there was no offence in it. George II. escaped from this dilemma by saying that he should be delighted to receive her Grace in his closet, but hoped to amuse her better than by the employment she proposed."

John, Lord Hervey, puts the case from the ministerial point of view, and fills in the picture of the pertinacious duchess. He says of *Polly* that it was less pretty than *The Beggar's Opera*, " but more abusive, and so little disguised that Sir Robert Walpole resolved, rather than suffer himself to be produced for thirty nights together upon the stage in the person of a highwayman, to make use of his friend the Duke of Grafton's authority, as Lord Chamberlain, to put a stop to the representation of it.* Accordingly this *Theatrical Craftsman* was prohibited at every playhouse. Gay, irritated at this bar thrown in the way both of his interest and of his revenge, zested the work with some supplementary invectives and resolved to print it by subscription. The Duchess of Queensberry set herself at the head of this undertaking and solicited every mortal that came in her way, or in whose way she could put herself, to subscribe. To a woman of her quality, proverbial beauty, and at the top of the polite and fashionable world, people were ashamed to refuse a guinea though they were afraid to give it. Her solicitations were so universal and pressing that she came even into the Queen's apartment, went round the Drawing-room and made even the King's servants contribute to the printing of the thing which the King had forbidden being acted. The King when he came into the Drawing-room, seeing her Grace very busy in a corner with three or four men, asked her what she had been doing. She answered, ' What must be agreeable, she was sure, to anybody so

* See Appendix, Note 4.

ANNE CATLEY.

From an etching drawn when she was thirty.

MRS. MATTOCKS.

From an engraving by Ridley, after Miller.

248]

humane as his Majesty for it was an act of charity,
and a charity to which she did not despair of bringing his Majesty to contribute.'

"Enough was said for each to understand the
other, and though the King did not then (as the
Duchess of Queensberry reported) appear at all
angry, yet this proceeding of her Grace when talked
over in private between his Majesty and the Queen
was so resented that Mr. Stanhope, then Vice-
Chamberlain to the King, was sent in form to the
Duchess of Queensberry to desire her to forbear
coming to the Court ; his message was verbal. Her
answer, for fear of mistakes, she desired to send in
writing, wrote it on the spot (see the letter quoted
by Mrs. Delany). . . . When her Grace had finished
this paper, drawn with more spirit than accuracy,
she gave it to Mr. Stanhope, who desired her to think
again, asked pardon for being so impertinent as to
offer her any advice, but begged she would give him
leave to carry an answer less rough than that she
had put into his hands. Upon this she wrote another, but so much more disrespectful that he desired
the first again, and delivered it.

"Most people," Hervey adds, "blamed the court
on this occasion. What the Duchess of Queensberry
did was certainly impertinent. The Duke of Queensberry laid down his employment of Admiral of
Scotland upon it, though very much and very kindly
pressed by the King to remain in his service."

Among other reasons alleged why *Polly* was refused, it was rumoured that Colley Cibber, out of
jealousy, had intrigued against it. There is no proof
of this, and it does not appear that Gay himself
thought so. Cibber defends himself in these words :
"The same Author, the next Year, had, according to
the Laws of the Land, transported his Hero to the
West Indies, in a second Part of *The Beggar's Opera* ;
but so it happened, to the Surprize of the Publick,
this second Part was forbid to come upon the Stage !
Various were the speculations, upon this Act of

Power ; some thought that the Author, others that the Town, was hardly dealt with ; a third sort, who perhaps had envy'd him the Success of his first Part, affirmed, when it was printed, that whatever the Intention might be, the Fact was in his Favour that he had been a greater gainer, by Subscriptions to his Copy, than he could have been by a bare Theatrical Presentation. Whether any part of these opinions were true, I am not concern'd to determine or consider. But how they affected me, I am going to tell you. Soon after this Prohibition, my Performance was to come upon the Stage, at a Time when many People were out of Humour, at the late Disappointment, and seem'd willing to lay hold of any Pretence of making a Reprizal. Great Umbrage was taken, that I was permitted to have the whole Town to my self, by the absolute Forbiddances of what they had more mind to have been entertain'd with . . . The report it seems that had been run against me was this ; That to make way for the Success of my own Play, I had privately found means, or made Interest, that the second Part of *The Beggar's Opera* might be suppressed. . . . This is so very gross a Supposition that it needs only its own senseless Face to confound it ; let that alone be my Defence against it."

The ever-ready poet peculiar to the times was of course to the fore, and his efforts are seen in a poem —for a wonder quite decent, but also somewhat dull— entitled *The Female Faction, or the Gay Subscribers.* The young Duchess of Marlborough is apostrophised thus : " First in thy list does great Almeria stand," and the dowager duchess, the haughty Sarah, is unkindly addressed as " Clodia, broke with the Disease of age." To the Duchess of Queensberry is inscribed the following :

" The gay Amanda let us now behold,
In thy defence a lovely banish'd Scold :
What tributary numbers can thy Muse
To this bright Championess of Wit refuse ?

To her who greatly Empire's Frowns defies,
And bids her *late Disgrace* now point her Eyes ;
Who makes her tender L(or)d her Quarrel join,
And the fair Honours of his P(os)t resign,
To let the Fools her Soul's high temper see,
That holds no sacrifice too rich, for THEE !
Point her each Beauty o'er and o'er again,
Strong as when first she charm'd in P(rior)'s strain,
When kind Mamma indulg'd her *Heart's Desire*,
And then, as now, she set the World on Fire."

The last phrase is in allusion to the lines with
which Prior's *The Female Phaethon* concludes :

" Kitty at heart's desire,
Obtained the chariot for a day,
And set the world on fire."

The Duchess of Bedford is termed " The Chaste
Calista," and the list of Gay's supporters is com-
pleted with " Florio and Clara," the newly married
Lord and Lady Essex.

Gay writing to Swift on March 18 says : " I
print the book at my own expense in quarto, which
is to be sold for six shillings with the music. . . .
Mrs. Howard has declared herself strongly both to
the King and Queen as my advocate. The Duchess
of Queensberry is allowed to have shown more spirit,
more honour, and more goodness than was thought
possible in our times. I should have added too more
understanding and good sense."

Swift was plain-spoken in his opinion of *Polly*,
and he puts this opinion in his letter to Gay of
March 19, remarking : " I had never much hope of
your vamped play, although Mr. Pope seemed to
have, and although it were ever so good ; but you
should have done like the parsons and changed your
text, I mean your title and the names of the persons."
Sir Walter writes in the margin of the volume already
mentioned : " The Dean's judgment was correct—
the second part of *The Beggar's Opera* is *crombe bis
colta*, and the ministry, as in many other cases, could
not have done Gay a greater service than by excluding

it from the stage and rendering it a point of party
thereby to encourage the circulation of it by subscription."

But in spite of King and Court, the Duchess
fought for Gay all the same ; she gave £100 for a
single copy of *Polly*, and thanks to her assistance,
and that of other ladies of influence, Gay netted
between £1,100 and £1,200—much more than *The
Beggar's Opera* brought him. All this squabbling,
since it put money in Gay's pockets, highly amused
the Twickenham coterie. " The inoffensive John
Gay," wrote Arbuthnot to Swift on March 19, 1729,
" is now become one of the obstructions to the peace
of Europe, the terror of the ministers, the chief author
of the *Craftsman* and all the seditious pamphlets
which have been published against the government.
He has got several turned out of the place ; the
greatest ornament of the Court banished from it for
his sake ; another great lady ;(Mrs. Howard, subsequently Countess of Suffolk) in danger of being
chassée likewise ; about seven or eight Duchesses
pushing forward, like the ancient *circumselliones* in
the Church, who shall suffer martyrdom on his
account first. He is the darling of the city. If he
could travel about the country, he would have
hecatombs of roast oxen sacrificed to him. Since
he became so conspicuous Will Pulteney hangs his
head to see himself so much outdone in the career of
glory. I hope he will get a good deal of money by
printing his play ; but I really believe he would get
more by showing his person ; and I can assure you
this is the very identical John Gay whom you
formerly knew and lodged with in Whitehall two
years ago."

When the nine days' wonder was over, and subscriptions had poured in, and the book been printed, we
have Arbuthnot writing to Swift on May 8 that " Mr.
Gay has gone to Scotland with the Duke of Queensberry. He has about twenty law-suits with the
booksellers for pirating his book." Pope had the

same experience at this time concerning *The Dunciad*, but as he dared not avow his name as the author he was not successful. The contrary was the case with Gay. Meanwhile Prior's "Kitty" continued to be contumacious, and not until 1747 was she reconciled with the King (the Queen of course was dead), when Anna Walpole wrote that the Duchess " has at last been at Court, a point she has been intrigueing these two years." *Polly*, considerably altered, was played in 1777 at the Haymarket Theatre, and according to Genest, the Duchess of Queensberry, then very aged, was among the audience. The play, however, was not approved, and was speedily withdrawn.

At the end of 1732 the author of *The Beggar's Opera* died, and it must be confessed that he paid the penalty of a life of ease and indulgence, alternated with periods of gloom, due to disappointed ambition and—overeating. He was then but forty-four, and his last letter to Pope shows pathetically how his bodily powers were reduced. He writes : " I find myself in such a strange confusion and dejection of spirits, that I have not strength enough to make my will, though I perceive, by many warnings, I have no continuing city here. I begin to look upon myself as one already dead, and desire, my dear Mr. Pope, whom I love as my own soul, if you survive me, as you certainly will, if a stone should mark the place of my grave, see these words put upon it :

" 'Life is a jest, and all things show it,
I thought so once, and now I know it.'

with what you think proper. If anybody should ask how I could communicate this after death ? let it be known it is not meant so, but my present sentiments in life."

He was mourned sincerely by his friends. Dr. Arbuthnot wrote to Swift on January 13, 1733 : " We have all had another loss, of our worthy and dear friend Gay. It was some alleviation of my grief to see him so universally lamented by almost everybody, even by those who knew him only by representation. He was interred at Westminster Abbey, as if he had been a peer of the realm, and the good Duke of Queensberry, who lamented him as a brother, will set up a handsome monument upon him."

In another letter, from Pope to Swift, we read : " It is, indeed, impossible to speak on such a subject as the loss of Mr. Gay—to me an irreparable one. You say truly that death is only terrible as it separates us from those we love, but I really think those have the worst of it who are left by us, if we are true friends. I have felt more, I fancy, in the loss of Mr. Gay than I shall suffer in the thought of going away myself into a state that can feel none of its losses. I wished vehemently to have seen him in a condition of living independent, and to have lived in perfect indolence the rest of our days together—the most idle, most innocent, undesigning poets of our age."

Gay's friend and patron, the Duchess of Queensberry, wrote to Swift : " Soon after the death of our friend, Mr. Gay, I found myself more inclined to write to you than to allow myself any other entertainment. If I have any good in me, I certainly learned it insensibly of our poor friend, as children do any strange language. It is not possible to imagine the loss his death is to me, but as long as I have any memory, the happiness of ever having had such a friend can never be lost to me." It may be said of Gay that he was fortunate in his death, as he was fortunate—in spite of his fancies to the contrary—in his life. He did not outlive his friendships, and he was spared the mortification of failure, for most assuredly he would never have followed up the success of *The Beggar's Opera*, or produced anything approaching it.

CHAPTER XXII

RIVAL POLLIES

A " Polly " charged with bigamy—The fascinating Miss Norsa—Her connection with Lord Orford—The fancy of noblemen for actresses noted
by Horace Walpole—The rival Pollies, Mrs. Cibber and Mrs. Clive—A
furious paper war—*Polly* and *Lucy* compared—The Licensing Act of
1737—What led to it

WITH the opening of Covent Garden in December
1732, the Opera commenced a new lease of life. Mrs.
Egleton, who had been identified with Lucy, died
in the early part of 1732. Various actresses followed
her in the part; but Lucy was always subordinate
to Polly, and the public did not care who played the
former, so long as they were satisfied with the latter.
Miss Warren imitated Miss Fenton. She quitted
the stage to " better herself." Whether she did so
may be doubted, to judge from the embarrassment
indicated in the following paragraph which appeared
in *The Daily Post* of December 6, 1736: " On
Thursday last, Polly Peachum (Miss Warren that was,
sister to the famous Mrs. Mapp) was tried at the
Old Bailey for marrying Mr. Nicholas, her former
husband Mr. Somers being living, and after a long
trial she was acquitted." Mrs. Mapp was, of course,
the famous " bone-setter," about whom one would
like to say a good deal were it germane to the matter.
   Miss Cantrell, who followed Miss Warren, achieved
but a *succès d'estime*, and Mrs. Thurmond, the wife
of the dancing master who wrote *Harlequin Jack
Sheppard*, was the Polly for five successive nights in
February 1732, but was not heard of again in the
part. Kitty Clive played Polly when the Opera was
produced at Drury Lane on September 12 of the
same year, 1732, but she does not seem to have

255

created a furore. Probably she had not the chance.
The Opera was put on at Drury Lane for one night,
and no doubt this was by special arrangement. If
Rich contemplated reviving the piece in his new
theatre, it was hardly likely he would permit the
attraction to be forestalled. It may be said, too,
that Kitty in this year having made a hit as Nell in
The Devil to Pay, was content to rest on her laurels.*

Not until Miss Norsa made her appearance did
the public have a Polly after their own heart. The
records are silent concerning Miss Norsa. Genest has
nothing to say about either her singing or acting,
but we may assume that she was a favourite from
the number of times she played Polly, the Opera
having a run of twenty nights in succession, and
Royalty honouring her on two occasions. Her benefit
later in the year realised £142, only a few pounds
less than the original Polly obtained when she took
her second benefit.

That Miss Norsa had her fascinations is pretty
certain, and it is equally certain that she exercised
those fascinations off the stage as well as on. She
attracted the attention of Lord Orford, Horace
Walpole's brother, and proved once more how lucky
Polly was. Miss Norsa was a Jewess, and, like most
of the daughters of Zion, no doubt had plenty of
musical ability. Lord Orford took her off the stage
with the concurrence of her parents, to whom he
gave a bond by which he engaged to marry her on
the demise of his wife. Peter Cunningham is the
authority for this statement, and it would have
been interesting if he had told us what penalty Lord
Orford incurred in the event of the non-fulfilment
of the contract. Old Mr. and Mrs. Norsa, no doubt
experienced in the art of driving hard bargains,
were not likely to overlook this important point.
Be this as it may, Lord Orford seems to have been
greatly attached to his Polly.

Horace Walpole was present at the trial of the

* See Appendix, Note 5.

CHARLES BANNISTER AS " POLLY."

From a mezzotint by J. R. Smith.

rebel lords in 1746, and made one of his sprightly comments. When the peers voted the unhappy noblemen guilty, using the formula " Guilty, upon my honour," Walpole seems to have been greatly amused, and wrote: " I was amused too, with old Norsa, the father of my brother's concubine, an old Jew that kept a tavern ; my brother as auditor of the Exchequer has a gallery along one whole side of the court. I said ' I really felt for the prisoners ! ' Old Issachar replied, ' Feel for them ! pray, if they had succeeded, what would become of all us ? " The witty Lady Townshend was of the party, and uttered one of her smart bon mots, remarking when she heard her husband vote, " I always knew my husband guilty, but I never thought he would own it upon his honour."

At this time it was quite the mode for noblemen to have their pet actresses, and no mock modesty was shown in such arrangements. Walpole writing on June 10, 1743, says: " Lord Walpole has taken a dozen to Starm, a small house about four miles from hence (Houghton, Norfolk), where he lives with my lady Walpole's vice regent (Miss Norsa) ; " and four years later (June 26, 1747) thus generalises the fashion : " This Lord (Lord Luxborough) keeps Mrs. Horton the player ; *we* keep Miss Norsa, the player ; Rich, the harlequin, is an intimate of all, and to cement the harlequinity, somebody's brother (excuse me if I am not perfect in such genealogy) is to marry the Jewess's (Miss Norsa's) sister."

The fair Jewess was one of the merry party in 1750 at Vauxhall, of which Walpole gives so vivid an account. " At last," he writes, " we assembled in our booth, Lady Caroline Fitzroy in the front, with the vizor of her hat erect, and looking gloriously jolly and handsome. She had fetched my brother Orford from the next box, where he was enjoying himself with his Norsa and *petite partie,* to help us mince chickens. We minced seven chickens in a china dish, which Lady C. stewed over a lamp with

17

three pats of butter and a flagon of water, stirring
and rattling and laughing, and we every minute
expecting to have the dish fly about our ears." All
that need be said—and, after all, it is something to
say—the eighteenth century knew how to find its
amusement, and did not scruple to take it when
there was the chance.

No actress of any standing who could sing (and
even those who could not) was able to resist the
temptation of playing Polly. It was the one part in
which all were anxious to shine. Hence the celebrated quarrel between Kitty Clive and Mrs. Cibber
which agitated the theatrical world in 1736–37,
supplied the newspapers with columns of controversy, and was the first of many rivalries of which
the ever-popular Opera was destined to be the cause.

The first intimation the public had that all was
not well within the green room of Drury Lane Theatre
was contained in a letter headed " Enormities
of the Stage," and signed " A Spectator," which
appeared in *The Daily Gazetteer* of November 4, 1736.
The Grub Street Journal, *The Daily Post*, and *Daily
Advertiser* contributed their quota of inflammable
material, and then appeared a series of articles commencing in *The Daily Journal* of December 6, headed
" The Occasional Prompter," the first of which sums
up the merits of the quarrel so well that we adopt
the writer's words. In alluding to " A Spectator's "
letter " The Occasional Prompter " says :

" This writer, in giving an account of the contest
between two actresses for the part of Polly, seems
to be of opinion that an injustice is done to Mrs.
Clive in attempting to take it from her . . . but
at the same time allows Mrs. Cibber in the hand-
somest manner all the merit she could have any
right to expect, never having at that time stepped
out of the *pathetic* and *tender* walk. This letter
drew a very virulent and long-winded reply from one
Mr. A. Z. on November 13, in *The Daily Advertiser*
and *London Daily Post*, in which Mrs. Clive is most

unjustly and unfairly aspersed. . . . Mrs. Clive answered this in the same two papers a few days after, and signed her name to it, in which she acquaints the town that *to oblige them* she was willing to play any part they should desire to see her in, but as it did not appear to be their desire she should give up the part of Polly, or perform that of Lucy, she thought she might withstand the cabals within doors against her, and therefore declares that *through choice she will never give up the part of Polly*, but that if Mr. Fleetwood orders her to study Lucy in conformity to her Articles and to avoid the penalty she would incur in case of her refusal, she is ready to perform it. She adds she is under an apprehension other Parts may likewise be demanded of her in favour of her Competitrix and that she never did or could refuse that of Lucy, not having received orders to study it. This is the sense, though not the direct words, of her reply. . . . The question, in short, is this : which would make the better Polly, Mrs. Clive or Mrs. Cibber ? It is that this latter, from having the appearance of more natural Innocence and Simplicity in her looks than Mrs. Clive, if natural innocence and simplicity are the essentials of Polly's character, would ; and the inference drawn from hence is that if Mrs. Cibber would make the best Polly, Mr. Fleetwood is justified in taking the part from Mrs. Clive in order to entertain the town better."

It seems to us that " The Occasional Prompter," with every desire to do justice to Mrs. Clive, forgot what was really the essence of the business—the natural repugnance of a clever actress, sure of herself and confident in her public, to giving up a leading character with which she was identified and taking a subordinate one in the same play. Human nature, and certainly not the nature of the fiery Kitty, would not be equal to the sacrifice. Whatever may be said about Polly, she is the principal character in *The Beggar's Opera*, it is she whom the audience want to see and hear, and Lucy is always second fiddle, no matter how distinguished may be her representative. To continue, however, with " The Prompter." He goes on to quote from a letter signed " Æquus " in *The Daily Journal* of November 13 to show Polly's real character ; and this letter is of special interest because it lets us know how Lavinia Fenton played the part. " Æquus " says :

" It has been a matter of a good deal of surprise to me to see what a false Notion the Generality of spectators have entertained of the character of Polly ; she is commonly thought to be a young *innocent* Girl made up of nothing but artless Simplicity and Nature, very fond *and tender*. Whether the *appearance* the first Polly made conveyed this Idea of *artless Innocence* in Polly, and stamped *that* character on her, I shall not determine ; but certain it is that this is the conceived *Idea* of her ; and all succeeding Pollies but *one* have copied from the first original exhibition of her, and given us, in spite of Nature and Truth, as *tender, soft* and *fond* a Fool as Heart could wish.

" Now the real character of Polly is very different from this ; and I dare answer for Mr. Gay he never thought of drawing such unnatural Creatures as our Pollies have made of themselves. . . . . Hear Mr. Peachum's Account of his daughter :

" ' PEACH : Lookye, wife, a handsome wench, in our way of business, is as profitable as at the bar of a Temple coffee-house, who looks upon it as her livelihood, to grant every liberty but one. My daughter to me should be like a court lady to a minister of state, a key to the whole gang.'

" Now let her Mamma speak :

" ' MRS. PEACH. : Mayhap, my dear, you may injure the girl : she loves to imitate the fine ladies, and she may only allow the Captain liberties in the view of interest.'

" And for fear we should not know what sort of Education she had been used to, the old Gentleman rejoins :

"'PEACH.: But 'tis your duty to warn the girl against her ruin, and instruct her to make the most of her beauty.'

"But to set this matter out of all doubt and to show she was THE VERY THING her Father and Mother would have her, let Polly speak for herself:

"'POLLY: I know as well as any of the fine ladies how to make the most of myself, and of my man too. A woman knows how to be mercenary, though she hath never been in a court, or at an assembly. We have it in our natures, papa. If I allow Captain Macheath some trifling liberties, I have this watch, and other visible marks of his favour, to show for it. A girl who cannot grant some things, and refuse what is most material, will make but a poor hand of her beauty, and soon be thrown upon the common.'

"Pretty, little, innocent soul! What a Pity 'tis she should be deceived by such a Rogue! *Risum teneatis, Amici!*"

"Æquus" denies poor Polly the possession of "a grain of nature, Simplicity or Innocence, and the acting that *formed Character*, on *Romance* and *low Life.* . . ." On the other hand, Lucy from the writer's point of view "is a thousand times more naturally *innocent* and *foolish*"; but strong passions get the better of her natural Temper and make her appear violent throughout. Hear her herself:

"'LUCY: 'Tis the pleasure of all you fine Men to insult the women you have ruined.'

"Polly in all the Play does not say so innocent, simple, natural and foolish a Thing. Consider her song. The first four lines show the tender, innocent, betrayed fond one:

"'How cruel are the traitors
Who lie and swear in jest,
To cheat unguarded creatures
Of virtue, fame, and rest!'

"What more pathetick! What more moving! But in an instant the violence of her Passion gets

the better of her natural softness, and she ends it in
an angry resentment :

> " ' Whoever steals a shilling
> Thro' shame the guilt conceals ;
> In love the perjur'd villain
> With boasts the theft reveals.'

"But go to the 11th scene, and this character
of Lucy will be set out of all Question :
" ' LOCK. : Whence came you, hussy ?
" ' LUCY : My tears might answer that question.
" ' LOCK. : You have then been whimpering and
fondling like a spaniel over the fellow that hath
abused you.
" ' LUCY : One can't help love, one can't cure it.
'Tis not in my power to obey you and hate him.'
" . . . If this character of Polly is her real one, and
that she is a romantick, amorous *whiner*, and not an
innocent, fond, artless girl, submit to the Judgment
of the Public whether it is to be play'd with real
Innocence or no. If it is *not*, I would then ask
what woman on either stage is most likely to look
and act the character ? I name none."

There is much force in this view of Polly's character, but it is incomplete. In spite of her immoral
surroundings and training, the girl might at the same
time have tenderness and real love for the handsome
highwayman. There is nothing impossible or unnatural in the apparent contradiction. There are
scores of Pollies in real life, who show devotion to
the men of their choice, and who to the world are
all that is designing, unscrupulous, mercenary, immoral
and faithless.

What added to the gaiety of the town was that
at the very height of the squabble a laughable affair
happened in the theatrical world abroad which was
at once applied to matters at home. " Last week at
the Opera-house in Paris," *The Grub Street Journal*
records, " the two famous rival Dancers Mademoiselles
Petit and St. Germain had some words behind the

scenes; from words they fell to blows, and their
fury hurried them on to the stage, where they fairly
box'd it out before the audience, who were much
better diverted by that scene than they would have
been by the piece itself. Miss Petit, who began it,
was immediately turn'd out of the Theatre." The
skittish poet of the period of course went to work
at once, and evolved "An Epigram on the late
Battle of the French Dancers at Paris, and the two
Rival Ladies (for the part of Polly) here." It ran:

> "Two Rivals in Theatrick Fame
>   Fell out in France—and fight;
> Two Nymphs in England did the same,
>   But, cooler, chose to write.
> Their Nature each example shows:
>   Courageous That, This Witty;
> The Frenchmen back their Cause with Blows,
>   But Englishmen with Treaty."

Nothing would have delighted an English audience
more than to see the ladies settle their claims to
"Polly" on the stage *vi et armis*, but Mrs. Cibber's
nature was anything but pugnacious. She does not
appear to have shown herself active in rivalry, and
if the truth were known we fancy that her good-for-
nothing husband, Theophilus Cibber, was at the
bottom of the business. From all accounts she
seems to have been gentle and sympathetic—that is,
if her singing and acting were any key to her character. Davies says of her: "Her great excellence
consisted in that simplicity which needed no ornament; in that sensibility which despised all art.
There was in her countenance a small share of
beauty; but nature had given her such symmetry
of form and fine expression of feature that she preserved all the appearance of youth long after she
had reached to middle life." Mrs. Cibber was the
sister of Dr. Arne and a most accomplished singer.
In 1736, however, she had had little experience as an
actress, and it was not to be wondered at that Kitty
Clive strongly resented being placed in the background

to make room for a raw recruit so far as the drama was concerned. In regard to her vocal abilities one need only mention that she was the first Galatea in Handel's cantata, and that he wrote the contralto songs in *The Messiah*, and the part of Micah in *Samson* expressly for her (*Dictionary of National Biography*), to indicate that she was not only an accomplished musician but had a voice of great compass. The music assigned to Micah is a sufficient proof of this. In regard to the first exponent of the part, however, we are faced with the usual contradiction. Vincent Novello in his edition of *Samson* (1850) says it was Miss Edwards, and quotes Handel's MS., on which in pencil are written (we give the words exactly as we find them) the names of " Mrs. Clive, Signora Avolio, Miss Edwards, and Boys, Mrs. Low." Mr. Novello claims for Miss Edwards the part of Micah. The point, however, is one which we are not called upon to settle.

One of the contributors to the controversy (*Daily Journal*, December 10, 1736) draws a picture of Mrs. Cibber which may not have been altogether fanciful : " There is, without denying Mrs. Cibber to be a very agreeable figure, a certain narrowness between her brows together with a sharpness of face that will hit to admiration that *angry resentment of wrongs* so strong in the character of Lucy, while her natural softness will touch Lucy's more tender and pleased moments with Macheath." The portrait of Mrs. Cibber (see p. 8) suggests a settled melancholy. It represents her in middle life, and it is little wonder that her face when in repose was sad, for she looked back upon a past which contained as unsavoury a scandal as woman ever endured. Her husband, who habitually ill-treated and neglected her, threw her for his own mercenary gain into the arms of a lover. The affair came before a court of law in 1738, when the jury showed their contempt for Theophilus by awarding him £10 as amply sufficient to heal his wounded honour.

INCLEDON AS MACHEATH.

From an engraving by H. R. Cook, after Clater.

Poor Mrs. Cibber had to suffer bitterly for her misconduct. The published report of the trial is as gross an example of what at the time was popular reading as can well be cited. The coincidence of dates would seem to show that in 1736–7 Theophilus was ready to stoop to anything to make money. Probably he imagined that if his wife could once play Polly she would oust Mrs. Clive and make more money, of which he of course would have the benefit. The wordy, windy letter he wrote to *The Daily Journal*, ostensibly in defence of his wife, suggests that he was the instigator of the cabals to which Kitty Clive alludes. It was hardly likely Fleetwood, the patentee, favoured Mrs. Cibber. She had played Desdemona once at the beginning of the season of 1736–37 on October 4, and however meritorious she may have been it did not follow she would play a part so vastly different as Polly. The boisterous Kitty, on the other hand, had been the mainstay of Drury Lane, and crowds were drawn to the house by her lively acting in *The Devil to Pay*, *The Virgin Unmasked*, and *The Beggar's Opera*. Though " Æquus " does not indicate by name the " one " who did not adopt the reading of Lavinia Fenton, it is very clear he meant Mrs. Clive. We may be sure that, if she had not the tenderness and simplicity of the original Polly, she made amends by her sauciness and piquancy. Moreover the public were unmistakably on the side of Kitty, as the following lines which appeared in *The Daily Journal* of December 14 show :

" To Mrs. Clive on the Ungenerous Treatment she has
lately met with.

" Take courage, Clive ! the tyrant of the stage
Shall never crush the Darling of the Age ;
Two other Houses would be glad to court thee :
Leave him—the Town will follow and support thee :
Despise his threats, the destin'd Forfeit pay,
Thy Friends will make amends another way :
And to his sorrow it will soon be found
For ev'ry Doit thou pay'st, He'll lose a Pound."

Mrs. Clive of course gained the day; it would have needed more than ordinary force to put down that "mixture of combustibles" as Davies called her, and she signalised her triumph by playing Polly on the last day of 1736, with Mrs. Pritchard as Lucy. Years after, the rivals were reconciled, Mrs. Cibber acting Polly and Mrs. Clive Lucy at Drury Lane on December 12 and 13, 1747, and again on October 15, 1748. Genest's words are : "Nothing probably would have induced Mrs. Clive to have resigned Polly to Mrs. Cibber; but as she had previously and of her own accord resigned the part to Miss Edwards (September 30, 1746) and played Lucy, she could not well object to Mrs. Cibber's Polly." Genest might have added that the Mrs. Cibber of 1747 was quite a different personage from the Mrs. Cibber of 1736. In the interval she had established her reputation as one of the finest emotional actresses of the day. Her Constance in *King John*, her Belvidera in *Venice Preserved*, and above all her Ophelia, surpassed all performances of previous actresses. It was no slight to Mrs. Clive when she played Polly. As to her rendering of the songs there could not be the slightest doubt of her superiority.

Between 1736 and 1747 Mrs. Cibber acted Polly thrice—the performances on December 14, 15, 16, 1745, in aid of what was called the Guildhall Veteran Scheme, a fund raised to assist those who had fought in the Scotch Rebellion—and her playing and singing probably convinced Mrs. Clive of her powers. On this occasion Rich gave the free use of Covent Garden Theatre, and the company their services. Mrs. Pritchard, who was afterwards so celebrated for her performance as Lady Macbeth, and who had not then turned her attention to tragedy, was Lucy, and she may have been as slim as forty years later she was the reverse. Horace Walpole spoke of her as "poor fat Mrs. Pritchard," and Hannah More, in describing the bigamy trial of the "Duchess" of Kingston, otherwise the adventurous Elizabeth

Chudleigh, compared her by inference to a bundle of bombazeen !

The year 1737 is memorable in the annals of the stage for the passing of the Licensing Act, which placed further restrictions on the already hampered " rogues and vagabonds." The anonymous author of one of Quin's biographies was very wrath with the author of *Tom Jones,* who he asserts was the cause of the Act being introduced.

" Colley Cibber tells us," he writes, " that a broken wit collected a fourth company, who for some time acted Plays in the Hay-market, which house the united Drury Lane comedians had quitted. This enterprising person (Henry F—d—g) had sense enough to know that the best plays with bad actors would turn but to a very poor account, and therefore thought it necessary to give the public some pieces of an extraordinary kind, the poetry of which he conceived ought to be so strong, that the greatest dunce of an actor could not spoil it. He knew, too, that as he was in haste to get money it would take up less time to be intrepidly allusive, than decently entertaining ; that to draw the mob after him, he must rake the channel, and pelt their superiors ; that to shew himself somebody, he must come up to Juvenal's advice, and stand the consequence. Such then was the nettlesome modesty he set out with ; upon this principle, he produced several frank and free farces that seemed to knock all distinctions of mankind on the head. Religion, laws, government, priests, judges, and ministers, were all laid flat at the feet of this Herculean satyrist, this Draw-cansir in wit, that spared neither friend nor foe. Who, to make his fame immortal, like another Erostratus, set fire to his stage, by writing up to an act of parliament to demolish it.

" The most remarkable of these politico-satyrical pieces were *Pasquin, The Historical Register,* and *Eurydice Hissed* ; but he did not confine himself solely to stage abuse ; for about the same time he

attacked Sir Robert W—— and in a most violent
manner in the paper called *The Champion*, written, as
the title set forth, by Hercules Vinegar : and, doubtless that laureat obliquely hints at the title when he
calls him the *Herculean Satyrist.*

" To Henry F—d—g then are we indebted for that
licensing act, and the theatrical power that is now
lodged in the licenser ; who exercised his authority
for the first time in 1738, upon *Gustavus Vasa*, a
tragedy, written by Mr. Brooke."

Mrs. Delany in one of her letters, dated April 22,
1736, touches on this subject in these words : " When
I went out of town last autumn, the reigning topic
was Farinelli; I find it now turned on *Pasquin*, a
dramatic satyr on the times. It has had almost as
long a run as *The Beggar's Opera*, but in my opinion
not with equal merit, though it has humour."

To what heartburnings and inconvenience this Act
led, the history of the drama in England bears ample
testimony. For years Sadler's Wells and other
theatres could not perform what it had become the
fashion to call the legitimate drama, and Elliston in
1808 was only able to put *The Beggar's Opera* on the
stage at the Wells by calling it a burletta, with the
dialogue thrown into a sort of jingling rhyme ! The
same ridiculous barriers compelled him to produce
Macbeth under the name of a Pantomime !

CHAPTER XXIII

THE BEGGAR'S PANTOMIME

The Beggar's Pantomime—Woodward's skit on the rival Pollies—Fielding's *Historical Register for 36* satirises the Italian Opera and the Clive and Cibber squabble—Woodward and Kitty Clive—Curious performance of *The Beggar's Opera* at Goodman's Fields Theatre—The eccentric Charlotte Charke's Macheath—An unsolved mystery.

THE quarrel between the ladies subsided so far as the combatants were concerned, but it was not allowed to rest. The controversy was continued in the newspapers, other matters were dragged in, and Rich saw a chance of attracting the public by burlesquing the quarrel, and with the assistance of his understudy " Lun Junior," otherwise Woodward, he brought out at Lincoln's Inn Fields *The Beggar's Pantomime or the Contending Columbines.* Woodward wrote the piece and played the principal male character, Harlequin Macheath. Woodward, however, had no intention of offending the ladies, and in his dedication to Mrs. Clive and Mrs. Cibber, he, writing as " Lun Jun.," said : " When I publicly declare this trifling piece was meant only to promote the theatre to which I belong, I hope you will have more good nature than to, imagine I designed to affront two ladies whom I am utterly a stranger to. Your *Paper War* making such a bustle about the town, and its being so much public talk of coffee houses, I thought it no bad scheme to make use of the opportunity and introduce something like *your Contention* upon our stage ; I immediately made use of the subject and (at a time when it was most alive) resolved to bring it out ; the Pantomime, songs, and scenery were all finished and ready to be exhibited in ten days."

Genest, while apparently in possession of a copy of *The Beggar's Pantomime*, which was printed and published at the time, had not before him all the particulars of its production on the stage. He gives the cast as follows : Harlequin Macheath, Lun Jun. ; Manager, Cox ; Beggar, Hewitt ; Deputy Manager, Mrs. Charke ; Squire Rustick, Yates ; Clown, Pinkethman ; Ghost of Gay, Lyon ; Polly, Mrs. Roberts ; A Pretender to Polly, Mrs. Hamilton. The part of Pistol, Genest adds, was omitted. As a matter of fact it had not been thought of, for reasons which we give presently. Genest speaks of January 3, 1737, as the first night, although he surmises that the burlesque may have been produced earlier. In this supposition he was right. December 3, 1736, was the date—just when the paper war was at its height. Rich possibly regarded the skit as an experiment, for it was advertised under its title only " with Polly and Lucy," no cast being given and no actors' or actresses' names mentioned. The *Pantomime* evidently caught on, and on December 8 we have the cast announced for the first time. It will be seen that it differs considerably from Genest's list. Mrs. Charke, Theophilus Cibber's extraordinary manwoman sister, did not appear for some days after the first production. The names given in *The Daily Post* run thus : Manager, Mr. Osborne ; Beggar, Mr. Hewitt ; Gamester, Mr. Dove ; Jenny Diver, Mrs. Dove ; Molly Brazen, Mrs. Haughton ; Suky Tawdrey, Miss Tollett ; Mrs. Slammerkin, Miss Thirnowetz ; Columbine Polly, Mrs. Hamilton ; Columbine Lucy, Mrs. Roberts ; Peachum, Mr. Rosco ; Lockit, Mr. Lyon ; Mat o' the Mint, Mr. Richardson ; Squire Rustick, Mr. Yate, and Clown, Mr. Pinkethman.

Theophilus Cibber's inane letter appeared in *The Daily Journal* of December 9 ; the shrewd Rich instantly made use of it to advertise his novelty further, and Cibber is introduced as " Mrs. Hamilton's husband," " Mrs. Hamilton " was supposed to repre-

sent Mrs. Cibber, and Mrs. Roberts personated Mrs.
Clive. The advertisement of December 11 has this
announcement tacked on to it : " With additional songs
in the character of Mrs. Hamilton's Husband occasion'd
by an accident that happen'd to him in Grub St.
on Thursday last (*i.e.* the date of Cibber's letter).
The part of Mrs. Hamilton's Husband in the character
of Spitfire by Mr. Bardin." *The Beggar's Pantomime*
was apparently of the nature of the modern *Revue* ;
it could be altered or strengthened to suit the progress
of events. Seemingly neither Spitfire nor his impersonator was adequate to the circumstances, and
on December 16 we have the following alteration :
" The part of Mrs. Hamilton's Husband in the
character of Pistol by Mrs. Charke." Pistol was of
course selected to take off Theophilus Cibber's
braggadocio and boasting. Mrs. Charke, whose career
was one of the most singular to be found in the history
of the stage, preferred to play a man's part both in
the drama and in real life, and no doubt she caricatured her brother pretty closely, for there was no
love lost between them. She remained in the piece
to the end of the run. From December 23 to 30
the *Pantomime* was advertised by its title only, but
on the 31st the names of the characters reappear,
together with " new songs and several alterations
and additions, particularly a sequel to the Contention
call'd *Pistol in Mourning* . . . with a new ballad—
Prologue to the Pantomime by Mrs. Roberts." By
the middle of January the affair had become stale,
and the last night was on the 14th.

The *Pantomime* as stated, was published, but we
have failed to find a copy in the British Museum,
and we fall back upon Genest for information. It
had a prologue set to the tune of *Chevy Chase*, and
Genest gives the following as the principal verses :

" Heav'n prosper long our noble King,
Our lives and safeties all !
A woeful quarrel late there did
In Drury Lane befall.

"To charm the Pit with speech and song
  Dame Cibber took her way ;
  Players may rue, who are unborn,
  The quarrel of that day.

"Cibber, the Syren of the stage,
  A vow to heav'n did make :
  Full Twenty nights in Polly's part
  She'd make the play-house shake.

"When as these tidings came to Clive,
  Fierce Amazonian dame ;
'Who is it thus,' in rage she cries,
' Dares rob me of my claim ? '
  .   .   .   .   .
"With that she to the green-room flew,
  Where Cibber meek she found ;
  And sure if friends had not been by
  She had fell'd her to the ground.
  .   .   .   .   .
"But now each loving spouse engag'd,
  In honour of his wife ;
  Each drew his mortal grey-goose quill,
  And writ away for life.

" At length bold Pistol (Cibber) thus did say,
  As one in doleful dumps,
' My wife shall have the part, or I'll
  My pen write to the stumps.'

" On this he writ at such a rate
  That in each dreadful page
  Truth, sense, and English all did fall
  The victims of his rage."

(The Manager decides in favour of Mrs. Clive.)

" ' O heavy news ! ' then Pistol cry'd,
  With that he wept full sore ;
' O heavy news ! ' his wife reply'd,
  Then fainted on the floor.

" Heaven save the King, and bless the land
  With plenty, joy and peace,
  And grant henceforth that foul debates
  'Twixt Actresses may cease."

Genest says that the first three scenes were in the
usual manner of a harlequinade, the fourth scene
taking place in Newgate. After the stage has been
kept waiting some time a Beggar enters in a hurry.

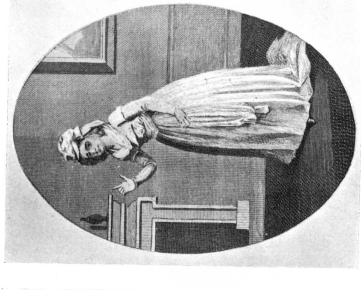

MRS. CROUCH AS POLLY PEACHUM.

From an engraving by Thornthwaite, after De Wilde.

MRS. MARTYR AS AURA IN "THE COUNTRY LASSES."

From an engraving by Leney, after De Wilde.

272]

"BEGGAR : Mr. Prompter! Mr. Prompter! (*Enter Prompter.*) What the Devil is the meaning of this stop! Have you a design to ruin me ? Why, the stage has stood this hour!

"PROMP. : I assure you 'tis none of my fault, but Mrs. Roberts and Mrs. Hamilton are quarrelling who shall do the first Columbine ; they scolded as long as they had breath, and now they have set themselves down to send letters to the public papers to inform the town of their ill-usage."

Mrs. Roberts and Mrs. Hamilton now contend in three or four pages of singing—the Ghost of Gay decides in favour of Mrs. Roberts—the piece then proceeds as a harlequinade till the next scene, when Pistol and his wife are discovered in mourning. If this was all, it looks as if *The Beggar's Pantomime* contained but a ha'porth of satire to an intolerable quantity of harlequinade. But doubtless it pleased the town.

Fielding in a comedy which he called *The Historical Register for 1736* (played at the Haymarket in 1737) also refers to the squabble. *The Historical Register* is a vehicle for gibing at everything that concerns the town. It skims the surface of fashion, and one has only to read between the lines to get a very fair idea of the theatrical and operatic topics that interested the *beau monde* at the time. One of the characters, Lord Dapper, says, in allusion to the decorations of Lincoln's Inn Fields Theatre (see p.68), " Here are no looking-glasses. I love Lincoln's Inn Fields for that reason better than any house in town." The chatter of the ladies is particularly sprightly, as may be seen from the following sample, the point of which the student of the history of early Italian opera will have no difficulty in appreciating.

"ALL LADIES : Was you at the Opera, Madam, last night ?

"2 LADY : Who can miss an opera while Farinello stays ?

"3 LADY : Sure he is the charmingest Creature.

18

"4 LADY : He's everything in the world one could wish.

"1 LADY : Almost everything one could wish.

"2 LADY : They say there's a Lady in the city has a child by him.

"ALL LADIES : Ha, ha, ha !

"1 LADY : Well, it must be charming to have a child by him.

"3 LADY : Madam, I met a Lady in a visit the other Day with three.

"ALL LADIES : All Farinello's ?

"3 LADY : All Farinello's, all in wax.

"1 LADY : O Gemini ! who makes them ? I'll send and bespeak half a dozen to-morrow morning."

Fielding has no mercy for Theophilus Cibber, whom, following *The Beggar's Pantomime*, he calls Pistol. Pistol enters with a Mob, which he thus addresses :

" PISTOL : Associates, Brethren, Countrymen and Friends,
Partakers with us in this glorious Enterprize,
Which for our Consort we have undertaken ;
It grieves us much, yes, by the Gods it does !
That we whose great Ability and Parts
Have rais'd us to this Pinnacle of Power,
Entitling us Prime Minister Theatrical ;
That we should with an Upstart of the Stage
Contend successless on our Consort's Side ;
But tho', by just hereditary Right
We claim a lawless Power, yet for some Reasons,
Which to our self we keep as yet conceaĺéd :
Thus to the Publick deign we to appeal ;
Behold how humbly the Great *Pistol* kneels.
Say then, Oh Town, is it your Royal Will,
That my Great Consort represent the part
Of Polly Peachum in *The Beggar's Opera* ? "
[*Mob hiss*

PIST. : Thanks to the Town, that Hiss speaks their Assent.
Such was the Hiss that spoke the great Applause
Our mighty Father met with, when he brought
His *Riddle* on the stage ; such was the Hiss
Welcom'd his *Cæsar* to the Ægyptian shore ;
Such was the Hiss in which Great *John* shou'd have expired.
But wherefore do I try in vain to number
Those glorious Hisses, which from Age to Age
Our Family has borne triumphant from the Stage? "

These allusions to Colley Cibber's failures, *Love in a Riddle* and others, were doubly charged, and must have wounded the father more grievously than they wounded the son.

Another shot at the Clive-Cibber squabble is fired later on, where Sourwit, a critic, says to Medley, the author of the Comedy—" Hey-day! What's become of your two Pollys? "

" MEDLEY : Damn'd, Sir, damn'd ; they were damn'd at my first rehearsal, for which reason I have cut them out ; and to tell you the truth, I think the Town has honour'd 'em enough with talking of them for a whole month ; tho' faith, I believe, it was owing to their having nothing else to talk of."

Woodward's protest that he did not know either of the ladies was intended to conceal the authorship of *The Beggar's Pantomime*. As a matter of fact he had acted more than once with the " combustible Kitty," and was likely to be able to banter her effectively. Tate Wilkinson mentions one play, Otway's *Friendship in Fashion*, for which both Woodward and Mrs. Clive were cast, written quite in the spirit of one of Mrs. Eliza Haywood's " smart " novels. " Be it noticed," remarked Wilkinson, quaintly, " Dame Clive was not blessed with beauty, though of infinite talents ; yet she unfortunately in that Comedy was ideally ravished twice or thrice before the fourth act ended, which the audience very properly judged to be too much for that lady's feelings, and not knowing what might truly happen in the fifth, they consequently put a violent and final stop to all further indecent proceedings." This is Wilkinson's version (*Friendship in Fashion*, by the way, is hardly so bad as he represents), and there might have been some reason other than consideration for Kitty which made the audience stop the play. The delicate (or indelicate) matters dealt with in *Friendship in Fashion* were not taken very seriously, or such a play as Fielding's *The Coffee House Politicians* would hardly have been produced. The theme of this may be gathered from the prologue put into the mouth of pretty Mrs. Younger, who had to ask :

> " Pray do all your frowns arise
> Because so much of rape and rape we bawl ?
> Or is it that we have no rape at all ?
> Indeed, our poet, to oblige the age,
> Had brought a dreadful scene upon the stage ;
> But I, perceiving what his muse would drive at,
> Told him the Ladies never would connive at
> A downright actual rape—unless in private."

The Rev. John Genest, the recognised historian of the stage, prints these lines without comment, and we follow his example. It may, however, be said that, in spite of the alarming title of *Rape upon Rape, or the Justice caught in his own Trap*, which it bears in addition to *The Coffee House Politicians*, there is very little harm in the play. It is merry enough after a fashion.

For the next two years the Opera was given a rest, being revived chiefly for benefits; but on October 17, 1740, it was produced for the debut of Lowe, who, according to Genest, for the first time on this date played Macheath. The Opera was acted several times. On December 31 it was brought out at Goodman's Fields Theatre, with Walker as Macheath, and " Polly—a Gentlewoman, her first appearance on any stage." The Opera was sandwiched between two parts of a concert, and in addition a " Pantomime Entertainment " was given, the performance concluding with *The Triumphs of Love*, a little pastoral very popular in both the eighteenth and seventeenth centuries. The programme was truly a liberal one, that is if *The Beggar's Opera* was played without " cuts."

Probably there was some special reason for the attraction, the advertisements in *The Daily Post* informing us that both the Pantomime and *The Triumphs of Love* " will be performed gratis by Persons for their Diversion." Wonderful to say, *The Daily*

Post (January 7, 1741) inserted a notice in addition to the advertisement as follows : " Last night *The Beggar's Opera* was perform'd at the late (why 'late ' ?) Theatre in Goodman's Fields, in which a Gentlewoman perform'd the Character of Polly and was generally esteem'd equal to any one who hath before appear'd in it." No doubt such an ample bill of fare attracted large audiences, and the hope expressed that " no Gentleman will take it ill that they are refus'd Admittance behind the Scenes, it being impossible to perform the Entertainment unless the Entrances are kept entirely clear," was probably not wholly unnecessary.

The Opera ran for thirty nights, and on January 15 gave place to *The Winter's Tale* (" not acted these hundred years "), also performed between the " divisions of a concert " and " with singing and Dancing adapted to the Play, particularly A song by the Gentlewoman who perform'd Polly." On January 27 the Opera was put on for one night, and this was the last of the " Gentlewoman." Curiosity was never gratified as to the name of the lady, and she remains unidentified to this day.

Lowe seems to have been the principal Macheath in 1742 and the two succeeding years. Two dates— April 29 and 30—are notable in 1744, Mrs. Clive on those days surrendering Polly to Miss Edwards (afterwards Mrs. Mozeen). It was a graceful act, and Kitty could well afford to do it, for she had made her reputation as the leading comedy actress of the day and was in no way remarkable as a singer, while Miss Edwards was an accomplished singer or Handel would not have written for her the elaborate music of Micah in *Samson* (see p. 264).

Macheath has always had a wonderful fascination for actresses who fancy " breeches " parts. The picturesque costume shows off the figure admirably, the dash and go of the character appeal to certain feminine temperaments, and the songs suit a woman as well as a man. It was not at all extraordinary

that Charlotte Charke, who was always at home in
male rôles, was anxious to show what she could do as
the dashing highwayman. She found her chance at
the Haymarket Theatre with " The Queen of Hungary's company of Comedians," who produced the
Opera on December 28, 1744. Genest gives this on
the authority of playbills in the British Museum ;
the newspapers of the period are silent on the subject.
Charlotte Charke, who possessed " a constitutional
tendency towards vagabondage," is in her extraordinary *Autobiography* provokingly reticent concerning
her theatrical career, and there is no mention in it
either of " The Queen of Hungary's Company " or
of the Haymarket Theatre. It should be pointed out
in passing that the present Haymarket Theatre is
not built on the site of the old one The first building, opened in 1720, was intended as a summer theatre
only, and for a long time was known as the Little
Theatre in the Haymarket, to distinguish it from the
Opera House. It was permanently closed October 14,
1820, and the theatre of to-day erected on a piece of
ground immediately adjoining and south of the old
site. Charlotte Charke, so far as we can ascertain,
played Captain Macheath but once.

Tate Wilkinson asserts that at Covent Garden in
1747 the Opera was put on with Beard as Macheath.
This is an obvious error, as Beard's time did not
come for some years later, although he seems to
have played the part on January 15, 1748, at Covent
Garden, and twice in 1749 at Drury Lane, Mrs. Clive
being Polly on the second occasion. Tate Wilkinson
says that the Opera was repeated several nights and
" drew more money than any other play to the house,
deserted as it was at that time." We can find no
confirmation of this either in Genest or in the newspapers of the period. Wilkinson probably confused
1747 with 1751, when public interest was revived in
a most extraordinary way, Lowe making a great hit
as Macheath.

It is rather singular that Genest does not supply

particulars of this revival, but the advertisements in *The General Advertiser* probably furnish the reason. The part of Polly was taken " by a Gentlewoman who never appeared on the stage before," and for this reason was ignored by the chronicler. The first performance was given on October 29, 1751, and concluded " with a country dance by the characters of the Opera." It ran for fourteen nights with but two interruptions. On the fifteenth night Polly was played by Mrs. Chambers. Whether she was the " Gentlewoman " who had hitherto appeared incognito we are unable to say.

CHAPTER XXIV

FROM COFFEE-HOUSE TO CORONET

The death of the Duchess of Bolton and marriage of Lavinia Fenton to the Duke—Anastasia Robinson, the first actress-peeress—The death of the Duke of Bolton—His laconic will—Long run of *The Beggar's Opera* with Miss Brent and John Beard—Nancy Dawson's hornpipe dancing a great attraction—Goldsmith's paper in the *British Magazine* on two rival Pollies, Miss Brent and Mrs. Vincent.

THE year 1751 was destined to be a notable one in the life of Lavinia Fenton. Twenty-three years had passed since she was the idol of the town, and when Charles Duke of Bolton took her from the stage her private life interested no one. She dropped naturally into domesticity, and there is every reason to believe, despite the sneers of Lord Hervey as to the Duke's " folly " and the shrugging of many shoulders among noble dames, that his Grace never had cause to regret his choice. It is certain she did not flaunt herself in any way, and was contented to live in retirement sometimes at Hackwood, the seat of the Paulets in Hampshire, or at Bolton Hall in the North Riding of Yorkshire, but mostly at Westcombe House, Greenwich, which the Duke leased for her and where she died.

The Duke's early marriage in 1713 with Lady Anne Vaughan, only daughter and heiress of the Earl of Carbery, an Irish peer, was an unhappy one. The marriage was forced upon him by his father, and when the latter died in 1722 the son and his duchess separated. Probably her Grace having considerable property of her own did not, after parting from her husband, trouble either Hackwood or Bolton Hall with her presence, and the Duke was free to do as he liked. Anyhow, the only definite fact which has come down to us is that, during the lifetime of the Duchess, Lavinia became the mother of three children.

Tate Wilkinson seems to insinuate that Lavinia made a compact with the Duke that when he became a widower he would make her his wife, but this is simply conjecture. It is certain, however, that his Grace was very anxious for the arrival of the day when he would be free to marry the woman of his heart, and when his duchess fell ill in 1751 he sent for his friend, the Rev. Dr. Joseph Warton, to whom he had previously presented a living, to go abroad with him and Lavinia, so that the marriage might be solemnised the very moment the news of the Duchess's death, which was daily expected, reached him.

Mr. Singer, Warton's biographer, in alluding to the Duke's hasty summons to the clergyman, says: " The pleasure which might have filled the mind of Warton upon the prospect of visiting the Continent must have been greatly abated by the unpleasant circumstances under which his presence was courted, and he had also to add to this the separation from his family. It was evident, however, that he could not refuse, without in some measure destroying his future expectations in that quarter, and the straitened income of his small living made an abandonment of his hopes of preferment hardly to be expected. They left England in April, and travelled by easy stages through the French provinces to Montauban, the Duke purposing to stay there some months. Warton, who had expected to visit Italy, and whose imperfect knowledge of French made his intercourse with society irksome, became tired of his situation, and returned home in September.

"The Duchess died in the succeeding month, and he immediately wrote to his patron asking his permission to return to him. But the Duke was impatient to be married, and had sent to Mr. Pevisme, the Chaplain to the Embassy at Turin, by whom the ceremony was performed at Aix in Provence." Dr. Warton, however, brought home with him a pleasant reminiscence of Lavinia (or it may have been an experience of after-years) when he wrote: "She was very accomplished, was a most agreeable companion, had much wit and strong sense, and a chaste taste in polite literature. Her person was agreeable and well made, though she could not be called a beauty. I have had the pleasure of being at table with her, when her conversation was much admired by the first characters of the age, particularly old Lord Bathurst and Lord Granville."

All that is to be learned about the Duchess's death is told in the following paragraph from *The General Advertiser* of October 8, 1751 : "Yesterday the corpse of her Grace the Duchess of Bolton was carried out of Town to be privately interr'd in the Family Vault belonging to her noble Ancestors in Llanvihanghl Church in the County of Carmarthen; which church was built by her Grace's great-grandfather, John, Lord Vaughan, Earl of Carbery. This good and excellent Lady was the Daughter and sole heiress of the Right Hon. John, Lord Vaughan, Baron of Mollingart, Earl of Carbery in Ireland, and Baron Emlyn in the County of Carmarthen. She was married to his Grace Charles, Duke of Bolton, in 1713, by whom she had no issue. Her Grace has left Golden Grove with the several Lordships and Manors adjoining and belonging, with all the rest of her real together with her personal Estate, to her Heir-at-law, the Hon. John Vaughan, Esq., Member of Parliament for the County of Carmarthen; who is a great-grandson to Sir William Vaughan, the next brother to John, Lord Vaughan, Earl of Carbery."

The Duke was twenty-three years older than his bride, but there was nothing about his marriage to cause any sensation. It was not even a nine days' wonder. No doubt everybody knew that he would make Polly his duchess at the very first opportunity. Mrs. Delany, writing to Mrs. Davies on November 16, hardly two months after the event (the marriage took place September 20, 1751) intimates as much : " You desire news from England—then a roundabout truly. All I know you shall, though it may be as old as Queen Elizabeth's death by the time it reaches you, or at least as old as the Duke of Bolton's marriage with Polly."

Lady Mary Wortley Montagu " improved " the occasion by indulging in some moralisings after her fashion. In one of her letters she wrote : " My poor friend the Duchess of Bolton was educated in solitude, with some choice of books, by a saint-like governess; crammed with virtue and good qualities, she thought it impossible not to find gratitude, though she failed to give passion ; and upon this plan threw away her estate, was despised by her husband, and laughed at by the public. Polly, bred in an ale-house, and produced on the stage, has obtained wealth and title, and found the way to be esteemed. So useful is early experience." Lady Mary omits to mention that the Duchess was very plain. Walpole does not, however, mince the matter. " Unluckily," he says, " she was a monster, —so ugly that the Duke, then Marquis of Winchester, being forced by his father to marry her for her great fortune, was believed never to have consummated." At the time of the Duke's marriage to Polly, Walpole describes him as " an old beau, fair complexioned, in a white wig, gallanting the ladies about in public."

Lavinia Fenton was not the first actress to be ennobled. That distinction belongs to Anastasia Robinson; but of the latter it may be said that she was more distinguished as a singer than as an actress. There is not the slightest parallel to be drawn between her and Lavinia Fenton either in their origin or careers. Anastasia was the daughter of a man of means and repute. Lavinia was " nobody's child," and had been dragged up, if not in " an alehouse," certainly in a coffee-shop. Anastasia had been carefully trained in her art, and had worked her way to the very front of her profession by sheer hard work and ability. Lavinia, on the other hand, favoured by Fortune, was simply hurried along the tide of popularity without any preparation, and her success was as unaccountable as it was ephemeral. Their suitors presented differences quite as striking. Lord Peterborough's method of wooing was not that of the Duke of Bolton. The story of Anastasia Robinson is worth contrasting with that of Lavinia Fenton. We are told by Dr. Burney that " Anastasia Robinson was of middling stature, not handsome but of a pleasing modest countenance, with large blue eyes. Her deportment was easy, unaffected, and graceful, her manner and address very engaging, and her behaviour on all occasions that of a gentlewoman with perfect propriety. She was not only liked by all her acquaintances, but loved and caressed by persons of the highest rank, with whom she appeared always equal, without assuming. Her father's house in Golden Square was frequented by all the men of genius and refined taste of the times. Among the number of persons of distinction who frequented Mr. Robinson's house, and seemed to distinguish his daughter in a particular manner, were the Earl of Peterborough and General H——. The latter had showed a long attachment to her, and his attentions were so remarkable that they seemed more than the effects of common politeness ; and as he was a very agreeable man and in good circumstances, he was favourably received, not doubting but that his intentions were honourable. A declaration of a very contrary nature was treated with the contempt it deserved, though Mrs. A. Robinson was very much prepossessed in his favour.

" Soon after this, Lord Peterborough endeavoured to convince her of his partial regard for her; but agreeable and artful as he was, she remained very much upon her guard, which rather increased than diminished his admiration and passion for her. Yet still his pride struggled with his inclination; for all this time she was engaged to sing in public—a circumstance very grievous to her; but, urged by the best of motives, she submitted to it in order to assist her parents, whose fortune was much reduced by Mr. Robinson's loss of sight, which deprived him of the benefit of his profession as a painter.

"At length Lord Peterborough made his declaration on honourable terms; he found it would be vain to make proposals on any other, and as he omitted no circumstance that could engage her esteem and gratitude she accepted him, as she was sincerely attached to him. He earnestly requested her keeping it a secret till it was a more convenient time for him to make it known, to which she readily consented, having a perfect confidence in his honour."

The Earl behaved very shabbily over the matter; apparently he was wanting in moral courage, and he certainly was indifferent to the reputation of the lady whom he had made his wife. At last, however, when in a bad state of health, and when probably suffering from an attack of nerves and conscience, he made ample reparation in the presence of his family, and all was well.

The Duke of Bolton did not follow the example of the Earl of Peterborough. He made no secret of his marriage with Lavinia Fenton (or Lavinia Beswick as some of her detractors preferred to call her), but it is hardly likely the marriage was approved by his own set. However celebrated " Polly Peachum " may have been in her own sphere, she was merely a " player " of low birth, and not a singer of world-wide reputation like Anastasia Robinson.

How the news of the marriage and consequent elevation of " Polly Peachum " affected the theatrical circles of 1751 we have no means of knowing. Probably it was the gossip of the green room for a few days and forgotten. All the principal partners in Polly's success of 1728—Walker, Hippisley, Hall,

Clark, Mrs. Egleton—were dead. Gay after " life's fitful fever " was sleeping well. Rich, her old manager, Quin and Macklin who had known her, alone remained. Apparently in her days of decorum and respectability she dropped acquaintance with the stage—unlike the merry and unconventional Harriet Mellon, who both as Mrs. Coutts and the Duchess of St. Albans never forgot her old comrades of the footlights. This aloofness may have been due to the scruples of the Duke of Bolton, but whatever was the cause there is no record of Polly Peachum, either as Lavinia Fenton, the inseparable companion of his Grace, or as his duchess, visiting the scene of her triumph or in any way acknowledging the source of her fame and fortune. Nor did the death of her husband after three years of married life make any difference in her complete retirement from things theatrical.

The Duke of Bolton died at Tunbridge Wells on August 26, 1754, and before his death he had the satisfaction of having had restored to him several minor posts of which he had been deprived, among them the lord-lieutenancy of the county of Southampton. In November 1745, having been promoted lieutenant-general, he raised a regiment of foot for service in the Rebellion, but was not called upon to take the field.

The Duke's will was as short as it could well be. We give an extract from the document deposited in the archives of the Principal Registry of the Prerogative Court of Canterbury, Somerset House, and we believe it now appears in print for the first time.

" *6th July* 1753.

" (Reg. 219 Pinfold).

" Charles Duke of Bolton, Knight of the Most Noble Order of the Garter. . . . It is my direction to be buried in my family vault at Basing co. South'ton at the discretion of my executrix . . . . all my estates real and personal whatsoever . . . .I give unto my dear and well beloved wife Lavinia Dutchess of Bolton and her heirs for ever. . . . I appoint her the s^d Dutchess of Bolton my s^d wife whole and sole executrix.

" BOLTON.

" MOR (MORGAN) KEENE.
" FRA^s MOORE.
" JOHN YOUNG.

" This will was proved at London on the 26th August 1754, by the Most Noble Lavinia Dutchess Dowager of Bolton, widow, the Relict of the Deceased and the sole Executrix named in the said will."

The terms of the will dispose of any doubts as to the estimation in which the Duke held the once famous Polly Peachum. The only thing he could not dispose of was his title, and as his three sons were born prior to wedlock the dukedom fell to his Grace's brother Harry, the father of Harry, sixth Duke of Bolton.

During the seven years following 1751 the Opera was continually being performed in London, but there was no run of any importance until two distinguished singers, Miss Brent and John Beard, were associated at Covent Garden Theatre in the season 1758–9. *The Beggar's Opera* became as popular as though it were a complete novelty, and it ran for thirty-seven (thirty-nine including benefits) nights with only one break. Polly and Macheath never had more competent exponents. Miss Brent was the favourite pupil of Dr. Arne, and a vocalist of no ordinary calibre. Her repertoire was exceedingly varied, ranging from Polly to Jephtha's daughter in Handel's oratorio. When Miss Brent was announced to make her first appearance Garrick went to hear her sing in private. He admitted her merit, but said he to Arne : " You know, Tom, all your geese are swans, and you ought to consider that after all music is at best but pickle to my roast beef." " By

Heaven, Davy," retorted Arne, "'your beef shall be well pickled before I've done." And Arne was right, as presently will be seen.

John Beard was equally accomplished. He was highly esteemed by Handel, and he created the title rôle in *Samson* in 1743. His aristocratic wife, whose marriage with the singer so excited Lady Mary Wortley Montagu's wrath, was dead at the time of the run of the Opera in 1758–9, and soon after he married Rich's daughter Charlotte, and at Rich's death became joint manager of Covent Garden Theatre with Bencraft.

Admirable as was the singing of Miss Brent and Mr. Beard, the British public, as it is wont to do, ran after its fooling, which was supplied by pretty and engaging and we may also add, fair and frail Nancy Dawson, who made a hit by dancing the hornpipe introduced into the Opera and drawing the crowds quite as much as Anne Brent and John Beard. The poet says as much in his lilting verse :

"Of all the girls in our Town,
The black, the fair, the red, the brown,
Who dance and prance it up and down,
    There's none like Nancy Dawson !
Her easy mien, her step so neat,
She foots, she steps, she looks so sweet,
Her every motion is complete,
    I die for Nancy Dawson.

"See how she comes to give surprise,
With joy and pleasure in her eyes ;
To give delight she always tries,
    So means my Nancy Dawson !
Was there no task t'obstruct the way,
No Shuter droll, nor house so gay,
A bet of fifty pounds I'll lay
    That I gain Nancy Dawson.

"See how the Op'ra takes a run
Exceeding Hamlet, Lear or Lun,
Tho' in it there would be no fun,
    Was't not for Nancy Dawson.
Tho' Beard and Brent charm every night,
And female Peachum's justly right,
And Filch and Lockit please the sight,
    'Tis crowned by Nancy Dawson.

MRS. BILLINGTON.

From an engraving by Ridley, after Cosway.

"See little Davy strut and puff:
'P—— on the op'ra and such stuff,
My house is never full enough,
A curse on Nancy Dawson!'
Tho' Garrick he has had his day,
And forc'd the town his laws t'obey,
Now Johnny Rich is come in play
With help of Nancy Dawson."

"Little Davy," indeed, could make no headway against the all-conquering *Beggar's Opera*, and Drury Lane could show hardly more than a beggarly account of empty boxes. "In vain did Garrick," says Davies, "oppose his Ranger and Benedick, his Hamlet and Lear to Polly Peachum; the public was this season allured by nothing but the power of song and sing-song."

Nancy Dawson was the daughter of a Clare Market porter, and left alone in the world at the age of sixteen she joined the company of a puppet showman, learned to dance, and was engaged at Sadler's Wells, being promoted to the part of columbine in her second year. She was introduced to Covent Garden by Ned Shuter, and on April 22, 1758, had a benefit, when *The Merry Wives of Windsor* was played. On October 10, 1759, Beard produced *The Beggar's Opera*, as already mentioned, the hornpipe in the third act being danced by Mr. Miles. Mr. Miles fell ill and Nancy Dawson followed him, and her engagement marked the good fortune which always attended the Opera. Her first appearance was on October 15— "(by desire) a hornpipe by Miss Dawson," as the advertisement in *The Public Advertiser* informs us. Her success was instantaneous, and she became "vastly celebrated, admired, imitated and followed by everybody." "The hornpipe by which she danced into fame," says *The Dictionary of National Biography*, was "performed to a tune which was fitted with words in the shape of a song called 'Ballad of Nancy Dawson,' the authorship of which is attributed to George Alexander Stevens. This tune was for a long time the popular one of the day. It was set

19

with variations for the harpsichord as Miss Dawson's
hornpipe, was introduced in Carey's and Bickerstaffe's
opera *Love in a Village*, is mentioned as ' Nancy
Dawson ' by J. Goldsmith in the epilogue to *She Stoops
to Conquer*, and in another unspoken epilogue to the
same play, and is still sung in nurseries to the words
' Here we go round the Mulberry Bush.' "

Nancy with all her powers of fascination had a
keen eye for the main chance, and the offer of a
higher salary tempted her the next year to transfer
her attractions to Drury Lane.   Beard was not to be
outdone, and he commenced *The Beggar's Opera* with
a Mrs. Vernon to replace the faithless Nancy.   The
promise of two *Beggar's Operas* at the same time was the
cause of much talk, and we have *The London Chronicle*
of September 16, 1760, writing as follows : " There
is likely to be as warm a contest between *The
Beggar's Opera* at both houses as there was some
years ago with the two Romeos.   Mr. Lowe is to do
Macheath at Drury Lane and Mrs. Vincent Polly.
She has already rehearsed it upon the stage, and in
the opinion of the connoisseurs who heard her will
form a most formidable competitor for the theatric
laurel with the Covent Garden heroine."

Drury Lane opened on September 23 and Covent
Garden on the 24th, and for a few nights both
houses were full.   Mrs. Vernon was quite as successful as Nancy, if we may judge from a paragraph
(Sept. 30, 1760) in *The London Chronicle*, which says :
" There seems to be as great an emulation reigning
between the two hornpipe dancers (Mrs. Vernon and
Miss Dawson) as the two Pollies.   Disputes run high
amongst the dancing connoisseurs, some preferring
the one and some the other.   Encore is the word to
both, and on Friday night the applause was so loud
and general to Mrs. Vernon during her performance
that neither she nor the audience could hear a note
of the music."

The rivalry between the two theatres did not last
long.   The managers probably found that the public

might have too much even of *The Beggar's Opera*. At all events, however graceful Mrs. Vernon may have been, she never attained the celebrity of Nancy, notwithstanding that she danced a hornpipe to music specially composed by Dr. Arne. No portrait of her exists, while no less than four prints were made of Nancy. We give reproductions (see pp. 184, 192) of two. One shows her dancing, and has the lines beneath :

> " Come all ye bucks and bloods so gim,
> Who love the rowling hornpipe trim,
> Behold how Nancy moves each limb—
> The charming Nancy Dawson.

> " How easily she trips the stage !
> Her heaving breasts all eyes engage,
> Love's fire she can best assuage—
> Oh charming Nancy Dawson !

> " Yet vainly she each breast alarms
> With all love's hoard of heavenly charms ;
> She's only for N—d S—r's arms—
> The smiling Nancy Dawson.

> " Tho' Poitier treads the passive air
> And Baker's always debonair,
> Yet none with Nancy can compare—
> The charming Nancy Dawson."

The Poitier alluded to was of course the French male dancer. About Miss Baker there is no uncertainty. She succeeded Nancy when the latter's popularity began to wane.*

The discrepancies which abound in theatrical records have not left Nancy Dawson alone. One would think that the allusions in the verses quoted would have settled any doubt as to the possessor of pretty Nancy's charms, but they did not satisfy a correspondent of *The Bristol Times*, who, writing somewhere about 1846, remarks : " Nancy Dawson is said to have been the mistress of Ned Shuter, an actor, but this is probably a mistake. Anne Catley the singer certainly enjoyed that distinction." The mistake is " probably " on the side of the correspondent. There is certainly no evidence that Anne Catley

* See Appendix, Note 6.

favoured Ned Shuter, but on such a delicate point it is impossible to be dogmatic.

The correspondent adds : " Nancy died at Hampstead May 27, 1767. She was buried in the church of St. George the Martyr, Queen Square, Bloomsbury, where there is a tombstone to her memory, ' Here lies Nancy Dawson.' " *The Dictionary of National Biography* puts her last resting-place in the quaint burial-ground of St. George the Martyr and St. George's, Bloomsbury, behind the Foundling Hospital, " where her tombstone may still be seen, though some scandalous lines originally inscribed thereon have been obliterated." The graveyard is now a recreation garden, and among the notabilities whose memories are preserved are Zachary Macaulay, the father of Lord Macaulay, and one of the granddaughters of Oliver Cromwell. But the name of Nancy Dawson, and that of another damsel who achieved celebrity in a different direction—Eliza Fenning, executed, after much controversy as to her guilt or innocence, for attempting to poison her master and mistress—are not to be found.

Ned Shuter, whose name is associated with Nancy Dawson, it is almost unnecessary to say, was the leading comedian of his time, and he certainly deserves a niche for saving Goldsmith's *Good-Natured Man* from damnation. His humorous presentment of Croaker turned a prospective failure into a success.

As for the Pollies in this theatrical duel, it is interesting to note that their rivalry was the subject of one of Goldsmith's characteristic papers written for Smollett's *British Magazine* of 1760. A discussion is supposed to be going on at Vauxhall Gardens between two visitors ; Goldsmith overhears their talk, reproduces it in his own charmingly unaffected way and enables us to form a fair idea of the respective merits of the two singers. The paper has until now never been reprinted, and we make no apology for giving the bulk of it.

" ' I own,' says he who spoke first, ' that Miss

Brent, by pleasing the town last season in *The Beggar's Opera*, has acquired a share of popularity, which may alone lead the injudicious ; but let us strip her of her theatrical ornaments, and merely as a singer compare her with her rival, Mrs. Vincent. I think it will be allowed me Mrs. Vincent has rather the most graceful person of the two ; even that consideration, trifling as it may seem, is of no consequence when we are considering the perfections of a female singer. In Italy, you know, sir, scarcely a lady dares appear even in a chorus, upon the stage, or as a public performer, without this natural advantage. Upon some of Miss Brent's notes there is also a huskiness, which her rival is entirely free from ; for you must confess that nothing can be clearer than Mrs. Vincent's voice. Miss Brent sometimes drives the feeling theatrical manner into affectation, for though a little of that manner is proper at all times, and is in fact the only thing in which the voice excels an instrument, yet in plain singing, where acting is not required, it may sometimes be carried to a ridiculous excess. Mrs. Vincent sings with more ease, fetches her inspirations quicker, more unperceived, and with a better grace than your new favourite. Though I must own that neither the one nor the other are, by any means, perfect timeists ; yet, in this respect, Mrs. Vincent has certainly the advantage, and is seldom guilty of blunders, which the other through haste, want of skill, or of time, sometimes commits. I have but one thing more to say in favour of Mrs. Vincent, which is that she would certainly appear to greater advantage were the music she sings more nicely adapted to her voice. Every judicious composer sets his music to the voice of the performer ; that which this singer chuses seems in general, taken by herself at a venture, or composed for her without a perfect knowledge of her excellencies. The lower part of her voice has a much finer body than the upper, which is rather too small, and has somewhat too much of the German-flute tone in it ; tho' she

has great command, yet her transitions are not perfectly graceful ; the music therefore adapted to her
would be composed of notes not reaching extremely
high, and not with difficult transitions. The music
composed for Miss Brent, on the contrary, is set with
perfect taste, and with a thorough knowledge of her
forte. That pretty song of Liberty, in particular,
both in delicacy and accompanyment, is far beyond
the song of Mrs. Vincent.'

   " Influenced by this, most of the company were
going to declare in favour of Mrs. Vincent, when the
other gentleman gave his opinion, as follows :

   " ' I allow the justice of almost all that has been
advanced, but I am of opinion Miss Brent is far
superior. It is true her voice is by no means so clear
as Mrs. Vincent's, nor have I ever heard any singer
equal that lady in this particular ; yet still Miss Brent
has much the best voice of the two, for it is at
once capable of a greater swell, and has a greater
body of tone. These two perfections are alone
sufficient to give her the preference ; but there is
another, in which she excels almost every singer. I
mean, that of her voice being perfectly in tune. I
cannot tell whether it be in reality so, but it would
seem by the exact tunefulness of her voice, that she
had not been entirely taught to sing from the harpsichord, for such as are wholly taught by that instrument, tho' they may be sufficiently in tune with
any instrument, yet by learning only to chime with
a chord, which from the nature of this instrument
is not quite perfect, they seldom arrive to that tunefulness which reaches the heart ; and hence we see
natural singers frequently more pleasing than those
who are taught. The lady I refer to seems to possess
all that makes sweetness of voice, at the same time
that she has acquired by art the perfect manner
of flattening those notes, which upon the voice of
every natural instrument, as the trumpet and horn,
are naturally too sharp. Her shake, tho' not perfect
(as it is in general too quick), is, however, much

superior to the other's, who is very faulty in this respect. Tho' she may sometimes feel too much, yet it must be owned that this is preferable to a total vacancy of sensibility, which is the other's case. Let us add to this, that the music we have now heard her sing is preferable to that sung by Mrs. Vincent, and I fancy upon the whole we shall find she affords the highest entertainment. I am sensible that both have faults which neither of us have mentioned; and one among the rest is in the execution of those holding notes of which they both seem so fond. They seem to think that all the art in this respect lies in beginning one of those tedious notes very soft, and then swelling it as loud as possible in the middle, then falling off, and so forth. These should never be continued without that softening which is taken from the tone below; which on the voice is capable of becoming every moment more distinct, till it at last falls naturally into the shake, which should not be of very long continuance neither. But I fear I tire the company. I shall only observe that the public are greatly obliged to both for one of its most innocent and highest amusements.' Just as he had finished, we were called away to hear the concluding song, which gave me such pleasure, I could not avoid concluding that she who sung last always sings best."

Miss Brent and *The Beggar's Opera* were much favoured by the fascinating and attractive Elizabeth Chudleigh, who in 1760 was closely associated with the Duke of Kingston, subsequently marrying him when she thought she had shaken off her matrimonial ties with Augustus Hervey, afterwards the Earl of Bristol, and thereby landing herself into serious trouble after the death of the Duke. Thomas Whitehead, the Duke's valet, who published a very entertaining and somewhat malicious account of his experiences with the Duke and the frolicsome lady whose escapades were the talk of the town, refers to *The Beggar's Opera* at this time, when it had such a run and when Miss Brent was the chief vocal favourite with the public.

" Miss Chudleigh and her party," writes Whitehead, " attended almost every night and drank tea
in their box, making such a noise and disturbing
both the performers and the audience so repeatedly,
that at last they were determined to rout her. This
they effected by giving her a smart paragraph in
the newspapers, after which she was received at the
theatre with hissings and groanings, and such strong
marks of disapprobation, that she and her whole
party were obliged to decamp before the opera was
over ; not appearing there for some years after."

Miss Brent was often a guest at the Duke of
Kingston's house in Surrey, Pierrepoint Lodge, where
Miss Chudleigh held high state.

Davies in his *Life of Garrick* says of this revival :
" Of all the entertainments of the stage, none has
been so properly serviceable to the players as *The
Beggar's Opera*. A new Polly or a new Macheath
has successfully given such a spirit and lustre to
that humorous dramatic satyr, that the public has
often run to see it for twenty or thirty nights successively. Miss Brent was deficient in beauty as well
as form to represent the amiable simplicity of Polly
Peachum, but such were the powers of her voice,
though in her songs she was absolutely wide of the
author's original design (who intended no more than
the giving a common ballad tune in the simplest
manner), that London seemed to be more enamoured
with *The Beggar's Opera* than when the principal
parts were originally acted by Tom Walker and Miss
Fenton."

Churchill honours both Miss Brent and Mrs.
Vincent with discriminating mention in the *Rosciad*,
and severely but not unjustly criticises Arne for
pandering to the Italian style of ornamental singing :

> " Lo ! Vincent comes—with simple grace arrayed ;
> She laughs at paltry arts and scorns parade ;
> Nature through her is by reflection shown,
> Whilst Gay, once more, knows Polly for his own,

Let Tommy Arne, with usual pomp of style,
Whose chief, whose only merit's to compile,
Who, meanly pilfering here and there a bit,
Deals Music out as Murphy deals out wit,
Publish proposals, laws for taste prescribe,
And chant the praise of an Italian tribe ;
Let him reverse kind Nature's first decrees,
And teach e'en Brent a method not to please."

The caricature entitled " Fitzgiggo," which we
reproduce (see p. 200), shows Miss Brent, Beard and
Tenducci in Arne's *Artaxerxes* with the house in riot.
The strife which convulsed the theatrical world in
1763 originated in the spite of a certain Fitzpatrick,
who posed as a critic, and fell foul of Garrick. His
insults provoked the publication of the *Fribbleriad*,
attributed to Garrick, in which Fitzpatrick appears
under the name of Fitzgigg, and the freedom with
which his person is described sent the would-be
critic thirsting for revenge. Garrick announcing full
prices when *The Two Gentlemen of Verona* was revived
gave Fitzpatrick his opportunity. He organised a
cabal, who raised a storm, and as the manager refused
to give way, the rioters broke the benches and lustres
and stopped the play. The next night Garrick was
received with shouts of " Will you or will you not give
admittance for half price after the third act of a play,
except during the first winter a pantomime is performed ? " and Garrick capitulated.

The cabal then opened fire on Covent Garden, and
Artaxerxes was not allowed to proceed. Beard took
legal proceedings, but ultimately he had to imitate
Garrick. The plate is interesting as showing the stage
of Covent Garden in 1763.

CHAPTER XXV

THE CURTAIN FALLS

Death of " Polly Peachum," Duchess of Bolton—Horace Walpole's insinuation—The Duchess of Bolton's will—Aristocratic prejudices against marriages with stage players—Lady Mary Wortley Montagu's bitterness —Westcombe House, Greenwich, the home of the Duchess—Its history and situation—Curious statement in *The New Monthly Magazine.*

IN *The London Chronicle* of January 24, 1760, appeared the following paragraph : " On Thursday died at Westcombe in Kent the Dowager Duchess of Bolton, by whose death a jointure of £5,000 per annum devolves to his Grace the Duke of Bolton." It sounds strange to read of "Polly Peachum" as a dowager, but as a matter of fact the appellation descended upon her at the death of her husband, his brother upon whom the title descended being already married at the time of his elevation. Nothing precisely is known of the dowager duchess's occupation, her amusements, her tastes, her movements, during her married life of three years and her widowhood of six. Her sons were grown up, and if Walpole may be believed she while a widow passed some time at Tonbridge, where she came under the influence of an Irish surgeon named Kelley.

Writing to George Montagu on January 28, 1760, Walpole says : " There has been cruel havoc among the ladies; my Lady Granby is dead, and the famous Polly, Duchess of Bolton, and my Lady Bessborough." A week later in a letter to Horace Mann he returns to the subject. " The famous Polly, Duchess of Bolton, is dead," he writes, " having after a life of merit relapsed into her Pollyhood. Two years ago, ill at Tonbridge, she picked up an Irish surgeon.

When she was dying this fellow sent for a lawyer to make her will, but the man, finding who was to be her heir instead of her children, refused to draw it. The Court of Chancery did furnish one other not quite so scrupulous, and her sons have but a thousand pounds a piece ; the surgeon about nine thousand." The reference to the Duchess's " Pollyhood " is quite in Walpole's sneering vein.

On this point Leigh Hunt aptly says : " There is no trusting to these pieces of gossip ; nor is any conclusion to be drawn from one part of a story, particularly a family one, till we know the other. Preposterous wills of all sorts are frequent, but ' a life of merit,' especially of kindly merit, is seldom closed by contradiction ; and supposing the statement to be true, the Duchess may have had other reasons for leaving no more to her children. They were the Duke's as well as hers, and may have been already provided for ; or she might have felt certain they would be so. In addition to the words ' a life of merit ' as affecting the Duchess of Bolton a strong though negative testimony to the good behaviour . . . of Lavinia towards the Duke in one whose memory was so sensitive on the point is observable in the very silence maintained respecting them (*i.e.* other ladies who married from the stage into the ' quality ') by Horace Walpole."

The genial essayist was right. The terms of the Duchess's will show quite clearly that she and the Duke had made provision for their three sons. We have extracted the document from the official records, and it is now printed for the first time. It runs :

" Prerogative Court of Canterbury. (Lynch 47). Will of the Most Noble Lavinia Dutchess Dowager of Bolton, widow and relict of Charles late Duke of Bolton. . . . The money in South Sea Annuities in names of Robert Henley, Sir Richard Hoare and Morgan Keene, Trustees of Settlement made by late Duke and myself, is to be for the benefit of

Charles Powlett and his two brothers, Percy and
Horatio Armand Powlett. . . . The settlement of
my house and lands at Westcombe, Co. Kent, I
confirm and I bequeath the furniture and farming
utensils to sd. Charles. I have the perpetual ad-
vowsons of the churches of Sherfield upon Loddon
and Itchin Abbas, Co. Southampton. I will my
exor. to present sd. Charles now Rev. Chas. Powlett
M.A. to sd. livings the first time they become vacant.
I am entitled expectant upon the decease of Geo.
Kelley of Tunbridge Wells, Co. Kent to reversion of
certain Manors in Co. Kent. I give all my interest
therein to said Geo. Kelley and heirs. To Rev. Chas.
Powlett £1000. To Mrs. Anne Sutherland £250. To
my Goddaughter Lavinia Cuddon, £100. Residue
to said Geo. Kelley, sole Exor.—L. Bolton.
December 6th, 1759. Wm Wizzell, Andr. Hatt.
Geo. Addams. Frances Lancaster.—Will proved
7th February, 1760, by the oath of Geo. Kelley, Esq.,
to whom as sole Executor, Administration was
Granted."

Walpole had a prejudice against the stage and
all that belonged to it. Rarely does he praise an
actor or actress, and when he does so it is with a
qualification, as in the case of Peg Woffington. Over
the handsome Irish actor who ran away with the
daughter of Lord Ilchester, the retailer of gossip was
terribly shocked, and called the marriage " the com-
pletion of disgrace—even a footman were preferable ;
the publicity of the hero's profession perpetuates the
mortification."

Walpole tells the story of the " sad misfortune "
in his own lively style. " The swain," he writes,
" had learned to counterfeit Lady Sarah Bunbury's
hand so well that in the country Lord Ilchester had
himself delivered several of O'Brien's letters to Lady
Susan ; but it was not till about a week before
the catastrophe that the family was apprised of the
intrigue. Lord Cathcart went to Miss Read, the
paintress : she said softly to him, ' My lord, there is

a couple in next room that I am sure ought not to be together. I wish your lordship would look in.' He did, shut the door again, and went directly and informed Lord Ilchester. Lady Susan was examined, flung herself at her father's feet, confessed all, vowed to break off, but—what a *but*!—desired to see the beloved object and take a last leave. . . . On Friday she came of age, and on Saturday morning—instead of being under lock and key in the country—walked downstairs, took her footman, said she was going to breakfast with Lady Sarah but would call at Miss Read's; in the street pretended to recollect a particular cap in which she was to be drawn, sent the footman back for it, whipped into a hackney chair, was married at Covent Garden church."

O'Brien was not the only member of the profession whose wife was a lady of title. John Gallini, manager of the Haymarket Theatre, married Lady Elizabeth Bertie, eldest daughter of the third Earl of Abingdon and added to the enormity of his crime by being a dancing master as well as an actor!

Lord Chesterfield placed actors in the same category as fiddlers. When Sheridan engaged Garrick to play in Dublin, the Earl was Lord-Lieutenant of Ireland. He condescended to be gracious to Sheridan, and "admitted him to the castle, but he took not the least notice of Garrick, carrying his rudeness so far as not even to return the great actor's salute." But even his condescension towards Sheridan had no sincerity. He professed the highest esteem for Sheridan and gave every encouragement to his plan of forming an academy to teach oratory, and on the actor-manager's departure enjoined him, "Never let the thoughts of your oratorical institution go out of your mind." "Yet," says Robert Hitchcock, "a few years afterwards, when Mr. Sheridan waited upon him in London to fulfil his promise, that celebrated patron of men of genius, the witty, the generous, the liberal-minded Earl of Chesterfield bountifully presented him with a *guinea* as his contribution towards one of the noblest plans devised by human wisdom." But could more be expected from the polite Earl of Chesterfield, who kept Dr. Johnson cooling his heels for hours in his antechamber ?

" I have been unfortunate in my own family," writes Walpole to Mann: "my nephew Captain Cholmondeley has married a player's sister." That player was the very Peggy whom he had disparaged as " a bad actress " ! We read in Taylor's *Records* that " Lord Cholmondeley, whose nephew had married Mrs. Woffington's sister, was much offended at what he conceived a degrading union in his family, but on being introduced to Mrs. Woffington some months after the match he was so much pleased with her that he declared, though he had been at first offended at the match, he was then reconciled to it. Mrs. Woffington, who had educated and supported her sister, coldly answered : ' My lord, I have much more reason to be offended at it than your lordship, for I had before one beggar to maintain, and now I have two.' "

When John Beard married, on January 8, 1739, the Lady Henrietta Herbert, widow of Lord Edward Herbert, second son of the Marquis of Powis, and daughter of James first Earl of Waldegrave, the marriage (ignored in all the peerages) excited the rancour of Lady Mary Wortley Montagu, who spitefully wrote that he was " a man of very indifferent character." This was a deliberate untruth. Lady Mary permitted herself to indulge in more manufactured scandal. " Lady Townshend has entertained The Bath with a variety of lively scenes ; and Lady Harriet Herbert furnished the tea tables here with fresh tattle for this last fortnight. I was one of the first informed of her adventure by Lady Gage (Lord Gage is one of the group on the stage in Hogarth's picture of *The Beggar's Opera*), who was told that morning by a priest that she had desired him to marry her the next day to Beard, who sings in the farce at Drury Lane. He refused her that good office, and immediately told Lady Gage, who (having been unfortunate in her friends) was frighted in this affair and asked my advice. I told her honestly that since the lady was capable of such amours I did not doubt if this was broke off she would bestow her person and fortune on some hackney coachman or chairman, and that I really saw no method of saving her from ruin and her family from dishonour but by poisoning her, and offered to be at the expense of the arsenic and even to administer it with my own hands if she would invite her to drink tea with her that evening." Amiable and generous Lady Mary!

It is doubtful whether the Duchess of Bolton was seen much in London, even when the Duke was alive. In spite of Tate Wilkinson's assertion that the Bolton family could testify to her good qualities, in all probability she was looked at askance. The fact that she was not of their order was sufficient to make her reluctant to meet them, and she could hardly help doing so if the Duke took her into society. It is pretty certain she was not presented at Court. The important part she played in the Opera which was so obnoxious to Sir Robert Walpole and the Queen would be an insuperable barrier. The softness and amiability which Hogarth so admirably indicates suggest that she was sensitive. One can imagine that she could be as easily moved to tears as to smiles. To quote Leigh Hunt once more, we read concerning her influence over the Duke that " her good qualities appear to have fixed a passion created perhaps by vanity. It is said that on his once threatening to leave her she knelt and sang ' Oh ponder well ' in a style so tender that he had not the heart to do it." Hunt does not give his authority for this statement, and it sounds slightly melodramatic, but it may be true. Whatever faults the Duke had, he was at least easy-going and good-natured.

The death of the " famous Polly," if one may judge by the absence of anything in the public prints beyond the barest reference, passed almost unnoticed. *The Public Advertiser* of January 29, 1760, has this : " We are informed that her Grace the late Duchess of Bolton has left behind her three sons, but bequeathed the bulk of her fortune to her physician. The jointure, which was considerable, descends with the title to his Grace Charles, Duke of Bolton." Not a word about the real point of interest—that she was the " Polly " on whom the town went crazy some two-and-thirty years before. Yet while she was lying in state after the fashion of the time *The Beggar's Opera* was being played at Covent Garden and the house was resounding with laughter and applause, as in the days of the " famous Polly Peachum."

She was buried at St. Alphege Church, Greenwich, a stately ornate structure in Wren's style, on February 3, and she lies in a private vault beneath the church. The vault was bricked up some thirty or forty years ago by order of the authorities, and the name and date of death were placed on the front of the vault. Sir Egerton Brydges in his edition of Collins' Peerage has the following concerning the Duchess's three sons : " Rev. Charles Powlett now living (1812), formerly Rector of Itchen, Hants, etc. ; second, Percy Powlett, a lieutenant in the Navy, deceased ; who was father of the Reverend Charles Powlett, Jun., now Rector of Stoke, near Alresford, Hants; third, Armand Powlett, in the Army, dead." There may be descendants of these Powletts now living, but we cannot speak with certainty.

Those who are acquainted with the surroundings of Greenwich Park will not need to be told of the ascending road which winds from uninteresting and somewhat frowsy East Greenwich, past the workhouse, to what is now called Westcombe Park Road. This ascending road is Vanbrugh Hill, and to the

MADAME MARA.

From an engraving by Ridley, after David.

right, some little distance along Westcombe Park
Road, is Vanbrugh Castle, built by the architect-
dramatist on the model, of all buildings in the world,
of the Bastille ! For some reason this conglomerate
turreted structure seems to have been regarded with
great favour by the architects of the eighteenth
century, for the tasteless Wyatt erected a "palace"
in what is now Kew Gardens for George III. in the
same style. Crossing the Westcombe Park Road
from Vanbrugh Hill, one enters a modern road
termed Vanbrugh Fields, leading to a picturesque
patch of heath now known as Vanbrugh Park. This
patch of heath is bordered to the south-east by a road
skirting the frowning wall of Greenwich Park; and
if not opposite the gate leading into the Park, not
far distant from it, stood Westcombe House, where
the Duchess lived with her husband and where she
died. In Hasted's *History of Kent* we read that " the
ancient house of Westcombe stood near the entrance
gate of the park, the wall round which was built by
Multon Lambarde about 1620. It was converted
into stables, on the front of which was inserted a
tablet displaying a plume of feathers and the date
1633. In 1854 the house and stables which stood
in the centre of the park were taken down, the foot-
path on the south widened as a road and the heath
alienated and covered with houses."

Hasted does not err on the side of lucidity, and
his reference to the " park " (what park ?) is confusing. He is strangely inaccurate when he comes
to speak of four houses which Vanbrugh built in the
immediate vicinity of Westcombe House. A footnote informs us that " Vanbrugh built four houses
under lease granted by the Biddulphs in 1717. He
and three of his brothers, Adam Leak and Dame
Elizabeth Biddulph, at one time occupied three
houses, and he built the arch on which is the date
1714. The two houses south of this arch were built
in 1719 for the Duchess of Bolton (Polly Peachum)
and Sir James Thornhill." The wording of this

20

perpetrates a ludicrous blunder, for in 1719 Lavinia
Fenton had no thought of becoming the Duchess of
Bolton, being then but eleven years of age! Probably
1719 is a misprint for 1729, but it should not have
been left uncorrected. One of these four houses still
remains, and is probably not altered very much from
what it was in the days of Vanbrugh. The arch
stood at the bend of the road called Vanbrugh Fields,
and was only pulled down recently.

Of Westcombe House Hasted says that it " was
owned by Sir Gregory Page of Wreckle Marsh in
Charlton, and was leased, among others, to the Duke
of Bolton, and that after the Duchess's death the
place was successively occupied by Lord Clive, the
Marquis of Lothian, and the Duchess of Athol." He
adds that the house was left to the Rev. C. Powlett
and that the lease expired in 1824. Standing on
the breezy little heath adjacent, one can well
imagine that in 1760, and indeed for a long time
afterwards, " the prospect from the terrace near the
house was very beautiful, commanding the windings
of the Thames with Shooter's Hill and the intervening
woodland." The windings of the Thames are now
invisible. The picturesque slopes to the river show
but chimneys and housetops, and the " intervening
woodlands to Shooter's Hill " have given place to
modern villas.

The writer of the description of Paul Sandby's
sketch of Westcombe House, which we reproduce from
Watts' *Views* (see p. 208), praises Westcombe House
and its surroundings. " An agreeable eminence," he
writes, " from which many picturesque views are
continually commanded, renders this seat peculiarly
happy in its selection. This building, though not
magnificent, may boast of elegance in the midst of a
thick and venerable Grove which rises to the eye with
an air of *propreté* more easily imagined than described.
The modest grounds around are laid out with so much
taste as to render them a perfect scene of rural
simplicity. The variety of floating objects observed

(from the front of the house) upon the Thames at a considerable distance off, and others from its serpentine course rendered much more brilliant and enlivening, must necessarily claim our attention, especially if we include a multitude of cattle continually grazing on each side of the river's verdant banks. Limehouse church affords us a *coup d'œil*, and carries the eye to the landscape of London with the adjacent hills of Highgate and Hampstead in the background terminating the view. Notwithstanding the vicinity of this Seat to the Metropolis, yet from the advantage of Greenwich Park on the left, Charlton to the right, and Blackheath to complete the whole, we may without hesitation pronounce it one of the most desirable spots in England." Watts' *Views* were published in 1777, when Westcombe House was in the possession of the Marquis of Lothian, and the house, in the arrangement of the grounds and the surroundings, were probably much as they were in Polly Peachum's time.

The prolix "Apology" for the stormy and adventurous life of the beautiful actress George Anne Bellamy contains a tantalising reference to the deceased Duchess. Foote, she says, occupied one of Sir John Vanbrugh's houses, and on one occasion she, accompanied by a Dr. Francis, paid the comedian a visit, riding to Blackheath on horseback. "We found with him," writes Mrs. Bellamy, "Arthur Murphy and an author named Cleland, and as we had arrived at this habitation of laughter early and there was no garden to walk in or lands to amuse us, by way of relaxation until the convivial meal made its appearance, the master of the house proposed going to the sale of the Duchess of Bolton's furniture. This celebrated lady had lately paid the debt of nature. . . . I wished to see her residence, and I therefore readily consented to the proposal and soon remounted horse." Dr. Francis, who appears to have been a kind of Pecksniff, had scruples about being seen with the actress in public (by which we may assume that the sale was likely to attract the " quality " to Westcombe House), although, as she complains, he did not mind accepting from her a box at the theatre, and she set off with the others, leaving the prudish doctor behind.

George Anne had here a chance of describing not only Polly Peachum's house but Polly's furniture. Alas! not a word has she to say about either. Had she been Horace Walpole, with what an informing description we should have been favoured! The absence of dates is one of the irritating features of Mrs. Bellamy's tedious *Apology*, and it is impossible to gather from the context anything to help one to form an idea when the sale took place. Nor are the newspapers of the period—so far as 1760 is concerned at all events—of any assistance. There is, indeed, one reference, not to the property of the Duchess but to that of the Duke, in advertisements in *The Public Advertiser* of June 1760, the first portion of which runs as follows : " To be sold by auction by Messrs. Prestage & Hobbs on Wednesday 25th June at their room, the end of Saville Row, next Conduit St., Hanover Square, the genuine and large sideboard of wrought and other plate of the most Noble Charles, Duke of Bolton, deceased, consisting of a large service of Gaderoon dishes and plates, tureens, dish covers, waiters, salvers, sauce boats, candlesticks, knives, forks and spoons, bread-basket, cruet frame, coffee-pot, saucepan, etc." So far as we have been able to trace, this is the last reference in the eighteenth-century newspapers to Polly's Duke and his affairs.

According to a letter in *Notes and Queries* (Series 5, vol. 1) Polly's favourite residence was in Wensley-dale, in Yorkshire, where the Duke had property ; and at Capplebank, says the writer of the letter, " there is still in existence (1874) a summer-house built for her by her lover, in which local tradition asserts she used to spend much time on her visits to the north of England, and which commands one of the

most extensive and varied prospects in the dale."
We have lighted upon no confirmation of this statement; Mr. J. S. Fletcher, who has packed his *Picturesque History of Yorkshire* with interesting facts, has nothing to say about it when he deals with Wensleydale and its neighbourhood.

Records are equally silent as to the Duchess's life at Westcombe House. The only reference to it is contained in a paragraph in *The New Monthly Magazine* quoted by Mr. Clark Russell in his *Representative Actors*, but unfortunately without any indication whereabouts in the many volumes of the magazine the paragraph is to be found. It runs as follows: " Miss Fenton, the original Lucy Lockit (*sic*) of *The Beggar's Opera*, who was married to the Duke of Bolton, became after her elevation so obnoxious to the lower orders about the place of her residence that they were with difficulty prevented from dragging her out of her coffin. The cause of this extraordinary antipathy is not exactly known."

The writer who could blunder so egregiously as to write Lucy Lockit instead of Polly is hardly to be regarded as an accurate and painstaking authority. There is probably not a word of truth in the story. Such an occurrence would surely have found its way into print. It was the sort of news the journals of the day delighted in. But diligent search has revealed nothing in confirmation.

CHAPTER XXVI

FAMOUS POLLIES

Anne Catley, a celebrated Polly—Her adventurous life—Her great popularity in Dublin in *The Beggar's Opera*—A furore over her Macheath—" Catleyfied " hair and the " Abington " cap—Anne Catley's audacity—A famous Polly and Lucy—Mrs. Arne and Mrs. Abington—The pianoforte first publicly exhibited at Covent Garden Theatre.

THE original Polly Peachum was dead, but *The Beggar's Opera* went merrily on with other Pollies eager to be famous. One of the most celebrated (if one-half of the amatory adventures related of the lady be true, "notorious" would be the more fitting word) was Anne Catley. Anne strangely resembled Nell Gwynne in her career, and there were also certain experiences which remind one of Lavinia Fenton. Like Lavinia and like Sally Salisbury, she had her imaginative biographer, and the style and certain of the material so much resemble each other that, had it been possible in regard to dates, the biographer might have been the same. Anne Catley, however, had this advantage over the other ladies: certain of her astonishing adventures, especially those in relation to Sir Francis Blake Delaval, a leading man of fashion of the day, and the Hon. Isabella Paulet, daughter of Lord Nassau Paulet, a branch of the Powlett stock, of which Lavinia's Duke was another, can be verified.

Anne Catley's origin was as obscure as that of Nell Gwynne or Sally Salisbury or Peg Woffington, certainly more obscure than that of Lavinia Fenton. She was born in an alley off Tower Hill in 1745, her father being a hackney coachman and her mother a washerwoman. Mrs. Catley washed for several of the officers quartered in the Tower, and as Nan took home the washing and was uncommonly vivacious she naturally attracted a good deal of attention. She was then ten years of age, and, as her biographer informs us, " her admirers increased with her years, the whole corps of officers regarded her with wishful eyes, and at thirteen many serious overtures of love had been made her." Like Sally Salisbury, Nan was ill-treated at home and went into the streets, where she sang about the public-houses. Just as Lavinia Fenton had a lover in the mercer's apprentice of Ludgate Hill, so Anne Catley had one in the person of a young linen-draper in the Minories. The biographer does not scruple to hint how Nan got her living, but we are not so much concerned with her private history as when she was apprenticed for seven years to one, Bates, " music master and chorus singer at one of the theatres," her indentures binding her father in a penalty of £200 in case she should run away or misbehave herself.

Nan, as may be imagined, paid very little attention to the restrictions sought to be placed upon her, and when she had been three years with Bates she made the acquaintance of Sir Francis Blake Delaval, who had heard her sing at Marylebone Gardens. Sir Francis was not only dissolute, but mean and dishonourable. He was closely associated with Samuel Foote, and between them, according to Anne Catley's biographer, they concocted a disgraceful plot to intrigue the Hon. Isabella Paulet into a marriage. The lady was rich and not handsome, and she was very credulous, constantly visiting a fortune-teller at Norwood. The fortune-teller was easily brought into the plot, the details of which had been arranged in concert with her. The scheme succeeded, Sir Francis married the lady, Foote was paid for his share in the transaction, and after a bitter experience of married life the lady was glad to be separated from her husband. It was soon after the separation that Sir Francis met Anne Catley and fell in love with her.

Then commenced a new plot, for which Anne may
or may not have been responsible. At all events,
we are told that, tired of Bates, she persuaded Sir
Francis to pay the music-master the penalty of £200,
for which her father was liable, and also £200 more
in consideration for her professional earnings during
the season. In addition she agreed to bind herself
apprentice to Sir Francis for the residue of the term.
Everything was done in proper legal form, and Anne's
father was given a deed to sign, by which she cove-
nanted not to leave Sir Francis's house ; Sir Francis
on his side covenanting to instruct her, or cause her
to be instructed, in the art of music.

Catley, who was in the service of Mr. Berkeley,
" an eminent Quaker in Cheapside," showed his master
the document before signing it ; and the Quaker,
seeing through the design, was much shocked, and
advised the father to commence a criminal prosecution against the parties, promising to supply him
with the means.

Now ensued a complicated legal battle, highly
amusing to read but too long to go into. All that
need be said is that the " offence alleged in the application was a conspiracy to debauch the daughter
of the prosecutor." Lord Mansfield, who presided
over the proceedings, was inclined to scold everybody
all round, and the upshot was " a rule for an information to be made absolute against Delaval, Bates,
and Frain, the attorney who had prepared the deed."

The consequence of this information, solemnly
pronounced by the Court of King's Bench against
the defendants, was a trial by a petty jury, during
which a number of *bons mots* were thrown out by the
counsel on both sides, and " received with great glee
and pleasantry by the learned judge, notwithstanding
the severity of his previous reprobation and grave
assertion of the Court of King's Bench being *custos
morum* of the nation." We will spare our readers
the infliction of specimens of these witticisms and
simply remark, in the words of the biographer, that

" this sport of the court and the unconcerned auditors was, however, of serious consequence to Sir Francis. He and the two defendants were found guilty by the jury, and in the ensuing term were heavily fined, the whole amount of which, as well as of the costs, which were considerable, falling upon him."

Although Sir Francis Delaval was Foote's friend and patron, friendship did not prevent the mimic from turning Sir Francis into ridicule—Foote's besetting sin. Tate Wilkinson relates how he happened to call on Sir Francis, with whom Foote and others were dining, and " as the circling glass went round, Mr. Foote grew more cordial and cheerful, and began speaking of tables in the first style of elegance in Ireland and Scotland—that several noblemen's houses in both places were supported with every luxury that a London table could furnish : for if London had the superiority in some particular articles, the other places had in greater perfection what London could not so easily purchase, which made the equality of good things more upon a level than the English would readily admit ; but to which Sir Francis would not assent. And as a trait I have before observed in Foote's character, when his real best friend Sir Francis Delaval left the room, where there were not less than eight or ten persons, each of whom he knew would relate again what he said, he burst into a loud laugh, and turning to me said : ' Wilkinson ! did you ever hear such a hound giving his sentiments on good tables and living ? Since my return from Ireland,' added Foote, ' I have had the mortification to dine here six times, and each day a d——d large loin of pork on the table, which he calls a dinner. By G—d, I'll not dine here again these three months ; for I suppose he means to run his loin of pork against *The Beggar's Opera* '—which had been acted a great number of nights at Covent Garden, Mr. Beard being Macheath, Miss Brent the Polly." Foote's sole merits were his humour and power of mimicry ; in other respects he was despicable.

The biographer is hardly kind to Anne. He represents her as ill-favoured and cursed with a temper, and perhaps he means to let her down lightly when he says " she was perhaps the only woman of easy virtue that ever received countenance on the stage from the modest women of Ireland ; but they looked upon her as an eccentric character, making proper allowances for her early habits, and imputed her failings to early misfortunes rather than to vice " —a somewhat backhanded compliment.

Whatever Anne Catley was in private life, and probably she was not worse than other ladies who could be named, she was the joy of the Dublin audience. In 1763 she appeared at Smock Alley (under Mossop's management) as Polly, and instantly became a decided favourite. Hitchcock in his *View of the Irish Stage* says that in 1764 the rage for Miss Catley was at this time so great that Barry, the manager of the rival house in Crow Street, was at his wits' end how to hold his own, and " conscious that his musical performers were not equal to those of Smock Alley, he boldly announced *The Beggar's Opera*, Captain Macheath by himself, Polly by Mrs. Dancer, and Lucy by Mrs. Abington." The experiment was successful, and it rested with Mossop to go one better. It was the fortune of *The Beggar's Opera* to excite rivalry wherever it went, and with success on both sides, thanks to its capacity for variety. Anne Catley had long drawn a full house as Polly, and now Mossop induced her to figure as " the rakish, joyous Macheath," and in the rearrangement of the cast Miss Dunlop played Polly. About the middle of the season there was a fresh shuffling of the cards. Mrs. Abington came to Smock Alley, and was the Polly to the Lucy of Signora Spiletta, a very capable actress and singer. She had a very imperfect acquaintance with English, but this was far from being a drawback. The absurdity of her pronunciation was in itself an attraction.

Constant repetition had no effect on the freshness of the Opera. In October 1765 Mossop opened the season with it, Miss Catley being again the Polly with Miss Thomas as Lucy. Hitchcock says that Anne " had at this time nearly arrived at the zenith of her reputation. . . . She drew as much money to the Irish theatre as any vocal performer ever did either before or since. . . . She played Polly, Macheath, and Lucy." Not only this, but (and it must have pleased her as much as her success on the stage) she set the fashion of dressing the hair, and the Dublin ladies had their locks " Catleyfied." Mrs. Abington had the same gratification in another direction. She first wore the " Abington cap," which became the rage both in Dublin and London.

Miss Catley, we are told, "was not beautiful, but pleasing. Her face was oval, her features *petite*, and her eyes small ; her forehead being remarkably high, she always wore her dark hair, which was thin and lank, caught down upon it like a fan, and as this mode gave a peculiar archness to the countenance," it was readily adopted, and, says Anne's too candid biographer, " remained in vogue for years among the lower classes of those ladies who stroll the streets." For the rest she was remarkably thin, her bones small, her skin brown and all covered with freckles, yet her *tout ensemble* was pleasing, when she was made up and on the stage (see illustration, p. 248).

We get a fair notion of her powers from an article in *The Maccaroni Magazine* : " As an actress she claims no title," declares the writer ; " as a singer she is at present the sweetest warbler on the English stage. Her voice is strong, clear, harmonious and expressive. In person she is well made ; her complexion is fair ; the next her eyes, which are lascivious and enchanting ; then her air, which to many is beyond expression. But not to touch upon her gallantries here, as it will be needless, so many anecdotes, etc., having been published concerning this lady ; therefore I only proceed with what nature

has endowed her with. She possesses lively spirits,
with a peculiar turn of wit; and, as Polly in *The
Beggar's Opera* says, 'she knows as well as any
woman how to make the most of herself.'"

Here is another word-picture of the Protean actress
from the pen of O'Keefe. He says: "Her person is
above the middle stature; though perfectly well made
she is not genteel, there being a carelessness in her
gait that too nearly approaches the hoyden. Her
countenance is remarkably pleasing and expressive,
and she has a wanton wildness in her eye that cannot
fail to captivate. Her mouth, from which the most
exquisite harmony flows, displays a set of teeth that
are unrivalled upon the stage, and adds charm to
a face uncommonly beautiful. She could not be
reckoned a first-rate actress, even in comedy, but her
singing brings her upon a level with our performers
now existing."

Boaden is much more enthusiastic over the lively
Anne than the writer in *The Maccaroni Magazine*.
He says in his *Life of Mrs. Jordan* " that there was
in her personal character a good deal of the careless
boldness of Woffington; like her, too, she was extremely handsome, and her eyes and mouth had a
peculiar expression of archness. She aimed at the
almost manly frankness of speech, and acted as one
superior to censure when she raised the wonder of
prudery."

Boaden alludes to her also in his *Life of Mrs.
Siddons* in the following terms, " To those who have
never heard Miss Catley I must . . . try to give some
notion of what was peculiar to her. It was the singing of unequalled animal spirits; it was Mrs. Jordan's
comedy carried into music—the something *more* that
a duller soul cannot conceive and a feeble nerve
dare not venture. Even at the close of her theatric
life when consumptive and but the ghost of her
former self, gasping even for breath and wasting her
little remaining vitality in her exertion, she would
make sometimes a successful attempt at one of her

former brilliant *rushes* of musical expression, and mingle a pleasing astonishment along with the pain you were compelled to suffer. No other female singer ever gave the slightest notion of her. She was bold, volatile, and audacious." It will be noticed that not two of Anne's admirers agree in their description of her charms, and the discrepancy is in itself a high compliment. It is clear that she was " infinite in her variety."

The Beggar's Opera from the days of Madame Violante's " Liliputians " had always been a great favourite in Dublin, and many other Irish Pollies could be mentioned, among them being: Miss Bridges at Crow Street, with Vernon, one of the best Macheaths of his day; Miss Green at Smock Alley, Miss Browne at the same theatre; and when in 1769 Miss Catley had lost some of her hold, Miss Ashmore came to the front and for some years was very popular.

Writing some years later, Michael Kelly, a favourite singer and composer of the day, makes a curious statement concerning Dublin and *The Beggar's Opera*. He says that the Opera " was prohibited by the Irish Government from being acted, which of course made the public more eager to see it." Kelly interested some influential people to bring pressure to bear on the authorities, the ban was removed, and the performance brought him an overflowing house. Kelly adds, " The managers ought to have been well pleased that I took this measure and carried it out, for ever since that time (1793) the piece has kept its station on the Irish stage." The Irish Government of that date would seem to have been as greatly afraid of Gay's satire as was Sir Robert Walpole.

Many stories have been told of Miss Catley's wit, which appears to have been of the boisterous character not far removed from that of the popular jest books of the day. Her biographer records how " the Reverend Dean Bailey was the principal superintendent to one of the public charities, and it having been determined that a concert should be performed

for the benefit of the Lying-in Hospital, the Dean, who
was principally attentive to this charity, took upon
him to engage Catley to sing at the concert and
wrote her a card to the following purport : ' Dean
Bailey's compliments to Miss Catley, and requests
to know when she can give him a night at the Lying-
in Hospital and her terms.'   On this card Nan put
a jocular interpretation, and returned for answer :
' Miss Catley presents her compliments to the
Reverend Dr. Bailey ; for three nights to come she
is engaged to particular friends, but on the fourth
she will be at his service.'   This produced a laugh
against the Dean, but in the end served the charity,
for which Nan sang gratis."

O'Keefe relates how on the first time of his
venturing into a theatre after the failure of one of
his musical plays Miss Catley accosted him from
a front row in the lower boxes loud enough to be
heard by all.   " So, O'Keefe, you had a piece damned
the other night.   I'm glad of it.   The devil mend
you for writing an opera without bringing me into
it."   " A few moments after Miss Catley had thus
accosted me," writes O'Keefe, " Leoni entered the
box with a lady leaning on his arm.   Miss Catley
catching his eye called out, ' How do you do, Leoni ?
I hear you're married—is that your wife ?   Bid her
stand up till I see her.'   Leoni, abashed, whispered
to the lady, who with good-humoured compliance
stood up.   Catley, after surveying her a little, said :
' Ha ! very well indeed.   I like your choice.' "   O'Keefe
adds : " She was one of the most beautiful women
I ever saw ; the expression of her eyes—her smiles
and dimples that played around her lips and cheeks
were enchanting.   She was eccentric, but had an
excellent heart."   The Catley certainly was never
slow to obey the whim of the moment, as for instance when in response to a " call " she curtseyed
but with her back turned to the audience !   And
they applauded louder than ever.   They understood
the vagaries of their favourite.

Not only in Dublin but in other parts of Ireland
The Beggar's Opera was the rage. The people took
to Gay's humour naturally—perhaps they recognised
in it something akin to their own. Dr. Johnson,
speaking of the many famous Irish actors and
actresses on the English stage, was of opinion that
" the Irish mix better with the English than the
Scotch do, their language is nearer to English ; as
a proof of which they succeed very well as players,
which Scotchmen do not."

At the time Anne Catley was scoring in Dublin
amateur theatricals were the rage all over Ireland.
Dr. Doran has recorded how Kilkenny, Lurgan, Cavan
and Dublin had their private stages.   He also adds
drily that " when the amateur actors played for
charity's sake, everybody took private boxes and
nobody paid for them."   In 1761 *The Beggar's Opera*
was played at the Duke of Leinster's seat at Cavan.
A reverend dean played Lockit, and had four lines
in the prologue (which he wrote and spoke) devoted
to himself, wherein he said :

> " But when this busy mimic scene is o'er
> All shall resume the work they had before ;
> Lockit himself his knavery shall resign,
> And lose the Gaoler in the dull Divine."

Anne Catley's last appearance in Dublin was in
September 1772, after which she returned to London
and played both Polly and Lucy at Covent Garden
in 1772, 1774, 1780, and lastly in 1782, when she
revived her impersonation of Macheath under circumstances and with a result to be recorded later on.

While the Opera with Anne Catley was triumphing in Dublin it was holding its own in London, Mrs.
Arne, an accomplished singer of the florid school,
which was then being revived by her husband, taking
the part of Polly to Mrs. Abington's Lucy and Vernon's
Macheath.   For some reason, which so far as we
know has never been explained, the ever-delightful
Mrs. Abington was always contented with the less

important character. Possibly she found its tenderness suit her style ; the great actress was too shrewd not to know when she was effective and picturesque, especially in dress. O'Keefe says of her that " her manner was most charmingly fascinating, and her speaking voice melodious. She had peculiar tricks in acting ; one was turning her wrist, and seeming to stick a pin in the side of her waist ; she was also very adroit in the use of her fan ; and though equally capital in fine ladies and hoydens, was never seen in low and vulgar characters."

On one occasion, however, she departed from her rule, and Mrs. Charles Mathews wrote severely that " Mrs. Abington (the original performer of Lady Teazle) in the latter portion of her dramatic life was tempted to throw aside feminine grace and delicacy so far as to exhibit herself as Scrub in *The Beaux' Stratagem* for her (pecuniary) benefit—a character," adds Mrs. Mathews, with a suggestion of spite somewhat unnecessary, " which, it may be said, she acted but too well." No doubt this was intended to apply to Mrs. Abington's low origin and her experience in early life as a waitress at a tavern. That she should have sprung from the commonest of surroundings to live to set the fashion to fine ladies of *ton* is one of the strange contrasts which are constantly to be met with in the history of the stage. Mrs. Abington, we read, "is the harbinger of the reigning fashion for the season—a very beautiful style of petticoat of Persian origin is amongst the last importations of this admired actress." Again, " Mrs. Abington, the pattern of fashion, has fallen into the absurdity of wearing red powder : her influence on the *ton* is too well known— let her at once deviate from this unnatural French custom, or, if she is determined to continue a *red head*, let her frizeur throw a little brick-dust on her arches (eyebrows)."

The vicious style of elaborate ornament which Arne too often adopted, whether to set the taste or

MISS MARY CATHERINE BOLTON.

From an engraving after De Wilde.

to follow it, had been allowed to creep into *The Beggar's Opera* and spoil the simplicity of the music, which is its chief charm. A letter in *The Theatrical Observer* of September 1767 gives us a very good idea how the Opera was performed at that time. "Undoubtedly," writes the correspondent of *The Observer*, " the exhibition at Drury Lane was rather weak than otherwise, for although *The Beggar's Opera* cannot but be allowed, by all who are in the least conversant with dramatic writing, to be a most masterly and great composition, yet the length of time it hath been wrought and the frequency of its having been acted not only in London, Dublin, and Edinburgh, but in every capital town and village in the three kingdoms, hath taken off the keenness of appetite with which people used to flock to see that piece in preference to almost any other; but at present nothing except a new Macheath or Polly, or a new method of wobbling out and Italianizing the songs can any longer excite the curiosity of the public to the repetition of *The Beggar's Opera*; and these stratagems, especially the last, have been practised with some success ever since our poor country people have taken it into their heads to relish everything foreign and ridiculous, slight their home manufactures, and think it absurd to pay for anything they understand. To do Mr. Vernon justice, he acted Macheath very well, Mrs. Arne and Mrs. Abington went through their parts with spirit and applause; but I almost beg all the fine singers' pardons, when I declare that I am no friend to the present manner of performing *The Beggar's Opera*, and that (to please me) I have seen it some years ago, infinitely better done and much nearer to the author's design, I am perfectly assured, than I did on Wednesday night last." This criticism, we venture to think, is both sound and just.

Macklin in his *Memoirs* enumerates all the best of the Macheaths up to his day. Among them were Vernon and Webster. Of the first we are told that

21

he was reckoned a good Macheath in his time, with musical knowledge equal to the part, but neither his voice nor his figure, was that of a highwayman; he "was a coxcomb of the first water, and whatever part he played he was for showing himself more than his author" (see p. 216). Macheaths would appear to have been endless in their variety. "Webster," says the critical Macklin, "was all *but* the character; a fine, sweet-toned manly voice, genteel deportment, etc., which made forcible impressions, but in his acting he was too much of a gentleman for Macheath. The man who lives months with women of the town and men of the road is not likely to acquire any other manners than a bold forward look and a free familiar impudence. Webster could not exactly compass this, and so far he failed in the eye of critical examination."

Another Macheath was Lowe, who had a fine voice, but had no musical science. When Handel quarrelled with Beard, he intended to engage Lowe for the oratorios, but finding him deficient in the requisite training, was obliged to make peace with Beard, who had both voice and talent. Lowe was once proprietor of Marylebone Gardens, but afterwards came down in the world, and John Taylor speaks of meeting him in a narrow lane near Aldersgate Street coming out of a butcher's shop with some meat in an old blue-checked handkerchief. Taylor says Lowe's name was found in all the old song-books of Vauxhall and Marylebone Gardens, and that a print was published of him as Macheath with Mrs. Chambers as Polly.

Of Beard it is said that, "though his singing and person were in character, he was deficient in speaking as well in the bold flashy gentility of deportment, which belong to the character. Lowe's voice was still more happy, but his expression less characteristic." Beard was fortunate in his management of Covent Garden Theatre, and retired with a handsome sum. It is worthy of note that during

Beard's tenure the piano was first publicly introduced to an English audience. We are told in
Lloyd's Evening Post of May 16, 1767, that after
Act I. of *The Beggar's Opera* " Miss Brickler will sing
a favourite song from *Judith*, accompanied by Mr.
Dibdin on a new instrument called Piano Forte."
The invention does not seem to have attracted any
attention. Probably in its rudimentary form it was
not regarded as an improvement on the harpsichord.

CHAPTER XXVII

TRAVESTIES OF *THE BEGGAR'S OPERA*

Opinions of Johnson, Gibbon and Boswell on the " morality " of *The Beggar's Opera*—Sir John Fielding's correspondence with Colman and Garrick—Colman's extraordinary travesty of the Opera at the Haymarket Theatre—Mrs. Billington and Miss George—a vocal contest between Polly and Lucy—Braham's revenge on Mrs. Billington—Charles Bannister's success as Polly—Colman's " Preludio "—Description of the travesty given by Adolphus—Mrs. Webb's enormous bulk—*The Ladies' Opera* at Covent Garden Theatre, with Anne Catley as Macheath—A failure—Death of Miss Catley.

WHAT with Anne Catley, Mrs. Abington, Mrs. Arne and Vernon, and possibly because of the Italianising of the simple melodies, the Opera became more than ever the rage in 1775. Boswell tells how in this year Dr. Johnson and Sir Joshua Reynolds, together with himself, were being entertained by Mr. Cambridge (the author of *The Scribbleriad* and other works) at his villa, the well-known Cambridge House on the banks of the Thames at Twickenham. The subject of *The Beggar's Opera* came up—as it was natural it should in a neighbourhood so closely associated with Pope and Gay—and " the common question whether it was pernicious in its effects having been introduced," Johnson remarked, "As to this matter, which has been very much contested, I myself am of opinion that more influence has been ascribed to *The Beggar's Opera* than it in reality ever had ; for I do not believe that any man was ever made a rogue by being present at its representation. At the same time I do not deny it may have some influence by making the character of a rogue familiar and in some degree pleasing." Then, collecting himself as it were to give a heavy stroke : " There is in it such a *labefactation* of all principles as may be injurious to morality "; and while the great lexicographer was pronouncing this ponderous judgment, Boswell and Reynolds and the rest of the company " sat in a comical sort of restraint, smothering a laugh, which we were afraid might burst out."

Boswell adds sententiously that in his opinion " not only are the gaiety and heroism very captivating to a youthful imagination, but the arguments for adventurous depredation are so plausible, the illusions so lively, and the contrasts with the ordinary and most painful modes of acquiring property are so artfully displayed, that it requires a cool and strong judgment to resist so imposing an aggregate; yet I own I should be very sorry to have *The Beggar's Opera* suppressed, for there is in it so much of real London life, so much brilliant wit, and such a variety of airs which from early association of ideas engage and soothe and enliven the mind, that no performance with the theatre delights me more." This was not Burke's opinion. He could see no merit in *The Beggar's Opera.*

Boswell's moralising never has anything particularly original about it. He has a way, as in this instance, of presenting a platitude as though he had made a profound discovery. It is pretty certain that the discharged servant who took to the " road " and became glorified—as " Sixteen String Jack," as many another footman without a character did—hardly required the example of rollicking Macheath to be convinced how easy it was to stop a coach and ease the terrified passengers of their purses and valuables—especially as there was generally a complaisant innkeeper handy, who would give the professor of the " High Toby " game shelter and secrecy in case of a hot pursuit.

In a footnote, Boswell quotes the opinion of " a very eminent physician, whose discernment is as acute and penetrating in judging of the human character as it is in his own profession." This authority remarked once at a Club " where I (Boswell) was, that a lively young man fond of pleasure and without money would hardly resist a solicitation from his mistress to go upon the highway, immediately after being present at the representation of *The Beggar's Opera*." The " discernment " of this " eminent physician " is not so evident in the conclusion he came to as Boswell imagined. The argument certainly has not the whimsical ingenuity of Gibbon's notion that *The Beggar's Opera* may perhaps have sometimes increased the number of highwaymen ; but otherwise it had " a beneficial effect in refining that class of men, making them less ferocious, more polite —in short, more like gentlemen." In other words, if you must be robbed on the highway it is preferable to be told to " Stand and deliver ! " by a highwayman who holds his pistol with an air, and prefaces his demand with a courtly bow, than to be compelled to hand over one's money to a vulgar ruffian. Sir John Fielding and other magistrates at Bow Street had, however, different views.

Richard Ryan says that during Mr. Colman's management of Covent Garden Theatre, the Magistrates of Bow Street, with wonderful regard for the public morals, wished to suppress *The Beggar's Opera*, and the following is the correspondence that passed on the subject :—" *From the Magistrates in Bow Street.* The Magistrates now sitting in Bow Street present their compliments to Mr. Colman, and acquaint him that on *The Beggar's Opera* being given out to be played some time ago, at Drury Lane Theatre, they requested the managers of that theatre not to exhibit the Opera, deeming it productive of mischief to society, as, in their opinion, it most undoubtedly increased the number of thieves ; and that the managers obligingly returned for answer, that for that night it was too late to stop it, but that for the future they would not play it, if the other house did not. Under these circumstances, from a sense of duty and the principles of humanity, the Magistrates make the same request to Mr. Colman and the rest of the managers of His Majesty's Theatre Royal, Covent Garden, the same Opera being advertised to be played before this night.—Bow Street, October 27, 1773."

To this Colman returned the following answer: " Mr. Colman presents his best respects to the Magistrates with whose note he has just been honoured. He has not yet had an opportunity of submitting it to the other managers; but, for his own part, cannot help differing in opinion with the Magistrates, thinking that the theatre is one of the *very few houses in the neighbourhood* that does not contribute to increase the number of thieves.—Covent Garden, Wednesday Morning."

The letters which passed between Sir John Fielding and Garrick on the same subject must have been highly amusing, if what is recorded in *The London Chronicle* be correct. We read : " It is humourously reported that the correspondence between Sir John Fielding and Mr. Garrick respecting *The Beggar's Opera* commenced with the former officially desiring of the latter that Macheath might be hanged agreeable to the dark complexion of his crimes. The manager in return pleasantly remarked that it did not suit his interest at present to carry conviction to such lengths, whatever might be the knight's, and therefore without he could point out how he might likewise gain four score hard pounds by every execution of his favourite hero he must beg leave to waive a ceremony so disagreeable in every point of view."

This retort hit the magistrate very hard, for Sir John, as indeed did other London magistrates, derived a part of his salary from fees derivable from prisoners. The words of Townsend, the famous Bow Street runner, may be quoted on this matter, as follows : " The plan used to be to issue warrants and take up all the poor devils in the streets, and then there was the bailing of them, 2*s.* 4*d.* each, which the magistrate had. In taking up one hundred girls

they would make at 2*s.* 4*d.* each—£11 13*s.* 4*d.*   They
sent none of them to gaol, for the bailing of them was
so much better."

This question of the effect of a stage play on the
morals of the public has been discussed over and
over again, and need not now be laboured.   Its
importance in the present connection is that it
kept alive interest in *The Beggar's Opera* : not only
those who saw no harm thronged the theatres where
the opera was performed, but also those who wanted
argumentative material with which to denounce it.

One of the characteristics of Gay's masterpiece
was its ready adaptability to suit the fancy of enterprising managers on the look-out for novelty.   It had
already been performed by children, more than one
actress had essayed Macheath, and it was left for
George Colman in 1781 to have " recourse to a most
whimsical and indecent mode," as Richard Ryan in
his *Theatrical Anecdotes* puts it, " of attracting visitors
to his theatre in the Haymarket—viz., by travestying *The Beggar's Opera,* that is by putting all the
female performers in the male parts and *vice versa.*"
" Breeches parts " were of course no innovation.
Had not Woffington made her great success as Sir
Harry Wildair, and had not pages innumerable been
represented by women ?   But to see female characters enacted by men was apparently too much for
some of the censors, forgetful that until the end of
Charles the Second's reign ladies were not seen on
the stage.   Kynaston, the handsome young man
who was so popular as a heroine, will of course be
remembered.

Colman's experiment was possibly suggested
by the success of Mrs. Kennedy, who (imitating
Anne Catley at Dublin) made a sensation by her
Macheath in London.   Mrs. Kennedy was a clever
Irish girl, once, like Mrs. Abington, a waitress in a
public-house.   She had so charming and fresh a voice
that her reputation reached Dr. Arne, who took her
under his tuition, and she came out in *The Beggar's*

MISS PATON.

From an engraving by R. Newton, after W. J. Newton.

Opera at Covent Garden in 1777 and introduced the now well-known song "A hunting we will go," composed specially for her by Arne. William Parke in his *Musical Memoirs* speaks of Mrs. Kennedy as possessing " one of the finest counter tenor voices ever heard. She was ungainly in figure and not favoured with beauty, and it was decided that her only chance was in some male impersonation, and so it came about that Macheath was selected for her debut." She afterwards sang a good deal at Vauxhall Gardens.

Advertising his venture in *The Morning Chronicle* of August 9, 1780, as " A favourite Pasticcio call'd *The Beggar's Opera*, the music compiled by Dr. Pepusch," Colman got together a very strong company at the Haymarket for his experiment. Mrs. Cargill was Macheath ; Mrs. Webb, Lockit ; and Mrs. Wilson, Filch. Charles Bannister was Polly ; his son John, Jenny Diver ; and John Wilson, Mrs. Peachum. Colman wrote a " Preludio " to introduce the novelty, and *The Morning Chronicle* in its notice of the performance gives the reason put forward by Colman for travestying what originally in some respects was in itself a travesty.

" *The Beggar's Opera*," says *The Chronicle*, " was certainly designed by Gay as a satire upon the taste of the times in which it was first brought forward ; at that day Italian operas were the idols of the public, and sense, sensibility, and humour were warbled off the stage by the dying airs of Senesino, Farinelli, and other fashionable foreign singers. Powerful as the satire originally was, it gradually lost its efficacy in proportion as the mode of representation became injudiciously refined, till at length what was meant as a piece of comic ridicule was converted into a serious sentimental performance, and instead of its being attended as a dramatic satire the sole allurement to the theatre wherein it was represented was a new or favourite singer in one or the other of the principal characters. Finding it in that state, Mr. Colman wisely lent wings to the author's

original intention by reviving the characters and
letting the men play those parts which are female in
their names and nature. But foreseeing there was
some danger in so violent an alteration in the cast,
he wrote a dramatic introduction to prepare the
audience for the burlesque manner in which they
were to see our old acquaintance appear, and gave it
the title of a new 'Preludio,' in which the excessive
love of the Italians for music, of the French for dancing, and of the English for newspapers and politics,
was ridiculed in the persons of Signor Scrapelli,
Monsieur Cabri, and John Bull. But the chief object
of the 'Preludio' was to satirise the performance
at the King's Theatre and pauperise those of its
rival house on the other side of the Haymarket."

Had this been written in the present day, Colman's ideas would have been put forward in the
form of an " interview." It may be doubted whether
the enterprising manager cared a button about
restoring *The Beggar's Opera* to its original object.
He wanted something startling to attract the town,
and he saw his way to this by turning the opera
upside down. At the same time there is something
to be said as to the opera having been " injudiciously refined." Miss Brent, Mrs. Arne, Mrs.
Billington, like Miss Anne Catley, did not look for
their success in the simplicity of the music and their
own self-restraint, but in the amount of ornamenta-
tion they could introduce. Catley had an amazingly
flexible voice, and was the first to sing a passage
staccato, to the horror of the believers in the orthodox
Italian school, which was nothing if not smooth.
She is reported by Parke to have sung the whole of
Fischer's Minuet staccato in the burlesque opera of
Tom Thumb, performed in the same year as Colman's
Beggar's Opera burlesque " with most extraordinary
power of voice and articulation, and in it was at all
times vehemently encored " ; and if she was in the
mood, Anne would not hesitate to play tricks with
the old English melodies of *The Beggar's Opera*.

A proof of the anxiety of the lady singers of the day to exhibit their accomplished vocalisation is to be seen in the curious contest which took place in Ireland in 1777 between Mrs. Billington and Miss George, who, says Parke, " had a voice of such extent that she sang up to B in alto perfectly clear and in tune, this being three notes higher than any singer's I ever heard. Mrs. Billington, who was engaged on very high terms for a limited number of nights, made her first appearance on the Dublin stage in the character of Polly, surrounded by her halo of popularity. She was received with acclamation and sang her songs delightfully, particularly ' Cease your funning,' which was tumultuously encored. Miss George, who performed the part of Lucy (an uphill singing part), perceiving she had little chance of dividing the applause with the great magnet of the night, had recourse to the following stratagem : when the dialogue ' Why, how now, Madame Flirt ? ' came on, Mrs. Billington gave her verse with great correctness and expression, and was much applauded. Miss George in reply, availing herself of her extraordinary compass of voice and setting propriety at defiance, sang the whole of her verse an octave higher, her tone having the effect of the high notes of a sweet and brilliant flute : the audience, taken by surprise, bestowed on her such loud applause as almost shook the walls of the theatre, and an unanimous encore was the result."

To be eclipsed in her own particular line—for Mrs. Billington had also a voice of phenomenal compass (Shield wrote for her a song which went up to G in alt., probably the highest vocal melody extant, not excepting the famous air for the Queen of Night in *Zauberflaute*)—must have been extremely galling. As for Mrs. Billington's rendering of the music of Polly, one can hardly believe she was contented to leave it unadorned, when we read that " her style was chiefly marked by an inexhaustible fund of ornaments, always extemporaneous ; not even a pencil memorandum of what she meant to do was ever made upon her singing copy ; she trusted to the suggestion of the moment, never sang the same song twice with the same ornaments, and never was known to attempt anything she did not completely accomplish " (see p. 288).

As the accounts of things theatrical rarely agree, to find another authority giving a different description of Mrs. Billington's method is only what one expects. Braham, whose voice rivalled the lady's in flexibility, once sang with her at Milan in an opera by Nasolini. The great tenor was rewarded by such thunders of applause at the rehearsal that the husband of Mrs. Billington, one Felissent, mad with jealousy, induced the composer to omit the grand scena in the second act he had written for Braham. The plot got wind, the public took up the matter, and at its first representation the opera was well hissed. The next day it was announced that the composer would complete his opera, and that the scena would be restored. Braham sang it magnificently, and it was received with enthusiasm. But Braham was not satisfied, and he conceived a plan of retaliation which none but he could have carried out.

" It was Mrs. Billington's habit," says the narrator of the story, " to study all her *rifiormenti*, which when once selected she seldom or never changed, and to rehearse her songs in a full voice and all her ornaments and cadences at length." Here of course is a flat contradiction, but let it pass. " Braham, whose *entrée* and first air preceded that of Mrs. Billington, listened to her roulades at rehearsal, learned them all by heart, and one night appropriated remorselessly all her well-studied graces to the adornment of his own song." Mrs. Billington refused to sing a duet with him in the next opera in which they performed together, but she was not one to bear malice, especially where a man was concerned, and the two were afterwards reconciled.

It is quite certain that at this period a meretricious style was adopted by nearly all the great singers, and it is not too much to hazard the opinion that Colman's desire to go back to the original simplicity of *The Beggar's Opera* was little more than a piece of advertising claptrap intended to justify the production of his topsy-turvy absurdity.

After its exordium *The Chronicle* proceeds to describe Colman's " Preludio." " The scene opened," we are told, " with a representation of the front of the Haymarket Theatre, and a dialogue between Townly (the supposed author) and the Beggar, and soon changed to the Orange Coffee-house, where the Beggar said a party of foreigners were assembled for the purpose of dancing his piece. Signor Scrapelli is there discovered, composing music with Signor Trebletti, and is disturbed in the midst of his performance by a musician attending upon Monsieur Cabri, who dances or rather capers to the time. The Italians stop their ears, cry out ' Execrable ! diabolo ! ' and interrupt the Prince of Capers, who quarrels with them for the interruption. John Bull calls for a glass of brandy and water, reads his paper as long as the noise will permit him, and then leaves the coffee-room, damning them all for a pack of outlandish fellows that will not let him enjoy his newspaper and stupid blockheads who have no heads for politics."

The Chronicle does not explain how Colman joined his Preludio to the opera, but this omission is supplied by *The Morning Herald,* which says : " The scene then changes to the Haymarket Theatre, and the Beggar calls on the Prompter to know why the performance was not begun, it being then considerably past the usual hour ? The Prompter tells him that there is a strange confusion among the comedians, that ' Polly ' was not above half shaved, that the carpenter had not made Mr. Bannister's jumps to fit him, and that Mrs. Webb could not get her coat and waistcoat on. . . . The music bell is then rung for the overture, but the Prompter observing a trapdoor up in the centre of the stage, asks the carpenter the reason of it. Honest Chip replies that he meant it for him to stand and prompt the opera, being instructed that everything was to be done exactly in the same manner as was usual on the other side the Haymarket. The Prompter bids him shut the trap, telling him that he shall stand in his own place and not attempt to follow the example of the other side of the street." Then the opera began.

The fooling was heartily enjoyed and received with unbounded applause. Adolphus in his *Memoirs of John Bannister* gives us a very good idea of the performance. He writes that " its extraordinary merit or its extreme whimsicality reconciled the audience even to this portion of its impropriety. Wilson's vulgarity in Mrs. Peachum was often ludicrous and effective, but if Sir Hugh Evans was shocked at the old woman who had a ' peard under her muffler,' the spectators of *The Beggar's Opera* had much more right to be so when Mrs. Peachum, holding her dress a little awkwardly, or swinging too heedlessly in her chair, let them perceive a pair of black plush breeches under her petticoats. They were not so much offended when Charles Bannister, managing his dress too carelessly, showed an ankle which, for its elegance, the fairest lady present might have wished her own.

" Edwin's Lucy was everything that a low virago transplanted from the bar to the high office of an inferior turnkey at Newgate could be expected to display. Her ludicrous grief, her vulgar rage, her nauseous fondness, and her petulant vituperation, were delineated even beyond the life. Those who witnessed it cannot easily forget the tone and spirit which he infused into the songs 'Thus when a good housewife sees a rat,' and ' I'm bubbled, I'm bubbled.' The line ' These fingers with pleasure could fasten the noose' was given with a most unfeminine energy.

" In the mock female characters, the achieve-

ment was Charles Bannister's Polly. Sir Joshua
Reynolds has observed that, whatever horrors an
artist may intend to display, his picture should
always represent some individual, or some object,
in which the eye could delight for its beauty. Gay
seems to have anticipated this idea in placing the
gentle, confiding, affectionate Polly Peachum in
the midst of his crew of dissolute ruffians and worth-
less strumpets. Had Charles Bannister, with his
ample, muscular, manly frame, and deep intonation
both in speaking and singing, attempted to mince
in his gait, or to ' aggravate his voice ' into any
feminine softness, the effect would, however successful for a moment, in the end have become tiresome
and disgusting. The public had been used to witness his imitation of the soprano of Tenducci, and
his Arionelli, a similar personage, in *The Son-in-law*,
but they were short and produced an effect very
different from that which would have attended a
repetition during three long acts. He appeared
overloaded, but not encumbered, by a complete
dress of white muslin, with a hoop, the middle of
which appeared tightly laced ; and however incon-
sistent his large size, a certain trick of his countenance, and his manly step, might seem when compared
with the delicacy of a young female, no antics or super-
added drolleries of his own drew down the senseless
laugh, so often a tribute to mere grossness and
absurdity. His ' big manly voice ' alone produced
a sufficient comic effect, his Caliban roar when
Peachum pinches his daughter to make her confess,
in the press-yard fashion, ' by squeezing an answer
from her,' and the deep intonation of her kindness
when she recommends a *repitatur haustus* from the
gin-bottle—' Give her another glass, sir ; my mamma
drinks double quantity whenever she is out of order,'
would have drawn a hearty laugh from the sourest
misanthrope. The songs, whether tender or spirited,
were given with the utmost taste and judgment, and
as much applause as could possibly be bestowed no

an attempt of the kind was readily given to Polly's
male representative (see p. 256).

(see p. 256)

" To the ladies in the travesty no less praise may
be assigned. Mrs. Cargill's small and unencumbered
figure made her a ludicrous contrast to Bannister,
who, when singing the line ' Fondly let me loll,'
hardly knew on what part of her diminutive person
to accommodate himself ; yet the sweetness and
spirit with which she gave the song more than reconciled, it captivated the public . . . Mrs. Webb showed
much ability in Lockit . . . but Mrs. Wilson, the
arch, comical little creature, nicknamed from the
colour of her locks ' the Goldfinch,' presented in
Filch the perfect personification of a hardy, expert
pick-pocket, and the genuine manners of a well-
plumed Newgate bird. So complete was the representation, that I remember hearing a lady remark
that, if she saw such a fellow near her in the street,
she should not require the admonition of a Bow
Street officer to ' take care of her pockets ' "—
ladies wore pockets in those days.

One can well believe that Mrs. Webb as Lockit
was very laughter-provoking. She was an enormous
woman, " one of the most bulky I ever saw," says
Parke, and after her Lockit she played Falstaff with
great success. One morning at rehearsal she com-
plained of a pain in the small of her back, and was
incensed beyond measure when some one inquired,
" Pray, Mrs. Webb, which is the *small* of your back ! "
Her fondness for bed and her love of eating sufficiently
explain the cause of her corpulency. It is said
that she used to recruit herself after the fatigue of
the week by lying in bed on Sundays and having
her dinner brought there, the dish consisting invariably—even in the dog days—of hot roast pork,
stuffed with sage and onions. In spite of her size,
or perhaps because of it, she was an immense favourite.

Mrs. Webb's husband, also an actor, matched her
in bulk, and the two were called " the jolliest couple
in the kingdom." The story goes that, being engaged

MADAME VESTRIS.

From Mr. A. M. Broadley's Collection.

at Southampton, Webb, who, like John Gilpin's wife, had a frugal mind, advertised for " an agreeable companion " to occupy a seat in their post-chaise and pay a third part of the expense. It so happened that the advertisement was seen by a portly Hampshire pig-herder, who, having finished his business in London, was tempted by the prospect of getting home cheaply, to call at Webb's lodgings. The three stared at each other, and the pig-herder burst out indignantly : " What, screw us into a post-chaise !— worse than three in a bed in the dog days. A hot bath would be an ice house to it. By the lord, if we were to make a grand set-out in a broad-wheeled waggon, it would certainly be stopped at the first weighing machine for being overloaded." The Webbs were not at all offended, asked the countryman to dine off a fine round of corned beef, and the pig-herder, when he got home, sent them in return a huge ham, which more than repaid Webb for the money he had spent in advertising.

During the brief season of the Haymarket, the Opera in its transposed version was played eighteen times, and the house opened with it in the following year. Towards the end of 1781 we find it advertised in *The Morning Chronicle* to be performed at Drury Lane in its original form, with Mrs. Cargill as Macheath, Moody as Peachum, and Polly a Miss Wheeler from Bath, " with accompaniments to the airs composed by Mr. Linley." It was now quite the thing to introduce dancing, and we have the announcement: " End of Act II., dancing by Miss Stagledoirs (surely a *nom de théâtre*), and in Act III. a hornpipe by Mr. Walker." In the meantime Anne Catley was content with Polly and Lucy, but Mrs. Cargill's rivalry tempted her to revive her Macheath success in Dublin. Her powers, however, were failing her, consumption was eating its way into her constitution, and possibly the Covent Garden manager, Harris, doubted whether by herself she would prove a formidable rival to Mrs. Cargill. He determined to

22

go one better than the composite performance at
Drury Lane, and announced that *The Beggar's Opera*
would be given by a company in which there would
not be a single male impersonator! This company
he called *The Ladies' Opera*. Miss Catley, it may be
mentioned, was supported by Mrs. Wilson and Mrs.
Webb from the Haymarket.

The Drury Lane version, with Mrs. Cargill, gained
a day's start, and on October 16 *The Morning Herald*
gave a notice of the performance. The critic was
very friendly towards Miss Wheeler from Bath as
Polly, and then, waxing facetious, remarked that
" Mrs. Cargill was all that we could wish in Captain
Macheath, and Lucy alone might differ with us in
opinion. Lucy was played by Mrs. Wrighten with her
usual humour, but might we not be permitted to
ask that lady one question? Was it envy or merely
the warmth of action which caused her to cough
so loud while pretty Polly was sweetly warbling
in the prison scene? If, as we suspect, it was the
latter, it were to be wished that in future she will
' moderate her heat,' and not deprive the audience
of those delicate sensations which Miss Wheeler
seems calculated to feel and to inspire."

On the following night *The Ladies' Opera* was
produced, and of its production we find *The Morning
Chronicle* saying : " The managers of Covent Garden
Theatre, willing to give every species of novelty to
the Town in their power, last night entertained
them with the new edition of *The Beggar's Opera*,
which, on account of all the parts being cast for
women, was performed for the first time under the
title of *The Ladies' Opera* with a new introduction.

" The introduction was no more than a single
controversial song, supposed to be between a man
and his wife, relative to the rage for theatrical novelty,
which afforded a few sallies of fancy on what might
be done by metamorphosing the principal actresses
of both theatres into male characters, and modestly
enough concluded that as *The Beggar's Opera* was

originally written to burlesque the Italian Opera, a continuation of that burlesque in another style might produce novelty and entertainment.

" The Opera then commenced, and though Miss Catley's Macheath was a *petit* one in point of figure and real importance, it was pretty and arch, and by throwing her usual originality of voice and manner into it, made it, on the whole, very laughable. The parts of Polly and Lucy were perhaps never better performed than by Miss Harper and Mrs. Kennedy. The latter introduced a new song into the second act, which from her admirable manner of executing it had a very pleasing effect ; the air likewise in the last act beginning with ' A curse attends that woman's love,' was sung, in a new style of composition, by Mrs. Kennedy and Miss Harper, and gained them very great and deserved applause. It is almost needless to speak of Mrs. Wilson and Mrs. Webb in Filch and Lockit, they having lately appeared to so much advantage at the Haymarket in those characters. The rest of the characters, allowing for the change of sexes, were as well as could be expected, not forgetting the female stage attendant, who from the novelty of bringing on and off chairs, tables, etc., produced almost each time an involuntary burst of applause. In short, the present performers and this opera bid fair to entertain the lovers of burlesque, and will be sure to please the lovers of true English singing."

The Morning Herald was not quite so complimentary to Miss Catley, nor so enthusiastic in its general criticism. It records that " last night *The Beggar's Opera* under the title of *The Ladies' Opera* was performed at this theatre (Covent Garden) by Ladies only. It was preceded by an introductory dialogue between Mr. and Mrs. Whitfield, about the privilege assumed by the ladies of wearing the breeches, and abounded in many witty turns and some strokes of the double entendre which excited some laughter and not a little tittering.

" Miss Catley performed the part of Macheath, but was by no means competent to the undertaking ; and the rest of the ladies who had boldly assumed the breeches only discovered their inability, except Mrs. Webb, who was perfectly at home in Lockit. Miss Catley's attempt in Macheath proved unsuccessful, and the appearance of the ladies without petticoats being no novelty, *The Ladies' Opera* last night, from the representation it met with, does by no means promise to become the rage of the winter season ! ''

Notwithstanding this adverse criticism, we are told in another column on the same page, that *The Ladies' Opera* " was received by a numerous audience with very great applause," and that " it is to be repeated on the morrow."

The reflections on Miss Catley caused some indignation among her friends, and we have a letter signed "Dramaticus" appearing in *The Morning Herald* of the next day to the following effect : " Mr. Editor, some parasite of the Drury Lane Manager's has availed himself of your absence shamefully to mis-represent the performance of *The Beggar's Opera* at Covent Garden, and I rely on your candour and impartiality to make it known by the publication of this card. It bears too managerical an aspect not to convince every reader from what quarter it originated, but I trust the world, after all fulsome puffing on one side the question, and mis-representation on the other, can never be brought to give the theatrical fame to the Polly and Lucy of Drury Lane in preference to those truly harmonious ones of Covent Garden."

Of course champions of the opposite house were up in arms, and the next day a " Lover of the Drama " rushed into the fray. He declared at some length that he never received more pleasure than he had from the representation of *The Beggar's Opera* at Drury Lane, and probably the correspondence would have continued after the fashion of such controversies but for the sudden withdrawal of *The Ladies' Opera*. Harris's experiment had proved a frost, and its dirge was sung by *The Morning Chronicle* in the following paragraph : " Catley's crest will be lowered by her failure in the part of Macheath. She was to receive ten pounds a night for her performance of the character each night she played it, over and above her weekly salary, which was not a very moderate one. Cargill, who was originally considered by the Covent Garden performers as Catley's pupil, has lived to beat her mistress."

The respective merits of the rival Macheaths were summed up in a letter in *The Town and Country Journal*, bearing somewhat hardly upon poor Anne, who was then nearing death's door ; let us hope the writer did not know this. His letter, apart from its criticism of the two ladies, is interesting from the point he makes relative to Macheath's dress. He writes : " The different metamorphoses which *The Beggar's Opera* has lately undergone clearly prove that burlesque and ridicule may be carried too far. It is more than probable that Mr. Colman took his idea of transposing the characters from males to females, and vice versâ, from the success Mrs. Kennedy had met with in Macheath ; the thought, however, appeared novel, and it succeeded beyond his most sanguine expectations.

"The managers of Covent Garden Theatre, unwilling to be outdone in invention, judged that, in representing all the characters by females, they would improve upon Mr. Colman's thought, and Miss Catley was chosen, at a very extravagant salary, to perform Macheath ; but her greatest admirers must own, that she neither looked, dressed, nor spoke the character, so as to convey the idea of a bold, enterprising, gentleman-highwayman. For what cause is best known to herself, she never changed her dress, but appeared in boots the whole time, as if she were just come off the road ; whereas Macheath always dressed previous to his going to

Marybone, as it is to be supposed he was there to meet some of the politest company about town; to whom he would take every precaution of not giving the slightest suspicion of his being a highwayman. The consequence was natural, and, as might be expected, the town was nauseated with the same un-natural hodge-podge, though dressed different ways, and they repaired to another table that was better served.

" In a word Miss Catley has been fairly foiled at her own weapons. She judged that by brazening out the part she was sure of success; whilst Mrs. Cargill, by studying nature, and pursuing the intention of the poet, not only succeeded in the same character beyond her friends' most sanguine expectations, but it is said that she looked so much ' the youth in a cart who has the air of a lord,' that she made some conquests amongst her own sex, who were unapprized of the deception."

All that remains to be said of Anne Catley is that she formed a connection with Colonel, afterwards General Lascelles, whom she subsequently married, and, says Boaden in his *Life of Mrs. Jordan*, "left a large family by him, four sons and four daughters—however her will was signed Ann Catley, and was written entirely in her own hand." Boaden speaks exceedingly well of her. " In the great relations of life," he says, " as a daughter, wife and mother and friend, she was in principle steady and exemplary," and he remarks that " she amply atoned in her maturity for the scandal she had excited formerly in society. She died of the fell disease which has claimed so many victims, and was but forty-four when she passed away."

Colman's experiment brought *The Beggar's Opera* once more into the forefront of London life and gossip. A very clever use of its apt humour is to be seen in a frolicsome *brochure* called *Miniature Pictures*, published in 1781—a predecessor in a way of the modern " Birthday Book." Quotations from the Opera were fitted to the characteristics of the notabilities of the day. More than six hundred personages were bantered in this way, and the happiness—and we may also add the freedom—of many of the similes must have added to the gaiety of the town. We cull a few samples. The somewhat mean Duke of Newcastle had the following applied to him :

> " The Miser thus a shilling sees
> Which he's obliged to pay,
> With sighs resigns it by degrees
> And fears 'tis gone for aye."

The Duchess Dowager of Argyll (once one of the beautiful sisters Gunning) was told that " when women consider their own beauties they are all alike unreasonable in their demands ; for they expect their lovers should like them as long as they like themselves." To Dr. Fordyce, the fashionable physician, was assigned the passage " The vigour and prowess of a knight errant never serv'd half the *Ladies in distress* that he hath done." Dr. Johnson came in for :

> " When you censure the age
> Be cautious and sage,
> Lest the courtiers offended should be."

The compiler was unkind, but not wholly inaccurate, when he placed under the name of saucy Anne Catley the line, " Thou wilt always be a vulgar slut, Lucy." John Wilkes is described as " of tried courage and indefatigable," and Mrs. Thrale is thus enjoined : " Let not your anger, my dear, break through the rules of decency." The constitutional nonchalance of the Cavendishes is well hit off in the stage direction applied to the Duke of Devonshire (" sits down melancholy at the table ") ; while of his duchess, the beautiful Georgiana, it is remarked gallantly that " You are always so taken up with stealing hearts." With the appropriate words " Rip out the coronets," applied to the Duchess of Kingston, of bigamy notoriety, and at that moment ending her restless and adventurous life in aimless wanderings on the Continent, we take leave of the *Miniature Pictures*.

CHAPTER XXVIII

FROM MADAME MARA TO MADAME VESTRIS

A tragedian's idea of Macheath—Garrick and Moody—Various Macheaths—Incledon : his coarseness and vanity—Notable Pollies—Madame Mara, Mrs. Martyr, Mrs. Dickens, Miss Bolton—Erroneous rendering of *The Beggar's Opera*—Braham's vicious influence—Mrs. Mattocks and Miss Paton—Bishop cuts the Opera down to two acts—Miss Stephens' triumph as Polly—Madame Vestris electrifies the public as Macheath—Sims Reeves the last of the Macheaths—Conclusion.

FAMOUS singers came and went, but the Opera continued to hold its own with undiminished lustre throughout the eighteenth century. Actresses were not satisfied until they had played both Polly and Macheath, actors whose proper rôle was tragedy had a secret belief that Nature had intended them for singing knights of the road. John Kemble, it is said, was very desirous of trying his hand at the character, but, according to Clark Russell's *Representative Actors*, was dissuaded from the absurdity. Another tragedian with similar cravings was Digges, who in the parts with which he was identified—among them Cardinal Wolsey and Cato—preserved all the stilted methods of his predecessors, and, to use Parke's words, was " as frigid as the vicinity of the North Pole." Notwithstanding this, his ambition was to play the gay and dashing highwayman, and he selected the Opera for his benefit. He was conscious of one drawback—he had never sung a song in his life. This, however, did not shake his resolve, and having learned one of the ditties, he sent for Shield, the well-known composer, to listen to him. According to Parke, this is how the tragedian rendered the

344

MADAME VESTRIS AS CAPTAIN MACHEATH.

From Mr. A. M. Broadley's Collection.

song "If the heart of a man is depressed with cares":

> "If the *heart* (*striking his left breast with his right hand*) of a man is depress'd with cares,
> The *mist* (*drawing his hands across his eyes*) is dispell'd when a woman appears;
> Like the notes of a *fiddle* (*imitating the action of playing one*) she sweetly, sweetly
> Raises his spirits and charms our *ears*" (*seizing his left ear with the thumb and finger of his right hand*).

It is hardly necessary to add that this strict adherence to suiting the action to fit the word did not win the approval of Shield, who was a fine singer as well as a good actor, and Digges selected some other play for his benefit. In the face of this it is difficult to understand O'Keefe writing, "Digges was the best Macheath I ever saw, in person, song and manner." One has to become accustomed to contradiction where *The Beggar's Opera* is concerned, but this one puts every other into the shade.*

Tate Wilkinson tells an amusing story apropos of the estimation in which the part of Macheath was held. When he was at Portsmouth at the same time as Garrick he had arranged for a benefit, and Garrick, taking a great interest in the young actor, suggested he should fix on a favourite character and do his best with it. When, however, Wilkinson repeated Garrick's suggestion to White, the manager of the Portsmouth Theatre, adding that Garrick had promised to be present, the provincial magnate was highly indignant. White had an affectation of speech in regard to the letter r, and he burst out thus: "Why is Mr. Wilkinson to appoint a play for this Mr.—Ga—ick? Who is Mr. Ga—ick? Mr. Ga—ick has no command over *my* company at Portsmouth." Then, gathering himself for a final stroke, he went on complacently, "Mr. Ga—ick cannot, I think, be displeased with *my* Macheath; though I want no *favour* from Mr. Ga—ick." The manager of course was all-powerful, and Wilkinson had to submit.

* See Appendix, Note 7.

The Beggar's Opera was announced; Mr. White cast himself for Macheath, Moody was Lockit, and Wilkinson had a very minor part. It had been noised abroad that the great Mr. Garrick was likely to be present, and the house was crowded in anticipation. The first act was finished, but no Garrick appeared, and when the second act commenced and the seats retained for the famous actor and his friends remained empty, the company roundly denounced Wilkinson for having deceived them, the manager being especially furious at having played so much of *his* Macheath and Mr. Ga—ick not present. However, about the middle of the second act Garrick's party entered, and all was well.

" Mr. Garrick," adds Wilkinson, " was so pleased with my friend Mr. Moody in Lockit, that he sent for him the next morning and engaged him for the ensuing season, at a salary of thirty shillings per week, because, he told him, he *loved to encourage merit!* " This offer, paltry as it was, found acceptance, and Moody did not regret it. He made his first appearance in London as King Henry VIII. (other authorities do not support Wilkinson in this), and was soon an established favourite, but not in Shakespearean parts. Character comedy was Moody's line.

Michael Kelly,* the composer of many popular songs, the delight of thousands in the early days of the nineteenth century, had more claims to the part than many who have attempted it. He writes in his *Reminiscences*: " In April 1789 I played Macheath for the first time for my benefit. Mrs. Crouch, Polly; and Mrs. Charles Kemble (then Miss Decamp), Lucy; both these ladies were inimitable. To play Macheath was the height of my ambition; I took all the pains I could, and no man had greater pains taken with him." Kelly was of course anxious to preserve the traditions, and if possible carry on the methods of Lowe, John Beard, and Vernon. To enable him to do this, John Kemble and Digges

* See Appendix, Note 8.

gave him imitations of these Macheaths—a statement which supports the assertion that both actors had studied the part. "There was also then in London," adds Kelly, "the celebrated Irish Macheath, and worthy man old Wilder, who had retired from the theatrical profession and was living in London. . . . Through his tuition I learned much, but my great support was the perfect recollection I had of Webster, who was certainly the best Macheath in the world. I acted the part a number of nights with Mrs. Crouch and Miss Decamp, the best acting Polly and the best Lucy I ever saw, or ever hope to see again" (see p. 272).

One of the singular characteristics of *The Beggar's Opera* is that its exponents, if we may believe their admirers, were almost invariably the best ever seen! It seems always to have pleased, no matter who played in it.

Incledon of course deserves more than a passing notice. He claimed to be the best singer of English ballads on the stage of his day, and with justice. He utterly despised the methods of his neighbour Braham (the two famous singers lived next door to each other at Brompton) in "Italianising" simple melodies. C. H. Wilson, who compiled a little volume of biographies of musical celebrities, attached to songs of the day, under the title of *The Myrtle and the Vine*, says, "The compass as well as the energy of his voice is very uncommon; he possesses such a volume of sound, which he often makes use of in a kind of furor to so great an effect as to almost lift us from our seats. Mr. Incledon, in order to let us hear how independent his voice is of the orchestra, will often give his audience a specimen . . . of his vocal abilities without the aid of music, and it must be confessed that few men but himself were ever so little in need of assistance from the band."

Incledon certainly gave the audience plenty of sound for their money. He was intensely vain of his voice, which no doubt was quite exceptional. Whether his style of singing would be acceptable to-day, save at a music-hall, is however, very doubtful. We are told in C. R. Leslie's *Autobiography* that " his pronunciation was thick and affected by something like a lisp, which proceeded from a roll of his too large tongue when he prepared for a forcible passage or was embarrassed by the word. In this way, too, he used to jump to his falsetto by octaves, for the tone (it was that of a rich flute) was so widely different from his natural voice, there could be no junction. His singing was at once natural and national. The hunting song, the sea song, and the ballad, given with English force and English feeling, may be said to have expired with Incledon." Incledon was, in fact, a valuable National asset up to 1815, when Waterloo terminated years of war, during which our patriotism must at times have sorely needed sustaining.

Off the stage Incledon could not always have been a pleasing companion. The critic whom we have just quoted, adds : " It is impossible to imagine anything more conceited or coarse than Incledon in private life as well as on the stage. . . . Some of his theatrical companions were one day discussing the qualities necessary to the performance of Macheath, when Incledon spoke : A man should be a gentleman, G—— d—— me, to play Macheath ; he should be a man of education (another oath); he should have fine manners (a still stronger) ; in short (with a most blasphemous adjuration), he must be Charles Incledon ! "

This superlative praise of himself was not supported by the opinion of others. While admitting Incledon was the best English singer in the ballad line the stage had perhaps ever seen, Cooke (*Macklin's Memoirs*) was not disposed to accept him as an ideal Macheath. In Cooke's opinion Incledon " wanted somewhat of a figure and a certain decision of character to set off the chieftain of a band of robbers ; who, like the chieftains of the early ages, are supposed to be elected to that situation for superior courage, figure, etc. etc." To judge from the portrait of Incledon as Macheath (see p. 264), dressed for the part in the fashion of the Regency, one would say that he wanted a good deal more than Cooke has here set down.

When Incledon was in the zenith of his fame he did almost as he pleased. Kemble sent to him to ask his aid as Hecate in *Macbeth*. This Charles was inclined to consider *infra dig*. " The national singer, d—— me, play this he-cat! The fact is, d—— me, you may tell Mr. Kemble, d—— me, that if he'll play one of the thieves to my Macheath, d—— me, *I* will play a He-cat or any cat he likes to his Macbeth, d—— me ! " (*Records of an Old Veteran*).

With Incledon are associated various Pollies of celebrity. There was Madame Mara, who figures in more than one of Gillray's cartoons, an accomplished singer, but hardly an ideal Polly (see p. 304). She was neither very handsome nor very slim, and she had a strong foreign accent. However, she sang in the Opera for twelve nights with Incledon in 1797, and received a very large sum to induce her, we presume, to abandon her legitimate rôle, which was not humorous opera. Lucy was played by Mrs. Martyr, a pretty woman with " a strong shrill powerful voice," says C. H. Wilson, adding, " There is a kind of hicky-hocky she often makes use of at the top of her voice which renders it ludicrous. Catley had much of this effect, but she had a better voice than Mrs. Martyr " (see p. 272).

Mrs. Dickons (formerly Miss Poole), a refined and pleasing singer, also sang with Incledon in the Opera, and another notable Polly was Mary Catherine Bolton, who resembled the original Polly in so far that her performance in the part gained her a titled husband in the person of Lord Thurlow, whom she married after not a very long stage experience. She came out in *The Beggar's Opera* after having sung at concerts, and her first appearance was very successful. Time, however, revealed certain drawbacks, to which the critic of *The Monthly Mirror*

of September 16, 1807, draws attention. He writes
of the performance at Covent Garden :

" Mr. Incledon's Macheath is full of merit. His
songs were given in the true English style conformable to the spirit of the opera, and to the great reputation which he has deservedly acquired in this part.
His acting here indeed is so very natural as to make
it no personal compliment to praise it according to
its merits. The reverse of this is the case with Miss
Bolton. Her figure is exceedingly pretty, and she
has improved a little in her acting, but there is an
air of gentility about her which makes her look unlike
any Polly Peachum except such a one as we might
expect to see at a private fashionable theatre. Some
of her airs she sang in a very pleasing manner, but
not always with proper taste. For instance, that
beautiful melody ' Cease your funning' was not executed with a due degree of plain simplicity, the neglect
of which has been a common fault of most of those
who have undertaken the part. The words put by
Gay into the mouth of the Beggar in the Introduction show how the songs should be sung and the
parts acted : ' This piece, I own, was originally writ
for the celebrating the marriage of *James Canter* and
Moll Lay, two most excellent ballad singers. It
hath been heretofore very well represented by ourselves in our great room at St. Giles'.' Miss Bolton's
ear is also defective, and under these circumstances,
as the player has been called a parrot, the critic
may fairly be a parrot too and cry (? not) ' Pretty
Poll,' but ' Poor Poll.' She is a very clever girl,
and her parts are improveable, but not unless she
thinks so" (see p. 320). (see p. 320)

It is interesting to note, from the critic's remarks at
the conclusion of the article, that the fashion of performing the Opera had reverted to the elaborate style
which Colman tried to kill. "It must be recollected,"
says the writer, " that we have considered *The
Beggar's Opera* as it is now soberly played . . .
but the original sentiments are at present seriously

delivered, and the actors, though some of them dress their characters ridiculously enough, and though they are well able to play the buffoon on other occasions, on this they are moderate, and their timidity is mischievous. It is fit and it would be a real treat *to have it acted* after the style of *Tom Thumb*."

The reason of the decadence is not far to seek. Since Colman's time the star of Braham had arisen. Great artist as he was, he was more anxious to please the ears of the groundlings than to adhere to the dictates of pure taste. He did not disdain to fritter away his splendid talents for the sake of his pocket. " Why do you not sing like that always ? " asked the Duke of Sussex, when a guest at the singer's house. Braham, who had sung his best and his simplest, replied : " If I had I should not have been able to entertain your Royal Highness to-night." The Rev. J. Young in his *Life of C. M. Young* says : " I have heard him sing the best sacred music at the house of friends whom he knew to be refined and fastidious musicians, and then his rendering of Handel has been glorious and worthy of his theme. I have heard him at an oratorio at the theatre the very next night sing the same airs to a mixed audience and so overlay the original composition with florid interpolations as entirely to distract the listener's attention from the solemnity and simplicity of the theme." Braham's vicious example spread, and Miss Bolton, like many another singer, did not escape the infection. We have discovered no record of Braham ever having played Macheath, but if he did so it is pretty certain that he would have ornamented the simple melodies out of existence. He was a poor actor, and it is doubtful if he ever attempted the part.

It would be a tedious task to enumerate all the Pollies and Macheaths who appeared before the public in the early part of the nineteenth century. There are, however, some notable exceptions. One was Mrs. Mattocks, who, in addition to her having played the part, supplies in her family a contribution to the history of the Opera. Mrs. Mattocks was before her marriage a Miss Hallam, whose father was the actor whom Macklin, during a paltry dispute at rehearsal, stabbed in the eye with a walking-stick (see p. 248). His brother, Adam Hallam, translated *The Beggar's Opera* into French, and taking his translation to Paris, tried to get it performed. The French managers, who had no scruple in altering *Hamlet* to suit their own tastes, were equally fastidious over *The Beggar's Opera*. They would have nothing to do with the play unless Macheath were made to pay the penalty of his misdeeds. Hallam refused to make any alteration, and brought the manuscript back to England. Richard Ryan speaks of a French version of the Opera being successfully produced in Paris, but Ryan's statements are not always remarkable for their accuracy.

Then we have Miss Paton, an infant prodigy, who blossomed into one of the most accomplished singers of her day. Like many other celebrated vocalists, she had a hard struggle before her talents were recognised. She was the daughter of an Edinburgh writing-master—which seems to have been a most lucrative profession in the modern Athens, if it be true, as her biographer tells us, that Mr. Paton's income was not less than £2,000 a year. After running her childish career, the girl came to London, but failed to impress any of the musical authorities. She went to Bishop, but he refused to take her as a pupil. None of the other professors, with a want of perception which does not say much for their judgment, would have anything to do with her; but, nothing daunted, she pursued her studies for three years, with now and then a lesson from Cruvelli. But she could not get an engagement, and in vain she offered her services gratuitously to almost every theatrical manager in London. At last her chance came. She appeared as Susanna in *The Marriage of Figaro*; Mozart's charming music suited her style, and she made a hit at once. She came out as Polly at Covent Garden on October 19, 1821, and her position was established. Miss Paton may be included in the list of Pollies whom marriage ennobled. She became the wife of Lord William Lennox; but, less fortunate than Lavinia Fenton, Mary Catherine Bolton and Catherine Stephens, her married life proved most unhappy (see p. 328).

Dr. Busby, in his *Anecdotes of the Concert Room*, tells of Miss Paton one of the stories which years ago were considered humorous. When at the Haymarket, she wanted to sing "A miser thus a shilling sees," at the end of the first act, a note higher, to which the stage manager immediately replied " Then, Miss, you must sing 'The miser thus a *guinea* sees.' " Old anecdote books are full of sad jests such as this. Smarter was the reply of Harris, the manager of Covent Garden, to some one who expressed surprise when he instructed Sir Henry Bishop (then of course Mr. Bishop) to cut down *The Beggar's Opera* to two acts— the form in which it has remained ever since. " What ! " said Harris to his expostulatory friend, " do you call it cruel, when you find a piece hanging, to cut it down ? "

In Bishop's revised version Macheath was Incledon, and Polly the incomparable Miss Stephens, over whom every critic waxed enthusiastic. One might quote pages of laudatory notices, but that which came from Leigh Hunt's graceful pen must suffice : " This most enchanting singer made her first appearance in the old sweet part of Polly in *The Beggar's Opera*, and we thought never sang so well. The beautiful repose of her acting, the irresistible way in which she condescends to beseech support when she might extort reluctant wonder, and the graceful awkwardness and *naïveté* of her manner, more captivating than the most finished elegance, complete the charm of her singing. The pathos of her 'Can Love be controlled by advice?' and 'Oh, ponder well,' the mingled satire and sentiment of 'Cease your funning,' and the fine bird-like triumph of 'He so

23

pleased me,' are like nothing else to be heard on the stage, and leave all competitors far behind."

For the third time Polly was a mascotte to her impersonator—Miss Stephens became the Countess of Essex when the Earl took her from the stage.

With Miss Stephens the line of the most celebrated of the Pollies may be said to have ended, but the Macheaths went on. The fascinating Madame Vestris, over whom the theatre-going public in the first half of the nineteenth century went mad, and whose life off the stage was the subject of innumerable stories and *bons mots* of a more or less lively description, which the students of *The Age* and other satirical papers of the times can discover for themselves, saw a fresh victory for her charms of face and figure in Macheath, and she out-Catleyed Catley in the furore that she created. One of her biographers wrote with a luxuriance seldom met with nowadays concerning her Macheath and Don Giovanni. " Lovely as she appeared," we are told, " in a woman's dress—all bewitching in her laced tucker and braided locks, she never reached the acme of her reputation till she threw off female delicacy, and undertook at once to teach us how women looked arrayed in breeches. Macheath was the first breeches part in which the Vestris made her appearance in Drury Lane. The beautiful proportion of her limbs, the manly nonchalance of her manner, and the arch way in which she played and gave the songs, made the audience forget she was a woman. This character raised her reputation above the reach of all her enemies. The town rang with her praise, and every print shop was decorated with her likeness." The following song made its appearance at the time, and we make no apology for giving it entire :

"What a breast !—What an eye !—What a foot, leg and thigh,
What wonderful things she has shown us !
Round hip, swelling sides, and masculine strides,
Proclaim her an English Adonis !

"In Macheath how she leers and unprincipled appears,
    And tips off the tumblers so jolly!
And then, oh, so blest, on two bosoms to rest,
    And change from a Lucy to Polly!

"Her very hair and style when coupled with a smile—
    Let a virgin resist if she can;
Her ambrosial kisses seem heavenly blisses—
    What a pity she is not a man!"

"Madame," adds Mr. Arthur Griffinhoofe (or
whatever may have been the author's name), "no
sooner appeared in breeches—no sooner had she
committed this breach of female modesty, than every
buck and blood in London crowded to the theatre
to see her. . . . When Madame performed Macheath
in Dublin to crowded and applauding audiences,
Lord Mathew observed to Dr. Durgin that her
appearance was not masculine enough to impress one
with the idea of the bold and daring highway robber.
'It is very true,' replied the doctor, 'but as small
as she is, I make no doubt if she told your lordship
to stand and deliver, you would very readily obey
and look d——d foolish when your purse was empty.'"

Another writer, who made considerable use of Mr.
Griffinhoofe's material in a volume of Memoirs
published some three years after, says, "To make
her stick to the breeches, Mr. Elliston voluntarily
raised her salary, and her Macheath continued to
attract overflowing houses." From an earlier biography, published in 1830 and "privately printed,"
we learn that "at Liverpool she came forth as
Macheath, and, as might be expected, attracted all
the taste of the town. She was placarded on every
wall, and her likeness stuck in every window of
every print shop. The town rang with her praise,
and for twenty-seven nights Macheath was received
with cheers by a Liverpool audience. She did not
attempt any other breeches character and," says the
author charitably, "left Liverpool with a tolerably
fair fame."

In much the same spirit an account is given by

Griffinhoofe of an unrehearsed scene at Covent Garden which must have equally puzzled and amused the audience. " As we wish to be impartial," the candid writer observes, " we are sorry to admit that Madame Vestris, notwithstanding her many good qualities, is in the habit of acting occasionally in a very tyrannical manner towards those whom adverse fortune has placed beneath her, should they be so unfortunate as to incur her displeasure. Of this overbearing conduct, the writer was an eye-witness one evening during the performance of *The Beggar's Opera* at the Theatre Royal, Covent Garden, in which our heroine sustained her favourite char-acter of Captain Macheath. The late Mr. J. Isaacs was cast for Mat o' the Mint ; Madame having performed Macheath for a number of nights at the Haymarket Theatre, did not think proper to attend even one rehearsal at Covent Garden. Mr. Isaacs studied the part allotted to him very carefully, and certainly no man could go on the stage more perfectly prepared, he having, to use a theatrical phrase, made himself ' dead up in the part.' It appears, however, that the prompt-book of the Haymarket had been slightly altered at her request, in order to bring into her part what is professionally termed ' a bit of fat,' alias ' claptrap,' of which alteration Mr. Isaacs was perfectly innocent.

" The performance at night proceeded steadily on till the scene where Macheath enters to the gang to give them instructions as to their respective routes, etc. In the midst of the dialogue Madame suddenly stopped, as if waiting for a cue. Poor Isaacs, being rather nervous, began to fidget, while Madame advancing towards him exclaimed with a frown, ' Go on, sir.'

" ' Madame,' replied he, ' I have given you the cue.'

" ' It is false, sir.'

" ' I beg pardon, Madame : I have not omitted a single word.'

"She answered in a tone so loud as to be heard by a great portion of the audience, ' I say it is false, sir, and I will not speak another line until I have my cue,' and carelessly tapping her boots with her cane, she swaggered up the stage, and seating herself on a table, sat for some time swinging her crossed leg to and fro. The audience now perceiving very clearly that something was wrong, began to express their disapprobation by violent hisses. Not knowing what else to do in the business, poor Isaacs commenced his solo 'Let's take the road,' of which the chorus finishes the scene.

"No sooner were they fairly off the stage than Madame, stepping up to Isaacs like a little fury, exclaimed, ' How dare you so insult me in this manner before the audience ! '

"' My dear Madame, nothing was further from my thoughts, nor can I even now imagine how I have displeased you.'

"' Very well. I tell you once more that I will never again go on the stage with a man who is so glaringly imperfect in his part.'

"' I beg your pardon, Madame, I am perfect to the letter. Indeed I have played the part so very frequently that I could almost venture to repeat it backwards.'

"' I don't care, sir, how often you have attempted the part. I have performed Macheath at the Haymarket and other theatres without any unpleasant occurrences taking place ; and had you, sir, been sufficiently perfect, it would have been so now.'

"' But, Madame, I can't be expected to be able to play a part by instinct, and had you attended rehearsal this mor——'

"' Sir,' interrupted she, ' I shall attend what rehearsals I think proper. Am I to be accountable to you for my actions ? I shall appeal to the manager to protect me from insult.'

"' I hope, Madame,' answered Isaacs, ' you will allow me to speak. So far from meditating insult, I was about to observe that if you had attended but one rehearsal, I would with pleasure have studied my part with the alterations marked in the Haymarket prompt-book.'

" ' Don't talk to me, sir. I tell you you can't know your part. There is no alteration in the Haymarket prompt-book; and I repeat, sir, that I will never again be seen on the same stage with you.'

" ' Upon my word, it's extremely hard to be accused so unjustly. Allow me to appeal to Mr. Parslow (the prompter), and if I have not spoken every line according to his books I'll not only be ready to make an apology, but to submit to any fine the management may think proper to inflict.'

" Mr. Parslow produced the books, from which it appeared that Mr. Isaacs was perfectly correct. Madame was ready to burst with rage and vexation, and on the call-boy informing her that the stage waited, it was with the greatest difficulty that the manager (the late J. Fawcit) could prevail on her to again appear before the audience. In the midst of the next scene her feelings seemed to overpower her —she burst into tears and rushed from the stage !

" Madame is an excellent actress ! After the lapse of a few minutes Mr. Fawcit came forward with an apology ; he said that Madame Vestris, having become suddenly seriously indisposed, claimed an indulgence of the audience. She would try to go through the dialogue if they would forego the singing. Thus through her own obstinacy the feelings of a worthy man (for that such was Mr. Isaacs none who had the honour of his acquaintance can deny) were keenly wounded, and the audience deprived of the principal portion of their entertainment ; as it is well known that the second act of *The Beggar's Opera* is nearly all vocal, which on this occasion was, for nought, omitted." Of course Madame's daring impersonation did not meet with universal approbation, and an actor named Archer, conceiving himself injured by the rivalry of Madame Vestris, plotted a cabal against her, and when she appeared she was greeted by Archer's partisans with cries of " Off ! Off ! No female in breeches ! " Proceedings were instituted, and the jury returned a true bill, but the matter does not seem to have been carried any further.*

Madame made her great success as Macheath in 1825 ; and in 1839, when the Opera was revived at Covent Garden, she played the part of Lucy to Miss Rainforth's Polly ; Mr. W. Harrison, afterwards associated with Madame Louisa Pyne in a meritorious attempt to establish English opera as a permanent attraction, was Macheath. The fortunes of Covent Garden in 1839 were at a low ebb, but the lucky star under which *The Beggar's Opera* was born came to the rescue, and the depleted treasury was re-filled.

The Opera was played twelve times in 1841 and twice in 1842, and then followed a blank of some years. No doubt it was revived at intervals, but not by any singer of importance, until the late Mr. Sims Reeves was asked to undertake Macheath—and he tells the story in the book of Reminiscences which he called *My Jubilee.*

" After singing much in Opera, Italian and English, I was invited to assume the leading part in what is really a comedy with songs, though *Beggar's Opera* is its historic name. This was something quite new to me. Edgardo, Carlo, Ernani, and the many impassioned lovers whom I had been in the habit of representing on the Italian stage, are never for a moment comic. For any of these characters to raise a laugh, a smile, or even the faintest symptom of hilarity, would be fatal to the impersonation. Macheath, on the other hand, may be as lively as he pleases ; the livelier the better.

" On one occasion, a member of my gang had taken the liberty of getting intoxicated. This, a robber of his kind might possibly have done in actual life. But his chief would not have allowed him to get drunk on duty ; and I was much put

* See Appendix, Note 9,

out when, playing the part of Captain Macheath one
evening on a provincial tour, I found one of my men
in a comparatively helpless condition from over-
indulgence in drink. The chorus of robbers had to
go off ; but my inebriated friend was either unwilling
or unable to make his exit. He was, at least, very
sluggish about it : and as his face was already turned
towards the wing I helped him off by means of a
kick, administered in a lively, devil-may-care style.
I had really rendered him a service by promoting
his exit, and but for me it would not have been made
at the proper time. He did not take this view of
the matter, and the next day summoned me to
the police court, when, after hearing my evidence, the
magistrate (evidently a lover of art) dismissed the
case."

No doubt this preliminary canter, so to speak,
enabled the great artist to see the possibilities of the
part, and later on once more London was swarming
to see *The Beggar's Opera*. In his autobiography
Mr. Reeves writes :

" Many as have been my successes in Italian
opera and oratorio, I never achieved a greater
triumph than that which I obtained at the end of
1878 and the beginning of 1879 at Covent Garden,
in *The Beggar's Opera*, *The Waterman*, and other
English works of the same class." " On the occasion
of playing Captain Macheath in *The Beggar's Opera*,
the house," wrote *Punch*, " was literally crammed
from floor to ceiling by an audience whose enthusiastic
temperature increased in a graduated thermometrical
scale, the over-boiling point being reached at the
back row of the upper gallery ; and this on a night
when, in the stalls and boxes, wrappers, fur-mantles,
and ulsters, were *de rigueur* on account of *de rigour*
of the cold, and when the Messrs. Gatti might have
made a considerable addition to their good fortune
by sending round the attendants with a supply of
foot-warmers, hot toddy, and mulled claret, and
other popular drinks at cheap prices. There he was,

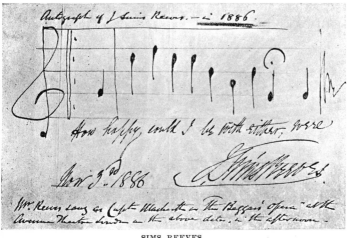

SIMS REEVES.

From a contemporary caricature-portrait in water-colours in Mr. A. M. Broadley's Collection,
cir. 1880.

bright and gay as ever, our *tenner* still unchanged, and equal to any number of the most valuable notes. . . . Let those who do not believe in a ' comic tenor ' see Sims Reeves as Captain Macheath, and they will then discover what magic there is even in a refrain of ' tol de rol, lol de rol, loddy,' when given by a tenor who is not impressed by the absurd traditional notion, that he is nothing if not sentimental.

" His acting of the celebrated song, 'How happy could I be with either! ' is full of humour, and his change of manner from ' tol de rol ' in a tender tone, when addressed to the gentle confiding Polly, to ' tol de rol ' with a true cockney chick-a-leary twang, when addressed to the vulgar Lucy Lockit, is a clever idea, most artistically carried out ; and then his dance up the stage while singing, giving his last note good and true to the end in spite of this unaccustomed exertion, as with a jump he seats himself in a natural, devil-may-care style on the table, was followed by an encore so momentous, that even he, the anti-encorist, was fain to comply with the enthusiastic demand ; so he repeated the two verses, the dance, and the jump, with as much freshness and vigour as though he had not already sung six songs— snatches more or less, it is true—and had got ten more to follow, with 'Here's to the maiden of bashful fifteen,' and a dance by way of *finale*."

November 3, 1886, marks the date of the final performance of *The Beggar's Opera*. It was revived at a matinée at the Avenue Theatre, ostensibly to give the friends of the veteran tenor an opportunity of seeing him in the character of the dashing highwayman. Mr. Reeves was then advanced in years, but his splendid " method " was unimpaired, his artistic instinct was as keen as ever, and only his incomparable tone had suffered. Those now living who heard Sims Reeves in his prime had the privilege of listening to the greatest tenor of his or any other day.

The Times in its notice of the matinée said of him : " He sings and acts Macheath in his own way . . . , the popular tenor was in good voice, and went through the part with unabated spirit from beginning to end." It was of course hardly possible to lavish enthusiasm over this solitary performance with all its drawbacks. The most important pronouncement of the critic was contained in the final words : " If one reads of the enormous success of the first production, which, as the wits of the time remarked, made Rich the manager gay and Gay the poet rich, one likes to contemplate the chance of a real revival of this the most English of all English operettas."

With this one must cordially agree. It is hardly conceivable that the play or opera—whichever may be its most appropriate title—which held its place on the stage for a century and a half, which probably has been played more often than any other piece that can be named, which has attracted nearly all the famous singers in the annals of English musical drama, which has never proved a failure when adequately performed, and which from first to last must have put thousands of pounds into the pockets of those concerned, should be allowed to remain in obscurity. One is tempted to say that age could not wither it nor custom stale its infinite variety. More than a century after its first production Henry Reeve in 1839, after seeing Vestris as Lucy and Miss Rainforth as Polly, wrote : " A charming performance ; the language so fine, the dialogue so witty, the music so enchanting. When Polly had done her last song we wished it all to begin over again. . . . *The Beggar's Opera !* May it last for ever ! " and we echo the wish.

Perhaps when eternal waltz tunes begin to cloy, and the music of the Futurists ceases to astonish and puzzle, it may occur to some manager that there is such a thing as simple unaffected English melody, and that abundance of it exists ready to hand in *The Beggar's Opera.* Maybe, too, some clever singer may be found capable of repeating the success of the original Polly Peachum and numberless other Pollies,

Luck has attended *The Beggar's Opera* from the day Gay put it on paper; it has revived the fortunes of drooping theatres more than once, and last but not least, three Pollies left the stage to wear a coronet. Is its wonderful vitality exhausted ? Has its career really ended ? We hope not.

APPENDIX

BELOW will be found a list of some of the actresses who have played Polly in the various revivals of *The Beggar's Opera* between 1728 and 1879. As the period covered extends to 150 years, the list is but an approximate one, nor could performances other than those in London (and a few in Dublin) be included. It is safe to assert that *The Beggar's Opera* has at one time or another been acted at every theatre in the provinces, but obviously it is impossible to do more than note the fact. Where the actress playing Lucy is of sufficient importance, her name has been given, while the Macheaths have not been forgotten. We may add that the dates attached to the names are intended for convenience in fixing particular periods. The days of the months are given when the performances were for benefits and special occasions.

Mrs. Barbier, Dublin	1728
Miss Warren, Lincoln's Inn Fields	1729
Mrs. Pullin, Haymarket	1729
Mrs. Woffington (as a child in " Liliputians," Dublin), 1728 ; London, 1732, and in Dublin between 1737 and 1740	
Miss Cantrell, Lincoln's Inn Fields	1729
Miss Norsa, Lincoln's Inn Fields, and Covent Garden (a run of twenty nights)	**1731–32**

Miss Norsa played Polly in " a serio-comico-farcical Elysian Ballad Opera in 2 acts called *Macheath in the Shades or Bayes at Parnassus.*" This was produced at Covent Garden Theatre on March 11, 1735. Stoppelaer was Macheath, and Lucy seems to have been cut out. It was played but one night, and of its nature or plot there is no record.

Mrs. Thurmond, Covent Garden and Goodman's Fields	1732
Mrs. Clive, Drury Lane	1732–36–49
The Opera ran for thirty nights at Goodman's Fields Theatre, the Polly being " a Gentlewoman " whose name was not published	1741
Mrs. Clive, Covent Garden . . .	1743–45
Miss Edwards (a pupil of Mrs. Clive, and afterwards Mrs. Mozeen); Lucy, Mrs. Clive . . .	1745
Mrs. Cibber, Covent Garden; Lucy, Mrs. Pritchard .	1745

Of Mrs. Pritchard it is recorded by Dr. Busby that she once went to see a play acted in a barn by a company of strolling players, and that she laughed so loudly and incessantly that she annoyed the audience, and one of the latter, knowing her, whispered to the orchestra—a solitary fiddler—that she was the great Mrs. Pritchard from London. " Then I'll give her a hint presently," said he, and immediately played the first tune in *The Beggar's Opera* :

> " Through all the employments of life
> Each neighbour abuses his brother."

"Come, let's be gone," said Mrs. Pritchard; "we're discovered. That fiddler is a clever fellow "; and as she crossed over the stage to the door, she dropped him a curtsey, and thanked him for his seasonable admonition.

Mrs. Cibber, Drury Lane ; Lucy, Mrs. Clive	.	. 1747
Mrs. Storer, Covent Garden . . .	.	. 1747
Mrs. Chambers	.	. 1751
Mrs. Davis	.	. 1752
Miss Brent, Covent Garden (a run of thirty-nine nights)		1759–60
Mrs. Vincent, Drury Lane (her first appearance on any stage)		September 23, 1760

Subsequently Mrs. Vincent played Polly in rivalry with Miss Brent.

Miss Anne Catley, Dublin 1763–4–5

Miss Catley was some time in London before she obtained an engagement, which only happened through Miss Brent neglecting to article in time. The acting manager at Covent Garden was instructed to engage her upon any terms, and he readily agreed to give her fifteen guineas a week.

Mrs. Abington, Dublin 1764

Other " Pollies " at the Dublin theatres between 1764 and 1770 were Mrs. Dancer, Miss Bridges, Miss Green, Miss Browne, Miss Duncan, and Miss Ashmore. The last-named was very popular. Mrs. Abington played Polly in Dublin occasionally. She was more often seen as Lucy.

Miss Wright, Drury Lane ; Lucy, Mrs. Abington .	April 14, 1766
Mrs. Arne, Drury Lane ; Lucy, Mrs. Abington .	1766–7
Mrs. Crawford, Haymarket	1767
Miss Macklin, Covent Garden (came out as Polly) .	1771
Mrs. Mattocks, Covent Garden . . .	1771

Mrs. Mattocks commenced her career as a singer, but won more fame as an actress. Boaden describes her as " the paragon and representative of the radically vulgar woman of any or no fashion, of whatever condition or age." Of her performance in *The Beggar's Opera* the critic of *The Theatrical Review*, October 28, 1771, said he " would like to see her in Lucy and not Polly."

Mrs. Sophia Baddeley 1770

Mrs. Baddeley played Polly in the provinces. It is said that when she appeared in the opera at Bath Dr. Herschell, afterwards the famous astronomer, was a violin-player in the orchestra, and at the first sight of her wondrous beauty he dropped his bow transfixed with admiration.

Mrs. Billington, Dublin and London (first appearance
    as Polly) 1777
Miss Harper, Haymarket 1778
Charles Bannister, Haymarket (in Colman's travesty
    of the Opera) 1780
Miss Wheeler, Covent Garden 1781
Miss Phillips, Drury Lane (Macheath, Charles Bannis-
    ter) . . . . . September 25, 1784
Mrs. Crouch 1789
Mrs. Dickons (first appearance Covent Garden)
    October 12, 1793

Mrs. Dickons was known also as Miss Poole. She made her reputation as an oratorio singer. Of her " Polly " we are told that " her vocal powers are calculated to appear to much greater advantage in parts requiring less simplicity. We speak of the character of Polly as it is now conceived, but according to the original design it would seem that it should be burlesqued, and Mrs. Dickons would do it admirably." It is curious to find the critic complaining because the music of Polly was given as it was written, and arguing that it ought to be burlesqued.

Mrs. Serres, Covent Garden . . . May 3, 1796

This lady subsequently achieved notoriety by her assertion that she was the legitimate daughter of the Duke of Cumberland. To her also has been attributed the authorship of *The Secret History of the Court of England* to which the name of Lady Anne Hamilton is attached.

Madame Mara, Covent Garden ; Lucy, Mrs. Martyr
    (a run of twelve nights) 1797
Miss Dixon, Covent Garden . . September 24, 1801
Miss M. C. Bolton, Covent Garden 1801
Miss Stephens (first appearance as Polly), Covent
    Garden . . . . . . October 22, 1813

She represented Polly at Farren's benefit, Covent Garden, June 19, 1821. Farren was Peachum and Madame Vestris Macheath.

Miss Paton, Covent Garden 1821–2
Miss Rainforth, Covent Garden ; Lucy, Madam Vestris 1839

Miss Rainforth played Arline in the production of *The Bohemian Girl* in 1843.

Madame Vestris 1848
Madame Cave Ashton, Covent Garden (Macheath, Sims
    Reeves) 1878

Among the Macheaths of celebrity, besides Walker, may be mentioned Charles Hulet, 1734 ; Leveridge, 1735 ; Quin (once only, March 19, 1730) ; Vernon, Webster, Lowe, Wilder (a great favourite in Dublin, who made his first appearance on December 17, 1756), West Digges, Dublin (1752) ; Barry, Dublin, 1764.

Webster, who was slim and thin-faced, " filled the house each night he played, and was the first favourite with the ladies of fashion in Dublin ; but vanity surely turned his poor head, for when singing his love-songs, instead of addressing Polly, and Rosetta and Clarissa, etc., on the stage, he turned his pleasing looks full upon Lady this, that and the other, in the stage boxes " (O'Keefe). Wilder was a great favourite in Dublin. " He was," says O'Keefe, " of a fine, bold, athletic figure, but violent and extravagant in his mode of acting." West Digges had a noble presence and fine figure, large and manly, a full, expressive, pleasing face and ruddy complexion. He was a prime favourite in Scotland, and thought so infallible that a man in the pit who had a book of the play, not being able to find the words that Digges, being imperfect in his part, was launching out, crammed it back into his pocket in anger, exclaiming, " The deil take these printers : they never print a book right ! "

John Beard appears to have played the part for the first time on January 23, 1742, at Drury Lane, and, with Miss Brent, was in the run of thirty-nine nights at Covent Garden in 1759–60. Michael Kelly, 1789. C. Bannister (to Mrs. Billington's Polly), May 18, 1789. Incledon. Braham (his performance as Macheath was by no means successful). Elliston, July 8, 1797. Trueman, Haymarket, August 11, 1803. W. Harrison, 1839. Sims Reeves, 1878–86.

The number of female representatives of Macheath shows in what high favour the part was regarded by the ladies of the stage. Besides Mrs. Woffington in her youthful days, we have Anne Catley (Dublin, 1765; London, 1781); Mrs. Kennedy (the first actress to play Macheath in London, 1777); Mrs. Cargill (1780); Mrs. Farrel, 1781; Miss Fontenelle (March 3 and 7, 1787); Miss Blake, Haymarket; Madame Vestris (according to Genest her first appearance as Macheath was November 4, 1820. The opera had not then been performed in London for seven years. In 1825 and in 1840–1 she again played the part with great success at Covent Garden). On October 23, 1821, a lady made her first appearance (and also her last) as Macheath at the Haymarket. "All the women of the town," says Genest, "were omitted except two—they got possession of Macheath's pistols, and Peachum with the officers entered immediately—nothing could be more flat."

24

NOTES

1. (See p. 99.)

"... This picture," J. Ireland says, "affords a good example of the dress and what was then called the dignified manner of the old school. That any woman should be enamoured of such a figure as Mr. Walker in Macheath, would excite a degree of astonishment, but to believe for a moment that so attractive a female as Miss Fenton should choose such an Adonis must, even in 1727 (? 1728), require a very large portion of dramatic faith."

2. (See p. 111.)

According to one authority Walker is said "to have thrown an easy and dissolute air into the character of Macheath, to which all his successors have been strangers." If this be so, Mr. Sims Reeves' impersonation was probably nearer to that of Walker than any of his predecessors. J. Ireland in *Hogarth Illustrated* flatly contradicts the above estimate of Walker. "The part of this hero of the highway being originally cast for Quin," he says, "proves the style in which it was thought right to play it. Walker was praised, for performing it with dignity!"

3. (See Illustration, p. 224.)

The "bottle trick" was a hoax perpetrated by Foote at the Little Theatre in the Haymarket in 1749. Advertisements announced that "a person" would go into "a common wine-bottle" in the sight of all the spectators, would sing in it, and that "during his stay in the bottle any person may handle it." The house was packed, but no one appeared on the stage, and the affair ended in the erecting of a bonfire in the street and the calling in of the Foot Guards to quell the riot. The caricature from which the plate is reproduced had the punning title "The Bottle Conjurer from Head to Foot, without Equivocation." The "Head" possibly is an allusion to the Duke of Montagu, who had the credit of being half crazy, and of having originated the hoax, and the headless man with the words "I have lost my head," may be intended for him. The central figure is presumably the Duke of Cumberland (to whom Gay dedicated his *Fables*), who was among the audience. The inscription on the drapery on the mast, " I have suffered £400—J. Potter," is a reference to John Potter, the proprietor of the theatre.

4. (See p. 248.)

Croker (*Lord Hervey's Memoirs of George II.*) says: "'Polly' is very stupid and equally inoffensive. . . . The piece seems to me to be as free from all political allusion as it is of any kind of dramatic merit. . . . Nor can I understand why the latter ('Polly') should have been prohibited, except to punish the author for his former sallies. Gay in a preface asserts that he had no political design, and certainly the printed piece justifies his statement."

5. (See p. 256.)

"One night when she (Mrs. Clive) was acting Sir Harry Wildair, she finished a scene with a prodigious thunder of applause, and running into the green-room, elate with joy, found Quin sitting there. 'Mr. Quin,' said she, 'I have played this part so often that half the town believe me to be a real man.' Quin in his rough-and-ready style made answer, 'Madame, the other half know you to be a woman.'" (Murphy.)

6. (See p. 291.)

Yates as a young man frequently danced a hornpipe in *The Beggar's Opera*. According to Genest he did so at Goodmans Field's Theatre, April 8, 1741, on the occasion of Miss Medina's benefit.

7. (See p. 345.)

The story is probably an invention. Parke could not have meant West Digges, who played Macheath in Dublin, 1752, and played it well.

8. (See p. 346.)

Kelly opened a music shop in Pall Mall, but failed through inattention. He was not much more prosperous when he went into the wine trade. With a sly allusion that Kelly was indebted to foreign sources for his musical compositions, Sheridan suggested that he should inscribe on his shop "Michael Kelly, Composer of Wines and Importer of Music."

9. (See p. 359.)

On November 4, 1820, the Opera was presented at Drury Lane, with an additional scene, Madame Vestris

playing Macheath, and Miss Kelly, Lucy. The additional
scene represented Marylebone Gardens as they were about
the time when *The Beggar's Opera* was written—Macheath
was betrayed by the women at these gardens instead of at a
theatre (Genest). According to the same authority, Madame
Vestris made her first appearance as Macheath on July 22,
1820. The opera had not been acted in London for seven
years.

AUTHORITIES

Adolphus, J. : " Memoirs of John Bannister." 1839.
Ambross, Miss : " Life of Miss Catley." 1790.

Baker, D. E. : " Biographia Dramatica." 1812.
Ballantyne, A. : " Voltaire's Visit to England." 1893.
Bellamy, Anne George : " Memoirs." 1785.
Bernard, J. : " Retrospections of the Stage." 1830.
Biography, National, Dictionary of.
Boaden : " Life of Mrs. Jordan."
— " Life of Mrs. Siddons."
Boswell, J. : " Life of Johnson."
Burney, C. D. : " History of Music." 1778.
Busby, T. : " Concert-Room Anecdotes." 1825.

Chetwood, W. R. : " A General History of the Stage." 1749.
" Cibber, Colley, An Apology for the Life of." 1740.
Cooke, W. : " Macklin's Memoirs." 1804.

D'Anvers, Caleb : " The Twickenham Hotch-Potch." 1728.
Davies, T. : " Dramatic Miscellanies." 1785.
— — " Life of Garrick." 1784.
Delany, Mary : " Letters." 1821.
Doran, Dr. J. : " Their Majesties' Servants." 1864.
Drake, H. H. : " Hasted's History of Kent." 1886.

Egerton, W. F. : " Memoirs of Mrs. Oldfield." 1731.

Forster, J. : " Life of Oliver Goldsmith." 1855.

Genest, Rev. J. : " History of the Stage." 1832.
Gilfillan, G. : " Life of Gay." 1859.
Griffinhoofe, A. : " Memoirs of Madame Vestris." 1806.

Hervey, Lord John ; " Memoirs of George II." 1848.
Hitchcock, R. : " View of the Irish Stage." 1788.
Hunt, Leigh : " Men, Women and Books." 1847.

Ireland, J. : " Hogarth Illustrated." 1791.
— — " Hogarth's Illustrations." 1794.
— S. : " Graphic Illustrations of Hogarth."

Kelly, Michael : " Reminiscences." 1826.

Leslie, C. R. : " Recollections." 1860.
Lowe, R. W. : " Biographical Dictionary of Theatrical Literature."

Macleod, E. H. : " The Beggar's Opera." 1905.
Mathews, Mrs. Charles: " Life of Charles Matthews." 1888.
Montagu, Lady Mary W. : " Letters." 1837.

Nicholls, J. : " Anecdotes of Hogarth." 1833.
— — " The Genuine Works of William Hogarth." 1808.

Parke, W. T. : " Musical Memoirs." 1830.
Pope, A. : " The Dunciad." 1736.

" Quin, James, Life of." 1766.

Reeves, J. Sims : " Life and Recollections." 1888.
— — — " My Jubilee." 1887.
Rockstro, W. S. : " A General History of Music." 1886.
Rogers, S. : " Table Talk." 1856.
Ryan, R. : " Dramatic Table Talk." 1825.

Scott, Sir W. : " Life of Swift."
Singer, S. W. : " Life of Joseph Warton." 1822.
Smith, J. T. : " Nollekens and his Times."
— R. J. : " A Collection of Newspaper Cuttings relating to
    the Stage." 1825.
— — " A Collection of Material for History of Stage " (MS.),
    Vols. v.–ix. 1825.
Spence, J. : " Anecdotes." 1820.
Swift, Dean : " Letters." 1741, 1764, 1805.

Taylor, John : " Records of My Life." 1832.
Thrale, Mrs. : " Autobiography." 1910.

Victor, B. : " The History of Theatres." 1738.

Walker, Charles : " Authentic Memoirs of Sally Salisbury." 1728.
Walpole, H. : " Letters."
Walsh, Rev. Dr. : " History of the City of Dublin." 1891.
Wheatley, H. B. : " Hogarth's London." 1792.
Whitehead, T. : " Original Anecdotes of the Duke of Kingston
    and Miss Chudleigh."
Wilkinson, Tate : " Memoirs." 1790.
Wilson, C. H. : " The Myrtle and the Vine." 1802.
Wright, W. H. K. : " Gay's Fables." 1889.
Wyndham, H. S. : " Annals of Covent Garden Theatre." 1906.

Young, J., Rev. : " Life of C. M. Young."

MAGAZINES

British Magazine. 1760.
Era Almanack. 1869.
European Magazine. 1807.
Maccaroni Magazine. 1773–5.
Monthly Mirror. 1807.
New Monthly Magazine. 1833.
Notes and Queries. 1874, 1895, 1903.
Theatrical Observer. 1767.
Universal Magazine. 1778.

NEWSPAPERS

Bristol Times. 1846.
British Journal. 1728–29.
Craftsman. 1728.
Daily Advertiser. 1736.
— Courant. 1726.
— Gazetteer. 1736–37.
— Journal. 1725–9, 1736.
— Post. 1721–2, 1726–8, 1736–41.
— Postman. 1710.

Evening Post. 1728.

Female Tatler. 1709.

General Advertizer. 1731–51.
Gloucester Journal. 1727.
Grub Street Journal. 1736–7.

Intelligencer. 1729.

Lloyd's Evening Post. 1767.
London Chronicle. 1759–60, 1769.

Mist's Journal. 1728.
Morning Chronicle. 1780.
— Herald. 1780.

Public Advertiser. 1760.
Punch. 1879.

Times. 1886.

Weekly Pacquet. 1714.

Anonymous

Abington, Frances, Life of. 1888.
Beswick, Lavinia, *alias* Fenton, *alias* Polly Peachum, Life of. 1728.
Catley, Anne, Life of. 1888.
— — A brief Narrative of the Life of. 1780.
Female Faction, The. 1729.
Miniature Pictures. 1781.
Peachum, Polly. Jests. 1728.
— — Letters in Prose and Verse. 1728.
— — Opera or Medley of New Songs. 1728.
Press Yard (Newgate), History of. 1717.
Prydden, Sarah (Sally Salisbury), Genuine History of. 1728.
Salisbury, Sally. Effigies—Parentage—Life, etc. 1722.
— — Tryal of. 1722.
Vestris, Madame, Memoirs of. 1839.

INDEX